SCOTTISH HISTORY SOCIETY

FIFTH SERIES

VOLUME 5

The Scottish Office

The Scottish Office
Depression and Reconstruction
1919–1959

edited by
Ian Levitt

★

★

EDINBURGH
printed for the Scottish History Society *by*
PILLANS & WILSON LTD., EDINBURGH
1992

British Library Cataloguing-in-Publication Data:
A catalogue record for this book is available
from the British Library

ISBN 0 906245 14 1

Printed in Great Britain

CONTENTS

ACKNOWLEDGEMENTS

This work would not have been possible without the active help and co-operation of many people. I would like to give special thanks to the staff of the Public Record Office, the Scottish Record Office, Cambridge University Library, the National Library of Scotland, Edinburgh University Library, Edinburgh Public Library and the University of Central Lancashire Library. I am also indebted to the Scottish Office Industry Department for permission to use currently closed files. In selecting material to be included, and in drafting an associated introduction, I was fortunate to be able to interview a number of people closely associated with the Scottish Office's work during the period under study. I remain grateful to these individuals for the clarification of the contemporary issues as they were then seen, and on the Scottish Office's administrative structure. I am additionally grateful to those who subsequently provided written comments on the selected material and on the introduction. Special thanks, however, must be given to Professor Roy Campbell for his early encouragement and then critical comment, Professor Michael Lynch and Dr Julian Goodare, who remained extremely patient throughout the work's final period, Stanley Henig, Dr Richard Hoyle, Dr Rex Pope and Dr Margaret Clark. Although I gave an understanding to those I interviewed that what they said would remain confidential, I feel I must depart from that undertaking in one case. Professor Tom Burns died shortly after we spoke, but, without his encouragement nearly twenty years ago, I would never have embarked upon a research career.

I.L.

Preston

INTRODUCTION

In November 1909 Harold Connacher, a senior clerk based at the Scottish Office in London, travelled north to open a branch office in Edinburgh's Parliament Square, aided by a number of junior officials. Mr Connacher's move was heralded as a small but significant step in the devolution of Government authority.[1] Established in 1885, largely from the Home Office, the Scottish Office was essentially a Whitehall department; it was there to ensure that Scottish interests were represented in the evolution of Government policy and in promoting Scottish legislation. Edinburgh, by contrast, remained the principal residence of other Government agencies, for instance the Local Government and Congested Districts Boards; but, four hundred miles away from the legislature, they monitored the quality of local administration rather than initiating any major changes of policy. 1906, however, saw the election of a Liberal Government committed to a wide range of social and economic reform, seen most dramatically in the creation of labour exchanges and national insurance, but also in other areas of social life, such as urban sanitation, poorhouse management and town and country planning.[2] Gladstone's 'night-watchman' state had given way to Lloyd George's 'managed interventionism'.

The gradual increase in Government power over the life of ordinary Scots had another, political by-product. In 1908, 1909 and 1913 back-bench Liberals pressed with increasing conviction for Home Rule, a Parliament in Edinburgh, linked by some federal structure to Westminster. Although the various Home Rule bills faltered, they served to underline another agenda behind Mr Connacher's move—a concern that whatever the political imperative,

1 *Scotsman*, Leader, 21 Oct. 1909. Liberal MPs had called for the transference of the Scotch Education Department from London to Edinburgh. The paper, however, suggested that there was a better case for Edinburgh having a branch of the Scottish Office. See also evidence of Sir James Dodds, Permanent Under Secretary for Scotland, 15 Nov. 1912. *Royal Commission on the Civil Service: Third Report, Evidence.* Cd. 6739 (P.P. 1913 Vol. XVIII).

2 I. Levitt (ed.), *Government and Social Conditions in Scotland, 1845-1919* (Scottish History Soc., 1988); I. Levitt, *Poverty and Welfare in Scotland, 1890-1948* (Edinburgh, 1988).

administratively at least the Scottish Office remained sensitive to any claims about distant, unresponsive government. The Office had remained one of the few Government departments without a branch in Scotland.

Harold Connacher's presence in Edinburgh, principally representing the Scottish Office on a number of committees and liaising with local 'interests', passed off without any great difficulty, and in November 1912 Lord Pentland, the Scottish Secretary, sought to increase the establishment by sending an assistant secretary to oversee a wide area of administrative business.[1] Dover House in London would thus be free to concentrate on Parliamentary business. Herbert Asquith, the Prime Minister, approved the proposal 'in principle in the interests of Government efficiency', but passed the matter to Lloyd George, the Chancellor of the Exchequer.[2] Lloyd George, however, disliked the possibility of a new separate Scottish Office emerging, and Lord Pentland was told:

> So long as the seat of Government and consequently the Secretary for Scotland are in London, it will be necessary that the Secretary for Scotland should have at hand and consequently in London the services of a staff which watches Scottish interests in Parliament much more effectively than would be possible from Edinburgh, which forms the channel of communication between the Departments resident in Scotland and the Secretary for Scotland, and by means of which he exercises control over them, and Scottish administration is kept in touch with other great departments of State.[3]

Instead Lloyd George offered Lord Pentland some additional clerks for Dover House.

Although the Edinburgh experiment was abandoned soon after, the discussion between Pentland, Asquith and Lloyd George had raised important issues about the political administration of Scotland and in particular the relationship of the Scottish Office to Whitehall, to the Edinburgh boards and to Scottish public opinion. On the one hand, there was the view that good Government in an expanding state meant devolving administrative (if not political) power nearer to the people. On the other, nothing should be done to diminish the authority of the Union: maintaining the Scottish 'interest' demanded close working with British and English institutions.

Despite recent interest in the issue of Scottish government and in Scotland's social and economic progress, it is surprising that little attention has been given to how twentieth-century government in Scotland has evolved or its

1 Minute of Sir James Dodds, 23 Nov. 1912, SRO, E824/4.

2 Lord Pentland to Lloyd George, Chancellor of the Exchequer, 23 Nov. 1912, SRO, E824/4.

3 Minute of Sir George Barstow, Second Secretary, the Treasury, 12 Dec. 1912, SRO, E828/4.

relationship to Westminster. Works abound on the policy and practice of most Whitehall departments, such as the Foreign Office, the Treasury and the Board of Trade. Nevertheless, apart from some official publications, most writings have been limited to particular historical episodes, cover political developments or discuss Scottish society and its economy.[1]

This volume of extracts from Scottish Office documents is an attempt to correct the lack of detailed knowledge of how Scottish administration interacted with the British State, particularly in the areas of industrial development, housing and health policy. No-one who has consulted Scottish Office Cabinet memoranda, or read *Hansard* or the contemporary press, can be in any doubt as to how central these issues became and remained to Scottish political development. Indeed, for the early period, the Scottish Secretary, by a simple count of memoranda, Parliamentary debates and leader comment, was in large measure a Minister for Housing. The volume begins in 1919, just after the first election fought on a popular franchise and at the same time as the establishment of a Board of Health. It ends in 1959, another election year which saw the Conservatives losing ground in Scotland, despite an overwhelming victory south of the border. It was also a time when the nature and direction of Scottish policy paused, as seen most dramatically in the withdrawal of plans to establish a Development Department.

The volume cannot, of course, cover everything that occurred. As a recent Public Record Office guide has noted, policy-formulation often takes place at *ad hoc* ministerial meetings with only a scanty record of what was said.[2] Additionally, much of the detail of Government was handled by junior officials and their records have rarely been retained.[3] Moreover, even where there are written records, for the historian, the full flavour of decisions and events is blurred by reporting conventions and civil service language. Thus Cabinet minutes, termed 'conclusions', rarely report the ministerial author of a comment.

1 Official publications include D. Milne, *The Scottish Office* (London, 1958) and J.S. Gibson, *The Thistle and the Crown: A History of the Scottish Office* (Edinburgh, 1985). G. Pottinger, *The Secretaries of State for Scotland, 1926-1976* (Edinburgh, 1979) was written by a former Departmental Secretary. Other recent works include I. Donnachie *et al.* (eds.), *Forward! Labour Politics in Scotland, 1888-1988* (Edinburgh, 1989); A. Dickson & J.H. Treble (eds.), *People and Society in Scotland, vol. iii, 1914-1990* (Edinburgh, 1992); M. Fry, *Patronage and Principle: a Political History of Modern Scotland* (Aberdeen, 1987); J.G. Kellas, *The Scottish Political System* (4th edn., Cambridge, 1989); J. Mitchell, *Conservatives and the Union* (Edinburgh, 1990).

2 B.W.E. Alford *et al.* (eds.), *Economic Planning, 1943-1951* (London, 1992), p. xi.

3 For Scottish Office retention policy, see SRO, HH1/680-2. In 1943, Tom Johnston agreed the first destruction schedule under the Public Records (Scotland) Act 1937. See also J. Imrie, 'Public registers and records', *Stair Memorial Encyclopedia of the Laws of Scotland*, vol. xix (Edinburgh, 1990).

Although Cabinet Committees are usually more extensive in reporting ministerial views, they too, if read literally, can often be misleading. For instance, at one meeting in 1938 Neville Chamberlain, the Prime Minister, and his Chancellor, Sir John Simon, spoke at great length against continuing the Special Areas Act.[1] Only two other ministers, John Colville, the Scottish Secretary, and Oliver Stanley, the President of the Board of Trade, spoke, and their comments in favour of the Act cover just a few sentences. However, Chamberlain clearly sensed that he could not carry the other ministers and quickly reversed his view in favour of the Act's continuation. Any reading of the documents must therefore appreciate the comments, style and format used by ministers and officials to write and communicate with each other.

The historian, and in particular the Scottish historian, faces another difficulty, the retention of records. Although substantially more departmental records have been retained at the Scottish Record Office than in the Public Record Office, there are important gaps. First, a wartime destruction order, for fear of incendiary bombing, resulted in the wholesale shredding of many Department of Health files. The papers of the Board of Health, 1919-28, have been especially affected.

A second difficulty is the policy for a department not to retain any Cabinet papers. The convention is that they are retained by the Cabinet Office and ultimately transmitted to the Public Record Office. However, the Public Record Office is in London, so whilst the historian of the English or British department has access to all the papers at the same location, the Scottish historian has to travel between London and Edinburgh. This point has been noted by the Scottish Office on several occasions since the passing of the 1937 Public Records (Scotland) Act, and was especially noted in the 1950s when public access to Government papers was greatly improved. The Scottish Office generally accepted that Government papers should be open for public consultation, but one official minuted:

> It will ... be necessary to safeguard the position of the Scottish Record Office in this matter. A complete set of Cabinet records will no doubt be transmitted to the Public Record Office, but it is equally essential, if public criticism is to be avoided, that copies of Cabinet records of particular Scottish interest should also be made available to the Scottish Record Office.[2]

1 Minute of the Depressed Areas Committee, 10 Nov. 1938, PRO, CAB 27/578 DA(34)15th.

2 Minute of Sir Charles Cunningham, Secretary, Scottish Home Department, 1 Feb. 1955, SRO, HH1/682. It was noted that neither the English nor Scottish Public Record Acts were limited in their application. United Kingdom departments could have their Scottish records transmitted to the Scottish Record Office, even if they had been held in a London office. This seems to have the intention of the Public Records Act, 1958, Schedule 1.

Following the Public Record Act, 1958, no such arrangement was made. Additionally, very few files which deal with Scottish Office discussion and correspondence just before submission of a Cabinet memorandum survive. Other departments seem to have adopted a more liberal policy, retaining many more 'fair copy' memoranda and final files before submission.[1] Thus in tracking the development of Scottish government the historian faces a number of hurdles: Scottish documents in different locations, the loss of documents of a type retained by other departments, and the nature and form of the written material. Nevertheless, the retained documents do narrate two interesting and interrelated tales: first, the gradual growth of government and its intervention into new areas of social and economic life, and, second, the definition and re-definition of Scottish departmental power *vis-à-vis* Whitehall.

The use of the term 'Scottish Office' requires explanation. The modern Scottish Office dates from September 1939, after the report of the Committee on Scottish Administration, chaired by Sir John Gilmour.[2] Before 1939 there were a number of distinct Scottish Departments and Boards, all very much under the political control of the Scottish Secretary, but without any unifying administrative structure. The Scottish Office in London was essentially a small, conventionally organised Whitehall department and dealt with such matters as the police, criminal justice, probation, local government, the prerogative of mercy and ceremonial matters.[3] However, the other departments, such as Health, Agriculture and Education, kept in touch with the Scottish Secretary through his private secretary and not the Scottish Office permanent under secretary. Scottish Secretaries usually asked the permanent under secretary for his views on major issues; but, as Sir Robert Horne once said, the 'semi-detached' nature of the relationship gave the impression of a 'ramshackle, disjaskit' executive.[4]

1 For instance, Cumbernauld: Proposed New Town, 1954-5, PRO, T 227/412.

2 *Administration*. Cmd. 5563 (P.P. 1937 Vol. XV).

3 Treasury Blue Notes: Secretary for Scotland's Office, 1920-1, PRO, T 222/469. The Scottish Office was also the parent department of the Scottish Boards dealing with prisons and borstals, fisheries, lunacy and mental deficiency. It was responsible for private bills, under the special Scottish Provisional Order Procedure, with a senior and junior advocate based in Edinburgh handling business in Scotland. Additionally, Dover House provided accommodation and services for the Scottish Education Department (where the Deputy Secretary was based) and for the Law Officers and their legal secretaries. The latter also acted as legal advisers to the Scottish Office and were the Parliamentary draftsmen for all the Scottish Departments. The Scottish Office provided the Scottish Secretary with private secretaries and routine assistance with Parliamentary work.

4 *House of Lords Debates*, Vol. 112, c.714, Re-Organisation of Offices (Scotland) Bill, Second Reading, 25 Apr. 1939.

The Gilmour reform altered the whole nature of Scottish administration, essentially bringing the Departments into a tighter, more cohesive relationship, with the Permanent Under Secretary of State at the head of a small private office in London. Most of the old Scottish Office's functions were transferred to the new Scottish Home Department, based along with the other departments in the new St Andrews House in Edinburgh.[1] After the merger, the term 'the Scottish Office' could be used generally to refer to all the Departments under the Scottish Secretary's political control, or more particularly the private office of the Scottish Secretary and the Permanent Under Secretary of State in London.[2] In this volume it is used in the former sense, but it should be noted that the Departments remained separate entities, with their own Secretaries and their own Vote. Subject to Ministerial authority they remained free to deal with other Departments in Whitehall as in the Civil Service generally. The Permanent Under Secretary's principal function was to provide advice to the Scottish Secretary where there was a difference of opinion between Departments, ensure they were informed of each other's problems and activities, and generally promote the 'Scottish interest'.

Each extract in the volume is prefaced with a short explanation indicating its context and, where appropriate, its consequence. As far as possible extracts have been selected that reflect discussion of social and economic conditions or statements of policy. Where papers appear in the Public and Scottish Record Offices, both are referenced. The remainder of this introduction provides an overview of the chapters.

Chapter One: The Nature of Government

The outbreak of war in 1914 brought in its wake a considerable upheaval in British political administration. Asquith's Liberal Government, after a succession of military débâcles, was replaced by a Coalition Government. By 1917, through a combination of personality and political intrigue, British Government was headed by Lloyd George and others determined to win the war. However, to secure victory, produce the munitions, commit an even larger military force and at the same time maintain public morale, Lloyd George had to begin to restructure Government. At one level he converted his secretariat

1 The Home Department also assumed administration of the Fisheries and Prisons Boards and provided 'common services' to the other Departments. The General Board of Control for Lunacy and Mental Deficiency continued to have a measure of independence but its Vote was borne by the Department of Health.

2 Treasury Blue Notes: Scottish Home Department, 1947, PRO, T 165/388.

into a fully-fledged Cabinet Office with general oversight of all Government activity.[1] Government was no longer a group of ministers meeting in Cabinet under the chairmanship of the Prime Minister; British Government was now led by the Prime Minister, assisted by other ministers. On another level, his new Ministry of Reconstruction spawned a whole set of domestic initiatives: a Ministry of Health to co-ordinate and extend health provision, unemployment insurance for all, and a crash post-war housing programme.[2] On yet another, the Haldane Committee was established to conduct a rigorous review of Government organisation and determine its guiding principles.[3]

The Scottish Office and Scottish Boards were not immune from these changes. During 1915, after the Glasgow rent strike, they became heavily involved in promoting the Rent Restriction Act and monitoring the militant shop stewards' movement. By 1917 they were busy developing a nascent health service and, in the wake of the Royal Commission on Housing, planning a post-war housing drive.[4] But despite the territorial nature of the Scottish Office's duties it remained strangely on the sidelines of British administration. On the one hand, Haldane virtually ignored the Scottish departments—indeed the Committee's principal recommendation, to organise departments according to services 'performed', rather than by 'persons or classes to be dealt with', seemed to run counter to the whole notion of a separate Scottish Office. On the other hand, Scottish officials played little or no part in early discussions about the nature and constitution of the reformed Ministries. This, in part, reflected the relatively 'anomalous' position of the Scottish Secretary.[5] Although all Scottish Secretaries since 1892 had been members of the Cabinet, they were not Secretaries of State and were paid on a lower scale. In fact, their Cabinet membership was seen by contemporary opinion as dependent on their personal relationship with the Prime Minister, a situation which many felt underlined their political 'inferiority'.[6]

1 P. Hennessy, *Whitehall* (Glasgow, 1989), ch. 2.

2 B.B. Gilbert, *British Social Policy, 1914-1939* (London, 1966).

3 *Report of the Committee on the Machinery of Government*. Cmd. 9230. (London, 1919). The Committee, under the chairmanship of Lord Haldane, was established in July 1917.

4 Memorandum by the Local Government Board (Scotland), Financing of Housing Schemes, 30 Oct. 1917, SRO, DD6/2203.

5 *Glasgow Herald*, 'History of the Scottish Office', 24 Apr. 1921. The Scottish Secretary's salary dictated the salary of his permanent under secretary, which in Whitehall terms meant that the Scottish Office was headed by a second secretary.

6 *Scotsman*, Speech by Lord Alness (Robert Munro), who added that Scotland was being 'kept in a subsidiary position unbefitting her dignity', 13 Mar. 1923.

In 1918 the Government's reconstruction discussion began to focus on the issue of co-ordinating local health provision and on the proposed post-war housing drive. In Scotland, as in England, a considerable campaign developed, from Labour, the medical profession and the health insurance lobby, to secure a Government department to administer the new services. At first the Cabinet remained uncertain that a Ministry of Health was appropriate, but in early July the political pressure and the logic of housing and health policy forced senior ministers to concede a Ministry Bill. Robert Munro, the Scottish Secretary, was immediately faced with difficulties. If the English were to receive a new ministry, Scottish opinion would want the same. But a Scottish ministry would mean the appointment of a Scottish minister with a larger budget and considerably more administrative staff than the Scottish Secretary. Who, the press asked, would be the senior minister, the Scottish Secretary or the Scottish Minister of Health, and who would be in the Cabinet?[1] It was unlikely to include both ministers. The Cabinet, as the extracts (pp. 74–5) indicate, agreed a compromise: a Board of Health, based in Edinburgh, but under the control of the Scottish Secretary. A new Parliamentary Under Secretary for Health, who would attend Board meetings, would take day-to-day responsibility for the implementation of policy.[2]

The 1919 Health Bill, then, was an important landmark in restructuring Scottish administration. It held much promise, but many voices remained convinced that, if the electorate was to be satisfied, some more substantial response was necessary. At one level, many felt that Lloyd George's restructuring of Government had not fully addressed the issue of Scottish administration. The Commons, for instance, which at the turn of the century had normally sat from February, now began the Parliamentary session much earlier. The increased legislation and the gradual extension of Government meant that the Scottish Secretary faced additional Parliamentary debates, questions and committees. He also faced new ministries with powers that touched on Scottish development—the Ministry of Labour, the Ministry of Mines and the Ministry of Transport. As one newspaper commented, the Scottish Secretary's task was 'more intricate and onerous', but at the same time his Office lacked Cabinet 'weight or prestige'.[3] Scottish legislation was, as often as not, dealt with by application clauses to English bills, with little Parliamentary time for discussion.

1 *Scotsman*, Leader, 29 Mar. 1919; *Glasgow Herald*, 'The Health Board and its Head', 31 Mar. 1919.
2 Formally the Scottish Secretary was President and the Parliamentary Under Secretary, Vice-President.
3 *Glasgow Herald*, 'The Scottish Secretariat', 21 Apr. 1919; 'Ministers and Salaries', 15 Dec. 1920.

In many areas of policy it was often complained that English concerns dominated.[1]

The Scottish Secretary's difficulty in Cabinet had been noticed on several occasions before 1914. In 1910, backbench Liberals, disappointed by Lord Pentland's apparent failure to obtain radical land reform, complained that his salary level, unlike that of the Irish Secretary, meant that few paid any attention either to him or to his officials.[2] The following year the MPs repeated the complaint and added that the low pay affected the quality of Scottish Office staff.[3] Such statements were probably associated with their desire to press Home Rule, but when the 1913 Bill failed to secure Government support the MPs changed their argument. The Scottish Secretary, they said, 'performed the duties relating to the Local Government Board, the Board of Education, the Board of Agriculture, the Home Office and the First Commissioner of Works' and if there was to be no devolution, Asquith, the Prime Minister, should at least recognise his position within the Government.[4] However, Asquith refused, arguing that a number of other 'competent' ministers on a similar salary had equally 'large and wide duties'.

The outbreak of war broke off further Parliamentary debate on Scottish affairs, but in 1917 the issue re-emerged in somewhat different terms. Scottish local authorities began to press hard for an adequately staffed Ministry of Reconstruction, with considerable powers.[5] Such concerns were echoed in Parliament where MPs complained about Dover House's relatively small staff and hinted that Scottish Departments seemed to lag behind others in preparing post-war plans.[6] The press, meanwhile, tapped a wider and more intangible concern. During the war, the *Glasgow Herald* noted, Scotland had remained astonishingly 'loyal', but after the Armistice domestic opinion seemed more restless and uncertain, an impression borne out by the almost immediate upsurge in industrial militancy.[7] The *Scotsman*, for its part, felt that the 1918 election

1 *Scotsman*, Leader, 6 Aug. 1919: supply debates were held on 'inconvenient, odd days where there was no other business'. Scottish MPs also complained that the 1919 supply debate, which was interrupted for two hours by a royal pageant on the Thames, was given no opportunity to make up lost time.

2 *Hansard*, Vol. 19, c.875, 18 July 1910, Supply: Scottish Estimates. There were also complaints that the Scottish Office was understaffed: *Glasgow Herald*, 'A Pressing Reform, Strengthening the Scottish Office', 31 Jan. 1910.

3 *Hansard*, Vol. 26, c.1249, 1 June 1911, Scottish Estimates, speech by J. Ainsworth (Argyll).

4 *Hansard*, Vol. 60, c.26, 23 Mar. 1914, Question from J.M. Hogge (Edinburgh, East); Vol. 63, c.1274, 18 June 1914, Question from W.A. Watt (Glasgow, College).

5 Levitt, *Poverty and Welfare*, 105.

6 *Hansard*, Vol. 107, c.1974, 4 July 1918, Supply Debates: Scottish Estimates, especially speech by Sir Godfrey Collins (Liberal, Greenock).

7 *Glasgow Herald*, 'Scottish Home Rule', 7 May 1924.

campaign had not gone well for the Coalition, despite its huge majority.[1] Apathy, it said, was more apparent than enthusiasm for 'reconstruction', especially amongst the newly-enfranchised workers.[2] It urged strong political leadership.

Munro, after the 1918 election, found himself under two quite distinct pressures: from Parliament, local authorities and the press, which continued to believe that Scottish administration was defective, and from the electorate, disorientated by war and apparently indifferent to plans for peace. Late in December, he wrote to Lloyd George outlining the case for his elevation to a Secretaryship of State, stressing the range and extent of the Scottish Secretary's work. An announcement, he said, 'would be very well received north of the Tweed, and would be generally interpreted as conveying some recognition of the great part played by Scotland in the War'.[3]

What influenced Munro to suggest a change in status? First, as he later commented, there was a practical concern. In the post-war world, where Government allocated a much larger share of the nation's wealth, it was important that Scotland should 'receive her due share of public moneys'.[4] A Secretary of State, permanently in the Cabinet and equal in rank with such ministers as the Home and Foreign Secretaries, would have 'weight and authority' to pursue Scottish interests, especially with the Treasury.[5] Second, he recognised that voter enfranchisement and new forms of industrial organisation had greatly altered Scotland's political economy; it was important to reconfigurate the symbols of Scottish political life.[6] A Health Ministry dominated by Labour and medical interests, he thought, would reinforce the sectional nature of Scottish society and might even add to pressure for Home Rule. By contrast, a Secretary of State offered the prospect of heightened political

1 *Scotsman*, 'The General Election', 16 Dec. 1918.

2 The electoral turnout had been one of the lowest ever, touching barely 60 per cent. In Edinburgh, election agents reported that working-class districts showed little evening 'congestion'.

3 Letter, 23 Dec. 1918, SRO, HH1/887. Munro indicated, in further support, that it was intended that his salary would be increased with the passing of the Health Bill, but a final decision had been delayed by the War Cabinet.

4 *Glasgow Herald*, 'The Scottish Office: Mr. Munro's Review and Retrospect', 17 Oct. 1921; see also his evidence to the Gilmour Committee, 12 Apr. 1937, SRO, HH45/65.

5 *Scotsman*, Speech, Scottish Grand Committee on the Board of Health Bill, 10 Apr. 1919. Although the Prime Minister decided Cabinet membership, it was unlikely that a Secretary of State would be excluded.

6 Munro later noted the 'paramount influence' of his Permanent Under Secretary, Sir James Dodds, in advice given. In private life Dodds acted as secretary to a literary society devoted to the works of the English romantic poet, W.E. Henley, and greatly admired R.L. Stevenson; see his obituary appreciation, *Times*, 30 Oct. 1934, and evidence to the Gilmour Committee.

integration, based on a 'practical, business-like' approach to Government; as the *Scotsman* commented, less 'sentiment', more 'reason'.[1]

Lloyd George appreciated the political significance of elevating the Scottish Secretary, but in a Conservative-leaning Coalition adopted a more cautious approach and committed the matter to ministerial review. The Treasury remained unsure that the Scottish Secretary's work merited an increase in salary. Scottish Coalition MPs, however, quickly sensed an altered mood and decided to support the proposal.[2] In July 1919, the Government agreed to introduce a Bill to increase the number of Secretaries of State, including one for Scotland. The Bill ran into the immediate opposition of Liberal MPs, many of whom, like Wedgwood Benn, the MP for Leith, had become incensed by the Government's policy of retrenchment.[3] How could the Government propose to increase the remuneration of certain ministers, but at the same time reduce social provision? The Bill was hastily withdrawn and a Select Committee established to review the position. The extracts (pp. 75-7) indicate the result: a Government in basic sympathy with the political need for change, but trapped in a wider debate about its Parliamentary support. The political issue of the Scottish Secretary was not that urgent.

The general reorganisation of Whitehall following the introduction of a Cabinet Secretariat and Haldane's dictum on organising Government services caused Munro more immediate administrative concern. First, despite what Lloyd George had said in 1912, the Scottish Office's control over Scottish administration had always been tenuous. Although the Permanent Under Secretary formed part of the Local Government Board and had a long-established right to see any paper before ministerial submission, he had little or no connection with the other Boards.[4] Moreover, the constitution of the proposed Board of Health further removed any direct link between the Scottish Office and domestic affairs; the Parliamentary Under Secretary of Health took the place of the Permanent Under Secretary. From July 1919 any papers for the Scottish Secretary on health, housing and unemployment were transmitted through his private office. Second, although this might have appeared more democratic, it

1 *Scotsman*, Leader, 27 Apr. 1920. Munro's own election campaign had laid special emphasis on 'ordered development': *Scotsman*, 'Mr Munro's Appeal for Unity', 25 Nov. 1918.

2 *Hansard*, Vol. 112, c.1947, 27 Feb. 1919, Question by Sir Henry Craik (Conservative, Scottish Universities); Vol. 117, c.780, 1 July 1919, Question from V. Henderson (Conservative, Glasgow Tradeston). In April Lloyd George received a memorandum from an all-Party group of 47 MPs supporting the proposal, shortly after a motion from the Convention of Royal Burghs.

3 *Hansard*, Vol. 119, c.280, 5 Aug. 1919, Ministers and Secretaries Bill, Second Reading. Benn had been amongst the memorialists.

4 Minute of G.O. Trevelyan, Secretary for Scotland, 25 Jan. 1895, SRO, DD5/439.

considerably detracted from the Scottish Office's ability to function. On one level, it had a duty to ensure that the Scottish Secretary could respond to any issue in the House. On another, it had a duty, as Munro pointed out, of 'keeping in touch' with other Departments to review prospective legislation and, if appropriate, secure its applicability to Scotland.

Munro's reaction was to propose a fundamental Scottish Office restructuring.[1] The Office would have three divisions, each staffed by new assistant secretaries. All would have access to the Scottish Secretary and be expected to provide him with advice on any relevant matter.[2] Such a restructuring, Munro felt, would underline the Scottish Secretary's ministerial importance both to the Cabinet and the Scottish public, the embodiment, voice and 'guardian' of anything Scottish at Whitehall.[3] It would complement his proposed elevation to a Secretary of State and maintain the 'centripetal' nature of British administration. The extracts (pp. 77-80) indicate the Treasury's response: an acceptance that some reorganisation was necessary, but a disinclination to believe that it should be more than minor administrative adjustment. Scottish policy, as distinct from British or English, existed only at the margins of political life—the Church, education and the law. The Scottish Office was not one of the 'chief departments of state'.[4]

Munro realised somewhat belatedly that the major obstacle to the reform he wished was the nature and constitution of the Boards.[5] Although he consistently opposed their integration into one department, the public had become accustomed to Edinburgh's administrative 'hierarchy'; they were essentially deliberative bodies, representative of a number of Scottish institutions.[6] On occasion they distanced themselves from Government decisions.[7] Sometimes,

1 Treasury letter, 14 Feb. 1919, PRO, T 162/494.

2 *Hansard*, Vol. 114, c.2395-6, 10 Apr. 1919, Board of Health Bill, Third Reading. The first assistant secretary would cover establishment, parliamentary procedures, crown matters, sasines, records, diplomatic business, church, law and justice; the second, local government, public health, elections, food, transport, employment, art and sciences; and the third, police, private legislation, finance, votes, loans and taxation. Previously the Permanent Under Secretary permitted only his assistant access to Munro.

3 *Hansard*, Vol. 127, c.2072, 16 Apr. 1920, Government of Scotland Bill, Second Reading.

4 Minute of R.S. Meiklejohn, Deputy Controller of Establishments, 24 July 1920, PRO, T 163/3/17.

5 Evidence to Gilmour Committee.

6 The Board of Health included Sir George McCrae (past member, Edinburgh Town Council), Sir James Leishman (health insurance), Sir Leslie Mackenzie (past local authority MOH), Dr J.C. M'Vail (health insurance general practitioner), E.F. MacPherson (advocate) and Muriel Ritson (Scottish Women's Friendly Society). It met each Friday to discuss policy and agree advice to ministers: SRO, HH1/472.

7 Levitt, *Poverty and Welfare*, 113. Here, the Board of Health raised objections to legalising relief to the able-bodied unemployed, despite Cabinet discussion in favour. The Board's objections, were, in fact, sustainable. Scottish parishes were too small to support the expenditure.

he found, they were unable to agree amongst themselves.[1] The period 1922-8 was therefore largely dominated by the political debate on the status, nature and mechanism of the Scottish Secretary's authority (extracts pp. 80-6). Lord Novar, Munro's Conservative successor, wanted Scotland administered from a directorate, but this had obvious undemocratic implications and was not pursued.[2] Adamson, Labour's pro-devolution Scottish Secretary, accepted the need for some change, but remained unhappy about substituting departments for boards, politically because they sat in Edinburgh and were generally regarded as 'Scottish', and administratively because it would have been difficult to replace them with Scottish administrative class civil servants.[3]

During Cabinet discussion on the Re-organisation of Offices Bill, Novar was also able to raise the issue of the Scottish Secretary's status. Although ministers again seemed sympathetic, the Treasury still maintained its hostility and the matter fell with Baldwin's first administration. Adamson showed some interest in the proposal and welcomed a deputation from the Convention of Royal Burghs, but the Labour Government fell before it could be considered in detail.[4] The issue resurfaced in February 1925 when the Convention again petitioned Baldwin for the status of the Scottish Secretary to be raised. Baldwin, with Conservative backbenchers also pressing the case, agreed that the matter deserved further consideration.[5] The issue, he said, was 'part of a much bigger question', keeping 'the people in good heart'. However, Baldwin found that other ministers who were paid on a scale similar to the Scottish Secretary also felt their work was equivalent to a Secretary of State and the matter was remitted to a small ministerial committee.[6] In the event, Baldwin, after visiting Scotland to assess its housing difficulties (see Chapter Three), felt that the Scottish case was strong, but not enough to raise the salary level. The Treasury still maintained that the Scottish Office did not have the same level of responsibility as the Home or Foreign Office.

1 When the Board of Health failed to agree, the Scottish Secretary 'shot their papers over' to the Permanent Under Secretary. See evidence of Sir John Lamb, Permanent Under Secretary, 1921-33, to the Gilmour Committee, 10 Feb. 1937, SRO, HH45/65.

2 Novar was even more contemptuous of the Boards, complaining that his political control was 'thin' and 'indirect'. He favoured 'centralising' their accommodation on a 'cheap, but convenient slum site': minute, 5 Jan. 1923, SRO, HH45/51.

3 Meeting of Lord Chancellor, Adamson, the Lord Advocate and the Treasury, 14 Mar. 1924, SRO, HH1/520. Adamson said that he faced a number of 'pressing problems': unemployment, health provision, local authority reform, and the fact that the Boards' staff were all executive grade officers.

4 Meeting, 14 Mar. 1924, SRO, HH1/887.

5 Meeting, 23 Feb. 1925, ibid.; *Scotsman*, 'Scottish Secretary's Status', 24 Feb. 1925.

6 Baldwin's Ministerial Salary Committee, Baldwin Papers, Cambridge University Library.

Gilmour's failure to increase his salary did, however, affect his view of departmental organisation. The Boards, with their distinct constitution, were clearly an impediment to his ministerial efficiency. The way forward, he argued, was to reorganise Scottish administration on more usual civil service lines with the Scottish Office clearly at its apex. It would enable the Scottish Secretary to reach 'rapid decisions' with the aid of 'highly trained civil servants'.[1] However, Gilmour, who was not noted for his political tact, announced during the Second Reading of his Re-Organisation of Offices Bill in 1927 that the new departmental structure would enable the interchange of officials between 'Scotland and the Head Office in London, and vice versa'. Such might have appeared administratively sensible to those in Whitehall, but it caused uproar in the Commons. Labour and Liberal MPs, in particular, raised three questions. Firstly, would the new departments be under the authority of the Scottish Office in London? Secondly, would English civil servants be transferred to hold senior Scottish positions? Finally, what faith would local authorities and others have that departments would understand the peculiarity of Scottish conditions? The Bill, Adamson said, summing up Labour's opposition, was an affront to 'national sentiment'; it would remove 'the last vestige of independent Government and nationhood'.[2] Conservative MPs remained strangely silent and the measure was withdrawn without a vote.

The Bill was re-introduced in the following year, but this time Gilmour qualified his proposals with two statements. First, the 'headquarters' of the new Departments would remain in Edinburgh; there was no intention to move them to London.[3] Second, in an apparent reversal of earlier policy, he said it was his 'ambition to centralise in Edinburgh all the Departments concerned with Scottish affairs' and added that he could 'visualise the linking up of Parliament and Dover House with a central office in Edinburgh'.[4] In effect, Gilmour retreated from his earlier statement. The Departments would remain separate entities with much the same relationship to Whitehall as before, the only difference being that instead of appointed board members the Departments would be headed by career

1 *Hansard*, Vol. 204, c.467-8, 23 Mar. 1927, Re-Organisation of Offices (Scotland) Bill, Second Reading.

2 *Hansard*, Vol. 204, c.476, Bill, Second Reading.

3 *Hansard*, Vol. 214, c.260, 28 Feb. 1928, Re-Organisation of Offices (Scotland) Bill, Second Reading.

4 In 1912 Lord Pentland agreed to accommodate all the Government's Edinburgh Departments in a new building on Calton Hill, including the branch of the Scottish Office. The post-war financial situation prevented the scheme from being fully revived until 1927: SRO, MW1/61. It is likely that the idea of an Edinburgh central office came from Patrick Laird, the Scottish Office establishment officer who was responsible for co-ordinating the projected Government offices on Calton Hill. Laird had a reputation of being 'creative'.

civil servants. At some future date the Government would 'contemplate' further reform.

On one level, Gilmour had failed to convince MPs and others that his reform would retain the essential Scottish element of British administration—its 'administrative individuality'. As his fellow Conservative, Noel Skelton, indicated, many felt that the boards brought a Scottish 'spirit' to Government and enabled the public to feel that it was their 'Government'—symbolically as much as administratively.[1] On another, Gilmour had not convincingly elaborated why appointing administrative-class civil servants to the Departments was necessary or fundamental to Scotland's interests.[2] His style and presentation had been somewhat functional. In fact, the argument for integration was far more succinctly presented by the Liberal Home Ruler, Sir Archibald Sinclair. If the Government would not pursue devolution, it was important, he said, to have a Scottish Departmental structure 'under the direction of a civil servant, who knows the ropes and knows his way about the Treasury'; that, he added, would 'give Scotland far greater administrative autonomy than she enjoys at present'.[3] Sinclair revised Munro's thesis; to secure a higher awareness and acceptance of Scottish needs within 'centripetalism', the Scottish Secretary should have a tighter, more cohesive administration.

Initially, the Scottish Office itself was not sure that moving some of its functions to Edinburgh would be either efficient or effective. There was concern over maintaining contact with the Home Office on matters of policing. In 1931, however, MacDonald appointed Sinclair as Scottish Secretary and Skelton as Under Secretary. The following year the Scottish Office began a more systematic review of Scottish administration, and the remainder of the 1930s was dominated by discussion surrounding its status, power and administrative structure.

As the extracts (pp. 80-100) indicate, the period witnessed a considerable change in attitudes towards Scottish administration, particularly from the Treasury. Part of the explanation can be attributed to the growth in Government; the early 1930s had seen considerable difficulty in maintaining Scottish Office

1 *Hansard*, Vol. 219, c.1955, 9 July 1928, Bill, Third Reading.

2 Gilmour subsequently agreed to staff the new Department of Health assistant secretary posts with Board executive grade officers, 'to avoid unecessary friction'. It is not known whether he considered recruiting from British and English departments: Departmental letter to Treasury, 14 Feb. 1929, SRO, DD1/31.

3 *Hansard*, Vol. 214, c.882, 5 Mar. 1928, Bill, Second Reading. The Bill received the Royal Assent in Aug. 1928.

liaison with local authorities, especially in distributing grant aid.[1] There had also been problems in progressing certain Bills and ensuring appropriate attendance at Cabinet Committees.[2] However, the fall of the Labour Government in 1931 had also created a vacuum in Scottish political life and the fervour of the ILP seemed, in part, to have been captured by the SNP, who appeared to do remarkably well in a number of by-elections.[3] Sir Godfrey Collins, the National Government's Scottish Secretary, like Munro before him, realised that there had to be a qualitatively different response, above and beyond some simple reorganisation of duties. The establishment of a new local government division based in Edinburgh was part of that response.[4] So too was the agreement to have a separate Scottish Special Areas Commissioner.[5] But Collins wanted an administration clearly under his control, which, in effect, meant the control of his Permanent Under Secretary; the Committee on Scottish Administration was essentially a committee to review how this could be achieved.[6]

The resulting Re-Organisation of Offices Act, the *Scotsman* noted with some satisfaction, offered the prospect of 'closer contact between the Departments and Scottish opinion' and 'a greater competence in stating the Scottish case at Westminster'.[7] Nevertheless the Re-Organisation of Offices Act was, as Tom

1 Minute of W.R.L. Trickett, Treasury, 23 June 1936, PRO, T 162/476.

2 Levitt, *Poverty and Welfare*, 191-2. The Poor Law Bill, after objections from MPs, was redrafted in Committee: Letter of R.N. Duke, Assistant Secretary to Treasury, 21 Aug. 1935, PRO, T 162/998. Duke complained that he was often obliged to attend meetings arranged at short notice because the Department of Health could not send someone from Edinburgh quickly enough. He 'did not feel he was a particularly useful Departmental representative'.

3 *Times*, 'Scotland and the State', 20 & 21 June 1938.

4 The office opened in Jan. 1935 and also provided a base for Ministers and officials to liaise more directly with Scottish interests on any matter of concern. Its assistant secretary was David Milne: SRO, HH45/115. Collins was also able to secure Treasury approval to recruit administrative-class officers into the Department of Health. He wanted 'officers of suitable quality, education and otherwise' to tackle housing and health issues. In late 1935 a principal, W.S. Murrie, was transferred from Dover House and an assistant principal, T.D. Haddow, recruited through Class 1 open competition: SRO, DD1/12.

5 The Scottish Office took little interest in the early discussions over the Special Areas. However, once it became apparent that new provision was likely, Percy Rose, the Assistant Under Secretary, alerted Skelton (10 Oct. 1934), who immediately 'reserved' the Scottish position: SRO, DD10/289. 'Minding' the Special Areas Commissioner became one of the Local Government Division's functions, something which Sir Arthur Rose always resented: *Scotsman*, 'Scottish Special Areas', 29 July 1936.

6 Sir John Lamb to Treasury, 13 Aug. 1934: PRO, T 162/998. Robert Munro, Lord Alness, was initially proposed as chairman, but J.A. Inglis, the King's and Lord Treasurer's Remembrancer, felt that he had 'the mind of a journalist' and Sir John Gilmour was approached instead: minute, 29 June 1936, PRO, T 162/ 476. Because of Gilmour's recent ministerial experience, Collins felt obliged to approach Tom Johnston as a member.

7 *Scotsman*, 'Scottish Administration; Under Secretary's Duties', 29 July 1938.

Johnston said, an administrative response to a political question.[1] Some, including Johnston, were not convinced that it was adequate. The *Glasgow Herald* felt that if the Scottish Office's work had become more complex, effective liaison was also dependent on a strengthened political secretariat.[2] Baldwin, it noted, had refused the appointment of a second parliamentary under-secretary, essentially believing that administrative integration would obviate its necessity; Chamberlain continued to resist, partly on similar grounds, but also because the Scottish issue never appeared to him to have much relevance to rational administration.[3] Baldwin, however, did recognise the anomalous position of the Scottish Secretary's salary. In October 1936 Sir Godfrey Collins died and the Prime Minister persuaded Walter Elliot, the Minister of Agriculture, to accept the Scottish Secretaryship. At the same time he also agreed to establish a Cabinet review of ministerial salaries, which after reviewing the work of a number of ministers agreed to raise, amongst others, the Scottish Secretary's salary.[4]

At the outbreak of war, Scottish administration certainly looked much stronger: the reformed Scottish Office ranked amongst the principal departments of state, it had acquired new functions, and it had a tighter and easily comprehended structure. However, the Act did not signal a 'revolution' in Scottish government.[5] In administrative terms only two new divisions were created: one at Dover House for Whitehall liaison, and the other at St Andrews House for general and 'penumbra' work.[6] What had changed were two things:

1 *Hansard*, Vol. 347, c.1851, 13 Dec. 1938, Re-Organisation of Offices (Scotland) Bill, Second Reading.

2 *Glasgow Herald*, 'Re-Organisation of Offices', 14 Dec. 1938.

3 It was amongst the Gilmour Committee suggestions, though not a specific recommendation. Baldwin refused Collins in 1935: minute, 21 Nov. 1935, SRO, HH1/896. Later Chamberlain specifically requested Colville not to raise the issue, as there was 'serious criticism of the already large number of MPs holding Government office' and it would have 'repercussions in Wales': minute, 19 July 1938, SRO, HH1/820.

4 Ministerial Salaries Committee, Dec. 1936, PRO, CAB 27/613 MS(36). The Committee reported that Cabinet ministers served in a dual capacity, as members of the Cabinet and as departmental chiefs, and recommended that each should receive £5,000.

5 *Scotsman*, 'Scottish Administration', 14 Dec. 1938.

6 Re-organisation of Offices, 1939-40, PRO, T 162/1009. The Home Department divisions were: A (London), Defence and Fire; B, Local Government; C, Police; D, Welfare and General; E, Establishment; F, Fisheries; G, Prisons; Dover House Liaison. Division D included the Special Areas Act, Highlands and Islands Development, Electricity Supply, Power, Rural Amenities, Scottish Travel Association, Scottish Committee for Art and Industry, Probation and Juvenile Delinquency. The Dover House officials were to 'attend the Scottish Secretary or Permanent Under Secretary when required, prepare briefs at short notice and take an active interest in all Parliamentary Bills'. In addition they had 'to maintain liaison with other Whitehall departments' and 'follow up any Cabinet Committee' matter affecting Scotland. Prior to reorganisation the divisions were: A, Defence and War Preparations (established 1937); B, Private Legislation, the Highlands and Power; C, Police and Prisons; D

first the relationship of the Departments to each other and to the Scottish Secretary, and second the status and authority of the Permanent Under Secretary.[1] Previously the Under Secretary held a position essentially junior to Whitehall heads and broadly equivalent to those in Edinburgh. After 1939 the Under Secretary held a position equivalent in status (and salary) to other principal Whitehall Departments and superior to those in Edinburgh.[2] His role at one level was to institutionalise Scottish 'sentiment' within Whitehall by maintaining an 'effective voice in the formulation of Government policy' and at another to translate the 'practicalities' of an integrated British administration back to Scottish opinion.[3]

The outbreak of war brought further Scottish Office developments to a virtual standstill. The Home Department found itself heavily involved in Defence of the Realm matters and the Department of Health in developing the emergency medical services. It was not until 1942, when the Government began discussion of post-war reconstruction, that the nature, status and functioning of the Scottish Office re-emerged as an issue. Tom Johnston, the Coalition's Scottish Secretary, had long taken a strong interest in promoting economic development and had pressed with some success the relocation of certain war industries.[4] But Johnston knew that Scotland's record in attracting new industries, particularly car and aircraft manufacture, was poor, and began to press for a redefinition of Scottish Office powers, especially on control of industrial development and town and country planning. The extract (pp. 100-4) indicates the response: a forceful statement that 'centripetal' economic management was necessary to persuade, encourage and perhaps direct industry north of the border. Moving to a system

(Edinburgh), Local Government, Special Areas Act and Economic Development (established 1935); E, Establishment, Court work, Home Rule and other non-statutory work. There were separate Prisons and Fisheries Boards. At reorganisation the Department of Health retained its existing divisions, Health Services, Housing, National Insurance, Public Assistance and Establishment. Its London liaison was handled by a principal (established 1937), not an assistant secretary as the Home Department.

1 The Act removed the anomaly of statutory functions being vested in a Department and not the Minister. It is arguable that the Act also created a climate were Departments were compelled to work more closely with each other and with London than in the past.

2 In 1937 Sir Horace Hamilton moved from Permanent Under Secretary at the Board of Trade to the Scottish Office. He retained his old and higher salary on a temporary basis until 1939.

3 Scottish Inter-Departmental Committee on the Gilmour Committee, Memorandum on the future of the Under Secretary of Scotland, Oct. 1937, SRO, HH36/1. In Parliament Archibald Sinclair called him the 'fifth wheel in the coach'. Willie Gallacher put it differently: he was the coach's 'brake', there to 'deaden' Scottish initiative. *Hansard*, Vol. 347, c.1859 and 1889, 13 Dec. 1938, Re-Organisation of Offices (Scotland) Bill. After 1939 the Under Secretary spent much of his time at Dover House, but held weekly meetings in Edinburgh.

4 Memorandum on Location of War-time Industry, for Scottish Council on Post-war Problems, 1 Feb. 1942, SRO, HH50/188. Council Meeting, 21 May 1943, SRO, HH50/177 SC(43)12th.

of 'parallel' administration was seen as counter-productive. Instead the Treasury believed that the Scottish Office should seek to improve its own administrative efficiency within Scotland to facilitate development, and between Scotland and Whitehall to ensure that any special interests or needs were adequately heard. By 1945 two new divisions had been established, one in the Home Department to co-ordinate economic development and the other in the Department of Health for town and country planning.

The post-war Labour Government's nationalisation plans were far-reaching and comprehensive; coal, gas, electricity, rail, road and air transport were all quickly brought into public ownership. However, unlike hospitals, these industries were organised on a British basis, though each had a Scottish division or a Scottish advisory council. At one level Labour's programme was popular. Virtually all the industries, after seven years of war, were severely under-capitalised, with pay and other conditions for workers poor. Nationalisation afforded an opportunity for much-needed development. Nevertheless, it meant the transfer of many private and local authority services to British boards. When, in early 1947, it became apparent that Scotland had not shared in the immediate post-war employment boom, Labour MPs, the Convention of Royal Burghs and the press, amongst others, began to voice concern. Socialist 'planning', it was said, had not brought the jobs.[1] Instead 'long distance' control had removed Scotland's ability to influence key investment decisions, allegedly seen in the failure to develop Prestwick as Britain's second international airport.[2]

At the same time a loose coalition of Scottish 'devolutionists', under the umbrella of the Scottish Covenant Movement, began a campaign for a separate Scottish parliament and secured considerable press coverage.[3] The 'Covenanters', many felt, had tapped a strong current of concern, which could conceivably be mobilised into a much larger campaign. Labour 'pragmatists' like Patrick Dollan, Glasgow's past Lord Provost, sensed that some positive Government response was necessary and suggested the creation of separate Scottish departments of British ministries under the control of Parliamentary Under Secretaries, who in turn would be responsible to the Scottish Secretary.[4] It had

1 *Scotsman*, Speech by Sir John Falconer, Lord Provost of Edinburgh, 1 Feb. 1947.

2 *Scotsman*, 'Scottish Survey; Scots Government', 24 Mar. 1947; *Glasgow Herald*, 'Scotland's Electricity', 28 Feb. 1947.

3 *Scotsman*, 'Scots Government', 24 Mar. 1947.

4 *Glasgow Herald*, 'Bottleneck at the Scottish Office', 7 Apr. 1947. Dollan was Chairman of the Civil Aviation's Scottish Advisory Committee.

proved impossible, he said, for the Scottish Office under one minister effectively to co-ordinate the activities of British departments within Scotland. An administrative response was, in itself, not enough.

Dollan's theme was picked up by a prominent Conservative politician, J.L. Clyde, who made it clear that the Conservatives remained opposed to any form of political devolution for three principal reasons.[1] First, much of Scotland's poor housing and health record was due to the impact of the depression reducing workers' wages. Without Treasury grants it would be difficult to maintain the necessary level of social investment. Second, industrialisation had meant that Scotland's economy was 'inextricably intermingled' with that of England and devolution might create an impediment to free trade. Third, a parliament would induce a 'provincial outlook' in the Scottish mind, like southern Ireland, and result in the Scottish 'voice' being excluded from post-war international 'councils', again to the detriment of its economy. Clyde suggested a different response that involved much more of 'the executive machinery being directed and operated in Scotland'. Two additional Parliamentary Under Secretaries should be appointed to take charge of 'defined departments'; that, he said, would enable the Scottish Secretary to exercise general supervision of Scottish affairs and 'give him more time to protect and enlarge Scottish rights in Cabinet'. Finally, he added that there was much to be said for 'a Finance Corporation for Scotland, administered through a Council of Industry, or similar body' to acquire industrial estates and generally encourage local enterprise. Clyde's views were quickly noted by the Conservative leadership and Sir Anthony Eden, although not pledging ministerial appointments, accepted the need to 'reduce Whitehall control' through 'administrative centralisation in Scotland'.[2]

Clyde effectively restated the position Conservatives had taken in the past. Much of the Scottish problem was really a problem of 'bigger' or 'greater' government, the natural progress of social advance. Amending the Government's administrative machine to meet the new exigencies was in itself wholly commendable. Clyde, however, went further than any previous Conservative spokesman; he openly advocated greater Scottish ministerial responsibility for economic development. The extent of responsibility was not precisely defined, but his position stood sharply at odds with the Treasury's wartime view. 1947 therefore saw three positions on Scottish administration being defined: the

1 *Scotsman*, 'Importance of Scottish Nationalism', 18 Apr. 1947 and 19 Apr. 1949. Clyde became Lord Advocate in 1951 and Lord President in 1954.

2 *Glasgow Herald*, 'Mr Eden on Scots Policy', 5 June 1947.

'Covenanters' pressing for the Northern Ireland solution, a parallel legislature; Dollan, following Johnston, in favour of Scottish ministerial control over British policy, a parallel administration; Clyde and the Conservatives loosely in favour of further 'decentralisation', a devolved administration. The extracts (pp. 104-40) show how much the issues went to the heart of Government in Scotland and how difficult it was to secure consensus.

The immediate response of Westwood, the Scottish Secretary, was to press for an increase in his ministerial team, very much on the lines Clyde had suggested. It met a hostile response from Sir Edward Bridges, the Head of the Home Civil Service, who could not see how a minister with unspecified responsibility for economic affairs would materially aid Government efficiency. The Scottish Office was told that the proposal was more likely to unsettle public opinion, cause further Government embarrassment and lead to calls for 'greater devolution'.[1] Westwood temporarily dropped the idea when Labour MPs began to press for an independent inquiry into Scottish affairs. Westwood again initially supported the proposal and found some support from Clement Attlee, the Prime Minister.[2] However, Herbert Morrison, Attlee's domestic manager, was quick to indicate his opposition. In fact, through the Lobby he also let the press know his opinions. There was, he said, 'no real demand for home rule', although the Government welcomed 'the case for lesser claims if they were more specific'. 'Post-war conditions', he added, 'make the time inopportune to bring devolution into prominence and perhaps sharp controversy'.[3]

In October Westwood became one of Attlee's casualties in the dollar-crisis Cabinet reshuffle, being told sharply that he was 'not up to it'. The appointment of Arthur Woodburn as the new Scottish Secretary was not unexpected. He had been Parliamentary Private Secretary to Tom Johnston and as a Parliamentary Under Secretary at the Ministry of Works had generally been hailed as a modest success.[4] Woodburn immediately dropped the idea of further ministerial appointments, but continued to press for some 'fact-finding' inquiry into Scottish affairs. He also added a new proposal, again from Clyde, but 'mulled over' in the Scottish Office: a Scottish Production Council to assist Scotland's

1 Bridges to Sir David Milne, 26 June 1947, PRO, T 222/1048. The proposal was very much Westwood's own.

2 Attlee minuted: 'While, I think, our Scots friends are apt to be unduly alarmed at Scottish Nationalism, I think it might be wise to have some kind of inquiry', 23 June 1947, PRO, PREM 8/658.

3 *Glasgow Herald*, 'Home Rule for Scotland', 1 July 1947; 'London Correspondent', 16 July 1947. Morrison was a fourth-generation Scot from Arran, with a certain fondness for Burns.

4 *Glasgow Herald*, 'Scotland's New Regime', 8 Oct. 1947.

economic regeneration. Morrison was not having any of this, and at a private meeting with Woodburn told him that public expectations of what Labour was prepared or able to do had risen to unacceptable levels.[1] At a time of national crisis, similar to 1931, Woodburn should remember where his loyalties should lie, his Party. Morrison had recommended Woodburn to Attlee in order to sell more effectively Labour's message that public ownership under a Government pledged to promote social justice was more likely to sustain Scottish economic advance than any inquiry or special initiative. Woodburn, a one-time radical contributor to *Forward* who had never fully recovered from MacDonald's 'treachery', hesitated and gave way.

The devolution issue re-emerged in early 1949 when the Covenant Movement began another campaign on the issue of Home Rule. The tactics adopted, including a suggested plebiscite, were more calculated than in 1947, aimed in part to broaden the Movement's legitimacy, but also to embarrass the Government by showing that its stance was unreasonable. The Government itself was less popular, and in Scotland Woodburn faced particular difficulties in maintaining the Scottish housing programme and inducing new industry north of the border. At the same time, the Conservatives had formalised their ideas on Scotland and announced their support for administrative devolution, much on the lines Clyde had suggested in 1947. In the face of these two opposing propositions, Woodburn reluctantly decided to maintain the Cabinet's 1947 line; it would have been politically difficult, he felt, to accept the Conservatives' proposals. It was a strange decision and one taken without considering the advice on offer from the Cabinet Office, where Bridges thought that some gesture (perhaps a Minister of State, an 'identical twin' based in Edinburgh) would do much to deflate the opposition, and from Morrison who felt that the 'Covenanters' were playing 'their hand' much more skilfully.[2] Woodburn was caught wrong-footed and after the 1950 election lost the Secretaryship.

Hector McNeil, his successor, came into office clearly briefed by Attlee as to his task: to defeat the Covenant movement and to counter the Conservatives.

1 It was widely reported that Woodburn was pressing for an inquiry into the treatment of Scottish business at Westminster, the comparative economic position of Scotland, the possibility of legislative devolution, or further administrative devolution through the appointment of a Minister of State: *Scotsman*, 'Devolution Inquiry', 6 Nov. 1947; 'Scottish Devolution', 14 Nov. 1947; *Glasgow Herald*, 'Scottish Fact-finding Inquiry', 7 Nov. 1947; 'Government of Scotland', 14 Nov. 1947. See also Notes on Draft Cabinet Paper, A. Johnston (Lord President's Office), 8 Nov. 1947, PRO, CAB 128/911. Bridges was not altogether opposed to the Production Council: minute, 30 Oct. 1947, PRO, T 222/1048.

2 Minutes of E.E. Bridges, 12 and 14 Dec. 1949, ibid.; minute of J.E.R. Pimlott (Lord President's Office), 14 Dec. 1949, PRO, CAB 124/60.

McNeil, whose background in journalism and foreign affairs gave him, perhaps, a broader perspective on Scottish affairs than his two predecessors, wasted little time in reformulating Labour's approach. He was only partially successful, for the Cabinet's left wing (especially Aneurin Bevan) remained opposed to any nationalist concessions—it was what they had fought the war against. At any rate the Covenant movement began to wane, partly because the press, and especially the *Glasgow Herald*, took a harsh line on the economic consequences of devolution, and partly because Scottish institutions became similarly concerned about the loss of Treasury grants.[1]

The Conservatives fought the 1951 election with a promise to implement their 1949 statements on Scotland. The issue of increasing the Scottish Office's ministerial team was included in early drafts of the King's speech.[2] At a political level, the Conservatives obviously felt that they had resolved the issue of ministerial strength. The Minister of State, based in Edinburgh, would deal with Scottish institutions with considerable delegated authority, whilst the Scottish Secretary and the additional Parliamentary Under Secretary could concentrate their activities on representing Scotland more effectively in Whitehall.[3] But the Conservatives had also inherited a Scottish Office still based on the 1939 administrative structure, albeit amended by Johnston.[4] The events of 1947 had left their mark on its psyche; Westwood's pursuit of two apparently conflicting objectives and then Woodburn's ignominious retreat were not signs of an administration in control or even one that knew its brief. The end of 1947 saw some administrative adjustments to staffing, but Woodburn proved as ineffective in reconfigurating the administration as he had been in maintaining his political influence.[5] Under McNeil, officials adopted a more active role in 'penumbra'

1 *Glasgow Herald*, 'Financial Policy', 20 May 1950; 'Covenant Questions', 2 June 1950; 'Facing the Past', 9 June 1950; *Scotsman*, 'Scots Government', 5 Apr. 1950; 'Covenant Progress', 24 Apr. 1950; 'Scottish Affairs', 10 May 1949. The Lord Provosts of Edinburgh and Glasgow and the STUC were amongst those who announced their opposition.

2 First Draft, 31 Oct. 1951, PRO, CAB 134/993 KSC(51)1.

3 *Scotsman*, 'Scottish Team, and Clearing House for Scottish problems', 10 Nov. 1951.

4 After 1945, the Home Department's Division A was subdivided and moved to Edinburgh. At the Department of Health the post-war social programme led to the establishment of two additional divisions each for Housing and Town and County Planning divisions and four for Health, with the loss of National Insurance.

5 In Dec. 1949, Sir Norman Brooke, the Cabinet Secretary, complained to Attlee that Woodburn's failure stemmed from 'not so much the failure of a United Kingdom Department to remember Scottish interests, but rather the failure of the Scottish Departments to secure that their views are heard at the formative stages of proposals which are devised in English Departments and have later to be applied to Scotland': minute, 14 Dec. 1949, PRO, PREM 8/1517.

affairs, which the Treasury noted, but they remained handicapped by Labour's preference for centralised planning.[1]

The prospect of a Royal Commission on Scottish Affairs was looked on with enthusiasm within the Scottish Office, but less so within the Treasury. The latter, although it accepted that the Conservatives had become electorally pledged, remained concerned over the Commission's outcome. The Treasury had no wish to see Johnstonian thought and language re-emerge with official sanction. The terms of reference were tightly drawn and its membership carefully selected to avoid overtly discordant views.[2] In July 1952 Lord Balfour was appointed chairman to 'review with reference to the financial, economic, administrative and other considerations involved, the arrangements for exercising the functions of ... Government in relation to Scotland'.[3] Nevertheless, the Treasury remained apprehensive over the issue of 'parallel' administration, especially as virtually all the early Scottish evidence remained critical of the current division of ministerial responsibility, particularly over trade and industry. In the event, Sir Edward Bridges decided to give evidence himself, much to the surprise of his colleagues who had assumed that the Treasury's evidence would be delegated elsewhere. His evidence, coming near the end of the hearings, was probably the Commission's turning point; only Tom Johnston's subsequent examination raised any discordant note, in favour of greater Scottish Office 'rights' at Whitehall, but not of further devolution of ministerial responsibility.

At one level, the Commission's report was 'barren'; 'parallelism' could not work within the British context.[4] At another, however, its negative tone also cast a spell over 'centripetal' administration; it had not worked to Scotland's advantage.[5] The Gilmour structure, a small London office to pursue liaison and

1 Economic Organisation Working Group (EOWG (50)26), 31 July 1950, PRO, T 222/324. Division I (Industry and Development) was primarily responsible for 'penumbra' affairs. Under its assistant secretary, one principal dealt with the Highlands and constitutional issues, whilst the other concentrated on the central industrial area.

2 SRO, HH41/1390. Sir David Milne revised the Commission's terms of reference over forty times before securing Treasury agreement. On no account would the Cabinet Office have Tom Johnston on the Committee.

3 Balfour was the nephew of Arthur Balfour, Prime Minister, 1902–5 and Foreign Secretary, 1916–19. He was chairman of the Scottish Special Housing Association, 1938–44, and of the Scottish Division of the NCB, 1946–51. The *Scotsman* considered that the Commission embodied 'neutrality' rather than 'distinction': 'Royal Commission', 27 July 1952.

4 *Scotsman*, 'Scots Devolution', 28 July 1954.

5 *Glasgow Herald*, 'Departmental Arrangements', 8 Dec. 1954.

a division in Edinburgh engaged in 'penumbra' affairs, was also seen to have disadvantages. One Treasury official noted:

> One of the main troubles seems to be that the Permanent Under Secretary of State has failed to keep in the 'Scottish Office' a good many of the co-ordinating functions which are properly his. There would be much to be said for the Scottish Office, rather than the Scottish Home Department, handling the non-statutory duties of the Secretary of State relating to trade and industry.... against the background of the manner in which extraneous duties have been added to the Scottish Home Department, there is much to be said ... that if highways are transferred to the Secretary of State, they ought not to be given to the Scottish Home Department: or, if they are, some of their functions (e.g. relating to the supervision of local government) should be transferred to (say) the Department of Health.[1]

The Treasury reluctantly recognised these issues. Once the Balfour Report was implemented and the functions transferred, it invited Sir David Milne to conduct an internal review of Scottish administration. The extracts (pp. 141-5) indicate the result: there was no unanimity over a restructured Department. Sir David Milne's memorandum, however, probably reflected wider views within Scotland. Labour, for instance, still regarded housing very much as a health issue, not one that was an adjunct of economic development.[2] Conservative views were little different. In 1959 a problem was recognised—that the structure of Scottish administration no longer matched economic circumstances; but an acceptable response remained unformulated.

Chapter Two: Employment and Industrial Development

At the outbreak of war in 1914 the Scottish economy was generally considered one of the world's great successes, based, it was said, on a unique combination of private enterprise, native entrepreneurship and craft labour. Its production of ships, the quality of its engineering products, its textiles and even coal-mining ensured substantial and growing employment, especially on the Clyde. There had been periods of economic depression, the last between 1907 and 1909, but to contemporaries the general trend of prosperity seemed unbroken. The war, in one sense, re-emphasised that prosperity: the military required virtually everything the shipyards, engineering works and other factories could produce. By 1918 few thought that the prosperity could continue without some

1 Minute of A. Johnston (Third Secretary), 3 June 1954, PRO, T 222/686.

2 *Hansard*, Vol. 565, c.39, 18 Feb. 1957, Housing and Town Development (Scotland) Bill, Second Reading, comments by Woodburn; Vol. 591, c.591, 10 July 1958, Supply: Scotland (Industry and Employment), comments by Fraser.

'adjustment', but most believed that a Coalition Government committed to a policy of national reconstruction would ensure the minimum of friction in the transition to peace. The reality was somewhat different. The structure of the British economy had been seriously undermined by the necessities of wartime production and by early 1919, with large numbers of demobbed soldiers out of work, strikes and rising inflation, the public's faith in reconstruction began to wane.

Before 1914 the 'economic' functions of the Scottish Secretary were not great and were further reduced by the Haldane Report which essentially sought to rationalise Ministerial responsibility for the conduct of Government business. By 1919 virtually all the Scottish Secretary's 'economic' functions, apart from agriculture and fisheries, had been transferred to other ministries.[1] The Scottish Secretary, however, did retain responsibility for monitoring the provision of local authority relief work. In the range of Government activity, this may not have appeared important, but it did mean that he could face Parliamentary questions on this and related 'penumbra' affairs.

The Government's post-war policy of economic retrenchment began in the summer of 1919 with a curb on profiteering, but took root more seriously the following spring when the Bank of England, fearful of the spiralling inflation, introduced tighter monetary controls on credit.[2] At the time, opinion generally welcomed the Bank's policy: deflation, it was said, would do much to restore Britain's balance of trade, seriously eroded by American imports and the loss of European markets.[3] Bonar Law, Stanley Baldwin and even the administration of Ramsay MacDonald that followed believed in much the same policy: strict control of public expenditure, tight monetary conditions and a return to the Gold Standard. Such a policy would restore Britain's status as a 'credit-worthy' nation, an essential element to any investment-led recovery.

1 This included the Ministry of Transport, which assumed responsibility for Scottish roads, piers, harbours, inland waterways and electricity, under the Ministry of Transport Act, 1919 and Electricity Supply Act, 1919. In both cases the Scottish Secretary was required to be consulted before the Ministry of Transport took action: Treasury Blue Notes, Secretary for Scotland's Office, 1920-21, PRO, T 222/469.

2 For general discussion of the period's economic policy, see D.H. Aldcroft, *The British Economy: Volume 1, 1920-1951* (Brighton, 1986); G.C. Peden, *British Economic and Social Policy: Lloyd George to Margaret Thatcher* (Oxford, 1991); S. Pollard, *The Development of the British Economy, 1914-1990* (London, 1992); J. Tomlinson, *Employment Policy: the Crucial Years, 1939-1945* (London, 1987). On Scotland, see R.H. Campbell, *The Rise and Fall of Scottish Industry, 1707-1939* (Edinburgh, 1980); G. McCrone, *Scotland's Economic Progress, 1951-1960* (London, 1965); A. Slaven, *The Development of the West of Scotland, 1750-1960* (London, 1975).

3 *Glasgow Herald*, 'A Check to Exports', 4 Apr. 1920; *Scotsman*, Leader, 1 Mar. 1920.

Throughout the early 1920s, Scottish opinion deviated little from British on either the causes of the consequent unemployment or the remedy. Scottish costs, it was said, remained comparatively high; to sustain any kind of growth based on investment, the press and Conservative MPs, in particular, remained convinced that Government policy should aim to rationalise much of the war-generated production capacity. The Government, they felt, should also aim to control other influences on production costs, especially local taxation and trade union power.[1] Within this circle of opinion there was never any thought of Scotland following a separate economic policy; too much of its trade was inter-dependent with England's.[2] A separate policy, it was believed, would have meant higher interest rates and probably taxation, which in turn would almost certainly have meant even lower levels of employment.

Nevertheless the severity of the immediate post-war slump, with unemployment rising in July 1921 to over 20 per cent of the Scottish workforce, caused alarm. As the extract (pp. 146-9) indicates, the Board of Health left the Scottish Office in no doubt that the domestic economy faced profound structural difficulties.[3] Scotland had too many coal mines, too many shipyards and too many export-orientated factories; it did not have enough capital or enterprise to sustain industry based on domestic demand. The immediate impact of the Board's survey, however, was muted. Although Robert Munro, the Scottish Secretary, along with other Ministers, was able to persuade the Treasury to extend the period of unemployment benefit and to provide local authorities with grants and loans to extend relief work, the Government remained convinced that retrenchment was the only method to restore 'equilibrium' and economic growth.[4]

Bonar Law's Conservative Government, elected in November 1922, was perhaps even more committed to fiscal control than Lloyd George's, and continued with the policy of deflation. Law's Scottish Secretary, Lord Novar, a pre-war Gladstonian Liberal MP, fully supported this policy, and entered office declaring that Scotland would soon benefit from a boom in private investment.[5] The Board of Health was quick to inform him otherwise, and Novar spent much of his fifteen-month tenure trying to convince the

1 *Glasgow Herald*, 'The National Purse', 1 July 1925; *Scotsman*, 'British Industry', 15 Sept. 1925.

2 For instance see comments by J. Kidd, *Hansard*, Vol. 127, c.2046, 16 Apr. 1920, Government of Scotland Bill; The Duchess of Atholl and Sir A. Hunter-Weston, *Hansard*, Vol. 173, cc.819 and 864, 9 May 1924, Government of Scotland Bill.

3 *Glasgow Herald*, 'Unemployment in Glasgow', 19 Sept. 1921.

4 B. Swann & M. Turnbull (eds.), *Public Record Office: Unemployment Insurance, 1911-1939* (London, 1975) and *Public Record Office: Employment and Unemployment, 1919-1939* (London, 1978).

5 *Scotsman*, 'Lord Novar's Return to Politics', 7 Nov. 1922.

Government that higher levels of relief work were politically as well as economically necessary (extracts pp. 149-56). Novar's basic difficulty was twofold: first his Cabinet colleagues, especially Neville Chamberlain, Minister of Health and then Chancellor of the Exchequer, remained unconvinced that there was any special political problem attached to Clydeside, and second, he seemed to wish for public investment in an industry, shipbuilding, that was readily acknowledged as having surplus capacity.[1] Unlike the English group of Conservative 'industrial' MPs, Novar had no ready scheme for investment in public infrastructure.

Novar's concerns were interestingly taken up by his Parliamentary Under Secretary, Walter Elliot, who during MacDonald's minority Government pressed for an inquiry into the possibility of the State re-equipping the Clyde shipyards.[2] The proposal was quickly rejected when the Conservatives re-entered office (extracts pp. 156-8). Rationalisation of plant and a reduction in wages remained the preferred option to recapture trade. Such thinking also dominated Government debates on the future of the Scottish shale oil industry (extracts pp. 158-62), and by 1925 any Scottish flirtation with economic interventionism had ended.

1927 saw something of a mini-boom in the British economy, and unemployment in the South-East of England fell to a post-war low of five per cent. In Scotland, even the shipyards had relatively full order books. Baldwin's Government felt more comfortable that its economic policies were working and with the collapse of the General Strike sensed a shift in popular perceptions. As a result, its view of the depressed areas altered. The Midlands and the South-East seemed short of labour, whilst a large number of miners (and in Scotland the Lanarkshire steelworkers) appeared content to survive on benefits and relief work. The Government's response was to promote industrial transference, training the redundant workers and moving them to where new jobs seemed to exist. It was a policy that the Board of Health took up with enthusiasm (extracts pp. 162-5): the removal of the unemployed would benefit both the individuals and their communities whose local taxation levels were at a historic high. It was also a policy that appeared to receive considerable Scottish support.

1 *Hansard*, Vol. 162, c.81, 26 Mar. 1923, Local Authorities (Emergency Provisions) Bill, Second Reading. Chamberlain felt that the unemployment was 'temporary' and that the Government's proposed extension of relief work loan facilities 'would alleviate any undue hardship'. The issue was of interest only 'to those Scots with an interest in dry subjects'.

2 *Hansard*, Vol. 176, c.2154, 30 July 1924, Ministry of Labour Supply Vote. Elliot commented that 'if we cannot stand on our feet in that industry the whole of our industry must sink, and the work of Great Britain with it.' He was particularly concerned to maintain naval supremacy.

The *Glasgow Herald* felt that the 'ordinary remedies' to cure unemployment 'would no longer suffice' and even Adamson, then a Fife miners' MP, called for more Scottish training centres to encourage workers out of the 'derelict' areas.[1]

The policy, however, was not popular amongst the unemployed, especially in Lanarkshire, where Government officials sent to assess the situation were heckled about its impact on the community and family life.[2] The Board of Health, nevertheless, remained adamant that transference was the only solution for the depressed areas and tried hard to persuade parish councils to cut poor law benefits to those reluctant to move. Threats of disturbances, mingled with a concern for family life, persuaded parish councils otherwise, and the policy of benefit-led transference was abandoned during MacDonald's second Government.

In the 1920s, apart from these limited forays into economic management, the Scottish Secretary's specific involvement with unemployment remained largely with public works, assisting the Ministry of Labour in processing local authority applications for grants and loans. Although Gilmour's steel housing programme (see Chapter Three) was also aimed at providing work for shipyard workers, he made it clear that economic development was not a major part of his brief.[3] In the 1920s, however, partly because of local authority caution (Scottish ratepayers were hard-pressed), partly because the grants favoured areas taking 'transferred' workers, and partly because of Scottish difficulties with Ministry of Labour liaison, expenditure on public works in Scotland fell below the unofficial 'Goschen' formula (11/80ths of the total).[4] The impact of this decline on unemployment is hard to assess, perhaps increasing it in 1930 by another 5,000, but the Scottish Office accepted that many local authorities remained perturbed by Whitehall's failure to appreciate their particular problems and difficulties.[5]

1 *Glasgow Herald*, 'The Problems of the Pits', 3 Apr. 1928; 'The Industrial Transfer Report', 24 July 1928. The *Scotsman* had called for such a measure some time previously, arguing that it was a waste of the Empire's 'capacity': 'Training the Unemployed', 21 Oct. 1925.

2 *Glasgow Herald*, 'The Unemployment Problem; Government Commission in Scotland', 27 Apr. 1928. The officials met local trades councils and other representative bodies.

3 *Hansard*, Vol. 183, c.183, 28 Apr. 1925, Adjournment Debate, Scottish Affairs.

4 Unemployment: Relief Schemes and Government Grants, 1925-34, SRO, DD10/170-191, 201. The Scottish share was put at 8 per cent.

5 Minute of Tom Johnston, Parliamentary Under Secretary of State, 20 Aug. 1930, SRO, DD10/187. Johnston suggested the establishment of a Scottish Advisory Committee based in Edinburgh and, reversing the existing practice, reporting to the Scottish Office before the Ministry of Labour. The protocol fell into disuse when the National Government withdrew unemployment grants in 1931.

When public works re-emerged in 1934, as part of the National Government's programme of reconstruction, this posed a problem for Scottish officials. A Government 'Public Works' Commissioner, working as originally proposed under the Ministry of Labour, might, the officials remembered, run into the same problems as in the 1920s. For the Scottish Office, there was the prospect of receiving the same criticism as before, from local authorities for not promoting Scottish needs, and from Whitehall for not organising a better Scottish response. Noel Skelton, the Parliamentary Under Secretary, and Sir Godfrey Collins, the Scottish Secretary, made it clear to Chamberlain that they would face severe difficulties, both with local authorities and with Scottish opinion, if the 1920s arrangements were reinstated.[1] The Government agreed to a separate Scottish Commissioner with a budget based on double the 'Goschen' formula, a significant achievement for the hard-pressed Collins.

It would be a mistake, however, to consider the Special Areas Act as a turning-point in Government attitudes towards regional policy. Chamberlain continued to believe that migration from the depressed areas was the only effective method to solve unemployment. The 1934 Act simply repackaged relief work under greater Government control, without any hint of introducing new industry. What had changed was the nature of the Scottish Secretary's brief: it now included economic development. This was seen in July 1935 when, for the first time, the Opposition called a Scottish Office supply debate on the Special Areas.[2]

That debate, and another a few days later, are interesting in that they demonstrate the beginnings of a distinctive Scottish attitude towards regional policy. Until then the view of the Scottish ministers, Collins and Skelton, was not materially different from Chamberlain's. Collins, however, quickly took note that opinion amongst the Government's Clydeside MPs had altered, and, perhaps equally importantly, that there had been a similar change of opinion in the Scottish press. The most critical comment on Government policy came from H.J.H. Scrymgeour-Wedderburn, the MP for West Renfrewshire, who during an Opposition debate on unemployment, contrasted the post-war growth of the South-East with the structural decline of Clydeside and stated:

> It should not be beyond the powers of the modern State to correct a mal-distribution of this kind, and to direct investment to those parts of the country where employment is most

1 Committee on the Reports of the Investigators into the Distressed Areas, 18 Oct. 1934 and 6 Nov. 1934, PRO, CAB 27/578 DA(34)2nd and 4th Meetings.

2 *Hansard*, Vol. 303, c.2064-2110, 4 July 1935, Supply: Committee—Scottish Estimates.

> needed and to check the unhealthy congestion of industry in the neighbourhood of London.[1]

The Government, he added, should consider establishing a holding company to finance industrial estates. The *Scotsman* spoke in a similar vein and commented, 'The public [now] look to the Government to initiate schemes which would be of permanent value in rebuilding industry in the distressed areas'. It added:

> New life is badly needed in these areas. It is very badly needed in Scotland. If the Government had put the Special Commissioner at the head of an Industrial Development Board with a competent staff and adequate financial resources, we might have had some hope.[2]

The view of the *Glasgow Herald* was similar:

> It was extremely important, for more orderly development than has taken place in the past, that changes must be planned and controlled. The powers of the Special Areas Commissioners are perhaps unnecessarily restricted and they are carrying out the kind of work which in all probability will sooner or later have to be attempted for the country as a whole.[3]

The mid-1930s therefore saw a change in Scottish attitudes towards economic development: a policy of Lowland 'clearance' was no longer acceptable. Why? First, the nature of the 1930s depression had wiped out the belief that the slump was temporary. In the 1920s the press and Conservative MPs generally felt that once trade union power had been curbed and public expenditure brought under control, the factors of production would adjust of their own accord. Second, throughout the 1920s, there was a widespread view, even from Labour MPs, that migration was the only option for the unemployed. The trade depression of the 1930s, however, was a world phenomenon. Rather than workers emigrating in large numbers, the reverse was true; many came back. The depression struck Canada, the United States and Australia even harder. Third, from 1932, the Government began a policy of trade protectionism and this tended to benefit the new consumer industries in the Midlands and the South-East. By contrast, Scotland was dependent on exports, and as virtually every

1 *Hansard*, Vol. 304, c.242, 9 July 1935, Unemployment and Distressed Areas Debate. He became Scottish Parliamentary Under Secretary in 1936.

2 *Scotsman*, 'Distressed Areas', 15 Nov. 1934; cf. 'Special Areas Report', 18 July 1935.

3 *Glasgow Herald*, 'The Special Areas', 18 July 1935. Both the *Scotsman* and the *Glasgow Herald* were in fact endorsing Sir Arthur Rose's first Report on the Scottish Special Areas, where he canvassed the possibility of wider powers.

other country also introduced trade tariffs, its economy saw a further reduction in its international market. In effect, this view was saying that the Government could not pursue a policy of domestic stability unaffected, as Elliot stated, by 'hasty external decisions', if at the same time it did not develop a policy that also recognised Scottish needs.[1] The Scottish economy needed new light industry aimed at the British domestic market.

These views soon became accepted Ministerial policy. Collins, Elliot and Colville, successively the Scottish Secretaries before the war, all pressed Chamberlain to modify his attitude and accept a more positive regional policy (see extracts pp. 165-77). Chamberlain's belief in migration, cheap credit and private led investment, however, never wavered and, as the extracts indicate, at every review he pressed for minimal Government involvement with industrial development.[2]

Three things stand out from the Government's discussions about the Special Areas. First, Scottish Office policy had shifted from viewing the 1934 Act as assisting the physical renovation of 'derelict' areas and restoring worker 'morale', to one that saw the Government as having an extended role in industrial planning.[3] Second, this view commanded widespread support. Although in public Scottish ministers accepted the Chamberlain line, in private their phraseology bore a certain similarity to Labour's.[4] It was also similar to that of the *Glasgow Herald* and the *Scotsman*, both of which openly advocated some form of national planning to 'steer' industry from the 'congested' South-East.[5] Third, during the Special Areas discussions, the authority of the Scottish Secretary not just to speak on economic development but also to indicate what would be the minimum acceptable as Government policy for Scotland grew. In 1937 Chamberlain had really wanted the Act discontinued, but instead found himself

1 *Hansard*, Vol. 330, c.1476, 16 Dec. 1937, Special Areas and Unemployment Debate. Sir Archibald Sinclair had resigned from the Scottish Secretaryship in 1932 because of the impact retaliatory tariffs would have on UK heavy industry, complaining that the Government's policy was 'an effective barrier' to their regeneration. *Hansard*, Vol. 303, c.204, 9 July 1935, Unemployment and Distressed Areas Debate.

2 His most resolute defence of policy can be found in *Hansard*, Vol. 321, c.1572-83, 12 Mar. 1937, Special Areas (Money) Resolution.

3 *Hansard*, Vol. 295, c.1365-70, 3 Dec. 1934, Depressed Areas Bill, Second Reading. Speech by Collins.

4 Patrick Dollan, Glasgow's Treasurer, described Government policy as 'offering a pancake to appease the hunger of an elephant': *Glasgow Herald*, 'Local Authorities and Special Areas Proposals', 2 Mar. 1937. Joe Westwood (Scottish shadow spokesman) thought that rearmament work only 'temporised' the situation: *Hansard*, Vol. 321, c.1569, 12 Mar. 1937.

5 *Glasgow Herald*, 'Keynes and the Slump', 19 Jan. 1937; 'The Block Grants', 2 Mar. 1937; 'The Industrial Magnet', 19 Jan. 1938; 'Scotland's Market', 10 June 1938; 'Planning for Scottish Industry', 10 Aug. 1938; *Scotsman*, 'Location of Industry', 9 Dec. 1937; 'Location of Industry', 31 Mar. 1938.

agreeing a new Act that included financing industrial estates. In 1938, it was the Scottish Ministers who were the most vociferous of the Ministers in ensuring the Act's further continuance. Colville realised that to have abandoned the Act before the Royal Commission into the Distribution of the Industrial Population reported would have tacitly undermined the case for positive intervention.

Nevertheless it would be a mistake to believe that the Scottish Secretary was widely recognised as an economic minister, or that his influence on the activities of other departments was widespread or significant. For instance, the Scottish Office pressed hard for, and was successful in securing, rearmament work for the Clyde. But much of the work (which greatly reduced unemployment) went to the established industries, the shipyards, engineering works and textiles.[1] The Scottish Office was less successful in securing the introduction of new industry. This, in part, reflected the established policy of the Cabinet's Defence Policy and Requirements Committee.[2] Apart from agreeing rearmament orders, it also set the criteria for the location of Government-sponsored war production factories. In early 1936 the Committee decided that to ensure a 'shadow' factory's 'effective' management it should be sited no more than 100 miles from its parent plant.[3] As most of the parent factories for aircraft production, cars and electronics, were in the Midlands and the South East, the Scottish Office found it difficult to argue for wider dispersal.[4]

The Scottish economy did not do particularly well out of the Second World War. Tom Johnston, who was appointed Scottish Secretary in February 1941, was by all accounts more energetic than his predecessor in pressing the Scottish case for war work. By spring 1942 he was able to claim some success, particularly in ensuring that existing plant was used to capacity, but although labour supply considerations meant later 'shadow factories' being sited further away from the South, the only major manufacturer induced north to Clydeside was

1 For an example of Scottish Office correspondence in securing contracts for Borders textile factories, see letters of C.C. Cunningham (Private Secretary to Scottish Secretary), SRO, HH36/139.

2 The Committee was established in early 1935 with ministers and officials from the Defence Ministries, the Ministry of Labour and the Board of Trade.

3 W. Hornby, *Factories and Plant* (London, 1958), ch. 9. Lord Swinton, Secretary of State for Air, was particularly concerned about compensation claims if the parent firm ran into financial difficulty: PRO, CAB 16/136 DPR 21st meeting, 25 May 1936. The Committee did have a Scottish representative, Lord Weir. Weir, in part, opposed the Bishopton site because the Clydeside rearmament programme had caused a shortage of skilled engineers, despite 15 per cent local unemployment: see comments, ibid., 20th meeting, 7 May 1936.

4 It was not until 1938 that a special War Office agent was appointed to liaise with Scottish firms, largely at the bequest of the Scottish Economic Committee: *Glasgow Herald*, 'Planning for Scottish Industry', 10 Aug. 1938.

Rolls-Royce.[1] Moreover, much to Johnston's embarrassment and the annoyance of Sir Stafford Cripps, the Minister of Aircraft Production, few Scottish manufacturers showed any interest in aircraft or other new forms of industrial production.[2] In total, the boost to post-war civilian production was not great, and most of the jobs created were for women. The result was to harden Scottish opinion. In April 1942 the Scottish Home Department initiated discussion within official circles about using Government contracts in the immediate post-war period to 'steer' industry away from the South-East, but found itself too far ahead of Whitehall thinking.[3] Other Government Departments, like the Board of Trade and the Ministry of Labour, had not fully considered their response to the Barlow Report. Nevertheless, throughout 1942 and 1943, Scottish Ministers continued to press their case.[4] The first issue they pressed was the strategic necessity for balanced industrial development. The concentration of war production in the South, they said, had not only given the enemy easy bombing targets but had also increased labour market 'congestion' and the public cost of supporting new communities. The second issue was the nature and extent of Government direction. Despite the creation of the Hillington industrial estate in 1937 and the exhortations of Government Ministers after 1941, English industrialists still felt reluctant to move. Some of this was attributed to Scotland's distance from London's consumer market, but there remained a hint of management wariness, especially over the Clyde's environment and its labour relations (see Chapter Three).[5] A positive regional policy meant tight control over London and Midlands building, financial incentives for factory building and the Government working much closer with industrialists to point out Scotland's cost advantages: relatively low wages, high levels of skill and no shortage of fuel or water. None of this involved compulsion, a key element in a free economy, but it did involve Government having a wider understanding of investment decisions.

1 Rolls-Royce's management was assured that the move would be temporary, for the duration of the war.

2 *Glasgow Herald*, 'New Industry', 12 May 1947.

3 Minute of A.J. Aglen, Assistant Secretary, Scottish Home Department (London), 3 June 1942, SRO, HH50/150. He was following up a suggestion of C.C. Cunningham, the Department's Under Secretary; letter, 21 Apr. 1942.

4 Reconstruction Priorities Committee, 13 July 1943, PRO, CAB 87/12 PR(43)13th.

5 *Glasgow Herald*, 'Scotland's Market', 10 June 1938; *Scotsman*, 'Scottish Industry', 10 June 1938; both noting comments by Lord Nigel Douglas-Hamilton, the Scottish Special Areas Commissioner.

The Scottish Office regarded the 1945 Distribution of Industry Act with some satisfaction.[1] Its administration largely embodied its wartime (and earlier) thinking. The new Scottish Development Area included the old Special Areas together with Glasgow, North Ayrshire and Dundee; the Board of Trade established a regional office in Glasgow; loan and other facilities were available to industrialists wishing to expand; factories were to be built in advance of demand; and Scottish officials had sight of and could object to any development plan throughout the UK. Although the Board of Trade assumed responsibility for the management of the Scottish industrial estates and held day-to-day responsibility for attracting new industry, the de-scheduling of existing ones could not be approved without the Scottish Secretary's agreement.

Nevertheless, as the extracts indicate (pp. 177-84), it soon became apparent that Scotland's share of new industrial building would not be enough significantly to reduce male unemployment or to stem growing Parliamentary and press criticism.[2] Scotland, it was reported, faced two particular difficulties: firstly, it had fewer redundant munitions factories suitable for conversion, and secondly, the Ministry of Works allocated materials on a 1938 basis, a relatively poor year for Scottish industrial building. Scottish Ministers responded robustly and, to obviate the reluctance of industry to move north, outlined a case for the Government establishing and maintaining its own factories. Such a policy, going beyond subventing risk capital, raised considerable alarm in Whitehall: even Labour had not fought the 1945 election on the partial (and regional) nationalisation of consumer and light industry. In the event, the dollar crisis intervened before the Ministers could press their case, but the 1947 discussions, for the first time, revealed a concern that the policy on distribution of industry was not as positive as perhaps Johnston had thought.

After the dollar crisis, Attlee's administration was export-oriented and made clear what it expected the Scottish contribution to be: whisky, coal and ships.[3] Factories that produced goods purely for domestic consumption, as was the case for most of the new industry, would be unlikely to secure a Government building licence. In 1948 the Scottish share of factory building slumped from over fourteen per cent to under seven per cent of all new starts, and during the remainder of the term of the Labour Government, never regained the Goschen benchmark. Despite Woodburn's belief (extract pp. 184-6) that the revised

1 Distribution of Industry Bill, 1945, SRO, DD10/576.

2 *Scotsman*, 'Scottish Industry', reviewing annual report of Scottish Industrial Estates, 24 Jan. 1947; *Hansard*, Vol. 432, c.148-58, 10 Feb. 1947, Adjournment Debate, Unemployment (Scotland).

3 *Scotsman*, Speech by Sir Stafford Cripps, Minister of Economic Affairs, Edinburgh, 18 Sept. 1947.

system of building control could operate to Scotland's advantage, Scottish officials remained less certain; their view of development in other regions was effectively obscured.[1]

1948 represented a watershed in post-war development and it meant a changed role for the Scottish Office. If, as the Ford case indicated (extract pp. 186-8), national economic needs no longer saw the distribution of industry in such strategic terms then, as contemporary comment noted, Scottish ministers and officials needed to adopt a different approach: one that by drawing in Scottish opinion, especially the SC(DI), the Scottish Board for Industry and the STUC, could present the case for marginal investment in political, as much as economic, terms.[2] The development of East Kilbride (extracts pp. 188-96) represented the first (and successful) attempt to pursue this new policy. Other attempts, such as securing a Clyde Tunnel, were less successful, but by the time the Conservatives entered office in 1951, the Scottish Office had established a much better understanding of how it should proceed.[3]

The Scottish Council's Report on local development, published in 1952, held little surprise for informed opinion (extracts pp. 197-9). The essence of its recommendations—Government assistance to support the 'developing' rather than the 'development' areas—had been widely canvassed in the press and in Parliament since 1945, if not earlier.[4] In 1952, however, the difficulty the Report created for Scottish Ministers lay principally in the fact that it misunderstood the nature of Government policy since the dollar crisis. Although in public Labour had stressed the importance of national planning, in private it had remained keen to maximise private investment, even at the expense of regional policy. The Conservatives dropped the pretence of 'national planning', but understood public sensitivity towards unemployment, especially if it was rising.

1 The Scottish Departments believed that unless a 'ring' was placed round London, deliberately restricting development, there was little chance of firms being attracted north: minute of H.S.F. Hetherington, Principal, Industry Division, Scottish Home Department, 1 June 1949, SRO, DD10/560.

2 *Glasgow Herald*, 'Chancellor of the Exchequer's Visit to Scottish Economic Conference', 21 May 1949; 'Scotland's Future', 23 Feb. 1950; *Scotsman*, 'Scottish Policy', 29 Nov. 1949. The Scottish Council (Development and Industry) had been formed in 1946 from an amalgamation of the Scottish Council on Industry and the Scottish Development Council, largely at the behest of the Scottish Office who wished to liaise with one authoritative body representing industry, the trade unions and local authorities in the shaping of Scottish policy.

3 Hector McNeil to Alfred Barnes (Minister of Transport) on the Clyde Tunnel, 29 Jan. 1951, SRO, DD12/1237.

4 *Scotsman*, 'Scottish Planning', 4 Oct. 1947; *Glasgow Herald*, 'Done on Paper', 10 Aug. 1946; 'State of the Nation', 14 Jan. 1950; comments by J. Maclay (Conservative, Montrose Burghs), *Hansard*, Vol. 409, c.837, 21 Mar. 1945, Distribution of Industry Bill, 2nd Reading. Personal communication of Tom Burns (Report's Secretary) to editor, 14 Jan. 1993.

For them, regional policy lay somewhere between helping industrialists relocate in areas where risk capital remained scarce and political common sense. General economic growth would come from private firms operating in a climate of Government fiscal prudence.

The Report, however, did help to crystallise Scottish thought. First and somewhat ironically, Scottish opinion became even more wedded to the Government promoting development; Scotland's share of new factories remained disproportionately low and the press, the STUC and MPs could not see how the Government's fiscal policy on its own would sustain an acceleration of factory growth.[1] Secondly, it was clear that there was not enough 'footloose' English industry on the move in any one year to make a significant difference to employment, even if building in the South-East was restricted.[2] Thirdly, it focused attention on the condition of heavy industry. Much plant, it was acknowledged, remained pre-war, but at the same time the coal-mines, shipyards and engineering works formed the backbone of the economy; new industry such as electronics and consumer goods had not gained any self-sustaining foothold. The Scottish economy would have to retain what it had, modernise it with Government assistance and extend it into 'secondary' and allied fields.

James Stuart, the Scottish Secretary, was aware that Scottish opinion remained uneasy and not altogether persuaded by the Government's strategy.[3] On entering office, although he had secured additional steel for the Clyde shipyards, the Government's anti-inflation policy had led to the suspension of the advance factory programme, restarted by Labour in 1950.[4] Stuart's principal priority therefore was highly political: demonstrating the Government's support for Clydeside, where most of the heavy industry and existing prosperity was located.

1 *Glasgow Herald*, 'State Funds for Factory Building', 9 July 1953. The paper felt that there was a shortage of private capital and that the Government's investment allowances were of 'slender' advantage. See also 'Towards a Balanced Economy' and 'Board of Trade President in Scotland', 5 Aug. 1953; *Scotsman*, 'New Industries', 5 Aug. 1953; 'Diversity of Industry' (reporting speech by President of STUC), 8 Apr. 1954; 'Economic Prospects', 16 July 1954; *Hansard*, Vol. 530, c.705, 15 July 1954, Supply Committee: Scotland, Industry and Employment, especially speech by J. Brooman-White (Stuart's Parliamentary Secretary).

2 Board of Trade Memorandum on matters arising out of President's Scottish Tour, 26 Oct. 1953, SRO, SEP4/315. New factories created about 50,000 jobs a year and although Scottish unemployment stood at 30,000, the Government had also to consider the needs of Wales, Northern Ireland, Lancashire and the North-East. In addition, some planned factories were simply extensions of existing ones.

3 *Hansard*, Vol. 517, c.1924-27, 14 July 1953, Speech, Supply: Committee, Scottish Affairs.

4 *Glasgow Herald*, 'Sharing Materials', 8 Mar. 1952; 'Scottish Industry: Trends and Portents', 25 July 1952. Between 1945 and 1950, the Clyde received 190 out of 228 Government-sponsored factories in Scotland.

The extracts (pp. 200-5, 211-13) indicate his influence in securing the Clyde Tunnel, retaining Scotland's nascent aircraft industry and preventing the de-scheduling of development areas.[1] However, Stuart knew that this would not be enough; the employment created neither sustained economic growth nor was large enough to signify any great political advance.

The ministerial decision to support Scotland's claims for the UK's fourth steel strip mill came as something of a surprise to officials (extracts pp. 205-10). The Ministers faced difficulties in pursuing their objective. First, making sheet steel was a complex process involving considerable managerial skill, which was predominantly located in the existing plants in South Wales. Second, the cost of steel was heavily influenced by the availability of coking coal and the plant's nearness to the car and other light industry markets.[2] Scotland had little coking coal and was further away from the Midlands, the centre of the British car industry, than were Wales or the North-East. Third, the iron and steel industry was a highly conservative body both in terms of investment plans and its view of Government. Nevertheless the projected £160 million available was Britain's largest single post-war investment and, as Stuart understood, its location was a political issue: the public viewed it as a guarantee of jobs, new industry and economic growth.

Stuart's successor, John Maclay, also understood the implications of the eventual Government decision, but by the time he took office, it was already apparent to the Scottish Office that South Wales was the preferred choice of the Iron and Steel Board.[3] But Maclay, unlike Stuart, faced a more serious internal problem: the Scottish economy, for the first time since 1945, showed signs of structural dislocation with a sharp rise in unemployment and emigration. Deputations from the STUC, Labour MPs and the SC(DI) on the need for advance factories, regional investment allowances and the strip mill became familiar.[4] Nevertheless, as the extracts indicate (pp. 213-23, 230-43), he faced

1 *Hansard*, Vol. 503, c.1636-43, 10 July 1952, Speech, Supply Committee, Industry in Scotland.

2 R.H. Campbell, 'Strip Mill: Pros and Cons', *The Banker*, cviii, May 1958.

3 Minute of Sir Charles Cunningham, Secretary, Scottish Home Department, 7 Jan. 1957, SRO, SEP4/2085.

4 *Scotsman*, 'STUC Plea for Industry', 8 Jan. 1957; 'Steel Expansion', 18 July 1957; 'Scotland Penalised', 25 Sept. 1957; 'No Assurances for STUC', 15 Oct. 1957; 'Prospect for Scotland', 2 Jan. 1958; 'STUC urges more Modern Industry', 13 Feb. 1958; 'Men out of Work', 25 Feb. 1958; 'Trend of Industry', 7 Mar. 1958; 'Unemployment Rate is twice that of UK: STUC', 13 Mar. 1958. In 1957 net emigration reached 36,000, a figure typical of the 1920s. Between 1948 and 1957 the numbers in employment in England increased by 8.5 per cent in comparison to Scotland's 3 per cent. This was attributed to Scotland's dependence on sections of traditional industry nearing the end of their productive life: Scottish Home Department Minute, 14 Nov. 1958, SRO, DD10/454.

a particularly difficult time persuading the Cabinet that the Scottish economy required special measures. This was sensed by the Opposition in Parliament whose previous lacklustre performance gave way to sharper and more frequent attacks on Government 'negligence', all targeted on the Scottish Office.[1]

By Spring 1957 Maclay's officials knew that Scotland's chances of attracting the strip mill were diminishing, partly because of economics, but also because they felt the Government that would be reluctant to force a Welsh company north of the border. Maclay was advised to pursue Colvilles, the largest of the Scottish producers, but Colvilles' own plan was to produce additional plates for the shipyards, a shortage of which, it said, had led to unemployment.[2] The production of some sheet steel was projected, but Colvilles' analysis of Scottish economic needs suggested that this would not be necessary until the mid-1960s.[3] As the extracts (pp. 223-9) indicate, the Cabinet stalled on a decision; Maclay insisted that a decision against Scotland would damage Anglo-Scottish relations, but Lord Mills was adamant that Grangemouth could not be supported. In the event Maclay's officials suggested a compromise: part of the project would be built in Scotland, if Colvilles agreed. Maclay, in turn, tackled the firm. At a private meeting with Sir Andrew McCance, the firm's Managing Director, Maclay was able to secure agreement that the long-term future of Scotland depended on a mill being established, though McCance still thought that the lack of a Scottish market made it economically unsound for a number of years.[4] After the meeting Maclay felt that McCance had shifted Colvilles' position and, taking the advice of his officials, promptly informed the Cabinet

1 During one Supply debate, Tom Fraser, the shadow spokesman, in a speech lasting 45 minutes, mentioned Scotland 58 times, steel 17, and employment 14. He also commented that the Government's anti-inflation policy should not apply north of the border: 'Scotland was utterly innocent and blameless for she has never had overfull employment or over-investment.' He added: 'There is one way, and only one way, in which to deal with Scotland's inherent difficulties and that is the construction of a mill to produce sheet.' *Hansard*, Vol. 573, c.1365-80, 18 July 1957.

2 Memorandum of Sir Charles Cunningham, Secretary, Scottish Home Department and John Anderson, Secretary, Department of Health for Scotland, 1 Apr. 1957 and Minute of Cunningham, 2 July 1957, SRO, SEP4/2085. The STUC's view was different. It believed that Colvilles' near-monopoly of Scottish production prevented development: meeting with Scottish Secretary, 14 Oct. 1957, SRO, DD10/440.

3 Initially the SC(DI), not wanting to embarrass Colvilles, refused to be drawn into supporting a Scottish mill, but after a full meeting of the Council, altered its view: meeting, 24 May 1957, SRO, SEP4/2085.

4 Minute of Maclay, 4 May 1958, SRO, SEP4/2090; for McCance's account, see P.L. Payne, *Colvilles and the Scottish Steel Industry* (Oxford, 1979). One of Colvilles' principal fears was the threat of renationalisation, which it felt would prevent raising the large amount of necessary capital.

that the firm did have an interest in producing sheet steel.[1] The firm, he added, would also want to be associated with any Government-sponsored scheme, preferably through a consortium. It was enough to break the deadlock; Mills baulked at further Cabinet division.[2]

Ravenscraig was essentially a political decision; few thought that it could work without the introduction of industry to consume its product.[3] But Maclay's actions on Ravenscraig, the shale oil mines, Prestwick and advance factories represented more than *ad hoc* activity to secure employment. In 1958 the Scottish Secretary became, *de facto*, the minister for Scottish economic development, and the Scottish Office, not the Board of Trade, the lead ministry to prevent unemployment and secure growth.

Chapter Three: Housing and Urban Development

It was one of the remarkable facts of nineteenth-century history that Scottish housing conditions, acknowledged by contemporaries as much worse than in England, remained out of the political arena until well after 1900.[4] At the time, this was ascribed partly to Scotland's speed of industrialisation, which had brought large numbers of relatively poor workers from Ireland and the Highlands into new urban and mining communities: popular expectations, it was said, remained low.[5] Part was also ascribed to a cultural preference for tenement living, with its alleged similarity to life in the 'walled' medieval town. Nevertheless, by 1914 most contemporary commentators felt a growing unease with the widespread slums, the overcrowding and the apparent deterioration in public health. They also noted the virtual cessation of building for the working

1 Minute of R.E.C. Johnston, Under Secretary, Scottish Home Department, 5 May 1958, SRO, SEP4/2090. The officials advised Maclay not to mention details of Colvilles' scheme, which was to cold roll imported English 'hot strip', in case the Ministers thought Scottish demand would be met.

2 Payne's account sets out the subsequent discussions with McCance, particularly over the size of the scheme and finance. McCance later denied that the the firm had been interested in producing sheet steel, but was left in no doubt that the Cabinet wanted all or some sheet production in Scotland, despite the economics.

3 *Economist*, 'Returns from Ravenscraig', 17 Jan. 1959. Financially the Treasury bore the risk if the strip mill did not reach profit, hence later Government attempts to introduce a car industry. The mill was essentially a nationalised plant managed by Colvilles.

4 For general discussion on Scottish housing during the period see: J. Melling, *Rent Strikes: People's Struggles for Housing in West Scotland, 1890-1916* (Edinburgh, 1983); R. Rodger, *Scottish Housing in the Twentieth Century* (Leicester, 1989); I.H. Adams, *The Making of Urban Scotland* (London, 1978); R. Smith & U. Wannop, *Strategic Planning in Action: the Impact of the Clyde Regional Plan, 1946-1982* (Guildford, 1988).

5 *Glasgow Herald*, 'Housing Shortage', 24 Jan. 1925; *Scotsman*, 'Scotland's Plight: Dearth of Houses', 21 Dec. 1925.

class.[1] A Scottish preference for the use of stone rather than brick, the relatively low wages and the peculiarities of the rating system meant that investors could secure better returns elsewhere.[2]

Asquith's Liberal Government recognised the problem, and in 1912, to offset growing disquiet that demand was outstripping supply, appointed a Royal Commission into Scottish Housing. The Commission's deliberations were interrupted by the war; by the time it reported in 1917, the Rent Restriction Act, the added years without building and the Government's need to maintain public morale had created a radically different political economy. The Commission recognised this, but it also recognised that in Scotland it was unlikely that the market could supply reasonably-priced 'working class' housing with contemporary standards of 'convenience' and 'comfort'.[3] The Coalition Government largely accepted the Commission's recommendations (extract pp. 244-5), but remained cautious over any long-term commitment to subsidising the market. The majority of the Cabinet, including the Scottish Secretary, expected that once the programme was complete, popular demands would subside and private enterprise would be sufficiently organised to reassert its historic role.[4] If the Government had any long-term responsibility, it was to supply housing for slum clearance: a much more restricted programme and one, politically, much easier to accept.

After the war, the Coalition was unprepared for the housing conditions it found, especially in Scotland. From 1920 a number of reports highlighted the poor physical capacity of the building industry; the housing programme never looked likely to reach its projected total (extract pp. 245-8).[5] In the event, the economic crisis intervened, and to control costs, the Government abandoned

1 Department of Health memorandum, 'Private Enterprise: Reasons for Failure', 26 Feb. 1941, SRO, DD6/1100.

2 Between 1900 and 1914 it was estimated that about 130,000 houses were built. *Hansard*, Vol. 170, c.1004, 3 Mar. 1924.

3 Using a standard of adequacy as less than three persons to a room, the Royal Commission estimated that 121,000 houses were required for the homeless, those in overcrowded conditions and for those occupying uninhabitable houses. However, Scotland also contained a higher proportion of one- and two-roomed houses than England, and for this it estimated that a further 115,000 houses would be required. In addition it estimated that 10,000 were required each year to meet demographic change and houses left derelict.

4 Munro suggested that assistance should be restricted to houses built within two years of the Act coming into operation. His fellow ministers preferred three years. Housing Bill Committee, 5 Mar. 1919, PRO, CAB 27/56. The local authority's contribution was limited to fourth-fifths of a penny rate on loans raised for a sixty-year period. The Exchequer grant covered the remaining estimated annual deficit.

5 See also *Report on High Cost of Building Working Class Dwellings in Scotland*, Cmd. 1411. The Report, published in June 1921, thought that the Scottish economy could support 25,000 houses in the period 1921-4, a remarkably accurate projection.

its policy of supporting building trade 'dilution' in favour of deflation.[1] Nevertheless, the decision to suspend the Scottish housing programme (extract pp. 248-9) came as a shock to Robert Munro, the Scottish Secretary, who had been assured that Scotland's special difficulties would mean the programme continuing, albeit on a different basis.[2]

Munro's successor in the Conservative Government of Bonar Law, Lord Novar, shared his initial reservations on subsidies and surprised the Cabinet by his market-oriented approach (extract pp. 249-50). Scottish local authorities took a different view; in meeting them, Novar reluctantly accepted that the Scottish housing market faced profound structural difficulties.[3] His problem in Cabinet was to persuade Neville Chamberlain, the lead minister for British housing policy, that Scottish conditions justified a special concession (extract pp. 250-3). Chamberlain saw the 1923 Bill, with its strictly limited subsidy, as a temporary device to continue the expansion of the building trade. His preference remained the encouragement of working-class owner-occupation, which in his view, could only come about by economies in construction and the withdrawal of state-assisted competition.[4] As Elliot, the Parliamentary Under Secretary, later explained to the Commons, the Scottish scheme was in direct conflict with that policy; moreover, it implied that the English taxpayer should subsidise Scotland to live in 'superior' accommodation.[5] In future, he added, Scottish Ministers could not argue for different treatment on the basis of 'architectural tradition' or 'climate', but 'by arguments of an altogether different order'.[6]

As the Opposition predicted, the 1923 Housing Act failed to induce any building boom. Labour's response when it entered office was hardly unexpected. The 1924 Housing (Financial Provisions) Act greatly increased the subsidy, and encouraged the local authority to take the 'lead' role in the

1 *Scotsman*, Leader, 15 July 1921.

2 *Glasgow Herald*, 'Economy and Housing', 8 July 1921. Under the restricted programme, 300,000 houses were built in the UK. The Scottish total, 25,550, was about 15,000 short under the 'Goschen' formula, a fact which Scottish opinion soon noted.

3 Notes on Deputation representing Scottish local authorities, 8 Mar. 1923, SRO, DD6/682.

4 *Hansard*, Vol. 163, c.303, 24 Apr. 1923, Housing (No. 2) Bill. The local authority could use the £6 a year subsidy for twenty years for their own building, or provide an equivalent lump-sum payment after the house was built, or provide an annual sum to the person who paid the rates, or meet loan charges on the cost of construction. Under the Act's slum clearance provision, the Treasury contributed up to one half the estimated average annual loss. Under the Act 34,000 'general needs' and 17,000 slum clearance houses were built.

5 *Hansard*, Vol. 163, c.1027, 30 Apr. 1923, Housing (No. 2) Bill [Money] Committee.

6 *Annual Report of the Scottish Board of Health, 1923*, Cmd. 2156, 128.

provision of 'general needs' working-class housing.[1] However, although the Minister of Health was John Wheatley, a Clydeside MP, Labour did little to consider the specifically Scottish issue (extract pp. 253-4). The Scottish Ministers assumed that the fifteen years' guarantee of work would suffice to ensure trade union co-operation and at the same time establish new Scottish suppliers of bricks, cement and plaster.

When the Conservatives returned to office later in the year, in addition to the technical problems of labour and material, Sir John Gilmour, the Scottish Secretary, faced two other major issues. First, despite the Wheatley subsidy, few local authorities showed any urgency in submitting schemes for Government approval, and those that did were reluctant to pursue the building programme with vigour.[2] Secondly, Gilmour understood that, unlike that of Baldwin, his Scottish 'mandate' was more precariously balanced, particularly in Glasgow where Labour remained the dominant party.[3] He told Chamberlain that British housing policy had barely 'touched the fringe' of Clydeside's difficulty: an additional programme was required, preferably using alternative methods of construction.[4]

The Government had not been unsympathetic towards alternative methods, but in all the schemes that had been approved, the technology was regarded as experimental and not designed for 'mass production' until its lifespan and costs had been fully assessed.[5] However, during the Lords' debate on the Wheatley Bill, Lord Weir, the Clydeside industrialist, suggested that his firm could produce large number of steel houses at reasonable prices, which could also reduce shipyard unemployment. Glasgow and other authorities thought the idea was interesting and proposed a number of schemes.[6] Weir imposed one condition on his firm's participation: to ensure the scheme's profitability, all

1 The Act provided a subsidy of £9 a year for forty years. Rents were to be similar to pre-1914 rents for working-class housing, unless the annual rate-borne expenses exceeded £4 10s per annum. The Act built 84,000 houses, the largest of the inter-war schemes.

2 *Annual Report of the Scottish Board of Health, 1924*, Cmd. 2416, 30-1.

3 *Glasgow Herald*, 'Unionism: the Scottish Secretary and Housing', 27 Jan. 1925. Speech to Glasgow Unionist Association.

4 *Glasgow Herald*, 'Scottish Secretary in Glasgow', 23 Jan. 1926; *Hansard*, Vol. 179, c.940, 16 Dec. 1924, Debate on Address. Gilmour was, in part, following up an election comment by Baldwin on the need for new construction methods with, if necessary, Government assistance: *Scotsman*, 'Socialists and Housing', 16 Oct. 1924.

5 Concrete was thought to have potential, but the durability of prefabricated blocks and poured concrete remained a problem. Timber was thought more appropriate for rural locations: HMSO, *A Guide to Non-traditional Housing in Scotland* (Edinburgh, 1987).

6 Labour, before it left office, established an inquiry into the issue: *New Methods of House Construction* (Two Reports), Cmd. 2310 and Cmd. 2334.

non-building labour (the majority) would be paid at shipyard (and lower) rates of pay. This infuriated the building unions, who sensed another attempt to introduce 'dilution' and threatened any local authority that continued the scheme with strike action. Gilmour's initial reaction was to support the local authority, but he then asked the Cabinet to consider the possibility of using the Government's Office of Works. Chamberlain, however, remained unconvinced. The Government would have to rely on the local authority for the provision of services, such as roads, schools and welfare clinics; without their support, the initiative 'was doomed to failure'. Gilmour, he added, should 'mobilise' public opinion behind Weir, particularly the 'housewife'.[1]

Nevertheless, by summer 1925, it was apparent that local authorities were not prepared to jeopardise their building programme; they remained sceptical about tenant satisfaction and the housing's likely lifespan. Gilmour, who had borne the brunt of five Commons debates on housing in eight months, felt the Scottish position was untenable and told Baldwin that without some action serious 'unrest' was possible.[2] Baldwin agreed and overruled Chamberlain's previous objection to a Government-financed housing association (extracts pp. 254-7). 'Discontent' through bad housing was understandable, he told an audience in Glasgow, and pledged a more lasting programme to 'eviscerate' inner city slums.[3]

The establishment of the Second Scottish National Housing Company represented more than a decision to build 2,500 houses. As far as Gilmour was concerned, the steel programme was a visible sign of what could be achieved; it provided, he felt, 'a strong stimulating effect' on the local authority.[4] On the other hand it had an impact on British policy (extracts pp. 257-60). Chamberlain believed that the growth of owner-occupation would dampen working-class hostility towards Conservatism and market forces.[5] Gilmour indicated that a

1 Memorandum, 'Weir Houses', 20 Feb. 1925, PRO, CAB 27/266 WH(25)3.

2 *Glasgow Herald*, 'Housing in Scotland' and 'Public Health', 21 July 1925.

3 *Glasgow Herald*, 'Baldwin and Housing Subsidy', 2 Oct. 1925; *Scotsman*, 'The New Housing Scheme', 19 Dec. 1925; 'Socialists and Housing', 21 Dec. 1925; *Times*, 'Poison and Antidote', 6 Oct. 1925; 'Houses for Scotland', 23 Dec. 1925.

4 Although tenants seemed satisfied, local authority estimates proved correct—each house was 25 per cent more expensive than brick. Because rents were kept similar to Wheatley levels (to encourage tenancy) and because of higher maintenance costs, the scheme remained unprofitable. In 1935 the Treasury wrote off arrears of accumulated interest and agreed to waive further interest for ten years. Scottish Housing: Treasury Blue Notes, 1950-1, PRO, T 165/216.

5 *Scotsman*, 'Dundee Slums', 16 Oct. 1925. In a speech during a tour of the slums Chamberlain said that he believed owner-occupation 'increased self-respect' and that workers were unlikely 'to lend themselves to any propaganda of a revolutionary or subversive kind'.

strictly market-led solution was politically counter-productive: Scottish problems were of a qualitatively different order to England's, and subsidies were required until the building trade could sustain an annual output of 25,000 houses.[1]

By 1929 England and Wales had seen nearly 1.5 million houses built. With costs falling, subsidies to meet 'general needs' seemed superfluous. However, the English record in providing housing for the slum tenant remained poor. MacDonald's second administration reversed the Conservatives' decision to withdraw housing subsidies and agreed an extensive programme of slum clearance. Unlike in 1924, Labour accepted the need for 'special treatment' for Scotland. Part of the argument of Adamson, the Scottish Secretary, related to the need to encourage slum tenants into the new housing, rather than moving to 'non-cleared' areas: as the extracts (pp. 261-5) indicate, the question was the level of rent such tenants could afford.[2]

The decision by the National Government to withdraw 'general needs' subsidies did not come as a surprise. By 1932, with interest rates and other costs falling, England saw a housing boom, especially in the South-East. In Scotland, the position remained unchanged (outside Edinburgh and a few other towns), and Collins, the Scottish Secretary, faced little difficulty in maintaining the general subsidy (extract pp. 265-8). The Government nevertheless realised that the boom had left much of the poorer working class untouched, especially those living in overcrowded housing, and with the Rent Restriction Acts still in force, it seemed unlikely that their needs would be met by private enterprise. The Government also recognised that the 1930 Act had a number of limitations, particularly over the grant available to local authorities. As the extracts indicate (pp. 268-72), discussions on the 1935 Housing Bill seemed to be dominated by a desire not to be outflanked by Labour.

The 1935 Housing Act was expected to provide a substantial boost to the housing programme, but during 1936 it became apparent that the Scottish building industry was still in structural difficulty, particularly over the supply of skilled labour. With the Government's re-armament programme competing for labour, this was not expected to improve.[3] Meanwhile, the Department of

1 *Hansard*, Vol. 189, c.1885, 18 Dec. 1925, Adjournment Debate; Housing.

2 The Act provided a grant of £2 10s per person displaced and rehoused, which could be increased by 15s for the acquisition and clearance of sites. Rents were limited by fixing the minimum rate contribution at £4 10s. Grants were payable for forty years. 58,000 slum clearance houses were provided under this and the 1935 Act.

3 *Glasgow Herald*, 'Relief of Overcrowding', 9 May 1936; 'Housing Progress', 8 July 1936; 'Labour Shortages', 18 July 1936. Under the Act 21,000 houses were built to relieve overcrowding.

Health published its estimate of Scottish housing needs.[1] A quarter of the population was housed in overcrowded conditions; to rectify this, a ten-year programme to build 150,000 houses would be required, in addition to the estimated 'normal' requirement of about 100,000. Such an output had never been reached before; indeed Glasgow, with about a third of the estimated need, had seen its programme decline to less than 2,000 per annum.[2] The Scottish situation stood in sharp contrast to England where boom conditions in private housing had given impetus to the domestic consumer market.

Labour, who had been remarkably quiet about housing, seized on the issue and, in Autumn 1936, began to press the Government for action.[3] Elliot, the Scottish Secretary, accepted that the situation was reminiscent of 1925 and announced his intention to boost the labour supply by seeking an extension of the apprenticeship programme and by reviewing the local authority grant. However, Elliot understood that the apprenticeship programme would have little impact until well after 1940. As for the housing subsidy, although inflation had removed much of its value, any increase without elasticity in the supply of labour and materials would be inflationary.[4] In a memorandum to Chamberlain he proposed using the Steel Housing Company to undertake a programme of between 2,000 and 4,000 houses per annum for seven years in areas where labour and housing need were most critical.[5] The Company could also be used to recondition about 50,000 existing slum properties.

Chamberlain ruled out reconditioning, on the grounds that it would remove existing property from the market and further encroach on building labour.[6] However, he did agree that the Scottish situation was critical, and that if the supply of labour could not be increased, a Housing Association, similar to one supported by the Special Areas Commissioner on Tyneside, should operate a limited programme in the Scottish Special Area.[7] The North-East scheme was

1 *Report on a Survey into Overcrowding in Housing*, Cmd. 5171.

2 Between 1930 and 1936, Scotland averaged about 20,000 houses per annum, two-thirds through the local authority.

3 *Hansard*, Vol. 318, c.2872, 18 Dec. 1936, Adjournment Debate: Scottish Housing. *Glasgow Herald*, 'Scottish Housing', 19 Dec. 1936; *Scotsman*, 'Scottish Housing', 19 Dec. 1936.

4 Minute of Craig Mitchell, Assistant Secretary, Housing Division, Department of Health, 24 Dec. 1936, SRO, DD6/1131.

5 'Housing in Scotland', 13 Jan. 1937, SRO, DD6/1131. The proposal would cost the Treasury about £250,000 per annum. The use of steel was ruled out, because of the re-armament programme.

6 Letter, 28 Jan. 1937, ibid.

7 The notion of a national housing corporation had been mooted by Labour in 1934. At the time Chamberlain maintained his previous opposition, believing its 'business' efficiency would be less than either private enterprise or the local authority. Housing Policy Committee, 13 Feb. 1934, PRO, CAB 27/565 H(34) 2nd Meeting. In 1937 Chamberlain was specifically against the Steel Housing Company,

confined to traditional methods of construction and had the normal Government subsidy, transferred by the local authority. But Elliot felt that Chamberlain had not ruled out other possibilities and in June 1937 the Treasury agreed to support an 'experimental' programme and provide an additional subsidy if the houses could not be let without loss.[1]

The agreement with the Treasury was limited to the Special Areas. Elliot was more interested in Glasgow, where, as he told one of his officials, 'it was a quarter of the problem for population, but two thirds of it in sentiment'.[2] He wanted to establish a Government Housing Board to build in areas of greatest need, arguing that it would also counter Scotland's apparent 'municipalisation' of housing. Elliot continued to press the case; as the extracts (pp. 272-8) indicate, a final agreement on an increased subsidy and a Housing Association, but not the Housing Board, was reached the following year.[3]

The 1938 Housing (Financial Provisions) Act visualised an extensive Scottish programme lasting until 1950, enough to meet the 'deficit' and a good part of 'normal' needs.[4] In the first phase, 1939-43, the local authority would build 20,000 houses per annum, private enterprise 8,000, and the Scottish Special Housing Association 7,000 (including 1,750 in Glasgow). The programme was expected to be broadly equivalent to Scotland's 'Goschen' share of new building. It was to act as a stimulus to domestic industry in the same way that it had in England.

In 1941 Tom Johnston established his Scottish Council on Post War Problems containing all surviving Scottish Secretaries. Amongst other issues, the Council considered the post-war housing programme. Early discussions largely repeated the position reached in 1939 with perhaps more emphasis on using alternative methods of construction and an enlarged role for the Housing Association.[5] It was estimated that wartime destruction, the lack of building and

partly because of its poor financial record, but also because he thought it might rekindle opposition more than a new Association.

1 'Note of Agreement with Treasury', 24 June 1937, SRO, DD6/1131. An additional subsidy was important, as the Housing Association could not levy rates to subsidise the housing account.

2 Letter to P.J.G. Rose, Assistant Under Secretary, Scottish Office, 2 Jan. 1937, SRO, DD10/171; Scottish Office memorandum, 21 Dec. 1937, SRO, DD6/1092. In 1924 Elliot argued for a 'Government Housing Commission', largely on the basis of providing 'continuity'; *Hansard*, Vol, 174, c.1099, 3 June 1924, Housing (Financial Provisions) [Money] Committee.

3 Sir John Simon, the Chancellor of the Exchequer, was extremely hostile to a statutory board replacing local 'effort', condemning it as 'an experiment in State Socialism': Letter, 29 July 1938, SRO, DD6/1092. The Special Areas Housing Association was reconstituted as the Scottish Special Housing Association in 1939.

4 *Hansard*, Vol. 349, c.1143, 4 July 1939, Supply: Committee—Health, Scotland.

5 T. Johnston, 'Note on Housing', 30 Dec. 1941 (SC(41)8) and 5 May 1942 (SC(42)12), SRO, DD1/66.

demographic demand meant a deficit of about 300,000 houses. On the basis of the 1938-9 programme, such a total was achievable, though Johnston knew that it would require continued support until the mid-1950s.[1] However, in 1942 the Department of Health conducted a further survey of housing conditions using higher standards of 'convenience', and this increased the deficit to 500,000.

By 1944, with popular expectation of Government action also growing, Johnston was faced with an altogether unprecedented problem. As the Department at the time noted, to achieve an annual output of 50,000 houses would require a substantial subsidy, the extension of the building trade, the use of steel housing as well as concrete and timber, and rigorous control of private building, both residential and commercial.[2] Johnston was adamant that such a programme should be planned (extract pp. 278-81), although the Cabinet remained concerned that the programme, as in 1919, was beyond the physical capacity of the Scottish economy. The Coalition agreed that local authorities could begin planning the post-war scheme in March 1944, on the understanding that subsidy arrangements would be fully reviewed as soon as the war ended. In 1946 the Labour Government announced a substantial increase in the subsidy, primarily to keep the programme going, but also to ensure that local authorities would build at 'affordable' rents (extract pp. 281-3). The subsidy was extended the following year when local authorities complained that post-war inflation would curtail the programme (extracts pp. 290-2). Labour, unlike Lloyd George's Coalition, remained committed to the provision of rented accommodation for the 'working classes'.

Before 1939 the Department of Health had shown little interest in encouraging new towns, already well established in England at Letchworth and Welwyn Garden City. This, in part, was ascribed to the fears of local authorities that they would lose industry and rates, but the Department also recognised a cultural resistance to 'planning' and the imposition of 'ordered' development on well-established community lifestyles.[3] Nevertheless, Johnston accepted the necessity of planning the physical landscape, both to secure 'efficiencies of scale' in the provision of services such as road building, electricity and water supplies, and to halt ribbon development. Regional planning advisory committees were established in

1 26,700 houses were completed in 1938, and the 1939 programme, until war broke out, was 10 per cent higher.

2 Minute of W.S. Murrie, Assistant Secretary, Department of Health, 7 Jan. 1943, SRO, HH50/153.

3 *Royal Commission on the Distribution of the Population* (London, 1938); Memorandum, Department of Health for Scotland (6 Oct. 1937), 31; Memorandum, the Association of Counties of Cities in Scotland (15 Dec. 1937), 229; *Glasgow Herald*, 'Planning the Clyde', 30 Sept. 1943.

1943 for the Clyde, the Forth and Tay basins, each employing a consultant to prepare a detailed plan. On Clydeside, Patrick Abercrombie, London's consultant, was appointed, not without some acrimony between the Clyde Committee and Johnston, who preferred the Scottish planner, Frank Mears.[1] Mears later became the consultant for the Forth basin. Their reports, which Johnston's successor Joe Westwood accepted, effectively established a physical plan for Central Scotland. As the extracts indicate (pp. 283-9), the proposed new towns were projected to house over 7 per cent of the Scottish population, and 25 per cent of Glasgow's.

This was a substantial departure from pre-war thinking, but what was perhaps even more significant was Westwood's acceptance of Abercrombie's total reassessment of Clydeside development.[2] In the inter-war period, Scottish opinion had largely seen the housing issue in public health terms, although Elliot also saw a link between development and indigenous economic growth. Abercrombie associated housing with economic development far more closely.[3] To him it was apparent that the Clyde's economy would face much difficulty adapting to the post-war world. First, it was clear that the traditional industries of coal, steel and engineering no longer had the same resilience. Further contraction in the coal industry was likely; in steel, unless new plant and markets were found, the same would apply. Second, the topography of Glasgow made it difficult to plan anything other than ribbon development, with all its problems of communications and supply of services. As for the surrounding towns, many lacked the kind of infrastructure that modern industry required—an integrated transport system, good-quality housing, and land for development. Third, the Clyde's workforce, trained in heavy industry and with a reputation for militancy, was not particularly attractive to new industrialists or the incoming skilled workers the industry required.[4] What Abercrombie thought necessary was a clean break with past traditions, the adoption of a 'wider vision', in which Government policy would instead 'impose a new order' on

1 Minute, Department of Health, 30 July 1943, SRO, DD12/92. The Committee were influenced by their Secretary, Sir William Whyte, Clerk, Middle Ward Lanark, who had served with Abercrombie on the Barlow Commission. Whyte thought that a report from Abercrombie would carry greater weight with the Treasury and the Board of Trade if it involved issues of finance and industrial location.

2 Leonard Silkin, the Minister of Town and Country Planning, was an enthusiastic supporter of new towns and the 1946 Act, which no doubt influenced discussion. *Hansard*, Vol. 422, c.1072, 8 Apr. 1946, New Towns Bill, Second Reading; Vol. 424, c.2339, 5 July 1946, Third Reading.

3 P. Abercrombie & R.H. Matthew, *The Clyde Valley Regional Plan* (Glasgow, 1946).

4 See Draft Memorandum of T. Fraser, Parliamentary Under SecreofState, on Development Areas Policy, 6 July 1946, SRO, HH36/58. The allusion in this and other contemporary memoranda was to a cultural dislike of the 'disputatious' Scottish workers.

the way the Clyde was housed and administered.[1] The future, he believed, lay in creating 'balanced industrial communities' surrounded by green belt, but 'integrated' through improved communications. This would induce a new spirit amongst Clydesiders, boost their morale and act as an incentive for English industry to move north.

Westwood's advocacy of Abercrombie was, like other aspects of Labour's post-war plan, abruptly halted by the dollar crisis. The attempts of his successor, Woodburn, to rekindle interest in a Renfrewshire new town for the steel industry fell victim to a mixture of political intrigue and financial caution (extract pp. 293-5).[2] With the Treasury, Clydeside MPs and local authorities against him, there was little that Woodburn could do. Although the regional planning programme was maintained, by the time Labour left office in 1951 the general idea of new towns spearheading Scottish development was almost moribund.[3]

In the immediate post-war years, public consciousness of new towns was diminished by Labour's inability to maintain the general housing programme. Through shortage of materials, difficulties over planning co-ordination and a 'ca-canny' attitude amongst the building trades, the programme failed to reach its target and was truncated still further by the dollar crisis (extract pp. 292-3).[4] The programme was restored in 1948 (extracts pp. 296-308), but Woodburn found Labour MPs anxious for its expansion, especially as the incidence of tuberculosis showed an increase at a time when it was declining elsewhere.[5] In July 1948 Woodburn secured an additional 1,000 temporary 'prefabs', but felt that more was required.[6] In December he gained Cripps's approval for 4,000 additional non-traditional houses (extracts pp. 298-300), but the following

1 *Glasgow Herald*, 'The Long View', 14 Oct. 1944; 'The Larger Vision', 16 Mar. 1946; *Scotsman*, 'Planning in Scotland; Housing in Clyde Valley', 14 Oct. 1944; 'Clyde Valley Plan', 16 Mar. 1946.

2 Under the Act, 'exporting' authorities were under no obligation to contribute towards housing costs. Glasgow opposed East Kilbride's designation, believing that it could rehouse at high density within its boundaries. It also refused to co-operate in the selection of tenants. For a discussion of Scotland's other designated New Town, Glenrothes, see R. Smith, 'New towns for Scottish miners: the rise and fall of a social ideal, 1945-1948', *Scottish Economic & Social History*, ix (1989), 71-9.

3 *Glasgow Herald*, 'Clyde Valley Development', 29 Aug. 1949; 'Clyde Valley Planning', 30 July 1951.

4 *Glasgow Herald*, 'Slow Bricklaying', 19 Apr. 1946; 'Housing Promises', 29 Jan. 1947; 'Housing Prospects', 10 Mar. 1947; *Scotsman*, 'Housing Set Back', 9 May 1947; 'Housing Deflation', 31 Oct. 1947. The Scottish proportion of UK completions, 1945-7, was about 9 per cent, but the majority, unlike England, were temporary houses. The shortage of materials was most acute for bricks and cement. Scotland had no cement production until the 1950s.

5 Letter of Craig Mitchell, Deputy Secretary, Department of Health, 17 July 1948, SRO, DD6/1461.

6 Letter of Central Economic Planning Section, 28 July 1948, ibid. The 'prefabs' were to be let to ordinary families, and the permanent houses they would have occupied to those with tuberculosis.

spring he advised his officials to seek economies in house construction to secure a larger total.[1] With these economies, Woodburn anticipated boosting the programme from 25,000 to 30,000 houses per annum, but in the event the sterling crisis intervened (extract pp. 301-3). Labour steadfastly maintained the Scottish programme at the lower level.[2]

At the 1950 party conference, the Conservatives pledged their next Government to a programme of 300,000 houses per annum. No specific Scottish total was mentioned, but when the Conservatives entered office they made it clear that they wanted to build as many as they could within a revised system of subsidies.[3] Although the Scottish subsidy may not have been at the level Stuart would have preferred (extracts pp. 303-5), it proved sufficient, with further economies in construction, to increase the rate of building. Most local authorities were under pressure to reduce waiting lists.[4] Nevertheless, Scottish Ministers were under no illusion that the enlarged subsidy was short-term and that the Government was pledged to market principles for all but the slum tenant. In 1950 Labour, as part of its post-devaluation retrenchment, had decided not to increase the 1946 subsidy in line with inflation.[5] This implied an increase in rents, but the Conservatives felt that this would remain politically difficult without a similar rise in the private sector. As the extracts (pp. 305-9) indicate, much of the discussion surrounding the Housing (Rent and Repairs) Bill was dominated by a desire to increase private rents at the same time as improving the quality of accommodation. Nevertheless Scottish Ministers remained cautious about restoring equilibrium in the private market without amending the

1 Minute of J. Hogarth, Assistant Secretary, Housing Division, Department of Health, 27 May 1949, SRO, DD6/1650.

2 The Scottish proportion of UK completions, 1948-51, was 12 per cent. A quarter were provided by non-traditional methods. Completions were higher than in 1936-9 and three times the level of 1921-4.

3 *Scotsman*, 'Housing Policy', 28 Nov. 1951; 'Housing Programme', 5 Dec. 1951; 'State of the Nation' (speech by Stuart), 26 Jan. 1952. Stuart initially wanted the subsidy limited to costs associated with the increased Bank Rate, largely to put further pressure on rents, but changed his mind after meeting local authorities: letter of W.G. Pottinger (Private Secretary) to Treasury, 6 Nov. 1951, SRO, DD6/1613.

4 Local authority completions in 1952-3 were 33,600, in 1953-4, 38,900, in 1954-5, 36,800 and in 1955-6, 31,500, which with private building was slightly more than the 'Goschen' formula. The programme was assisted by capital restrictions in other programmes, such as factories, schools and hospitals.

5 Letter of McNeil, 23 Nov. 1950, SRO, DD6/1161. To avoid restricting lettings to those who could afford increased rents, Glasgow sought an increase in subsidy.

Rent Acts: the sector had seen little investment since 1915, and the sanitary state of much tenement property fell well short of contemporary standards.[1]

The Conservatives entered office a little unsure about new towns. They knew that many of the cities were congested and lacking in amenity, but feared that the additional cost of constructing new towns might preclude development elsewhere.[2] However, at the end of 1951 the Cabinet accepted that there was little prospect of abandoning the investment already made and agreed to support the existing programme. The Government also agreed to introduce a Town Development Bill for England, negotiated with London by the previous Labour administration. The Bill enabled 'congested' local authorities to enter into agreements with others (primarily those with labour shortages) to receive their 'overspill', but with much less Government assistance than the 1946 New Towns Act.[3] However, Stuart believed that Scottish employment conditions were different to those in the Midlands and the South-East, and rejected its application to Scotland.[4] His priority was to encourage local authority building, especially on Clydeside.

Nevertheless the Department of Health remained concerned about Glasgow, where the city's development plan covered only a proportion of the estimated need and where, according to officials, available land would be exhausted by 1959. In September, Tom Galbraith, one of the Parliamentary Under Secretaries, met Glasgow Corporation at his own initiative and suggested that it might use other local authorities to rehouse its 'overspill'.[5] The Government, he said, would look favourably on adapting the 1952 Act to Scotland. Glasgow declined the offer, partly because of money, but also because it believed that it could rehouse within the city, either by building to high density or through boundary extension. The Minister did not give up, and the following February persuaded the reconstituted Clyde Valley Committee that Glasgow was in difficulty.[6] A

1 *Scotsman*, 'The State of Scotland' (speech by Stuart), 31 Jan. 1953; 'Prevention of Slums: Earl of Home's View', 10 Nov. 1953. Liability for owners' rates was abolished in 1957. Under the 1954 Act, 761 grants were awarded between 1954 and 1958.

2 *Hansard*, Vol. 424, c.2513, 5 July 1946, Comments by J.S. Reid (Scottish Spokesman), New Towns Bill, 3rd Reading. *Scotsman*, 'Scottish New Towns', 30 Aug. 1952.

3 Memorandum by Harold Macmillan, Minister of Housing and Local Government, 21 Nov. 1951, PRO, CAB 134/907 HA(51)3rd.

4 *Hansard*, Vol. 496, c.135, 26 Feb. 1952.

5 SRO, DD12/250; *Glasgow Herald*, 'Glasgow and the Clyde Valley', 15 Sept. 1952.

6 Meeting, 23 Feb. 1953, SRO, DD12/251. Galbraith approved its re-establishment in December 1951, principally to assist building co-ordination: minute, 5 Dec. 1951, DD12/650.

month later Stuart wrote more formally and invited the Committee to re-examine the feasibility of a new town.[1]

The change in attitude represented a fundamental shift in policy towards Scotland's post-war reconstruction. At the time, it was probably understood only by a few of Stuart's advisers. Unlike the 1946 Act, which relied largely on the voluntary movement of tenants and industry, Scottish policy after 1953 stressed compulsory clearance. Stuart had three reasons for this. First, he realised that a failure to sustain Glasgow's programme would cause political difficulties, especially as the worst of the housing need elsewhere was being met: the Conservatives' hold on Clydeside was tenuous.[2] Second, Stuart also realised the fiscal consequences of maintaining the local authority as the principal provider of housing.[3] If the subsidy arrangements were reflected elsewhere, then the Government's ability to reduce taxation, a key element in its election manifesto, would be severely impaired. Third, he recognised the impact of the local authority programme on Scotland's political economy. Most of industrial Scotland, including Glasgow, was Labour-controlled. As Elliot had predicted in 1937, Labour increasingly used low rents to maintain its electoral support.[4] An unelected new town corporation, free from local politics, offered the prospect of more direct control over the large 'overspill' programme of some 100,000 houses. It also offered the prospect of introducing economic rents to a key sector of Scottish political life.

However, Stuart realised that new towns were also relevant to the economy. Since 1945, the Scottish economy had not enjoyed the same success as England or even Wales.[5] Unemployment stood at twice England's level. Additionally, the report on Local Development published by the SC(DI) in 1952 broadly reflected the trend of Scottish thought, although rejected by the Government.[6] The Report effectively restated Abercrombie on a Scotland-wide basis. Glasgow's 'overspill' should be settled in areas most likely to achieve economic

1 Letter of G.H. Kimpton, Under Secretary, Department of Health, 2 Mar. 1953, ibid.

2 *Glasgow Herald*, 'Work and Homes for Scotland', 5 Feb. 1953. The paper castigated the Scottish Office for being 'too timid to formulate a plan to make dispersal possible'. 'Vigour and imagination' were required.

3 Minute, 12 Sept. 1952, SRO, DD6/1566.

4 Minute of Craig Mitchell, 24 Mar. 1953, SRO, DD6/1616. A number of authorities, for instance Armadale, had net rents (after allowing for owners' rates) below the statutory allowance required for their Repairs Account. Stuart, however, remained nervous about taking direct action.

5 See Chapter Two below, especially pp. 175-6, 200, 213-14.

6 The Report attracted considerable support from Scottish officials and also from two Parliamentary Under Secretaries, T. Galbraith and J. Henderson-Stewart: Development Area Review, September 1952, SRO, SEP4/587.

growth—the Borders, the Moray Firth, Strathmore, in fact anywhere other than Glasgow.[1] In 1953, Stuart, like Westwood before him, accepted that housing development could be used to give Scotland a 'new look' to attract English industry.

The shift in policy was soon evident in Cabinet, where Scottish Ministers made it clear that they felt Scottish difficulties required special consideration and probably finance.[2] The Ministers were aided by the Ministry of Housing, whose new towns were proving slow to develop, and at the end of 1953 the Cabinet accepted that further development might be necessary (extracts pp. 310-16). Nevertheless the Treasury remained unconvinced by Stuart's arguments, and suggested adapting the Town Development Act with its limited grant aid.[3] The Department of Health rejected this outright: without a new town, there was no guarantee that a co-ordinated programme could be established within the political timescale.[4] The Clyde Valley Committee had recommended the building of a new town (Cumbernauld) under the provisions of the 1946 Act, a suggestion that Scottish opinion generally welcomed.[5] However, Stuart's greatest difficulty remained Glasgow. Although it revoked its decision against 'overspill' in 1953, it remained suspicious of Conservative motives and refused any contribution towards the proposed development.[6] After much discussion with the city, Stuart secured an agreement which limited Glasgow's financial involvement to its existing statutory rate contribution.[7]

The decision to support Cumbernauld represented a considerable achievement for Stuart, and paved the way for the 1957 Housing and Town Development Act (extract pp. 316-19).[8] Nevertheless, the statute fell short of

1 *Glasgow Herald*, 'Regional Planning—The West's Time for Decision', 3 Feb. 1953.

2 Comment, Galbraith, Economic Policy Committee, 13 May 1953, PRO, CAB 134/846 EA(53)16th.

3 Official Meeting, Department of Health and Treasury, 29 June 1954, PRO, T 227/412.

4 The Department also argued that there was no guarantee that other local authorities would introduce economic rents. Similar logic was used to reject Glasgow administering Cumbernauld as a 'detached burgh'.

5 *Glasgow Herald*, 'Glasgow's New Town', 19 Aug. 1953; 'Rehousing Glasgow's Overspill', 16 Jan. 1954; *Scotsman*, 'New Town at Cumbernauld', 19 Aug. 1953; 'Congested Glasgow', 27 Apr. 1954. Houston was preferred by the Department of Health, but had a marginal Conservative constituency with a well-organised agricultural lobby.

6 Letter of Stuart to Butler, 23 Nov. 1954, PRO, T 227/412. Glasgow revoked its decision on the assumption that Cumbernauld would be built under the 1946 Act, so that it would have no financial liability.

7 Stuart met Glasgow on 4 Mar. 1955, without consulting the Treasury: PRO, T 227/412. Before the meeting, Glasgow faced a sustained political and media campaign, which dubbed its development plan 'laisser-tomber'.

8 *Glasgow Herald*, 'Balanced Communities New and Old', 29 Apr. 1955; 'Cumbernauld New Town', 13 Dec. 1955; 'Glasgow's Overspill Problem Unique' (speech by H.R. Smith, Secretary, Department of

committing the Government to creating Cumbernauld as a new town with a 'balanced' industrial structure. The Treasury, before and after the Cabinet decision, remained adamant that it would not provide assistance to move industry from one part of a Development Area to another, or to subsidise factory rents.[1] In the event Cumbernauld saw little 'parallel movement' of industry and population, and the town found its development dependent on external investment.[2]

By the mid-1950s, private enterprise in England was sufficiently organised to sustain a growth in owner-occupation, and the Treasury began to call for restrictions in the local authority programme. Although Stuart accepted the rationale for a reduction in the subsidy, he also understood Scottish sensitivity towards maintaining the building programme, especially as Scotland's share of new building began to fall below the 'Goschen' formula.[3] As the extracts indicate (pp. 319-28), the late 1950s saw a determined attempt to retain the Scottish programme at about 25,000 houses, sufficient to meet the unmet need and allow the new towns to grow.[4] However, the Government remained committed to cuts in taxation; the Cabinet found the case for differentiation in policy difficult to accept, despite only half of Johnston's programme being completed.

Chapter Four: Health and Welfare

One of the principal reasons for the reform of local government in 1889 was a desire to improve the state of Scottish public health.[5] Over the next twenty years, the new county structure, with its power to remove those suffering from

Health), 13 Jan. 1956; 'Scottish Proposals for Town Development' (Final Report of Clyde Valley Committee), 17 Jan. 1956.

1 Board of Trade minute, 12 Aug. 1955, PRO, T 227/412. The Board of Trade were less sure, but felt constrained by the Distribution of Industry Act which limited subsidies to 'incoming' industry.

2 Glasgow redevelopment probably reduced inner-city employment by about 20,000. Some firms whose premises were demolished had been closely integrated into the city's industrial structure, which Cumbernauld could not replace, whilst others found the 'economic' rents prohibitive, despite the compensation offered.

3 *Scotsman*, 'Housing Record', 6 Feb. 1956; 'Housing Policy', 4 Apr. 1956; 'Local Authority Housing', 4 Aug. 1956.

4 *Scotsman*, 'Brake on Housing', 12 Nov. 1957; 'Housing Trends', 1 Feb. 1958.

5 For general discussion on health provision, see B. Abel-Smith, *The Hospital, 1800-1948* (Harvard, 1964); C.L. Dunn, *The Emergency Medical Services* (London, 1952); A. Land, R. Lowe & N. Whiteside, *The Development of the Welfare State, 1939-1951* (London, 1992); A. Macgregor, *Public Health in Glasgow* (Edinburgh, 1964); G. McLachlan, (ed.) *Improving the Common Weal: Aspects of Scottish Health Services, 1900-1984* (Edinburgh, 1987); C. Webster, *The Health Services Since the War* (London, 1988).

infectious diseases to purpose-built 'isolation' hospitals, substantially improved Scottish life expectancy. At the same time, with the arrival of safer surgery and higher standards of clinical knowledge, accommodation in voluntary hospitals increased. The Poor Law, long regarded as a residual service for the 'less deserving', also saw an expansion of care.[1] For contemporaries, such developments came as little surprise: Scottish medicine, with its fine tradition based on the four university medical schools, was internationally renowned. The growth of hospital provision was matched by developments in the community, where many local authorities began to experiment with child welfare clinics aimed at improving the quality of care for mothers and their infants. After a long campaign, tuberculosis was declared a notifiable disease in 1905; a hospital-based system of care gradually expanded. For a variety of illnesses and diseases, a combination of medical technology and institutional care seemed to offer the possibility of a substantial reduction in the death rate and a permanent improvement to Scotland's health.[2]

The war inevitably interrupted developments, and many hospitals were taken over by the military. However, further advances in medical techniques, the war losses and the general increase in the standard of living all had an impact on popular expectations; the creation of the Board of Health in 1919 confirmed the view that modern society required higher levels of health care, facilitated by Government.[3] By the early 1920s, with the assistance of Government grants, virtually the whole of Scotland was covered by a child welfare service. At the same time the Board established a number of inquiries into health provision, including one on the co-ordination of services and another on public administration. Lloyd George's Government, in the wake of the wartime Maclean Report on the break-up of the Poor Law, remained committed to an overhaul of local government and the integration of health care into one authority.[4] The existing services, divided between the local authority, the education authority and the parish, produced overlaps in provision and hindered co-operative development.[5]

1 In 1890 the number of beds in voluntary hospitals was 6,000, in public health wards 1,500 and in the poorhouse infirmary 4,500. In 1914 the totals were 10,500, 7,900 and 6,900.

2 The average Scottish infant mortality rate in 1891-5 was 126 deaths per 1,000 births (English rate 151); in 1911-15, 113 (110); in 1921-5, 92 (76); in 1931-5, 81 (62) and in 1941-5, 68 (49). Slum districts generally had rates twice the national average.

3 *Report of the Consultative Council on Medical and Allied Services on a Scheme of Medical Service for Scotland*, Cmd. 1039 (Edinburgh, 1920).

4 *Report of the Committee on Transfer of Functions of Poor Law Authorities in England and Wales*, Cd. 8917 (London, 1918).

5 Scotland had about 800 parish councils, 400 public health local authorities and 37 education authorities,

In 1921 the Government recognised the disruption to the voluntary hospital. By way of 'reparation', it agreed to establish a Hospital Commission to distribute grants to those most affected by military use and lost income.[1] Although co-ordinated by the Ministry of Health, the Commission aroused little comment, largely because it was seen as being managed by the voluntary hospitals.[2] The Ministry, however, liked the idea of a Commission: it brought them into regular and more formal contact with one of the principal providers of health care, and they sought to retain the link after the Commission's original function ceased. A permanent British commission implied similarity of conditions in both England and Scotland; as the extract indicates (pp. 329-32), Scottish opinion remained steadfastly opposed to a common policy. The Scottish system was based on the pre-eminence of the four university medical schools, and the voluntary hospitals remained suspicious of any link to a county-based structure, with all its connotations of local authority control and its 'threat' to clinical freedom. Novar agreed that a separate 'co-ordinating body' was necessary, but the issue became submerged in Government difficulties elsewhere and did not resurface until after Labour entered office (extract pp. 333-6).

Adamson, Labour's Scottish Secretary, accepted the necessity of a co-ordinating body but saw the issue in broader terms than the Ministry of Health. He agreed that an inquiry into Scottish hospital services should also take account of the statutory sector. The Board of Health had, for some time, been concerned about accommodation for 'general' medical needs, particularly as the finances of the voluntary hospitals appeared less secure than in England.[3] It had also received a report on local health administration from its consultative council.[4] The Report largely reaffirmed the view of the Maclean Committee and recommended that every integrated service should be based on a minimum population of 50,000, which in Scottish terms would reduce the number of authorities from over a thousand to forty. The Report was broadly welcomed, and underpinned parallel discussions on local government reform.[5]

each providing health care to various patients. Different members of the same family could be treated by different authorities.

1 *Report of the Committee on Voluntary Hospitals*, Cmd. 1335 (London, 1921).

2 *Scotsman*, 'Lord Cave's Committee', 15 July 1921.

3 Traditionally, Scottish hospitals relied on donations and legacies more than patient fees and subscription income. Many, like Edinburgh's Royal Infirmary, were prohibited by charter from charging fees. In the 1920s, income from legacies fell, and workers' subscriptions were affected by unemployment.

4 *A Reformed Local Authority for Health and Public Administration* (Edinburgh, 1923).

5 *Glasgow Herald*, 'Health Services', 21 July 1923; *Scotsman*, 'Health Administration: Position of Parish Councils', 2 July 1923.

Sir John Gilmour, the next Scottish Secretary, shared Neville Chamberlain's belief that reform to improve efficiency would do much to improve the quality of services. As a Conservative, however, to be seen to promote radical reform at the expense of tradition was a problem (extracts pp. 336-7).[1] In 1924 a Public Health Bill to provide insulin to diabetes sufferers had been strongly resisted by local authorities, largely because the Bill also 'contemplated' the development of other rate-aided services for non-infectious diseases.[2] In the event the Conservatives postponed discussion on reform, partly because they felt that public opinion was unformulated and partly because they saw difficulty in untangling the existing system of Government grant aid and local rates.[3] Gilmour remained concerned about the position of the voluntary hospitals, whose pre-eminent position in meeting 'general' needs had been underlined by the Hospital Inquiry Committee.[4] He was also concerned about the development of specialist services such as maternity care and tuberculosis (extracts pp. 338-49). Scottish rates for infant and maternal mortality were significantly higher than those in England (a reverse of the position before 1914), and Gilmour was under pressure from Labour to announce special initiatives.[5] Chamberlain remained convinced that 'rationalisation' of local government would greatly assist development, and had some difficulty in accepting Gilmour's view that the financial position of the Scottish voluntary hospital was materially worse than in England.[6]

In Spring 1928 the Cabinet approved Chamberlain's Local Government Bill for England and Wales. It was a sweeping reform, recasting the system of grant aid and the unification of local services. With fee and subscription income

1 Speech to the Royal Sanitary Institute, *Scotsman*, 21 July 1925.

2 Adamson had been unable to secure grant aid, largely because in England the power to provide medicines to 'poorer inhabitants' under the 1875 Public Health Act was not grant-aided. There was no equivalent provision in Scotland. Memorandum, Public Health (Scotland) Amendment Bill, 27 Feb. 1924, PRO, CAB 24/165 CP(24)141. The Bill passed its third reading in the Commons and was reintroduced by the Conservatives in 1925, but restricted to the provision of insulin.

3 *Scotsman*, 'The Hospital Inquiry', 19 Jan. 1925; 'Voluntary Hospitals', 15 Aug. 1925; *Glasgow Herald*, 'A Hospital Policy', 8 Feb. 1926.

4 *Report on the Hospital Services of Scotland* (Edinburgh, 1926).

5 *Hansard*, Vol. 182, c.1942, 6 Apr. 1925, and Vol. 198, c.1425, 22 June 1926, Scottish Board of Health Supply Votes. The Board's application of Government economy measures in 1921-4 and 1925-6 had restricted the growth of child welfare schemes and reduced the Scottish share of grants below the 'Goschen' formula.

6 The Government rejected the English inquiry recommendation for 10,000 additional beds, largely because voluntary hospitals reported an increased flow of income. The Scottish proposals were for a subsidy three times the 'Goschen' formula.

growing, English voluntary hospitals appeared unconcerned about a challenge from a rate-aided hospital system. Accommodation had been substantially improved.[1] In Scotland Gilmour found the situation more difficult: there was opposition to the amalgamation of local authorities. Labour, in particular, thought that it went against Scottish traditions of local democracy.[2] Voluntary hospital managers also voiced concern about their sector's future position in meeting 'general' needs.[3] In the event Gilmour trimmed, setting the minimum population for a health authority at 20,000, not the 50,000 recommended in 1923 (extracts pp. 349-52). Initially he also excluded the development of a 'general' medical service; however, after a petition from Glasgow and other authorities, he agreed to introduce an amendment to the Scottish Bill on the understanding that the local authority would first seek co-operation from the neighbouring voluntary hospital.

The 1929 Local Government Act was essentially a political compromise, more so than the English Act, but Gilmour and his immediate successors thought that administrative action would do much to ensure voluntary and local authority co-operation.[4] However, by the mid-1930s it was evident to the Scottish Ministers that they faced three difficulties in securing an integrated service, despite further official exhortation.[5] First, the scale of unemployment in Scotland affected the flow of voluntary income, and opposition to rate-aided competition grew. A number of extensions based on fee-paying patients ran into difficulty, most notably the Glasgow Victoria Hospital and the Greenock Infirmary. Second, local authorities, heavily burdened with Poor Law and other welfare payments, showed no inclination to combine with others to develop hospital services. A significant number, particularly in Lanarkshire, positively refused to co-operate with Department of Health initiatives. Third, their concern about rate levels also affected the growth of community health services, and a number indicated that without additional grant aid further developments were unlikely.[6]

By the mid-1930s it was also evident that the broad indicators of public health had not significantly improved.[7] In maternity provision, the mortality rate had even increased. For Collins, the Maternity Services Bill (extract pp. 352-5)

1 Ministry of Health, *Voluntary Hospital Accommodation in England and Wales* (London, 1928).
2 *Hansard*, Vol. 223, c.859, 3 Dec. 1928, Local Government (Scotland) Bill, Second Reading.
3 *Glasgow Herald*, 'The Hospital', 25 June 1928.
4 *Annual Report of the Department of Health, 1931-2*, Cmd. 4080 (Edinburgh, 1932).
5 See the Department's Consultative Council Report, *Hospital Services in Scotland* (Edinburgh, 1933).
6 Departmental letter to Convention of Royal Burghs, 17 Aug. 1936, SRO, DD5/131.
7 *Hansard*, Vol. 303, c.1422, 28 June 1935, Supply: Committee—Health, Scotland.

represented the first instalment of a much larger 'assault' on health conditions.[1] It also represented the first occasion when the necessity of an enhanced Scottish grant for health care was formally acknowledged.

At the end of 1936 the War Office began preparations for civilian defence in the face of anticipated hostilities, and established an inter-departmental committee to plan an emergency medical service. The Committee estimated that there could be 300,000 civilian casualties within the first two weeks of war; on its calculations, the UK was short of about 96,000 hospital beds (after allowing for some less urgent cases to be sent home).[2] This casualty figure alarmed the Committee, who had seen the impact of bombing on morale during the Spanish Civil War. For speed of action they recommended that the Government, rather than the local authority, should plan the emergency accommodation.[3] The Committee thought some beds could be found by extending existing hospitals or converting other buildings such as poorhouses and asylums, but if additional accommodation was necessary it agreed to site new hospitals to serve a number of authorities.[4]

Planning the Scottish programme proved more problematic than the English, largely because the majority of the better hospitals (and beds) were located in the four cities, themselves likely targets of enemy action. Outside the cities the accommodation varied in both quality and extent; the Department found that it could not secure sufficient hospital beds for the estimated number of casualties.[5] For Colville the Committee's recommendations represented an opportunity to overcome some of the existing Scottish difficulties and, as the extracts indicate (pp. 355-7), his plan preferred allocating the expenditure to new hospitals. In England, once the accommodation was built, the Ministry of Health transferred management to the local authority, but in Scotland, with a history of failed co-operation, Colville preferred to retain control. The Emergency Service was, in all but name, a Scottish Hospital Authority.[6]

1 Collins was awaiting the report of the Committee on Health Services, which he expected to recommend that the Government should assume powers to ensure local co-ordination, aided by the National Insurance Fund. By the time the Committee reported (July 1936), the Government's attention was directed to planning for war. Collins and his immediate successors also pursued the Special Areas Commissioner to establish, in partnership with local authorities, a number of hospitals. War intervened before the programme was realised.

2 Report of the Committee on Imperial Defence: Sub-Committee on the Co-ordination of Medical Arrangements, 11 Mar. 1937, PRO, CAB 16/171 CMA 9.

3 Committee Minute, 30 July 1937, PRO, CAB 16/171, 9th Meeting.

4 Report, 25 Oct. 1937, PRO, CAB 16/171, CMA 12.

5 Comments on Report to Ministers, Mar. 1938, PRO, MH 76/95. The accommodation inspected was described as 'horrible'.

6 The Department urged that the hospitals should have a 25-year life: PRO, MH 76/240, 245. They

In 1943, shortly after the publication of the Beveridge Report on Social Security, the Coalition Government began to discuss the post-war health service. There was general acceptance amongst Ministers and officials that the voluntary hospital, even in England, would not survive without a firmer financial basis.[1] The public's expectation of adequacy in health provision had increased. However, the Ministry of Health, reflecting English opinion, favoured a county-based system of co-ordination, with additional funding derived from the proposed new system of compulsory national insurance. The development of services would be very much locally determined. As the extracts indicate (pp. 357-65), Johnston thought such a system inappropriate to Scotland, partly because the smaller local authorities had little knowledge of managing a 'general' service and partly because GPs were resistant to local authority control (as consultants had been in the 1920s). The Reconstruction Committee broadly accepted that joint hospital boards were more appropriate to Scotland, but the Ministers found it difficult to agree on the exact relationship between the voluntary and local authority sectors. Nor could they resolve the scheme's financial basis, especially the use of the National Insurance Fund. Labour believed that a reformed system of national insurance was unlikely to meet all aspects of need, and was adamantly opposed to the imposition of a means test.[2] Conservatives thought that the proposed scheme would place the voluntary hospital, with its tradition of clinical excellence, in a subordinate position, and weaken the quality of care provided.[3]

When Bevan's proposals to 'nationalise' the hospital service and make treatment free at point of delivery arrived in the Department of Health in September 1945, its Ministers immediately recognised the advantages for Scotland. Treasury support for health expenditure seemed a more reliable source of funding than donations, intermittent fees and rates from impoverished local authorities. Westwood had an easier passage than Bevan in securing an agreement with the medical establishment, partly because Bevan conducted the principal discussions ahead of Westwood, but also because Westwood based the Scottish scheme on the four university medical schools and their associated hospitals (extracts pp. 365-8).[4] Effectively the scheme was based on the tradition of the

contained about 20 per cent of Scottish beds. The Department also took a calculated decision to site the hospitals near railway lines for casualty evacuation, and in locations suitable for post-war use.

1 Department of Health minute, 24 Sept. 1941, SRO, HH65/93; minute, 31 Mar. 1943, SRO, HH65/93, 101/1.

2 Notes for Johnston's meeting with Labour MPs, 9 Nov. 1943, SRO, HH65/93.

3 See meeting with Johnston, 16 June 1944, SRO, HH101/5.

4 *Glasgow Herald*, 'Scottish Health Bill', 22 Apr. 1947. Younger consultants who had first-hand experience of the Emergency Scheme, in particular, were less concerned about hospital 'nationalisation'.

eminent specialist, the university teacher and the consultant, and incorporated the Conservatives' view of quality into the core of provision. Attlee thought the Scottish scheme better than Bevan's and personally congratulated Westwood on his achievement.

The passing of the National Health Service Act marked an important turning point in Scottish health policy. The removal of charges from general practitioner, dental, ophthalmic and hospital care proved extremely popular and, in some respects, greatly increased public awareness of health and expectations of minimum provision.[1] Nevertheless, the Department of Health understood that there were gaps in the quality of provision, despite the additional accommodation provided by the emergency service; the public were as sensitive to waiting lists as they had been to the payment of fees. The Department's priority for capital expenditure was largely for the upgrading of poorhouses and mental asylums and for the establishment of general hospitals where local agreements had proved difficult to secure (extracts pp. 368-72). Achieving the programme seemed feasible but, as the next three extracts indicate (pp. 372-8), financial issues, particularly over pay and the 'restructuring' of staff, dominated ministerial discussion.[2] Although the Health Ministers prevented the Government from reneging on free treatment, they were forced to accept severe restrictions in the capital programme.

To the Treasury, the events of 1949 brought home the reality of managing a State-organised service where resource allocation was determined by public demand rather than by rational planning. Cripps, the Chancellor, was determined to bring the Health Service budget into the usual framework of Government accounting. The removal of Woodburn as the Scottish Secretary assisted his task, as Hector McNeil took a less ideological view of Health Service development. For McNeil, the Government faced two key issues in discussing the future of the Health Service (extract pp. 378-82). First, there was a necessity to educate the public about the relationship between the country's economic capacity and available resources; second, the Government had to be clear on its priorities, especially as medical science was bound to advance public expectations.[3] Nevertheless, in the face of objections from Bevan and other Ministers, the Cabinet accepted that introducing charges remained politically difficult, and

1 *Glasgow Herald*, 'Social Services', 24 Sept. 1947; 'Progress Report', 15 Jan. 1949.

2 The issue was aggravated in England by the independence of the teaching hospitals under separate Boards of Governors.

3 Memorandum of Department of Health, May 1950, and McNeil's letter to Herbert Morrison, 19 May 1950, PRO, CAB 124/1187. The Department recommended 'manpower ceilings' to force hospital authorities to use staff 'more efficiently'.

agreed to submit the issue to a small Ministerial Committee. In the interim the Health Ministers were invited to control costs by administrative means. The 'supplementary' services saw a reduction in demand and costs, but McNeil was also able to achieve a modest success in controlling the hospital budget, largely due to the tight management structure of the regional board.[1] The administrative controls were not sufficient to appease the Treasury (or convince McNeil); in April 1951, the Cabinet agreed on charges for prescriptions, spectacles and some other items.[2] Bevan's resignation from the Cabinet was not altogether unexpected, but the subsequent political upror was a salutary reminder that the public generally supported a comprehensive service based on need.

Following the outbreak of the war, the incidence of tuberculosis in Britain began to increase, reversing the trend of the previous twenty years. In part, this was attributed to wartime conditions and the Government introduced a number of special initiatives, including additional hospital accommodation, higher levels of public assistance and a pilot programme of mass radiography.[3] In England this resulted in a reduced incidence, but in Scotland the numbers continued to increase, especially on Clydeside.[4] The Department was alarmed, and although further hospital accommodation was secured, nurses proved difficult to recruit.[5] The waiting list for treatment continued to grow. As the *Glasgow Herald* reported, the control of tuberculosis in Scotland remained an 'aspiration' rather than a 'reality'.[6]

In July 1950 a number of press articles indicated that the decline of tuberculosis in Europe had resulted in empty accommodation in Swiss sanatoria, and urged the Ministry of Health to offer treatment there on 'humanitarian and medical grounds'.[7] McNeil took up the idea and pressed both the curative and publicity benefits on Cripps and Bevan: the public appeared exasperated by Government inaction (extracts pp. 382-6). The Ministry of Health remained

1 Memorandum, Estimates and Economies in Scotland, 20 Feb. 1951, PRO, CAB 134/519 NH(51)5.

2 McNeil also favoured the introduction of dental charges.

3 Memorandum of W.R. Fraser, Secretary, Department of Health, 17 July 1942, SRO, HH102/116. The first Scottish mass miniature radiography set was allocated to Glasgow in June 1944, followed by Lanarkshire.

4 An inquiry established by Woodburn reported that a contributory factor was probably nutrition: *Tuberculosis in Scotland* (Edinburgh, 1951).

5 Minutes of N.W. Graham, Assistant Secretary, Health, 3 Sept. 1946 and 3 Oct. 1946, SRO, HH102/251. Nurses feared infection, and for career reasons preferred employment in general wards.

6 *Glasgow Herald*, 'TB in Scotland', 7 July 1949; see also *Hansard*, Vol. 466, c.2492-2500, 7 July 1949, Adjournment Debate, Tuberculosis, Glasgow.

7 Articles appeared in the *Spectator* and the *Economist*. See also *Scotsman*, 'Swiss Sanatoria Beds', 1 Aug. 1950.

uncertain of the scheme's value, partly because of cost, but also because they had some doubts about the standard of care.[1] However, after his officials visited Switzerland, McNeil publicly announced his interest and immediately attracted favourable press reviews.[2] The scheme, selecting on the basis of need and not the ability to pay, was evidence of a 'democratic' health service. With some reluctance the Ministry of Health agreed to establish their own scheme, and the first Scottish patients, suitably photographed, flew out in June 1951.

In December 1950 McNeil also insisted that additional accommodation was found in 'general' hospitals, using their existing staff. By early 1955 the Department of Health reported that the waiting list for treatment had significantly declined.[3] In November the Swiss scheme was withdrawn, 1,000 patients having been treated. However, the Department knew that significant numbers remained undetected, partly because it took some time for the characteristics of the disease to be identified, but also because many still regarded the disease with a degree of fatalism. Initially the Department proposed to continue with its community radiography surveys, but, with an eye on raising public consciousness, Stuart wanted something more visible. As the next extract indicates (pp. 386-8), Stuart, assisted by other Ministers, began an intensive campaign, first in Glasgow, Scotland's 'blackspot', and then other cities. This was widely applauded, and succeeded in producing a high rate of response for examination.[4] By the end of the decade, and with the arrival of new antibiotics, tuberculosis ceased to be a major health concern.

The Conservatives had fought the 1951 election committed to the Health Service, but equally pledged to maintain it within the nation's 'economic capacity'. Charges were introduced for dental care in 1952, but the Cabinet, wary of the public's reaction, decided to seek other controls through administrative action. Nevertheless, shortly after the 1955 general election, the Treasury initiated discussion on containing public expenditure, 'in the light of continuing balance of payments problems', and a special Cabinet Committee was established to review Health Service and other social expenditure. Stuart took the opposite position to McNeil. Government controls, particularly over

1 Departmental minutes, 19 July 1950, 28 Feb. 1951, SRO, HH162/316.

2 Report of N.W. Graham and Dr I.M. Macgregor, 16 Oct. 1950, ibid.; *Glasgow Herald*, 'Tuberculosis', 2 Nov. 1950; *Scotsman*, 'TB in Scotland', 2 Nov. 1950.

3 Minute, R.P. Fraser, Assistant Secretary, Health, 11 Mar. 1955, SRO, HH102/317; see also *Hansard*, Vol. 538, c.1883-93, 22 Mar. 1955, Adjournment Debate, Tuberculosis, Scotland.

4 *Scotsman*, 'All Out Attack', 22 Feb. 1956; *Glasgow Herald*, 'Campaign against TB', 22 Feb. 1956. The radiography units, mobilised from all over the UK, were likened to a 'Panzer' attack on the City.

wages, had reduced the Health Service's share of national expenditure, and he thought that the priority was to allocate resources in line with the 'natural' advance of medical knowledge.[1] In the face of sustained opposition from Stuart and the Minister of Health, the Cabinet abandoned the prospect of radical change (extracts pp. 388-94).

At the beginning of 1955, with a planned reduction in public sector housing, Ministers agreed to restart the hospital building programme frozen by Labour in 1949.[2] An extensive programme of modernisation was begun. However, in 1958, the Treasury sought to impose another squeeze on expenditure, largely to reduce taxation. As the final extract indicates (pp. 394-5), Maclay successfully opposed the restriction of expenditure in Scotland. In 1959 the Department of Health announced proposals for new hospitals and other extensions in areas where pre-war agreements had proved difficult to secure.

Conclusion

It was a general dictum within the civil service that twentieth-century government should be based on the widest possible administrative capacity combined with the gradual acquisition of specialist knowledge.[3] Unless there were 'special features', this tended to imply the establishment of departments on a British rather than a territorial basis. But the Scottish Office was never simply an ordinary department of state; it had also been created to symbolise the uniqueness of Scottish culture, incorporate Liberal devolutionists into the Union and keep Scottish interests in touch with Westminster. The Haldane Report may have represented high efficiency in administrative development, but, as the Treasury later acknowledged, it conveniently overlooked the 'peculiarities' of Scottish sentiment and the 'delicate' balance that past Scottish Secretaries maintained between unionism and nationalism.[4]

After 1918, with the growth of Government and extension of the franchise, senior officials in the Scottish Office and other informed opinion believed that if this balance was to be maintained the role of the Scottish Secretary would have to alter. Labour, whose position in the polls did not yet reflect its industrial strength, felt uneasy about Westminster's ability to deal quickly and effectively with Scotland's growing housing and health problems. As Munro pointed out, a devolved assembly would mean the abolition of the Scottish Secretary and

1 Scottish Office minute, 6 Dec. 1955, SRO, SOE 6/5/57.

2 *Glasgow Herald*, 'Investing in Success', 10 Feb. 1955; *Scotsman*, 'Hospital Services', 10 Feb. 1955.

3 Minute of W.S. Murrie, Secretary, Scottish Education Department, 4 Feb. 1953, SRO, HH41/690.

4 Notes on Government Organisation: Regional Organisation, June 1946, SRO, HH1/1231.

with it his ability to act as the 'guardian' of the Scottish interest. The 'practicalities' of the situation suggested a different response: less emphasis on the devolution of political authority and more on the Scottish Secretary advancing Scotland's material interests. London and the British Government remained at the hub of an extensive diplomatic and commercial network.

Between 1918 and 1959 there were sixteen Scottish Secretaries. Some, like Sir Archibald Sinclair and Walter Elliot, entered office with an established political reputation, but either resigned or were removed to another Ministry before they could achieve what they intended.[1] Others, such as Lord Novar and Hector McNeil, were unlucky to enter short-lived Governments. In all only six, Munro, Gilmour, Collins, Johnston, Stuart and Maclay, remained in office for more than four years. Any assessment of how, and in what way, Scottish administration altered during this period, is therefore conditioned by the facts of ministerial life in party Government. Nevertheless, a number of Ministers did make a distinctive contribution to the Scottish brief, expanded its administrative capacity and enhanced its power, and the rest of this conclusion is devoted to a fuller assessment of this.

As the early extracts here suggest, Robert Munro faced three particular difficulties in convincing the Coalition that Scotland's political economy demanded a special response. First, the orientation of Lloyd George's Government reflected the concept of the British military interest: war-time mobilisation had dictated commonality of social and economic policy. Thus, as Munro discovered, whilst ministers might have been sympathetic to the political arguments for upgrading the Scottish Secretary's status, they remained trapped within a particular mode of thought. The principal Whitehall ministries held the greatest influence on British policy, whether it was health, employment or trade. Second, the disparate nature of Scottish administration and the distance of the Boards from London greatly reduced Munro's ability to impose his political authority and achieve a co-ordinated response.[2] There is no record of the Board Chairmen and the Permanent Under Secretary ever meeting to discuss Scottish affairs. Third, the Scottish Office, one of Whitehall's smallest Departments, was not known for its high calibre of staff and was generally regarded as a 'backwater',

1 Towards the end of his eighteen-month tenure, Elliot proposed a special Cabinet Committee on Scotland to discuss housing, health and employment, but Simon, the Chancellor of the Exchequer, felt the time inopportune: letter of Simon, 18 Feb. 1938, SRO, HH36/120. Neither Elliot nor his successor, Colville, were felt to make much impression on the Cabinet.

2 Non-Departmental Organisations, 3 Jan. 1945, PRO, CAB 87/72 MGO 61.

a place, as one assistant secretary noted, to end one's career.[1] The Boards, for their part, were seen as a refuge for political patronage, rather than administrative ability.[2]

The economic crisis of 1921 caused the Scottish Office additional concern, but Munro continued to meet Cabinet resistance. On the one hand, there was a widespread belief that the Scottish economy required 'adjustment' both by migration and by wage reductions. On the other, the Act of Union had introduced a unified system of 'imperial' taxation and it was difficult to suggest reasons for differentiation in policy, especially for the Scottish industrial worker.[3] Munro left office with little conceded.

The 1922 General election saw the ILP capture ten out of Glasgow's fifteen seats and confirmed the view that Scotland's old political economy had been swept away, though contemporary opinion remained uncertain of the new. The *Scotsman* thought that the election heralded a period of instability, with Clydeside opinion open to many 'narrow and peculiar influences'.[4] Novar, after some hesitation, recognised that the Scottish brief had altered, but he too found the Cabinet (and especially Chamberlain) unpersuaded of any special political danger. Nevertheless Baldwin remained unsure of his party's strength in Scotland; after 1924, Gilmour's message that only a strong and identifiable Scottish administration could contain 'centrifugalism' seemed to make sense.[5] The steel housing programme certainly deflated the Opposition and added weight to those who saw Government-supported provision as an effective antidote to Scottish 'extremism'.[6] The concomitant elevation of the Scottish Secretary into a Secretaryship of State underlined a shift in Whitehall thought;

1 Letter of G.A. Steel, 14 Mar. 1922, PRO, T 162/494. Steel, a Scot, tried to avoid being transferred to a Scottish Office vacancy.

2 *Scotsman*, 'Scottish Board of Health', 14 Nov. 1923 (reporting petition from Civil Service Union).

3 There was a long history of special treatment for the Highlands, but it was not seen as part of the normal market economy.

4 *Scotsman*, 'The Election in Scotland', 17 Nov. 1922.

5 Gilmour, who sat for Glasgow Pollock, had a long record of concern over the Clyde's political stability and refused the Scottish Secretaryship in 1922 because Law would not officially endorse an anti-Labour coalition of Conservatives and National Liberals, something that Baldwin did in 1924. See letter to Munro, on Sinn Fein activity in Glasgow, 20 Dec. 1920, SRO, HH55/68; *Scotsman*, 'New Secretary for Scotland', 24 Oct. 1922; *Hansard*, Vol. 174, c.790-871, 9 May 1924, Government of Scotland Bill, Second Reading, especially speech by H. Craik (Conservative, Scottish Universities) who commented on the 'diversity of interests' in Scotland, the 'racial composition' in industrial areas and the 'local concentration of specialist industry'. Craik had been Secretary to the Scotch Education Department, 1885-1904.

6 *Times*, 'Steel Houses', 8 Jan. 1926; 'Steel Houses', 6 Mar. 1926.

Scotland's principal Minister held the same rank as other 'great Ministers of State'.[1]

Gilmour's subsequent introduction of a departmental system heralded a significant change in administrative structure, but in terms of general policy the remainder of the 1920s was dominated by an assumption that economic normality was within reach. It was not until Collins arrived at the Scottish Office in 1932, at the height of the Depression, that further developments took place. Collins had resigned the Coalition whip in 1921 on the grounds of the Government's inability to reduce taxation and its failure to secure international peace.[2] Collins, by inclination an Asquithian Liberal, also disliked German war reparations, believing that they destabilised one of Britain's important trading partners.[3] In the early 1920s such views were unfashionable, but by the 1930s they had become accepted wisdom for the group of politicians surrounding Chamberlain. As a result Collins attracted considerable respect for his political judgement. He also attracted respect for holding his Greenock constituency against Labour opposition. Greenock, with its heavy unemployment and high density of slum housing, ought to have been natural Labour territory, but, through a mixture of good fortune (the Communists usually fielded a candidate) and personal style, Collins continued to increase his share of the vote.

Collins saw that the Government would have to go beyond projecting an identifiable Scottish administration: to reduce Scotland's material deprivation and 'dampen the spirit of nationalism' it was necessary for the public to be convinced that Whitehall recognised higher levels of Scottish need.[4] In the 1920s Scottish Secretaries had generally been concerned to ensure that Scotland received its appropriate grant aid, normally assumed to be equivalent to the 'Goschen' formula for the distribution of education expenditure. However, they had usually remained reticent about pressing the issue, largely for fear of a political backlash in England. With some grants already above the 'Goschen line', but others below, it was, as one official wrote, 'a two edged weapon' only to be 'unsheathed' in extreme cases.[5] It was possible that some Scottish needs would fall below the formula. Collins rejected that approach: future settlements

1 *Scotsman*, 'Scottish Affairs', 24 Feb. 1929.

2 *Glasgow Herald*, 'Sir Godfrey Collins and the Government', 11 May 1921. Collins told his constituency that 'what the country wants is peace abroad, economy at home, lower prices, freedom of trade with emancipation from Government interference and from the restrictions imposed by too far a numerous bureaucracy'.

3 *Glasgow Herald*, 'National Finance', 13 July 1921.

4 Letter to Chamberlain (the Chancellor), 1 Nov. 1932, SRO, DD5/558; letter to Baldwin, 28 Nov. 1935, SRO, HH1/896.

5 Minute of T.D. Fairgrieve, Principal, Scottish Office, 27 Sept. 1926, SRO, HH65/51.

would have to be seen by Scottish opinion as 'above the line'.[1] An erstwhile believer in a reduced role for Government, Collins sought a new faith for the industrial worker: collective security through administrative action. For the National Government it was a strategy that held much appeal, with a reformed Scottish Office, based in Scotland, institutionalising domestic sentiment.

Tom Johnston entered office in 1941 with a reputation as one of Labour's most effective front-bench spokesmen and an efficient political administrator.[2] Although not carrying the same intellectual grace as Elliot, Johnston's speeches displayed an uncanny ability to sense an opponent's weakness, and in a few short, but brutal sentences shake their political credibility. However, Johnston's political faith in independent socialism had been badly shaken by Labour's 1931 election defeat; after his re-election in 1935, his speeches were tinged less with idealism about Scottish traditions and more with the material issues of employment, housing and health. He was particularly keen to demonstrate the advantages of planning.

In 1941 Johnston felt that Scottish affairs remained at the margins of Whitehall thought and that few other Ministers considered Scottish needs independently from British considerations. Part of this was ascribed to the wartime structure of Cabinet Government which excluded the Scottish Secretary from formal membership of virtually all but the Civil Defence Committees.[3] Part was also ascribed to the evolution of all-UK Departments to assist with wartime mobilisation—war planning in the 1930s had looked to the First World War as a guide to 'efficient' government. However, Johnston also felt that it reflected the relative failure of the 1939 Re-Organisation of Offices Act on its own to improve the Scottish Secretary's political position. If the Act was to achieve its intention, an identifiable national administration aimed at Scotland's material position, much would depend on the Scottish Secretary talking up the brief and developing a parallel system of administration.

1 Over time, Scottish officials were expected to achieve grant aid settlements of at least 'Goschen plus two per cent', about fourteen per cent of programme expenditure.

2 G. Walker, *Tom Johnston* (Manchester, 1988). In the 1929-31 Government, Johnston was Parliamentary Under Secretary of State for Scotland, and then Lord Privy Seal. In 1939-41 he was Scotland's Regional Commissioner concerned with Civil Defence and the emergency. Johnston was technically responsible to the Home Secretary (the Minister for Home Security), but his office was staffed from St Andrew's House and worked in close contact with the Scottish Departments.

3 J.D. Cantwell, *The Second World War: a Guide to Documents in the Public Record Office* (London, 1994). The Scottish Secretary was not a member of the Lord President's Committee which co-ordinated domestic policy (including economic development), but received its papers and could attend when the case warranted.

To achieve this, Johnston sought to shift the emphasis of Scottish administration. First, he wanted to organise Scottish opinion more effectively into one voice, whether it was from the Highlands, the health services or industry, and channel it through the Scottish Secretary.[1] The Scottish Committee on Post War Problems, comprising all the living ex-Scottish Secretaries, represented the political apex of that voice, but Johnston also established and re-invigorated a number of boards and advisory committees. Second, Johnston wanted his officials, armed with a unified view of opinion, to take the initiative in pressing the Scottish case at Whitehall, even before other ministries had begun discussion on policy. Third, he thought that Scottish needs would best be served by the Scottish Office generally taking over powers from UK Departments, especially those covering economic development. Locating Scottish administration nearer the source of domestic production seemed to make sense. Johnston may have rejected 'wee free' socialism, but to the Treasury he introduced the notion of 'wee free' administration.

Johnston's strategy had some effect, though not as much as contemporary thought accorded him. His early success was the rebuffing of Lord Reith's attempt to establish a UK Planning Authority. Johnston maintained (as Collins had in 1934 with the Special Areas Commissioner) that a British Department would face severe problems working with Scottish local authorities.[2] This was followed by the establishment of the North of Scotland Hydro-Electricity Board, against the opposition of those who wanted one electricity authority for Britain. Johnston argued that the Board would spearhead Highland economic regeneration and stem the flow of migration. His greatest disappointment was the failure to secure additional powers over economic development, but the Government remained convinced that centripetal economic management was the key to post-war reconstruction.[3]

Joe Westwood and Arthur Woodburn found it difficult to follow in Johnston's footsteps, but in a Cabinet committed to nationalisation and dominated by ministers such as Herbert Morrison, Aneurin Bevan and Sir Stafford

1 Minute of Sir Horace P. Hamilton, Permanent Under Secretary of State, Scottish Office, 27 Mar. 1943, SRO, HH36/18; evidence (in camera) of Johnston to the Balfour Commission, 17 Dec. 1953, SRO, HH41/691. The newly-established Scottish Home Department was said to be particularly effective in its liaison arrangements.

2 Letter, 24 Sept. 1941, SRO, DD12/41. Johnston wrote that the proposal would cause an all-party 'howl'.

3 Johnston, however, insisted that the Scottish Office be 'associated' with regional policy, and became a member of the Distribution of Industry Committee at its establishment in October 1944.

Cripps, maintaining the Scottish interest was never going to be easy.[1] Woodburn's principal difficulty was not so much maintaining the 'Goschen' formula in the distribution of Government funding, or securing the satisfactory adaptation of British legislation to Scotland, but his unwillingness to be seen pressing Scottish claims for special treatment.[2] His successor, McNeil, understood the issue of visibility and sensed the necessity of ensuring a greater presence in Government.[3] His more abrasive tone certainly had an effect and greatly revived Scottish Office morale, but the Government fell before the strategy could be fully tested.

James Stuart's appointment as Scottish Secretary in 1951 came as a surprise, not least to himself, and initially he seemed unsure of the brief.[4] However, like Johnston, he was an experienced political administrator with a reputation for political toughness and a known sensitivity towards Scottish devolution.[5] He also came into office with additional Scottish Office Ministers, thereby enabling him to concentrate less on the minutiae of purely Scottish business and more on Cabinet Government.

Like McNeil, Stuart accepted that the Scottish brief required greater visibility. For him the central issue was the need for the Government's Scottish policy to be 'inventive', so as to dampen the demand for political devolution.[6] The Covenant Movement had shown that Scottish sentiment remained a strong and powerful force, though in Stuart's view it hindered a rational assessment of Scotland's place in the post-war world. Stuart's assessment was highly materialistic and reflected other concerns in Scotland. One, that without substantial investment in factories, roads and housing, the Scottish standard of living would decline.[7] Two, that a Scottish administration, 'parochial' in orientation and

1 In July 1945 Westwood became a member of the Lord President's Committee. In October 1947 the Committee lost its responsibility in economic affairs to Cripps's Economic Policy Committee. There is no record of the Scottish Secretary attending the Committee in 1947-51.

2 *Scotsman*, 'Scots Socialists', 27 Oct. 1947; 'The Woodburn Plan', 31 Jan. 1948; 'Scotland at Westminster', 24 Dec. 1949; *Glasgow Herald*, 'Scotland's Future', 23 Feb. 1950. Only in roads and civil aviation was investment 'below the line'.

3 *Hansard*, Vol. 494, c.481-90, 21 Nov. 1951, Speech, Supply: Committee—Scottish Affairs.

4 *Scotsman*, 'Appointment of Stuart', 31 Oct. 1951; 'Scottish Team', 10 Nov. 1951.

5 *Scotsman*, 'Unionist Policy', 18 Oct. 1951; 'New Cabinet', 31 Oct. 1951. Stuart had been the Government's Chief Whip during the war and was the principal author of the party's Scottish policy document in 1949. He was also chairman of White's, a club favoured by Conservative MPs.

6 *Glasgow Herald*, 'A Second Look at Administration', 19 Aug. 1952; 'The Business of Government', 6 Oct. 1952.

7 *Glasgow Herald*, 'The Chancellor of the Exchequer visits Scotland', 21 May 1949; 'After Catto', 10 Mar. 1952; 'Scotland's Finances', 29 Jan. 1954; *Scotsman*, 'Scottish Housing', 4 Nov. 1949; 'Challenge to Industry', 20 Sept. 1952.

detached from Britain's new alliance with America and Europe, would almost certainly result in less investment and a consequent reduction in trade. As Lord Home, Stuart's Minister of State, put it, economic power lay in 'large systems'. For the Conservatives, it was difficult to see how a separate legislature could maintain the same influence on policy and events as a Scottish Secretary in a British Cabinet.[1] It might diminish access to power.

Stuart approached Cabinet Government in a different way to his predecessors. His tactic was to ensure that the Scottish Ministerial team attended any Cabinet Committee meeting where business might affect Scotland, irrespective of formal membership. The period witnessed considerably more Scottish memoranda on virtually everything that might lead to investment: roads, factories, new towns and the Health Service.[2] Stuart understood what appealed to Scottish opinion—'beef tub' politics—and his message to the Cabinet was clear: to satisfy 'sentiment' the Government must produce visible symbols that administrative devolution could work.

Maclay entered office in the aftermath of Suez and in a Government determined to restore its political credibility. Part of his difficulty with the Scottish brief stemmed from his predecessor's successes; the principal environmental diseases seemed under control, agreement had been reached on Glasgow's overspill, and the recommendations of the Balfour Commission were being implemented. But it also stemmed from a realisation that the Scottish economy faced a structural difficulty with a decline in demand for its staple industry. Maclay's problems were further compounded by the Macmillan Government's determination to reduce taxation (and hence public expenditure) before the next election. As Labour and Conservative MPs sensed, a diminishing 'pot' of regional aid meant that even fewer firms were likely to be redistributed from the south of England.[3]

These difficulties had an impact on the structure and functioning of the Scottish Office. Much of what Stuart achieved was due to the ability of his senior officials to anticipate Cabinet discussion and draft appropriate letters and memoranda outlining the Scottish case.[4] Nevertheless, Scottish officials noted a

1 *House of Lords Debates*, Vol. 174, c.392-8, 20 Nov. 1951. Speech by Lord Home, Self-Government for Scotland Debate.

2 Scottish Ministers frequently attended the Economic Policy Committee, though not formally amongst its members.

3 *Hansard*, Vol. 594, c.832, 4 Nov. 1958, Comment by J. Dickson Mabon (Labour, Greenock), Debate on the Address; Vol. 602, c.1500-06, 14 May 1959, Speech by Lady Tweedsmuir (Conservative, South Aberdeen), Supply: Development Areas (Policy).

4 By the mid-1950s a number of senior officials had served in other Whitehall departments and in the Cabinet Office.

significant hardening in the Treasury's attitude towards regional investment and Scottish claims for special treatment.[1] Public investment in housing, roads and factories, it argued, should follow where industry wished to develop—and its preference was the south of England. A Scottish Office aiming to maintain a special relationship with Whitehall and to secure additional grants was of little use if the Government believed that political conditions had changed. At the same time Scottish officials noted a hardening in domestic opinion, with a renewal of nationalist 'sentiment' and a more 'truculent' labour movement.[2] On the one hand Maclay's Ministry demonstrated the spectacular success of the reformed Scottish Office—new hospitals, new towns and Ravenscraig; but on the other it demonstrated that something fresh was required. 1959 represented the high tide of Labour Unionism and a watershed in Scottish development.

1 Minute of R.E.C. Johnston, Under Secretary, Scottish Home Department, 6 Aug. 1958, SRO, DD10/369; see also *Times*, 'Underemployed Areas', 31 July 1958.

2 Minute of W.G. Pottinger, Under Secretary, Scottish Home Department, 5 Mar. 1959, SRO, DD10/110/2. The Scottish Home Department was said to be on 'good terms' with George Middleton, the STUC's General Secretary.

Chapter One
THE NATURE OF GOVERNMENT

THE SCOTTISH SECRETARY AND CREATING A BOARD OF HEALTH, 1918-19

In 1918 a campaign developed for the establishment of a Scottish Ministry of Health. The first extract is from the minutes of the Cabinet's Home Affairs Committee which had already approved a Ministry for England. The second is from a later meeting clarifying the establishment of a Board of Health for Scotland. Its six members were to be drawn from the existing Local Government Board, the National Health Insurance Commission and the Highlands and Islands Medical Board under the Presidency of the Scottish Secretary and the vice-presidency of the Parliamentary Under Secretary for Health.

Minute of the Cabinet Home Affairs Committee, on Creating a Scottish Ministry of Health, 18 July 1918.

The Secretary for Scotland said that the demand for the unification of the Health Services was as strong in Scotland as elsewhere, but whereas some were in favour of setting up a separate Minister for Health for Scotland, others would be satisfied if the Secretary for Scotland performed the duties of the Minister of Health. Inasmuch, however, as the Secretary for Scotland was already charged with heavy responsibilities, the suggestion had been put forward that there should be a Parliamentary Under-Secretary for Scotland. The proposal had proved to be generally acceptable, and no opposition to it was anticipated from any quarter of the House of Commons. He had set out in his memorandum the modification which he suggested should be in the draft Bill so as to combine in a Ministry of Health *inter alia* the functions of the existing Local Government Board for Scotland and Insurance Commission for Scotland, and to provide for the appointment of a Parliamentary Under-Secretary.

The Committee approved the Scottish application clause as drafted by the Secretary for Scotland with the exception of the clause proposing to raise the status of the Secretary for Scotland, which it was thought should form the subject of a separate Bill. [PRO, CAB 26/1 HAC 3rd:2.]

Minute of the Cabinet Home Affairs Committee, on Creating a Scottish Board of Health, 6 February 1919.

Mr Munro pointed out that the changes in the title of the Bill from 'Ministries of Health' to 'Ministry of Health' might cause objections to be raised in Scotland. It might even raise the question as to whether there should be a separate Bill for Scotland.

Dr Addison explained that the new title had been adopted purely as a matter of convenience. As a matter of fact, however, it was the more correct, as there would be only one Ministry of Health, the corresponding body for Scotland being a Board. [PRO, CAB 26/1 HAC 19th:1.]

MINISTERIAL SALARIES AND THE STATUS OF THE SCOTTISH SECRETARY, 1921

In Autumn 1920, because of Parliamentary opposition to its cost, a Bill which would have created five additional Secretaries of State was withdrawn and the matter remitted to a Select Committee. The following March, after it reported, Lord Linlithgow indicated to Lord Birkenhead, the Lord Chancellor, that he intended to ask a question in the Lords about the Government's intention. The first extract is from Birkenhead's subsequent Cabinet memorandum. The second is from the minutes of a Ministerial Conference on the matter and the third from a later Cabinet conclusion. The Irish Secretary received a salary of £5,000.

Memorandum by Lord Birkenhead, Lord Chancellor, on Secretary for Scotland, 11 March 1921.

LORD LINLITHGOW yesterday had put down a question in the House of Lords to ask whether, in view of the recommendations of the Remuneration of Ministers Committee, it was proposed during the present Session to raise the status of Secretary for Scotland.

Lord Linlithgow postponed his question at my request and to meet my personal convenience, and he has put down the question again without fixing a day on which it is to be asked. It would not be reasonable that he should be expected to allow any long delay to interpose before he brings the matter forward, and it will not then be possible to ask for further postponement.

It is therefore, in my view, imperative that the Cabinet should arrive at a decision on the answer to be given to the question when it is asked.

The question has several times formed the subject of discussion in both the Lords and in the Commons, and the utterances of the Prime Minister, of Mr. Bonar Law and myself, acting upon the advice given to me by the Scottish

Office, appear to me to commit us irrevocably. I think it is sufficient on this point to cite the answer given by the Prime Minister to the question asked on the 22nd July, 1920, by Mr. Wallace:-

'The Government recognise fully the justice of the demand unanimously made by Scottish Members that the status of the Secretary for Scotland should be raised to that of a Secretary of State. The Government hope to deal with the subject in the Autumn Session.'

On the 22nd June, 1920, in answer to a question asked by Lord Linlithgow, I myself said:-

'I, and I think most Ministers, have very great sympathy with the case put forward by the noble Marquis. I myself have not been able to understand what historic accident deprives Scotland of the status and importance which is supplied by the representation of a Secretary of State ... It has always seemed to me difficult to answer the question as [to] the relative expenditure [on salaries] in the cases of Ireland and Scotland respectively.'

It appears to me that in the face of these declarations, it is extremely difficult for me, when pressed by Lord Linlithgow, to do otherwise than give a further promise on behalf of the Government.

Apart from these commitments, however, the case appears to me to be a strong one upon its merits.

The Select Committee of the House of Commons on Remuneration of Ministers [December 1920] made 'a special recommendation that the Secretary for Scotland and the President of the Board of Education be raised to first class. In the former case, a Lord Advocate on being appointed Secretary for Scotland has had to sacrifice 3,000l. of his salary, the superior position being paid less than the lower.'

The Secretary for Scotland receives a less sum per annum than his Under-Secretary, the President of the Board of Health or the Secretary of the Scottish Education Department. He, is in fact, in a position which is scarcely analogous to that of any one English Minister, for he combines in his own person the functions of the Secretary of State for the Home Department, Minister for Education, Minister of Health, and the Minister of Agriculture, each of those Departments in England being controlled by a separate Minister who is a member of the Cabinet. In addition, he controls some ten other Boards in Scotland. In fact, it may be said that, whatever claims may be put forward by other Ministers in respect of the importance of their respective Departments, the Secretary for Scotland represents not a Department but a country.

In these circumstances, I hope very earnestly that I may be placed in a position in which, when Lord Linlithgow's question is again put, I shall be able to give an affirmative reply. [PRO, CAB 24/121 CP (21)2714.]

Conference of Ministers on the Status of the Secretary for Scotland, 6 April 1921.

The Committee was reminded of the pledge which had been given from time to time to introduce legislation on this subject, and also that Mr. Chamberlain recently circulated to the Cabinet a Memorandum (Paper C.P.—2789) covering the Report of the Select Committee on the Remuneration of Ministers.

After some discussion, in which it was pointed out that it would be most difficult to find time for the passage of an opposed Bill during the present Session, the Committee agreed:

(a) That the Lord Chancellor should reply to Lord Linlithgow's question in the House of Lords to the effect that the Government had definitely decided to avoid, if possible, an Autumn Session, but that if the Bill altering the status of the Secretary for Scotland was unopposed the Government would undertake to pass it into law. If, however, the Bill was opposed from any quarter, the Government could not undertake to find time for the passage of the Bill;

(b) That negotiations with possible opponents should be entered into on the above basis, with a view to the Bill being treated as unopposed. [PRO, CAB 23/25 CC(21)22 Appendix III (10).]

Cabinet Conclusions, on the Status and Salary of the Secretary for Scotland, 4 July 1921.

With reference to Cabinet 22(21), Appendix III (10), the Cabinet were reminded that during the impending debate on the Scottish estimates it was probable that the status and salary of the Secretary for Scotland would be raised and attention called to the repeated declarations of the Government on the matter. The proposal to raise the status and salary of the Secretary would probably receive the unanimous support of the Scottish members, but might be opposed by 'anti-waste' Members, who would take advantage of the proposal, if made, to create prejudice against the Government quite independently of the merits of the question. It was fully recognised that very specific declarations of the Government's intentions had been made by the Lord Chancellor in the House of Lords on behalf of the Government, but that the atmosphere at present was particularly unfavourable to proposals to increase ministerial salaries. [PRO, CAB 23/26 CC 2(21)57.]

THE SCOTTISH OFFICE: APPOINTING A THIRD ASSISTANT SECRETARY, 1921-2

In December 1920 the Scottish Office requested the appointment of a third assistant secretary to complement two others appointed in 1919 as part of a general office reorganisation. The first extract is from a Scottish Office letter to the Treasury after the Treasury had reviewed the Office's work and rejected the request. However, Robert Munro, the Scottish Secretary, subsequently met Sir Robert Horne, the Chancellor of the Exchequer, and agreed that as Sir James Dodds, the Permanent Under Secretary, was on sick leave due to near blindness, a temporary appointment should be made. In August Dodds retired and the Scottish Office sought a permanent appointment. The second extract is taken from a Treasury minute on the subject and the third from the letter of Sir John Lamb, the new Permanent Under Secretary, to the Treasury, after the request had been refused. Munro discussed the matter again with Horne and in April 1922 a 'supernumerary' appointment was made.

Letter of P.J.G. Rose, Assistant Secretary, the Scottish Office, on the Appointment of a Third Assistant Secretary, 20 January 1921.

Let me say at once that I do not think that the amount and character of the work falling to the officials above the rank of Senior Clerk [Principal] have yet been sufficiently appreciated. Mr. Rae's colleagues have gained their information about the work of the Assistant Secretaries mainly as incidental to their examination of the work of the Senior Clerks and the Accountant. A large part of the Assistant Secretaries' work, however, is done in committees, conferences and interviews, of which there are only brief records in ordinary files. The work done on the plane above the Assistant Secretaries has, of course, not been examined at all. It includes a great deal in which the Secretary for Scotland and his chief advisers would like to have more assistance from the Assistant Secretaries if they were not already over burdened.

We fully realise that any substantial diminution in fresh Government legislation will *pro tanto* be a relief. It is, however, to be remembered that recent legislation will bring a volume of administrative work, that in refusing demands for legislation the Government is frequently committed to the appointment of Commissions etc. and other measures which make a heavy tax upon Departments, and that in such a period of industrial and social stress as apparently lies before us, a Department such as the Scottish Office must expect to be faced with special duties in connection with strikes, land troubles, police matters and the like. [PRO, T 162/494.]

Minute of W.P. Johnston, Assistant Secretary, the Treasury, on Appointing a Third Assistant Secretary at the Scottish Office, 12 December 1921.

There are certain features about the work of the Scottish Office which incline to render the staff top heavy as compared with their Departments engaged on direct administrative work, but full allowance was made for these peculiar features in the re-organisation scheme approved by the Treasury. It was also recognised that new duties had been permanently imposed on the Department since pre-war days, such as the duties consequent upon the passing of the Representation of the People Act and the Temperance (Scotland) Act. On the other hand the higher staff is largely engaged upon questions which have already been thrashed out by the higher staff of the Departments in Edinburgh. Very often indeed the Scottish Office act merely as a Post Office and forward proposals to the Treasury in the exact form in which they were submitted from Edinburgh.

... The general restriction of Government activity as a result of the need for economies will affect the Scottish Office not only directly by also indirectly through the diminished activities of the Edinburgh Departments. When other Departments are cutting down staff to the greatest possible extent it is hardly reasonable for the Scottish Office to press for further additional staff over and above the generous increases shown in the table above [19 compared with 13 in 1914]. Such increase in the bulk of the work as can be shown is not in any special degree higher than that of other Government Departments. We should indeed be breaking faith with other Whitehall Departments who, at our request, have been reducing their number of their Assistant Secretaries, if we were to agree to an additional post of this grade at the Scottish Office. [PRO, T 162/494.]

Letter of Sir John Lamb, Permanent Under Secretary for Scotland, on the Appointment of a Third Assistant Secretary, 7 February 1922.

With regard to the comparisons suggested in Mr. Scott's [Under Secretary] letter between the staff sanctioned in 1921 and the establishment of this Office before the war and in 1919, I am to point out that the present higher staff (excluding the third Assistant Secretary) numbers 14 as compared with 14 in 1919 and 12 or 11 in 1914 (according as the Accountant is or is not included). I am also to observe in this connection that for many years the administrative staff of this Department was maintained at so low a level that the work could only be overtaken with any reasonable degree of efficiency by means of excessive efforts on the part of the higher staff including a considerable amount of attendance on Sundays. Assuming that the volume of work is to continue at anything approaching its present level, the time has come, in Mr. Munro's judgement, when it is no longer physically possible for this strain to be borne without jeopardy to the service of the Government and to the health of the senior members of the staff. The post-armistice questions to which their Lordships allude, have been succeeded by other questions of no less complexity and importance, and at the present time the work of this Office is probably heavier than at any time in the past and shows no signs of diminishing, but rather the contrary. It was suggested by their Lordships' representatives in the discussion a year ago that the work of this Department would be lightened in future by the fact that a period was being entered upon in which new legislation was to be confined to their narrowest possible limits. Even during 1921 when it was an instruction that legislation was to be drastically curtailed, the legislation in which this Department was involved, either separately or jointly with other departments, was considerable, and one measure—the Licensing Act, 1921,—has added substantially to the duties of the Secretary for Scotland and his principal officials. It is now clear that, for some years to come, the volume of legislation which this Department will have to consider will be a heavy one. Mr. Munro fully appreciates that a reduction of Government expenditure, especially in the form of grants administered under departmental regulations and control, will, in many cases, be accompanied by a limitation of the activities of Government Departments which will in turn facilitate a reduction in staff. The Scottish Office, however, falls only in a slight degree within the class of departments to which these considerations apply. With the exception of the Police Grant, the expenditure from the Votes of this Department is relatively small. Its work arises very largely from the necessity of securing the necessary readjustments in laws, regulations, institutions and administrative arrangements which are called for by changing circumstances affecting the people of Scotland in their life and their occupations. With the exception of functions which are assigned for the whole of Great Britain to departments like the Post Office, the Secretary for Scotland is responsible for the whole range of Scottish administration. He has, therefore, to consider questions arising over a very varied field of administration and of legislation, public and private. He is constantly being called upon to consider questions which are not assigned to him by any existing legislation and also to assist with information and advice other departments whose field of operations extends to Scotland. There is no prospect that the necessity for dealing with this class of work will be diminished by the reduction of national expenditure which is at present being undertaken. On the contrary, there is a great accumulation of work of this class which presses for consideration and action and which will not materially affect, or be affected by the aggregate amount of national expenditure. [PRO, T 162/494.]

AMENDING THE BOARD OF HEALTH, 1922-3

In February 1922 the Coalition Government's Committee on National Expenditure, under the Chairmanship of Sir Eric Geddes, recommended that the Board of Health be reduced from six members to three. At the same time one of the Board's members resigned through ill-health. The first four extracts indicate Scottish Office discussion on the subject, which resulted in the publication of a Bill to reduce the Board to three. The following year the new Conservative Government published a Bill to reorganise a number of Scottish Departments. It included a clause to drop the Board's medical qualification. The fifth extract indicates the Scottish Office response when objections were raised by a number of County Councils.

Minute of Sir John Lamb, Permanent Under Secretary for Scotland, on Amending the Board of Health Act, 24 February 1922.

... owing to Dr. McVail's resignation there is at present only one medical member. If this vacancy is not to be filled up, it will be necessary to regularise the position by means of amending legislation. My own view is that a Board of 6 members is larger than necessary and power should be taken to reduce the numbers as opportunities arise. I think we should aim at a reduction to 3. The Geddes Cmttee make a recommendation to this effect.

I suggest that a Bill on the lines of a draft B. should be proceeded with. It does away with the need for a second doctor and for a legal member. It would, of course, be competent to appoint a medical man or a lawyer to any vacancy which might arise, but the professional qualification would not be obligatory—the hands of the Secretary for Scotland would be free. In this connection it is to be noted that the Bd. has now a legal branch, and this renders the presence of a legal member less necessary. Moreover, it may be easier to get the assent of the medical profession to the dropping of the medical members if we also do away with the requirement of the legal member. If you approve of action on these lines, I suggest that the draft Bill should be submitted to the Bd. for their views. [SRO, HH1/468.]

Minute of Robert Munro, Secretary for Scotland, on Amending the Board of Health Act, 24 February 1922.

I approve. This Board is too unwieldy in number: I think three members would be quite sufficient. Proceed as suggested. [SRO, HH1/468.]

Letter of E.B. MacPherson, Legal Member of the Board of Health, on Amending the Board of Health Act, 12 March 1922.

Unless it is absolutely necessary from a Parliamentary point of view I think it would be a mistake to tie the hands of the Secretary for Scotland as to the appointment of future members of the Board. From an administrative point of view I think it is a mistake that in a Board which it is contemplated should eventually be reduced to three there should necessarily be a technical member either Medical or Legal. It by no means follows that members either of the Medical or Legal profession are necessarily the best administrators. The medical interests of the Board would be sufficiently preserved by the large staff of doctors who would advise the Board members upon medical matters in the same way as the legal staff would advise on questions of law. I think that the fact that there must necessarily be a Medical member of a Board of three gives undue preponderance to the medical practitioner upon a Board which while dealing very largely with matters of medical interest, is concerned with many other matters of equal importance. There may often be vacancies to fill which from an administrative point of view could be better filled by laymen and I think it would be better to give the Secretary for Scotland a free hand to appoint the best man or woman. It seems to me that the Bill as introduced should contemplate this and that only in the event of Parliamentary pressure proving too strong should the proposed proviso be inserted. [SRO, HH1/468.]

Minute of P.R. Laird, Assistant Secretary, the Scottish Office, on Amending the Board of Health Act, 16 March 1922.

... in view of the points brought out [by the letter of Sir Leslie MacKenzie, the Medical Member, on the likely opposition of the Health Insurance lobby] it would appear to be undesirable to raise controversy on this Bill by disturbing the present requirement of medical representation on the Board. At the same time I cannot help feeling that if ever the Board were reduced to 3, the necessity of appointing a medical man leaves the selection of a strong Board rather narrow and that it would be better to have a well-paid post of chief medical adviser as in the Ministry of Health. [SRO, HH1/468.]

Minute of P.R. Laird, Assistant Secretary, the Scottish Office, on Text of Reply to County Councils on Amending the Board of Health Act, 31 October 1923.

The question of including a medical member of the Scottish Board of Health was fully gone into in connection with the proposed Scottish Board of Health Bill. At that time [1919] and in the [1922] Economy Bill provision was made for one medical member, but the decision was reversed when these matters were absorbed in to the Re-organisation [of Offices] Bill.

I think we might reply that their representation is noted. The Secretary for Scotland [Lord Novar] considers, however, that a statutory requirement that one medical member of a Board of 3 should be a medical man might on occasion be found unduly to prejudice the constitution of a strong administrative B. and that it is advisable that the field of choice should be as unrestricted as possible. Point out that should the Board at any time not include a medical member, it would none the less have the assistance of expert medical advisers. [SRO, HH1/51.]

RAISING THE STATUS OF THE SCOTTISH SECRETARY, 1923-6

The first extract here is from a Home Affairs Committee minute in 1923 after it had already agreed to introduce Lord Novar's Re-Organisation of Offices Bill. The second and third extracts are from Treasury minutes on the Bill. The discussion on the Scottish Secretaryship was truncated with the fall of Baldwin's Government, but the issue re-emerged in 1925 when the Convention of Royal Burghs petitioned Sir John Gilmour for such a change. The fourth extract is from a subsequent Cabinet meeting. A Bill was introduced the following April.

Minute of the Cabinet Home Affairs Committee, on Appointing a Secretary of State for Scotland, 11 July 1923.

Arising out of the foregoing Minute a short discussion arose on the desirability of raising the office of the Secretary for Scotland to the dignity of a Secretary of State. It was suggested that the Re-Organisation of Offices Bill and the economies to be made thereunder would afford a suitable opportunity of carrying out the change of status, it being understood that the increase in salary would not be made during the tenure of the office of the present Secretary. The Committee, after a brief discussion, agreed—To ask the Chairman [the Home Secretary] to discuss the matter with the Prime Minister and Lord Novar. [PRO, CAB 26/5 HAC 13(23).]

Minute of I. Brierley, Assistant Secretary, the Treasury, on Appointing a Secretary of State for Scotland, 21 August 1923.

Bill as agreed, but Home Affairs Committee raised the question whether economies to be affected by the Bill might not justify raising again the proposal to make Secretary for Scotland a Secretary of State of Scotland and increase his salary to £5,000. I don't know whether there is any serious idea of such a proposal in what is supposed to be an economy Bill. In any case economies are all very small and such an increase would possibly outweigh the lot of them. [PRO, T 163/18/9.]

Minute of James Rae, Deputy Controller of Establishments, the Treasury, on Appointing a Secretary of State for Scotland, 22 August 1923.

Drawn Sir R. Scott's and Sir Warren Fisher's attention to above. No further action at present stage required. The Secretary for Scotland will undoubtedly get his £5,000 sooner or later—but the Bill does not supply the justification. The latter arises mainly out of national sentiment. [PRO, T 163/18/9.]

Cabinet Conclusions, on Appointing a Secretary of State for Scotland, 16 December 1925.

The Cabinet agreed—That it was desirable that the Secretary for Scotland should have the status of Secretary of State and that, subject to the King's assent, the Prime Minister should take the necessary steps to bring this about, including legislation, if necessary in the forthcoming Session.

The Prime Minister informed his colleagues that the Secretary for Scotland had waived the question of any increase in emoluments in the case of the present holder of the office. [PRO, CAB 23/51 CC 13(25)59.]

CREATING A DEPARTMENT OF HEALTH, 1924-8

In November 1923 the Civil Service Union petitioned the Government for the Board of Health to be re-established as a Department. The first four extracts indicate the Labour Government's response when it decided to reintroduce Lord Novar's Bill. The Bill fell with the Government. In 1927, however, Sir John Gilmour, the Scottish Secretary, finally agreed to abolish the Boards of Agriculture and Health and replace them with Departments. The fifth extract is from his Cabinet memorandum seeking approval to introduce the necessary Bill. The Bill ran into difficulties during its Second Reading and was withdrawn. An amended Bill was introduced the following year and the next extract, taken from Government explanatory notes, indicates the reasoning behind the amendment.

Minute of the Cabinet Home Affairs Committee, on the Re-Organisation of Offices Bill, 29 February 1924.

Attention was directed to the contention that the occasion of the Bill should be taken to determine the arrangements under which the Scottish Board of Health now operate, and to put that Department in charge of a Permanent Secretary.

The Committee agreed to recommend to the Cabinet—To approve the introduction in the House of Lords of the Re-Organisation of Offices (Scotland) Bill ... on the understanding that the attention of the House would be drawn to the fact that the Government proposed to continue the Scottish Board of Health on existing lines. [PRO, CAB 26/6 HAC 4(24)7.]

Cabinet Conclusions, on the Re-Organisation of Offices Bill, 5 March 1924.

The Cabinet were informed that in the course of Parliamentary debate it was by no means improbable that amendments would be moved suggesting the abolition of some of the Scottish Boards and their attachment to the Departments of the Under-Secretaries. The Secretary for Scotland undertook to give careful consideration to this question. [PRO, CAB 23/47 CC 18(24)15.]

Minute of J.E. de Watteville, Principal, Scottish Office, on the Re-Organisation of Offices Bill, 15 April 1924.

Lord Novar as you no doubt are aware favoured the abolition of the Board and the substitution of a Director and assistant Director. This proposal would no doubt be similar in effect except that there would be a 'Secretary'.

Against the proposal we must consider the national sentiment which is I fancy favourable to the Board system—and, somewhat stronger, the sentiment of an authority actually in session in Scotland.

In favour I think saving of time might be expected, and saving in the preparation of material. A saving on the salary list might be effected. The objection to the method of appointment of members would be got over. Direct touch between the Minister and the administrative staff would be more fluid—and would probably be on the basis of visits to London instead of vice versa.

Generally the proposal is attractive from the point of view of administration, but I hardly think it is practical politics at the moment. [SRO, HH1/521.]

Minute of P.R. Laird, Assistant Secretary, Scottish Office, on the Re-Organisation of Offices Bill, 22 April 1924.

I think your minute gives a fair valuation of the pros and cons. [SRO, HH1/521.]

Memorandum by Sir John Gilmour, Secretary of State for Scotland, on the Re-Organisation of Offices (Scotland) Bill, 4 March 1927.

However suited the Board system may have been to Scottish needs in days when there was no Secretary for Scotland, and however suitable it may still be in cases where it enables the Government to utilise the services in administration of men of affairs not in the whole-time service of the State, I am satisfied that there is no advantage, under modern circumstances, in administering such services as health and agriculture through a Board rather than through a Civil Service Department on the ordinary lines, with a single Head directly responsible to the Secretary of State for Scotland.

I propose therefore that the powers and duties of the Scottish Board of Health and the Board of Agriculture for Scotland should at a convenient date be transferred to corresponding Departments of Health and Agriculture. These proposals are in line with the recommendations of the Royal Commission on the Civil Service [1913] and I hope that in principle they will be acceptable to Scotland. [PRO, CAB 26/9 HA(27)17.]

Government Explanatory Notes, Re-Organisation of Offices (Scotland) Bill, 17 February 1928.

The main object of the first three clauses of the Bill is to substitute with respect to certain Departments in Edinburgh the ordinary Civil Service system for what is known as the Board system: the change is in accord with recommendations of the Royal Commission on the Civil Service and has the merits of ensuring a more effective responsibility for action and advice, of diminishing the possibilities of appointments being made for political or similar reasons and of facilitating interchange of personnel between the Scottish Office and Departments in Edinburgh. The unified control in each Department will not, of course, in any way preclude recourse being had to expert advice whether from outside or within the Department.

This part of the Bill has however since the Second Reading Debate on the 23rd. March evoked a certain amount of opposition from bodies outside the house, mainly those connected with the work of National Health Insurance; it has mistakenly been supposed the conduct of affairs is being removed from Edinburgh to London and that matters relating to health in Scotland will be dealt with by a Department in less intimate touch with local conditions and requirements. In order to remove this misapprehension the words 'The Offices of the said Departments shall be situated in Edinburgh' have been inserted, in accordance with a suggestion made by the Convention of Royal Burghs, at the end of the first sub-clause.

The Bill does not, it should be explained, in the slightest degree affect the existing position as regards the ultimate responsibility for the administration of the Departments with which it deals: the Secretary of Scotland is now, to the same extent as under the Bill, the Minister of the Crown responsible to Parliament and the country for all services administered by those Departments and for laying before Cabinet any proposals relating to policy: the sole effect of the Bill is to adjust the machinery with which the Minister works. It cannot be too emphatically stated that there is no intention whatever of removing the machinery from Scotland to London, and the Bill clearly does not suggest anything of the sort. [SRO, HH1/526.]

A SCHEME OF ADMINISTRATIVE DEVOLUTION FOR THE SCOTTISH DEPARTMENTS, 1932

In October 1928, in response to a suggestion from Sir John Gilmour about the possibility of 'centralising' all Scottish Departments in Edinburgh, Patrick Laird, the Scottish Office Establishment Officer, prepared a memorandum indicating how it might work in practice. The proposal was not pursued, but in 1932 after discussion with Noel Skelton, the Parliamentary Under-Secretary, Laird was asked again to resubmit his ideas and the following is an extract from his memorandum.

Memorandum by P.R. Laird, Assistant Secretary, the Scottish Office, on Administrative Devolution, 17 November 1932.

In my memorandum of 1928 I suggested possible methods of giving effect to a scheme for transferring a considerable proportion of Scottish Office administrative work to Edinburgh. The work in question falls into three main groups (a) Local Government work, of a kind similar to that falling on the Ministry of Health in England; (b) work corresponding to that of the Home Office in England, which is partly (i) connected with local administration, e.g. police, administration of the Licensing Laws, the Shops Act and other statutes regulative of public liberties, and partly (ii) directly executive, e.g. in regard to the administration of justice, the Royal prerogative etc., etc.; (c) work connected with the organisation of legal services and departments, e.g. the Sheriff Clerk Service, the Court of Session and Justiciary, the Register House, some of which corresponds to work of the Lord Chancellor's Department in England.

The Memorandum discussed various methods of effecting administrative devolution: (i) by transfer to an existing Edinburgh Department, particularly the Department of Health, (ii) by the creation of a new Scottish Department of 'Home Affairs', (iii) by establishing a branch of the Scottish Office in Edinburgh. To all these proposals I found there were substantial objections. Assuming, however, the adoption of one method or another, I outlined a scheme by which the Scottish office in London would consist of the Under Secretary of State and a small staff engaged almost entirely on liaison duties and recruited from officers with experience in one or other of the Edinburgh Departments.

It was pointed out that the problem of devolution would have been considerably simplified if the logical course had been taken, on the establishment of the Departments of Health and Agriculture, of vesting all their powers in the Minister, and if *all* the principal Edinburgh Departments could speak in the name of Secretary of State.

Administrative devolution has now become a live issue,[1] and it is desirable to survey the possibilities further.

It must be pointed out first of all that the trend of events in recent years rather points to the conclusion that, so long as there is a United Kingdom, administrative convenience would be better served by a concentration of certain services in London than by further devolution in Edinburgh. For example, the big problems of agriculture are so closely connected with Imperial and foreign relations that it is impossible to avoid the transaction of a large part of business in London. Similarly Mr. Duke [Assistant Secretary] holds that it would be impossible, in present conditions, to work the administration of the police effectively from Edinburgh, owing to the necessity of daily consultation with the Home Office and other Departments here. Similar situations arise frequently in the case of health, housing, fisheries.

Obviously, however, it is not practical politics to suggest, for example, that any part of the functions of the Department of Agriculture should now be transferred to the Ministry or assumed by the Scottish office in London; and if this is granted, I feel that a general scheme of devolution ought not to be subject to exceptions (e.g. police administration) on grounds which would apply equally to services in which devolution is a *fait accompli.*

It is well known that the 'Board System' in Scotland had its origins in days when there was no Secretary for Scotland. The executive in effect delegated to quasi-independent bodies the administration of affairs with which it was imperfectly acquainted.... The logical course, on the abolition of the Board of Health and Agriculture and the Prison Commissioners would have been to vest all their powers and duties in the responsible Minister. It is not at all the same thing to vest powers and duties in a 'Department acting under the direction and control' of the Minister. Such a Department must remain a separate entity, separate from any other Department in the same position *and separate from the Minister....* In essence, therefore, though not in form, it may be said that the 1928 [Re-Organisation of Offices] Act perpetuated the Board system, in so far as it did not weld the Secretary of State into one entity with his machinery.

The clean method of overcoming all these difficulties is to make one fold as there is one shepherd, by a general transfer of the powers and duties of departments to the Secretary of State, so that all the departments concerned would be in effect 'the Scottish Office' or 'the Department of the Secretary of State for Scotland'. Under such a scheme the Minister could make whatever arrangements for departmental

1 [Added text, foot of page:] The Committee on Local Economy (Scotland) makes a definite recommendation for the establishment of a branch of the Scottish Office in Edinburgh.

organisation might be best suited to times and circumstances. Any branch of work could be undertaken in London or Edinburgh according to requirements, and all official letters, whether from London or Edinburgh, would go in the name of the Secretary of State. [SRO, HH1/799.]

SCOTTISH SENTIMENT, THE SPECIAL AREAS COMMISSIONER AND ECONOMIC DEVELOPMENT, 1934

In October 1934 the Cabinet agreed that a Committee of Ministers should review proposals for the depressed areas. The Committee met and agreed that four areas, including part of Lanarkshire, should receive Government funding to improve their economic position. To facilitate the work, a Commissioner for the Special Areas, responsible to the Minister of Labour, was to be appointed. The first extract is a note of reservation to this recommendation by Sir Godfrey Collins, the Scottish Secretary. The Cabinet asked the Committee to reconsider the issue and this was remitted to the latter's Sub-Committee. The second extract outlines the Sub-Committee's discussion. Subsequently the issue was discussed at a private meeting between the Scottish Secretary and the Minister of Labour and the third extract indicates their recommendation, which the Cabinet accepted. The Unemployment Assistance Board (UAB) was under the control of the Minister of Labour.

Minute of the Cabinet Committee on the Reports of the Investigators into the Distressed Areas, Minutes, 22 October 1934.

The Secretary of State for Scotland desires to reserve for the moment questions such as his relations with the Commissioner and possibly whether the appointment of a separate Commissioner for Scotland should not be contemplated. [PRO, CAB 24/251 CP (34)227.]

Committee on the Reports of the Investigators into the Distressed Areas. Vol. II. Proceedings and Memoranda, 6 November 1934.

The SECRETARY OF STATE FOR SCOTLAND stated that after careful consideration of the whole problem he had come to the conclusion that there should be a separate Commissioner for Scotland, independent of the Commissioner proposed to be set up to deal with the Depressed Areas in England and Wales. He advocated this proposal on political as well as economic grounds. In the first place, the question must be regarded as being partly one of sentiment: but consideration had undoubtedly to be given to this aspect of the matter. The Government scheme would be open to very severe criticism in Scotland if Scottish sentiment on this point did not receive adequate recognition by the appointment of a separate Commissioner. On the administrative side, he felt that though it could not perhaps be said that the scheme would actually work better with an independent Scottish Commissioner, yet there was much to be said for this point of view, having regard to the different forms of local government in Scotland, and the fact that the bulk of the work of many Scottish Departments was conducted in Edinburgh rather than in London. On the whole, therefore, he felt that the administration of the scheme would certainly not be made more difficult by the appointment of a separate Scottish Commissioner; and from all points of view he had come to the conclusion that the Government's scheme could not successfully be handled in Scotland except on that basis.

The MINISTER OF LABOUR [Oliver Stanley] reminded the Committee that there would in any case be a local representative of the central Commissioner in each of the four Distressed Areas to which the scheme would apply. He saw practical difficulties in the separation of the Scottish part of the scheme as proposed by the Secretary of State for Scotland. First, there was the difficulty of dividing up the funds to be set apart for the Commissioner. Secondly, the whole presentation of the case would be more complicated if Scotland were to be treated separately. It was to be remembered that it was not a question of dealing with the whole of Scotland, or with the whole of England, but with certain limited areas, of which only one was situated in Scotland. It hardly seemed reasonable that there should be an independent Commissioner in Scotland under whom there would be placed only one area in Lanarkshire and the adjacent counties.

The SECRETARY OF STATE FOR SCOTLAND said that on the financial side he recognised that there might even be some loss as a result of a division of funds between England and Scotland. For instance, some concession might have to be made on the proportion of eleven eightieths of the total amount which Scotland might normally claim.

The MINISTER OF LABOUR said he attached considerable importance to maintaining unity of control. It would be difficult to have to work with two Commissioners, instead of one. He enquired whether it would meet the difficulty if the Scottish representative were to be called Deputy Commissioner and the area representative in England, Assistant Commissioner.

The SECRETARY OF STATE FOR SCOTLAND said he felt this would hardly meet the political difficulty which this question would raise.

The UNDER-SECRETARY OF STATE FOR SCOTLAND [Noel Skelton] emphasised the importance of the different administrative system in Scotland ...

The MINISTER OF LABOUR pressed the Secretary of State for Scotland to consider the possibility of solving the problem by giving the Representative in Scotland a different status from those in the three English areas. If, however, the Secretary of State insisted upon a Commissioner in Scotland being entirely independent of the Commissioner in London, he thought it would have to be considered whether the former should be responsible to the Secretary of State rather than to the Minister of Labour.

The PRESIDENT OF THE BOARD OF TRADE [Walter Runciman] said he would be disposed to sum up the view of the Committee on this subject as follows: there was greater administrative convenience in having a single Commissioner, but politically there was a great deal to be said for a separate Commissioner for Scotland. [PRO, CAB 27/578 DA(34)4.]

Minute of the Cabinet Committee on the Reports of the Investigators into the Distressed Areas, Minutes, 12 November 1934.

Following the discussions which have taken place between the Chancellor of the Exchequer, the Secretary of State for Scotland and the Minister of Labour, the Committee have again considered the reserved matters ... and have reached the following conclusions.

The Committee are of the opinion that there should be a separate Commissioner in Scotland who should be responsible to the Secretary of State for Scotland in the same way as the Commissioner for England and Wales will be responsible to the Minister of Labour.

The relations between the Minister of Labour and the Commissioner in England and Wales, between the Secretary of State for Scotland and the Commissioner in Scotland and between the UAB and both Commissioners should be broadly as follows.

'The Commissioners will have wide discretion. While their general policy will be subject in England and Wales to the general control of the Minister of Labour, and in Scotland to the general control of the Secretary of State for Scotland they will act in close association with the UAB in all their experimental work which affects the welfare of the unemployed themselves. The Board will, however, have no particular concern in the Commissioners' activities in facilitating the economic development of the areas. In these activities the Commissioners will work in close association with other Departments, if any, concerned.' [PRO, CAB 24/251 CP (34)254.]

NEVILLE CHAMBERLAIN AND A SCOTTISH DEVELOPMENT BOARD, 1935

In July 1935 the Scottish Special Areas Commissioner suggested the establishment of an Economic Planning and Research Board, with wider powers than his Office, to stimulate industrial growth. A similar suggestion for Britain was also made by Lloyd George, the Liberal leader, and, within the Cabinet, by Lord Eustace Percy, the Minister without Portfolio. Percy, in particular, suggested that a new Special Areas

Board could deal with roads, town planning, industrial estates and public assistance. At the same time the voluntary Scottish Development Council asked the Government for a grant to extend its publicity work. The first extract is from a Scottish Office minute on these proposals. The second is from the response of Neville Chamberlain, the Chancellor of the Exchequer. The third is from the Scottish Secretary's revised proposal, which the Cabinet accepted. In 1936 an Economic Committee of the SDC was established.

Minute of P.J.G. Rose, Assistant Under-Secretary of State for Scotland, on the Proposal to appoint a Scottish Development Board, 24 July 1935.

... Sir A. Rose's suggestion is somewhat on lines which S. of S. has been considering for some time. If this suggestion is to be supported the Chancellor will no doubt want reasons to justify simultaneous grants to (1) the Planning and Research Body, (2) the Scottish Development Association. *Prima facie* he may think there is an appearance of competing activities and duplication of grants. Similarly, Sir James Lithgow and his colleagues may be afraid that the proposed Planning and Research body will overlap the Scottish Development Association.

In these circumstances it is desirable to consider the relation of the two subjects and to see whether any such Planning and Research Body as Sir A. Rose suggests can be worked by, or co-ordinated with, the S.D.A. In other words, can the S.D.A. undertake the functions suggested by Sir A. Rose (so far as approved), or take a considerable share in them?

The programme outlined in the application for a deputation [from SDC] appears practically limited to propaganda and publicity. It contains little hint of the reconstructive work which S. of S. and Sir A. Rose have in mind.

The real question seems to be what view should be taken of the malady from which Scottish industry is suffering. If it is merely a passing illness, then recovery may be hastened by the proposed propaganda and publicity as a kind of tonic. But if the malady is a serious one due to unhealthy conditions inside the patient and prejudicial conditions outside him, then this propaganda and publicity will have little effect unless accompanied by something directed to a real cure.

The question, therefore, arises in connection both with the deputation and with Sir A. Rose's Report whether further measures are necessary for exploring defects in Scottish industry and prejudicial conditions outside it and for trying to find remedies. The Government have rejected the principle of Mr. Lloyd George's Development Board but it may be possible to devise some useful machinery which will not be similarly open to objection. [SRO, DD10/301.]

Minute of the Cabinet Committee on the Special Areas Commissioners' Reports, Statement of Neville Chamberlain, Chancellor of the Exchequer, 8 October 1935.

He did not agree with the statement [of Lord Percy] that local government in the special areas has become static. In his opinion the problem of the Special Areas showed signs of being substantially reduced, and in future it might well be a problem of one or two special areas and a particular part of the other areas. He did not think that there was much anxiety about the future position of the Tyne, the Clyde and the Lanarkshire areas. These districts would benefit very materially from other proposals [rearmament] now under consideration ...

The political effect of substituting entirely new machinery for the Commissioners would be very bad indeed. The Commissioners had been working for less than a year and their supersession by the Special Areas Board would be regarded as an admission that the Government's policy had failed. Moreover, it would be said that the Government have not given the Commissioners a real chance to try out their experiments.

The proposals themselves were open to grave objection. They involved the splitting up of the functions of Local Authorities and the handing over of certain of these functions to the proposed Special Areas Boards. This was bound to arouse great resentment on the part of Local Authorities in the area, and that resentment would no doubt take active and obstructive forms. If [the] proposal had been to introduce, as a purely temporary measure, some system to supersede bankrupt Local Authorities, there would have been much to be said for it from the point of view of securing an improvement in local government administration, but such a proposal could not be confined to the Special Areas, and its wide extension would mean widespread political criticism and opposition. The scheme was open to all the political and other objections without securing any real improvement in local government. Moreover, it involved interference with the Departments of Central Government, such as the Ministry of Transport, which would have much to say against the transfer of certain of its functions [roads] to the proposed Board.

In short he did not regard the scheme as a practicable one. Its adoption would mean waste of time and energy and duplication of effort. It would bring the Government into acute conflict with Local Authorities, and would do nothing to improve the condition of the Special Areas. Accordingly he felt unable to support the proposals. [PRO, CAB 27/578 DA(34)7; SRO, DD10/170.]

Memorandum by Sir Godfrey Collins, Secretary of State for Scotland, to the Cabinet Committee on the Special Areas Commissioners' Report, 16 October 1935.

My suggestion is that we should strengthen the Scottish National Development Council. To accomplish this I would give the Council a Government grant to enable it to employ an adequate staff and generally to extend its work and activity.

(1) That the Council would appoint a Special Committee representative of industry, finance and transport who would explore the field and suggest and endeavour to promote measures for industrial development;

(2) that while the field would cover the whole of industrial Scotland, special consideration would have to be given to the question of the special areas; and

(3) that the Council would act in close liaison with the Commissioner for the Special Areas and with an intelligence or 'clearing house' branch of the Scottish Office in Edinburgh. (This Branch would, of course, work in co-operation with the Ministry of Labour and the Board of Trade.)

The Council would not be subject to Government Control and the Government would have no responsibility for such proposals as the Council might make or such action as they might take.

With the Development Council strengthened as suggested above there would be no need to appoint a new ad hoc body for the purposes suggested by the Scottish Commissioner. [PRO, CAB 27/578 DA(34)9; SRO, DD10/170.]

APPOINTING A COMMITTEE OF ENQUIRY INTO SCOTTISH ADMINISTRATION, 1935

The following extract is from a Scottish Office minute in November 1935 outlining the case for a Committee of Enquiry into Scottish Administration. A week later the Scottish Secretary, Sir Godfrey Collins, agreed that a Committee should be appointed, but asked his officials to seek Treasury sanction to settle its membership and terms of reference.

Minute of R.N. Duke, Assistant Secretary, Scottish Office, on a Committee of Enquiry into Scottish Administration, 21 November 1935.

Now that the General Election is over, it seems desirable to give further consideration to the question of appointing a Committee to review the whole field of Scottish administration.

An enquiry of this nature is desirable because the present organisation of the Scottish Departments—and in particular their arrangements for liaison in London—are by no means satisfactory; and the opportunity—which will arise in 1939—of concentrating the larger Edinburgh Departments in one modern building, makes it convenient to consider now what measures of general reorganisation should be undertaken. An enquiry into this question was foreshadowed by Sir Godfrey Collins when he opened the Edinburgh Branch Office on 15 February last and in the course of his speech remarked:

'If we are to reap the full benefit from concentration of all the big Scottish Departments in one large modern building, it will be necessary to undertake some comprehensive review of all our Scottish administrative arrangements, including the important question of our representation in London. I visualise the Scottish Office in London developing into a centre for responsible representatives and liaison officers from each of the Departments—an advance headquarters thrown forward from our new base upon Calton Hill.'

I suggest the following terms of reference for any Committee which may be appointed:-

'To enquire into and report upon the responsibilities and organisations of the Scottish administrative Departments under the control of the Secretary of State, the distribution of duties amongst these Departments, their relationship to the central executive Government, and the arrangements under which liaison is maintained between Edinburgh and the central executive Government: and to recommend what changes, if any, should be made, whether legislative or administrative, more particularly with a view to ensuring (a) the highest efficiency when it becomes possible to concentrate the larger Edinburgh Departments in one modern building: (b) the elimination of unnecessary and (so far as practicable) of over-lapping of responsibility: and (c) the most effective performance of the administrative functions of the Departments and the seat of Government.' [SRO, HH45/61.]

A NEW OFFICE FOR THE SECRETARY OF STATE FOR SCOTLAND, 1936

In June 1936 the Scottish Office finally agreed with the Treasury the terms of reference and membership for the proposed Committee on Scottish Administration. They broadly followed the lines laid down in Duke's minute (see above) with Sir John Gilmour appointed as chairman. The following is an extract from the evidence submitted to the Committee by the Scottish Office. The Committee's report largely embodied the scheme of reform outlined.

Evidence of the Scottish Office to the Committee on Scottish Administration, November 1936.

In visualising the extent and nature of Scottish Office work it is necessary to keep in view certain general points:-

(a) The duties are of great diversity ... They include however no big block of executive work (such as, for example, National Health Insurance) necessitating the employment of a large number of subordinate staff on routine duties—and this explains both the relatively small total strength of the staff, and the relatively high proportion of senior staff.

(b) Some of the Scottish Office duties fall under the head of control and liaison work in relation to Edinburgh Departments. Thus the Scottish Office provides administrative and other staff in London to undertake liaison work for the Department of Agriculture for Scotland: and in the case of the Fishery Board for Scotland, Prisons Department for Scotland and General Board of Control for Scotland, etc., its functions extend beyond liaison and embrace general direction and control.

(c) Most of the Scottish Office duties consist however of work for which the Department alone is responsible. It is directly responsible for most of the 'Home Office' work in relation to Scotland (e.g. police, criminals, Prerogative, betting, liquor and licensing, shops, theatres and cinemas, ceremonial matters, Royal patronage questions, advertisement regulation, Parliamentary elections and registrations of voters, etc.): for much 'Ministry of Health' work (e.g. local government, local finance, rating and valuation, byelaws, rent restriction, etc.): and much work which is either peculiar to Scotland (e.g. church questions) or is comparable with some work performed for England and Wales by the Lord Chancellor's Department (e.g. Sheriff Clerk Service, appointments to Sheriffs, appointments and establishment work in relation to the Court of Session and legal departments, etc.)

(d) As the Office of the one Cabinet Minister representing Scotland, the Scottish Office is in practice called upon to deal with a considerable number of questions of an extra-statutory nature which do not strictly fall within the scope of its Departmental responsibilities. In the Cabinet the Secretary of State for Scotland is the mouthpiece of Scottish opinion, and he is expected to express Scottish views on many questions which do not directly concern the Department for which he is responsible.

(e) The Scottish Office is regularly consulted by 'United Kingdom' Departments on points arising out of the Scottish application of 'United Kingdom' legislation, although such legislation may be on a subject for which the Scottish Office has no responsibility. In practice it is necessary for the Scottish Office to watch all legislation, if only to ensure that the question of application is duly considered, and, where necessary, properly done. Moreover, the Scottish Office is frequently consulted by 'United Kingdom' Departments in order that these Departments may get the benefit of local knowledge on particular points.

(f) There is an increasing tendency among Scottish people to appeal to the Secretary of State on all questions affecting the social and economic life of Scotland; and this tendency has been reflected in an extension of the sphere of the Scottish Office activity. For example, the Economic Committee for Scotland (a Committee of the Scottish National Development Council) was appointed in 1936 in consultation with the Secretary of State for Scotland, and works in liaison with the Parliamentary Under Secretary of State for Scotland and the Edinburgh Branch of the Scottish Office ...

(g) From time to time the Scottish Office is saddled with responsibilities which in England are laid upon a 'United Kingdom' Department. A recent example is the Special Areas (Development and Improvement) Act, 1934, which placed the Scottish Commissioner under the general control of the Secretary of State for Scotland instead of the Minister of Labour, who controls the English Commissioner.

(h) There is a tendency on the part of the public to regard the Scottish Office as a kind of central bureau for information on any legal, administrative, social or economic questions affecting Scotland, and this involves work outside the sphere of Departmental responsibility—even if only in the way of sending negative replies, or of considering whether a particular representation should be forwarded to another Department and, if so, which Department ...

[*Liaison with other Departments*] The Permanent Under Secretary of State, besides being head of the Scottish Office, is *in practice* called upon to act as head of the Civil Service in relation to all Scottish Secretary of State Departments. He is regularly consulted by the Prime Minister's Secretariat, Departments of The King's Household and other Royal Households, the Treasury (and in particular the Permanent Secretary to the Treasury) and the Secretary of State on personal questions affecting the heads of Scottish Departments generally or the Scottish Civil Service as a whole. He and the Assistant Under Secretary of State are expected by the Secretary of State to keep themselves informed of important developments affecting all branches of Scottish administration. He submits to the Secretary of State answers to parliamentary questions affecting all Scottish Departments. He and the Assistant Under Secretary of State are at times called upon by the Minister to advise on matters concerning Departments other than the Scottish Office. He is at the right hand of the Minister, and it is natural that the Minister should invoke his assistance in considering any subjects of special difficulty or importance.

... *The Department of Health for Scotland.* This Department conducts its Parliamentary, Ministerial and liaison business independently of the Scottish Office. Some of its work however, borders on that of the Scottish Office or other Edinburgh Departments, and this at times involves some action by Scottish Office staff in the direction of co-ordination. The Department has no officer resident in London. Much of its business is accordingly done by written submissions which reach Ministers through their Private Secretaries—and only occasionally involve consultation with members of the Scottish Office staff. Such submissions and other 'health' papers are kept in the Private Secretaries' branch. Liaison and Parliamentary work, in so far as not done by the Private

Secretaries, is done largely by frequent visits to London of the Secretary to the Department, and of other responsible officials of the Department.

[*Conclusion*] The new 'Office of the Secretary of State for Scotland' may be visualised as a confederation of four large Departments [a Home Department, a Department of Health, a Department of Agriculture and Fisheries, and a Department of Education] under the leadership of the Permanent Under Secretary of State and a Deputy Under Secretary of State. The success of such an organisation will largely depend upon the maintenance of the importance of the Individual Departments, and of their Departmental heads. The Permanent Under Secretary of State (even with the assistance of a Deputy) cannot act as a bottleneck through which the stream of all 'Secretary of State' departmental activities must flow. Departmental heads must continue to be responsible for their respective Departments ... It will be the duty of the Permanent Under Secretary of State ... to act as the head of the Civil Service in relation to all Scottish 'Secretary of State' Departments; to give inspiration and leadership to the Departments: to co-ordinate their activities: and to act as right-hand adviser, over the whole field of Scottish administration, to the Secretary of State. If he were to intervene in Departmental activities, it should only be on broad questions of policy ...

The creation of the 'Office of the Secretary of State for Scotland' will involve some breaking down of departmental water-tight compartments. The interest of the Office as a whole will take the place of departmental interests. Duties will from time to time be distributed, or re-distributed, to Departments in the light of what is best for Scottish administration generally. Transfers of personnel between one Department and other will be made whenever such transfers are desirable in the interests of the service as a whole. [SRO, HH45/64.]

CONCENTRATING SCOTTISH ADMINISTRATION, 1938

The Committee on Scottish Administration reported in September 1937 and the Scottish Office established a Committee of officials under Sir Horace Hamilton, the Permanent Under Secretary, to consider its recommendations. The first extract is from their Report. Walter Elliot, the Scottish Secretary, approved their recommendations and the second extract is from his successor's Cabinet memorandum seeking leave to introduce the necessary legislation, which was granted.

Report of the Inter-Departmental Committee on the Recommendations of the Committee on Scottish Administration, 17 December 1937.

We discussed the proposal which was rejected by the Committee that there should be one Department of the Secretary of State instead of the four recommended. It was, however, generally agreed that public opinion would be against such a merger as it would be more difficult to explain that the disappearance of independent Departments with a Secretary in charge of each would not involve down-grading. Ministers, we thought, would find it difficult not to accept what the Committee proposed on this point.

... The Committee ... supported their recommendation for a superior officer [as head of the new Scottish Office] by a reference to the 'peculiarity of the functions of the Secretary of State that, quite apart from his statutory duties, he has a large nebulous sphere of duties in which he is supposed to represent the Scottish point of view and to safeguard Scottish interests. The well defined duties of the Secretary of State are thus surrounded by a large penumbra of other duties which may not require Departmental action and may well lie outside the recognised province of any of the four major Departments'. The Committee argued that in such cases the Secretary of State could not reasonably be expected to get all the advice he required from the Departmental Secretaries. We agree with this conclusion.

We agree with the Committee that the chief adviser's services should be most valuable in important cases where co-ordination of departmental policy is necessary or when the Secretary of State has to consider a question not within the competence of any Department. His advice would also be available when a question arises as to the allocation of new duties to departments or when Departments hold differing opinions.

The Committee consider that a designation other than Under-Secretary of State would be more appropriate for an officer free from Departmental responsibilities. They suggest the title of Permanent Secretary to the Secretary of State. They appear to have reached their conclusions largely by reference to 'past associations'.

We venture to think that change of title is unnecessary. The Committee do not say what they mean by 'past associations'. No doubt, however, they had in mind the so-called domination of the Scottish Office under present arrangements of which the Under Secretary of State may have been regarded as a symbol. If so, the future position will be amply safeguarded without a change of title. The creation of a Scottish Home Department, equal but not superior in status to the other three major departments gets rid of any domination of the Scottish Office. Moreover, the acceptance of the doctrine of the full responsibility of Secretaries for their Department's work and the re-definition of the Under-Secretaries' functions will complete the process of insulation. [SRO, HH45/34.]

Memorandum by John Colville, Secretary of State for Scotland, on Scottish Administration, 20 July 1938.

The aim of the Committee was to improve the organisation of the Scottish Departments and to facilitate the concentration of Scottish Administration in the new building. Under their proposal there would be four major Departments in Edinburgh, namely, the existing Departments of Agriculture, Education and Health, and a Scottish Home Department which would replace the present Scottish Office. These Departments would be in charge of a Secretary directly responsible to the Secretary of State for Scotland for the work of his Department. The organisation of certain smaller Departments would be improved by associating them more closely with one or other of the larger Departments. Appropriate arrangements would be made for the discharge by officers of the Department's concerned of work which requires to be done in London, including Parliamentary and Liaison work. The Secretary of State would have available to assist him an officer of high rank, whom, the Committee suggests, might be designated 'Permanent Secretary to the Secretary of State'.

... In regard to the recommendations that do not require legislation, the most important is that relating to the appointment of an officer of high rank to assist the Secretary of State ... I agree that a chief adviser is required who could take a wider view than the Secretaries in charge of Departments, and who could assist in co-ordinating their work. On the other hand, I see no reason for adopting the title for this post of 'Permanent Secretary to the Secretary of State' suggested by the Committee, and I propose to retain the title of 'Permanent Under Secretary of State for Scotland' which is now held by the permanent head of the Scottish Office. The Treasury share this view. [PRO, CAB 24/278 CP (38)176.]

THE MACHINERY OF GOVERNMENT IN SCOTLAND, 1943

In December 1943, Thomas Johnston, the Scottish Secretary, submitted a memorandum to the Ministerial Machinery of Government Committee on Government administration in Scotland. Apart from presenting a factual account of Departmental responsibilities he also stated his intention to submit another note outlining the case for the further transfer of functions. The matter was remitted to the Official Committee on the Machinery of Government and the following is an extract from their Report. In the event the Ministerial Committee undertook no further discussion of the matter.

Report of the Official Committee on the Machinery of Government, on the Machinery of Government in Scotland, 24 December 1943.

The position of Scotland as a constituent part of the United Kingdom, governed by the same Crown, Parliament and Cabinet as England, but administered to a large extent by separate Departments, animated by an intense local patriotism and 'sense of difference', yet at the same time (with insignificant exceptions) by an entire devotion to the Union and 'sense of oneness' with its other constituent parts, is probably unique in the history of modern government. The system, as we know it to-day, rests on a balance (not always very stable) between sharply contrasted centrifugal and centripetal tendencies—imperial achievements shared with England; bitter memories of Scottish history contrasted with a common-sense appreciation of present-day facts; strong cultural differences co-existing with considerable economic interdependence. The present system is, in fact, a striking example of the peculiar British gift for reconciling incompatibles by an illogical compromise.

We mention these underlying factors since they assume importance whenever controversy is aroused and they point to certain general conclusions:-

(a) In the circumstances, the machinery of government in Scotland cannot be designed on entirely logical lines. Tidiness and ideal efficiency must sometimes give way to the claims of national sentiment. (b) The logical defects of the system will be overlooked only so long as it works. If the administration of those Scottish services which are based upon London fails to take proper account of Scottish differences and Scottish susceptibilities the centrifugal tendencies will be strengthened and the balance disturbed. (This is a point glanced at by the Secretary of State in paragraph 3 of his Note.) The same result will follow if, in the case of all new Government services resulting from increased State intervention in the life of the community, administration is concentrated, however logically, in London to an extent and in a manner which affronts Scottish opinion.

(c) On the other hand division of responsibility in the economic sphere between England and Scottish Ministers may be not only inconvenient but actually inimical to the best interests of Scotland herself, if the result is to deprive Scotland of her proper place in the minds of those primarily responsible for the central planning of Britain's economy.

In paragraph 5 of his Note the Secretary of State mentions the view that 'today Scotland expects that the central administration of her domestic matters will be based on Edinburgh rather than on Whitehall unless there are overriding reasons to the contrary'. This might be read as having far reaching implications and we ourselves would put it rather differently. It must be remembered that the separate administration of Scottish services merely because they affect Scotsmen cuts across the dictum of the Haldane Committee, now universally accepted as sound, that the distribution of business between administrative departments should be governed by the nature of the service to be rendered and not according to the persons or classes to be dealt with. (The Haldane Committee rather dodged the implications of their dictum in the sphere of Scottish administration and Scotland finds almost no mention in their Report.)

Our view would be that the first considerations must be efficiency of administration and the general interest of the country as a whole and of Scotland in particular; if these considerations suggest that a particular service should be administered by a Department covering the whole country—and they will not always do so—it should next be considered whether the strength of Scottish traditions and sentiment in the particular field is such as to make it expedient that the service should be separately administered for Scotland, or at least devolved on a regional basis. We do not read the Secretary of State's Note as implying anything essentially different from this.

Towards the end of the nineteenth century when the advances of Government policy lay mainly in the field of education and other social services and the development of local government, and hardly at all in the field of commerce and economics, it was natural that almost all new Government powers should be granted as respects Scotland to the Scottish Secretary. At that time, moreover, Scotland's population bore a respectable relationship to England's, and with the booming of the heavy industries round the Clyde, which created so much of Scotland's wealth, Scotland was not much dependent economically on England. But now, when Scotland's population has dwindled relatively to England's (it is now little more than half the population of London), when Scotland's heavy industries have suffered severe depression, and when, most important of all, the Government has widely extended its activities in the economic and industrial spheres and is preparing to an increasing extent to plan the allocation and development of the human and material resources of the country as a whole, the case for separate administration in Scotland has in many respects grown weaker rather than stronger.

Nevertheless, there does remain in the case of Scotland (and in passing we may say that we do not think that this is true of Wales) a substantial part of Government activity which may be administered separately, not merely without harm, but with much real advantage. It is natural and right that there should be separate administration for Scotland in those fields where there are distinctive Scottish traditions, law, history, or methods; for example, education, the control of local government structure, the health services, the administration of justice and of the legal services, ceremonial matters and cultural institutions, such as the National Library, Museums and Galleries. The same considerations may well apply to certain future Government activities; and we do not exclude the possibility that, consistently with what we have said above, there may well be some functions now dealt with by Whitehall Departments which might well be transferred to the Secretary of State.

We think it important to emphasise the desirability of single administration in matters which are likely to be the subject of national economic planning. The march of progress has made the island smaller, and it will in the future be a much more compact economic unit. It is to Scotland's interest that her needs and resources should be considered at the same time and in the same place as those of the rest of the country, and we should expect this view to be shared by a considerable body of realistic and forward-looking opinion in Scotland itself.

As regards *location of industry*, for instance, it is obvious that if Scotland were outside the responsibilities of the Board of Trade new businesses started by English capital would be directed on a choice between, say, the Humber and the Tyne; with nation-wide responsibilities the Board will have to consider whether the Clyde would not be more suitable than either. If the Secretary of State were responsible for location of industry in Scotland he would never hear of such a case at all, unless there were elaborate (and probably not wholly effective) liaison arrangements involving friction and waste of effort.

It is true that the *Special Areas* legislation set up a separate Scottish Commissioner responsible to the Secretary of State, whereas the Commissioners set up in the rest of the country were responsible to the Minister of Labour. But some of our evidence suggests that this was by no means a satisfactory arrangement.

Similarly, it seems clear that national man-power and employment policy must be administered as a whole, and that there should be a single administration of the nation's transport system and raw material resources such as coal and timber. (The question is before the Ministers but we, for our part, see no sound case for a separate Forestry Commission in Scotland.)

... we [do not] at all differ from the remarks of the Gilmour Committee about the Secretary of State's general position as 'Scotland's Minister'. We do not mean that he ought, or could reasonably be expected, to disinterest himself in the commerce, industry, man-power and general economic development of Scotland; merely that generally speaking he should not be directly responsible for administration in these spheres. That he should keep himself informed through such bodies as the Council of State and the Scottish Council on Industry, should stimulate his colleagues in Scotland's interests, advise them on Scottish aspects of national plans and on appointments of Scottish representatives on national bodies, and in general, act as Scotland's mouthpiece in the Government—all this is entirely desirable; and Ministers will no doubt wish to propose that the Secretary of State should be associated with standing Cabinet Committees whose work affects Scotland, even at points where the Secretary of State's statutory responsibilities are not engaged. But if he is directly responsible in all matters which affect Scotland's welfare, Scotland is likely on balance to lose rather than gain. Moreover, the burden on the Secretary of State personally, already prodigious, would be well-nigh intolerable; his staff would be loaded with a bewildering variety of work on much of which they could not acquire and bring to bear the necessary concentrated knowledge and efficiency; either it would be done less well than in the larger and less wide-ranging English Departments or else it would merely reproduce work which might without difficulty have covered Scotland as well as England in the first place; delays, overlaps and inconsistencies would be inevitable. [PRO, CAB 87/72 MGO 36.]

SCOTTISH MINISTERIAL ARRANGEMENTS, 1947

The extract here is from a draft memorandum submitted to the Cabinet Office by Joseph Westwood, the Scottish Secretary, on the issue of a appointing a second Scottish Cabinet Minister. He wished their comments before formally submitting it to Clement Attlee, the Prime Minister. Some discussion then ensued on whether a formal Cabinet or official inquiry should be established, with the Cabinet Office making clear that they 'were not enamoured' with the proposal. It felt that the Government's legislative programme would slow and that the appointment might 'raise the demand for greater devolution'. However, at the beginning of July, as discussion of appointing a wider inquiry into Scottish devolution was being mooted (see below), Westwood left the minute 'in suspense'.

Draft Minute of Joseph Westwood, Secretary of State for Scotland, on Scottish Ministerial Arrangements, June 1947.

I am sorry I must trouble you further about Scottish Ministerial arrangements.

The object of this minute is to discuss briefly the nature of the Ministerial responsibilities of the Secretary of State for Scotland, and to invite your consideration of the question whether a second Scottish Minister could be appointed and vested with authority sufficient to enable those responsibilities to be shared.

From its very nature the office of the Scottish Secretary carries with it Ministerial responsibilities which are exceptionally wide and varied. The Secretary of State is by statute responsible for agriculture, fisheries, forestry, education, health, housing, town and country planning, local government, police, prisons, the legal services, hydro-electric development and a wide range of miscellaneous functions. In addition, he is expected to take an active part in the consideration of economic questions affecting Scotland—particularly in relation to the Development Areas and the Highlands and Islands—and, more generally, to keep a vigilant eye as 'Scotland's Minister' upon all aspects of Government activity in and affecting Scotland.

The personal responsibility of the Secretary of State in relation to this wide range of subjects is bound to be onerous; and his position is not eased by the fact that Parliament and the central machinery of Government are in London, while the Scottish Departments for which he is responsible are located in Edinburgh. This geographical difficulty is met so far as possible by special liaison arrangements and frequent travelling, but cannot of course be eliminated.

These conditions are accentuated to-day when new approaches to social and economic problems are being made and the volume of legislation has increased. In recent years heavy additional responsibilities have been placed upon the Secretary of State in a variety of fields, including forestry, hydro-electric development, town and country planning, health, housing, agriculture and education.

During the war Parliament sat on only three days a week; there were no standing committees and little legislation; the Secretary of State was not a member of the War Cabinet; and the volume of business under his charge was reduced by the virtual cessation of many peace-time services. Despite this and the fact that the appointment of a second Parliamentary Under-Secretary of State was authorised in 1942, my predecessor found the strain of his office severe. Now Parliament sits on five days a week and has a full programme of legislation, in much of which the Secretary of State has to take an active interest. The standing committees, including the Scottish Grand Committee, are fully employed. The Secretary of State is a member of the Cabinet, and, of course, of a number of its committees. All services for which he is responsible are in full operation, and in addition there are many new and important policies now in hand, such as the organisation of the national health service and the development of education and agriculture and town and country planning.

My experience has been that Parliamentary business and the work of the Cabinet and its committees require Scottish Ministers to be in London on at least four days in every week. Even so, it has been very difficult in practice to provide for necessary attendance at standing committees simultaneously considering Bills of Scottish interest. This leaves the Secretary of State at most one and half working days a week during the Session for Departmental discussions, consultations with Local Authorities and other interests, and public engagements in Scotland. In present circumstances I can see no prospect of any increase in the amount of time available for such duties in Scotland without detriment to Parliamentary and Cabinet work in London.

I have carefully considered to what extent the position would be eased once the Solicitor-General for Scotland is in Parliament and if, in addition, the number of Parliamentary Under-Secretaries were increased. I am very conscious of the help I have received from the Lord Advocate and the present Scottish Joint Parliamentary Under-Secretaries; and in particular of the fact that during the past year a special measure of responsibility for housing has been carried on by an Under-Secretary. But in the light of the actual experience I am clear that the extent to which responsibilities of the Secretary of State can be discharged on his behalf by a Law Officer or by Junior Ministers is necessarily limited; and I feel that the time has come when some new and move effective means should, if possible, be found of relieving the Secretary of State of part of his Ministerial responsibilities.

The course which personally I should like to suggest for your consideration is the appointment of a second Minister for Scottish Affairs—of Cabinet rank—if not actually in the Cabinet, and the assignment to that Minister of a substantial part of the statutory responsibilities of the Secretary of State. There are great practical advantages in the present system under which the statutory responsibility for the various functions of Government separately handled in Scotland is placed upon 'the Secretary of State'. I think it is important to retain these advantages, and I should not, therefore, advocate a complete transfer of functions, amounting to severance, such as is provided for in the Minister of the Crown (Transfer of Functions) Act. What I have in mind is an arrangement whereby, at the instance of the Secretary of State, a new Minister could be given formal authority and responsibility for the discharge in his name of specified statutory responsibilities of the Secretary of State. A Minister of State for Scottish Affairs, to whom specified duties could be assigned as a matter of Departmental organisation, might perhaps be appointed without new legislation. Since, however, the bulk of the Secretary of State's responsibilities are placed on him by statute, assignment of duties without statutory authority for their discharge would not, in my view, be the best solution, and I feel that fresh legislation under which full responsibility could be assigned to a new Minister would be preferable. I would suggest that such legislation should enable the Secretary of State by Order (which could be varied as circumstances might require) to assign to a new Minister certain of his statutory responsibilities. The two existing Under-Secretary posts would remain unaffected, except that one Under-Secretary might work under the new Minister, leaving the other to assist the Secretary of State. [PRO, T 222/1048.]

LABOUR AND A FACT-FINDING ENQUIRY INTO SCOTTISH DEVOLUTION, 1947

After the 1945 General Election a considerable campaign developed to secure Home Rule, especially from the Scottish Convention, an all-Party alliance which sought a federal system of government. In June 1947 John Taylor, Secretary of the Scottish Council of the Labour Party, wrote to Herbert Morrison, Lord President of the Council, repeating a request made the previous October for the establishment of an independent inquiry into Scottish Administration. Morrison sent a copy of the letter to Joseph Westwood, the Scottish Secretary, asking for his comments, and the first extract is his reply. Morrison appears not to have replied, but Lord Elibank, a Conservative Peer, indicated that he would submit a question in the Lords asking the Government's intentions. The next extract is from Westwood's second letter to Morrison enclosing a draft temporising reply for Elibank. The third extract is Morrison's reply. The fourth is from Westwood's next letter to Morrison. The final extract is from a minute of Norman Duke, the Home Department's Secretary, to Westwood summarising the position reached at the end of September, after a meeting had been agreed between the two Ministers and the Labour MPs. However, before a meeting could take place, Westwood was replaced in a Cabinet reshuffle aimed at making way for 'younger men'.

Letter of Joseph Westwood, Secretary of State for Scotland, to Herbert Morrison, Lord President of the Council, on an Enquiry into Scottish Devolution, 27 June 1947.

Thank you for your letter of the 20th June enclosing a copy of the letter which you received from Mr. John Taylor, J.P.

I have discussed his letter with officials of the Scottish Group of the Parliamentary Labour Party and the conclusion which I have come to is that the best course would be to tell Mr. Taylor that we are prepared to set up an independent committee to enquire into the administrative set up in Scotland and to make recommendation as to whether and to what extent further legislative devolution of Scottish affairs is necessary, practical and advisable, whilst retaining the integrity of the United Kingdom.

My own feeling—and that of party officials with whom I have discussed the matter—is that an enquiry by an independent committee is the only way to deal with the criticisms which are levelled at the Government to the effect that Scotland's affairs are subject to too much central control from Whitehall. [PRO, CAB 124/911.]

Letter of Joseph Westwood, Secretary of State for Scotland, to Herbert Morrison, Lord President of the Council, on a Fact-finding Enquiry into Scottish Devolution, 21 July 1947.

I wrote to you on the 27th June about the request submitted by the Executive Committee of the Scottish Council of the Labour Party and the Scottish Parliamentary Labour Group for the appointment of an independent committee to conduct a fact-finding enquiry into the general question of Scottish devolution.

As I indicated in my letter [of 27 June] to you I do not think that we can avoid instituting some sort of enquiry on this subject; and in view of the representations recently made by the Scottish Labour interests it would be well, in my view, if we could announce before 30th July that we intend to set up a fact-finding enquiry in accordance with their request.

The precise scope and form of the enquiry will require careful consideration; and whatever the terms of reference, implications affecting other parts of the country may be inevitable.

In these circumstances I appreciate that an immediate decision may not be possible and I enclose a draft reply to Elibank [for 30th July] which has been prepared on that assumption. [PRO, CAB 124/911.]

Letter of Herbert Morrison, Lord President of the Council, to Joseph Westwood, Secretary of State for Scotland, on a Fact-finding Enquiry into Scottish Devolution, 25 July 1947.

In reply to your letter of the 21st July I have no points to raise in the draft reply to Lord Elibank which you enclosed. It seems to me to leave the position sufficiently open.

As I understand the position, the Labour Party Policy Committee were going themselves to conduct a fact-finding enquiry into the general question of Scottish devolution and to present the results to the Scottish Executive. I feel that we ought to await this report before we take any steps ourselves.

I should like to have a word with you some time about Government policy over this field since I think we should be very cautious about embarking on enquiries until we are quite clear in our minds where we want to get to at the end of the day. The whole subject is difficult and arouses great feelings and if we start up enquiries without a clear idea of our own policy we may be forced into courses of which we strongly disapprove. I should, for example, hope that you would resist any form of legislative devolution which reproduced in Scotland the kind of arrangements in force in Northern Ireland. There may be material for investigation into the field of government which comes within the province of the Secretary of State as distinct from U.K. Ministers since to some extent the present position is the result of haphazard development rather than of any coherent policy. Here again, I think we ought to have our own ideas reasonably clear before we discuss the matter with others. I feel grave doubt whether any useful purpose will be served by an enquiry into the administration of the socialised industries in relation to Scotland at the present juncture. For better or worse a framework has been set up in the various nationalisation measures and it will not be possible to do anything about that framework until there has been practical experience of its working over a number of years.

There is one last point I should like you to be thinking over. We seem so far to have failed to get across to Scottish opinion the merits of the present arrangements such as they are and the difficulties of the various alternative proposals that are canvassed. We have not really done enough to combat the sense of injury and grievance against the present machinery of government which is widespread in Scotland. There is a big public relations job here which ought to be tackled before it is too late. [PRO, CAB 124/911.]

Letter of Joseph Westwood, Secretary of State for Scotland, to Herbert Morrison, Lord President of the Council, on a Fact-finding Enquiry into Scottish Devolution, 30 July 1947.

Thank you for your letter of 25th July about the general question of Scottish devolution.

The terms of the temporising reply to Lord Elibank which accompanied my last letter to you on this subject were agreed with the Treasury, and the reply was duly given today by Lord Morrison in the House of Lords.

I agree that we ought to discuss the question of Government policy over this field, and I should welcome the opportunity of a meeting at a mutually convenient time which would enable us to go into the question fully. In this connection I may say that in putting forward the request of the Scottish representatives I did not contemplate any enquiry into the question of Parliamentary devolution, or even into the present division of functions between Great Britain Ministers and the Secretary of State. I appreciate, too, that a review of the machinery of the Boards of socialised industries at this time would not be free from difficulty. At the same time it is clear, I am afraid, that much of the present agitation centres around this question, and the whole matter will require very careful handling.

If you feel that the proposal of the Scottish Labour representatives for an enquiry should first be considered, in consultation with them, by the Policy Committee of the Party for the country as a whole, I should in no way dissent from that course.

On the question of putting over our position to Scottish opinion, I have for long been convinced of the necessity for this being done, and I have given a good deal of attention to the methods to be adopted. Having regard to the whole history of the idea of devolution in Scotland, the problem is one of unusual difficulty. To begin with I have tried to get the facts of the situation established. In a series of speeches, beginning with one at the New Year in Scotland, a 'state of the nation' address given to representatives of the local authorities at the City Chambers, Edinburgh, I indicated the lines on which our programme was developing, and the steps which we were taking to ensure that within the arrangements for Great Britain as a whole there should be the greatest practicable devolution of authority and provision for dealing with special Scottish conditions. I supplemented this by meetings with the Scottish Council of the Labour Party, and with the Editors of Scottish newspapers, in St. Andrews House and elsewhere. I then had the White Paper on Industry and Employment prepared, and followed it up with the popular version 'Scots at Work'. The whole point of my efforts was to get the Scots accustomed to the Labour attitude towards major Scottish affairs, and to realise that it is consistent with, and designed to secure, the best interests of Scotland. Having regard to all the circumstances I do not think that any more effective steps could be taken so far.

We have now reached the stage when it would be well if exposition of the facts could be supplemented by further evidence, in the form of concrete results, of the Government's goodwill to Scotland. Too often in the past beneficial actions have appeared to have been extracted from us unwillingly.

Your own recent decision to locate important research stations in Scotland is a good example of the sort of thing that is needed. And if a favourable decision can be reached soon on the question of the future of Rosyth Dockyard, this will also be of great assistance.

The more concrete results of this kind we can produce the better. I am doing all I can myself so far as the work of the Scottish Office is concerned. But important parts of the field are covered by Great Britain Ministers, and it is essential that they, too, should do their utmost to see that the needs of the Scottish position are kept fully in view. [PRO, CAB 124/911.]

Minute of Sir Norman Duke, Secretary, the Scottish Home Department, on the Demand for an Enquiry into Scottish Affairs, 20 September 1947.

The proposal which the Scottish Executive and Groups have been pressing without success on the Policy Committee and the Lord President during the last two years would appear to involve a comprehensive independent enquiry into the political, constitutional and economic relations between Scotland and England, and into the question whether legislation should be proposed for the purpose of establishing a Parliament and a Government in Scotland with powers to deal with Scottish domestic affairs. This is precisely what the Scottish Convention are out to secure and they have recently asked the Prime Minister to receive them in a deputation on proposals which they have prepared for such legislation. Whatever the merits of the constitutional arrangements at present in force in relation to Northern Ireland—and there are special reasons for their existence there—they leave financial control substantially with London. The adoption of any similar system here would place Scotland in a subordinate position, dependent on London for finance, and the resultant friction might well give rise at no distant date to claims for a separate fiscal system and separate commercial Customs and tariff policies.

The essential fact is that in trade, industry, finance and defence, the life of Scotland is very closely linked up with that of England and Wales; and these economic and other vital links could hardly be broken or even weakened without a risk of serious effects on the economic interest of both countries.

In his speech at Edinburgh on 17th September Sir Stafford Cripps [President of the Board of Trade] pointed out that the need for integrating the economies of the two countries was never greater than today, when Great Britain as a whole is fighting for its economic life. There is no question of one or other of the two countries surviving if the other goes down. The small island of Great Britain constitutes a single economic unit and we all stand or fall together.

The Lord President (in his letter to you of 25th July) has already uttered a warning about the danger of embarking on enquiries without a clear idea of where they may lead at the end of the day. The whole subject is difficult and arouses deep feeling and if enquiries are started up without a clear idea of the objective, the Government may be forced into courses of which they would strongly disapprove. The Lord President expressed the hope, for example, that any suggestion for reproducing Northern Ireland arrangements in Scotland would be resisted. He also expressed a grave doubt whether any useful purpose would be served by an enquiry into the administration of socialised industries in relation to Scotland at the present juncture. For better or worse a framework has been set up in the various nationalisation measures and it will not be possible to do anything about that framework until there has been practical experience of its working over a number of years.

This is the background of the situation against which you are now asked to press the Government to institute an enquiry which could not be confined to administration but would inevitably extend to industrial, economic and constitutional questions.

This in no way precludes every effort being made to secure the maximum degree of administrative decentralisation in relation to trade and industry compatible with the needs of efficient organisation. As Lord Morrison [Government Spokesman in the Lords] pointed out in his reply to a question asked by Elibank in the Lords on 30th July, the Government have been at pains to see that within the administrative arrangements for Great Britain as a whole there is the greatest practical devolution of authority and provision for dealing with separate Scottish conditions. All Departments concerned with trade and industry are represented in Scotland by responsible officers to whom is delegated authority to enable Scottish business to be settled on the spot. The arrangements for the conduct of Scottish business are, and will continue to be, kept under close review so as to ensure that the machinery of the various Departments and of the boards of socialised industry is properly related to Scottish needs.

In the circumstances it may be felt that the wisest course will be to concentrate on these immediate concrete issues rather than to press for an enquiry into economic and administrative relations between Scotland and England at this stage. But, if, notwithstanding these considerations it is felt that for political reasons the Cabinet should be asked to institute an enquiry, you will no doubt impress on the officials attending the meeting that if they wish you to put up proposals to the Cabinet, they must first supply you with a reasoned memorandum, setting out the specific grounds on which they consider that their proposal for an enquiry should be put forward together with the precise questions which they consider that an enquiry should cover. [SRO, SOE1/110.]

THE SOCIALISED INDUSTRIES AND SCOTTISH DEMANDS FOR DEVOLUTION, 1947

In October 1947 Arthur Woodburn was appointed Scottish Secretary and he immediately asked his officials to prepare a memorandum on Scottish affairs for the Cabinet. A draft was submitted to Herbert Morrison, the Lord President, for comment. It included proposals to enlarge the work of the Scottish Grand Committee, initiate a fact-finding inquiry into devolution and establish a Scottish Production Council which would work 'in close touch' with the Secretary of State for Scotland, the Minister of Economic Affairs and other bodies 'to stimulate and co-ordinate the development of industry'. The first extract is from Morrison's letter of comment and the second from Woodburn's subsequent reply. The third is from Woodburn's eventual Cabinet memorandum, adjusted after a meeting with Morrison. His five proposals were accepted without reservation, but a sixth, brought up in discussion to establish a committee of inquiry into Anglo-Scottish financial relationships, was rejected as the Cabinet felt its 'advantages' would not 'justify the effort' of civil service time. A White Paper on Scottish Affairs (Cmd. 7308) embodying the agreed recommendations was published in 1948.

Letter of Herbert Morrison, Lord President of the Council, to Arthur Woodburn, Secretary of State for Scotland, on Scottish Devolution, 13 November 1947.

I have been looking at the draft memorandum on Scottish Devolution which you were good enough to send me. I think that the paper will be a useful means of bringing the main Scottish issues before the Cabinet.

I have one or two points I should like to raise on the latest draft which, I think, is dated 7th November.

I am a little unhappy about Paragraph 7. As you know, I have never been too clear what field was to be covered by a fact-finding enquiry and in particular whether it was to cover legislative devolution as well as executive devolution. In any event, any enquiry would almost certainly stray beyond the facts into the contentious field of policy. I have, therefore, been wondering whether you ought not to make an effort to induce the Scottish Labour Party to accept your Scottish Grand Committee scheme as the best that can be done for the present. If you enlarge the scope of the Scottish Grand Committee in the way you propose *and* at the same time seem to open the door to further wide and unspecified concessions to be achieved after the fact-finding committee has completed its work, you may set afoot an agitation for concessions on a lavish scale which you will not be able to control.

In regard to the proposal for enlarging the scope of the Scottish Grand Committee [Paragraph 12], I feel that we shall have to consider whether the House should not be entitled to reverse a decision of the Scottish Grand Committee on a second reading of a Bill if it were adverse to the Government. This of course could be represented as seriously reducing the value of deliberations of the Scottish Grand Committee and we shall have to be very careful how we worded the matter.

On Paragraph 13 I shall, at a later stage, have to discuss with you the extent to which the new procedure makes it possible to have separate Scottish Bills where at present there is the U.K. Bill with a Scottish application clause. You will understand that I should have to resist any proposal for a wide extension of the practice of having Scottish Bills, since the report and third reading stages would be taken on the floor of the House of Commons and might take up a good deal of time which we needed for other business.

Lastly, I would suggest that paragraph 17 might be recast. As drafted, it is open to the objection that you seem to be adding yet another consultative body to several that exist at present. I quite understand that you will wish to be in close touch with Scottish developments for which U.K. Departments are primarily responsible and that you would like to have periodical meetings with the Scottish representatives of U.K. Departments and of socialised industries. If you can secure the assent of the U.K. Ministers to this, could you not have periodical meetings without describing the meetings as a formal Committee or Council? [PRO, CAB 124/911; SRO, HH36/92.]

Letter of Arthur Woodburn, Secretary of State for Scotland, to Herbert Morrison, Lord President of the Council, on Scottish Devolution, 25 November 1947.

I am much obliged for your letter of the 13th November about the draft memorandum on Scottish devolution.

As regards the points made in the fourth paragraph of your letter, I agree with what you say and I am revising the memorandum accordingly.

As regards the fifth paragraph, the number of Scottish Bills to be referred to the Scottish Grand Committee will be under the control of the Government. Accordingly the situation at any time will be one for adjustment between the

Secretary of State and the Legislation Committee. I entirely agree that I must not encroach on the general pool of Parliamentary time.

As regards the last paragraph of your letter, I have revised the part of the memorandum and the relative appendix so as to propose the setting up under my chairmanship of a Scottish Economic Conference consisting of the chief representatives of Great Britain Departments and of the executives of the socialised industries in Scotland. I enclose the revised wording for your consideration.

This leaves two difficult questions which I should like to have an early opportunity of discussing with you. The first is whether we should publish an annual White Paper about Scotland's economic position and, if so, what its scope should be. The second is the even more difficult question of an enquiry, with which you deal in the third paragraph of your letter.

In order the facilitate discussion I enclose a brief note summarising the general point we have reached, with specific reference to those two points. Perhaps our Secretaries could, if you agree, arrange a meeting at a mutually convenient time for us to meet?

Note for the Secretary of State's discussion with the Lord President

Motions by Lords Lindsay and Elibank for 2nd December in the Lords. Lord Morrison is doing his utmost to secure postponement of any Debate.

The Secretary of State is to see the Sub-Committee appointed by the Scottish Labour Party Executive before settling the terms and scope of his Paper to the Cabinet.

Anxious to consult the Lord President in the first place as to the best line to take at the meeting.

The Secretary of State proposes:-

(a) acceptance of the Opposition Motion which would provide for discussion of Scottish estimates in the Scottish Grand Committee;

(b) amendment of Standing orders so that, in suitable cases and subject to appropriate safeguards, a Scottish Bill may be referred for consideration in principle by the Scottish Grand Committee;

(c) in association with the Minister for Economic Affairs, the Secretary of State should seek to bring about a greater co-ordination of economic affairs in Scotland. This to be secured through the creation of a Scottish Economic Conference consisting of the chief representatives of Great Britain Departments and of Boards of socialized industries in Scotland, which would meet from time to time under the Secretary of State's chairmanship.

(d) an annual White Paper dealing with industry and employment in Scotland. It would be for consideration, in consultation with the Economic Section of the Cabinet and the Great Britain Departments concerned, whether this should be limited to a survey of the past year's achievements, or whether it should attempt to deal with the future on the lines of the Economic Survey for Great Britain.

(e) The Treasury might be asked to produce an up-to-date statement, similar to that published in 1931, showing the general financial relationship of Scotland to the United Kingdom in terms of revenue and expenditure;

In addition to these proposals the Scots Labour Party representatives may insist that a review of the executive machinery of Departments and the Boards of socialized industries in Scotland is necessary.

If this is to be conceded, it could only be done in either of the two following ways:-

(1) by the appointment by the Government of a Committee with some such terms of reference as the following:- 'To review the machinery of Government Departments and State-appointed bodies for the exercise of their functions in Scotland; to consider the principles of organisation upon which provision for decentralisation of administrative and executive authority in relation to different functions has been made, and whether in the interests of efficient organisation any changes in these arrangements are desirable and practicable; and to report', or

(2) by (i) a review by the Machinery of Government Committee of the machinery of Government Departments for the exercise of their functions in Scotland, with a view to seeing whether the administrative arrangements of the Departments are sufficiently decentralised; and (ii) a review by the Committee on Socialised Industries of the executive machinery of the responsible Boards with a view to seeing that in each case it is sufficiently decentralised. [PRO, CAB 124/912; SRO, HH36/92.]

Memorandum by Arthur Woodburn, Secretary of State for Scotland, on Scottish Demands for Home Rule or Devolution, 6 December 1947.

Summary

All political parties in Scotland, including the Labour Party, are taking part in an agitation for a greater measure of Scottish control over Scottish Affairs. For the reasons discussed in the Memorandum I submit the following proposals as immediately necessary:-

(1) that on agreed occasions Scottish Bills should be referred to the Scottish Grand Committee for debate before the Second Reading is taken formally in the House of Commons;

(2) that up to four days should be allocated in the Scottish Grand Committee, in addition to the normal Supply days in the House of Commons, for discussion of Scottish Estimates;

(3) that a Scottish Economic Conference should be established under the Chairmanship of the Secretary of State;

(4) that an annual review of Scottish economic affairs should be made and presented to Parliament;

(5) that special attention should be given to the arrangements for decentralisation of executive responsibility in Scotland.

Public opinion in Scotland

... With the advent of the Labour Government, it was confidently expected that further steps would be taken to increase the degree of control over Scottish affairs. But the Labour Government has deliberately established the socialised industries, in which Scottish local authorities and companies had shown considerable enterprise, on a Great Britain basis; and has been portrayed as having failed to make adequate statutory provision for responsible administration of Scottish business in Scotland. It has been represented that Scottish enterprise in civil aviation was contemptuously suppressed; and that there was undoubtedly deep resentment of the centralised set-up of British Transport. It is the treatment of the socialised industries—or the way in which that treatment has been represented and exploited—which has been largely responsible for bringing matters to a head.

The demand for an enquiry

Members of all groups, and many people outside the groups, with the united support of the Press, are calling, with a remarkable degree of unanimity, for an inquiry into the facts and considerations bearing on the question of Scottish devolution.

... In face of the position in Scotland, and of the feeling in both Houses of Parliament, I take the view that it would be ultimately highly dangerous to the relationship of Scotland if the Government were to adopt a purely negative attitude. But the suggestions as to the terms of reference of such an enquiry are varied and seldom well-defined. They range over the desirability of further legislative and parliamentary devolution; the facts of the financial relationship of Scotland and other parts of the United Kingdom generally; the machinery of government in Scotland; and the arrangements for the administration in Scotland of the nationalised industries. If any Committee of enquiry were appointed it would have to include members from both sides of the Border and of varying political views, and such members might well be found to have strongly held opinions on the subject of Scottish Nationalism. The possibilities of fundamental disagreement are therefore obvious. It is unlikely that any enquiry, however wide its scope, would satisfy the varying and far-reaching demands which have been made; and the time required for detailed investigation of all aspects of the position would in any case mean much delay. I feel, therefore, that the time is not opportune to set up a formal committee of enquiry and that it is more important to concentrate on practical measures which can be taken immediately.

Legislative and Parliamentary Devolution

I think that any proposal to set up a separate Scottish Parliament should be resisted, and that we should concentrate on meeting the desire of Scotsmen for more control over their own affairs by making greater use, within the present Parliamentary system, of the Scottish Grand Committee for the consideration of (a) Bills and (b) Estimates. I believe that this would be satisfactory to the bulk of moderate opinion in all parties in Scotland.

As regards *Bills* I have set out ... draft Standing Orders ... under which the House would be able to decide, on the motion of a Minister, to refer a Scottish Bill to the Scottish Grand Committee for consideration in principle. Where a Bill has been so referred, the House could, on its return, decide without debate and, if necessary, by division, to give or not give it a Second Reading. The House would retain the normal Report and Third Reading stages.

The types of Bills to which it would be suitable and convenient for the Government to apply this procedure would be (1) Bills of a technical nature only applying to Scotland, which, though debatable, are not controversial in a party sense. (2) Bills which repeat for Scotland legislation already passed by the House for England and Wales. (3) Bills which are at present allocated to the 'if there is time' category ...

As regards *estimates* the Opposition ... [has proposed] that, on the motion of a Scottish Minister, Scottish Estimates might be referred, in whole or in part, to the Scottish Grand Committee for consideration. After such consideration, the Estimates would come formally before the Committee of Supply in the ordinary way. I think this proposal should be accepted, with a limitation to four in the number of days which can be spent by the Scottish Committee on Scottish Estimates ...

Scotland's Economic Position

The primary concern of those who are pressing for a review of administrative arrangements in Scotland is with the economic affairs and with the organisation of the socialised industries. In view of this I propose, as an immediate step, the creation of a 'Scottish Economic Conference' representative of all Departments, all agencies with economic interests in Scotland, including the socialised industries. The Conference, which would sit under my Chairmanship, would have the following objects:- (a) To provide a forum for the discussion of economic questions affecting Scotland, and so to enable all concerned to keep themselves informed of developments in all fields. (b) To enable the Secretary of State to keep himself in closer and more personal touch with all Scottish economic questions and to advise Ministers concerned, particularly the Minister for Economic Affairs.

The machinery of Government and the Socialised industries in Scotland

The foregoing proposals are unlikely to be regarded as a complete answer by those who criticise the present machinery of Government administration in Scotland ... I am at present preparing a comprehensive statement of the organisation which Government Departments have set up in Scotland for the discharge of their functions; this will show a wide measure of devolved responsibility and the facts could if necessary be published. In the first place, however, I think that they should be examined interdepartmentally.... As regards socialised industries, I should propose to say that the new Boards are in the course of developing their own organisations within the wide limits of discretion given to them by Parliament, and that the Government will keep under observation the general pattern of these arrangements as they are worked out, in order to ensure that they are properly related to Scottish needs. [PRO, CAB 129/22 CP (47)323; SRO, HH1/1231.]

GOVERNMENT ORGANISATION IN SCOTLAND, 1948

As a result of the Cabinet's deliberations (see above) the Home Department conducted an inquiry into the extent of devolved Government in Scotland and a factual memorandum was prepared for its Secretary, Charles Cunningham. The following extract is from his subsequent minute to Sir David Milne, the Permanent Under Secretary of State.

Minute of C.C. Cunningham, Secretary of the Scottish Home Department, on Reviewing Government Organisation in Scotland, 9 February 1948.

The memorandum discloses a considerable variety both in the type of organisation maintained in Scotland by these Departments and in the rank and responsibilities of the officers in charge of them. Some variety of administrative organisation is to be expected from the variety of the functions exercised by different Departments; and some diversity of status among the Scottish heads of these Departments is inevitable in view of the diversity of responsibility. But the memorandum shows differences which are not thus accounted for. We find the Ministry of Works, for example, with an Under Secretary in charge of the whole of their organisations in Scotland and in a position to deal in Scotland with any question affecting the Department. In direct contrast we find the Ministry of Transport with no single officer in charge of their organisation in Scotland and with no officer at all in a position to deal authoritatively in Scotland with certain aspects of the Department's work. The Scottish officers of the Board of Trade and the Ministry of Supply have no responsibility for many aspects of the work of their Departments; and in the case of the Ministry of Supply [their Scottish office] is in charge of an officer of lower status than the Ministry of Works and there are branches of the Ministry's work which are not under that officer's control.

It seems clear that the Ministry of Works pattern is that to which it would be desirable that other Departments should, as far as possible, conform. One officer of high status is in charge of the whole of the Department's activities in Scotland and has a wide measure of delegated power. He can deal authoritatively in Scotland with any question affecting his Department; and he is of a rank to speak with authority in London in the shaping of his Department's policy.

The circumstances of other Departments differ, but their present arrangements have never, so far as is known, been reviewed against the background of Scottish aspirations to have Scottish affairs dealt with as far as possible in Scotland and considered by the Government on the policy level with full knowledge of Scottish conditions. The time for such a review seems opportune and [the] memorandum provides a factual basis on which it could be begun.

There are two long term problems to which I should also like to call attention.

(1) Sooner or later the allocation of Ministerial responsibility for Scottish business must be reviewed. The broad guiding principle [since 1885] has been to give the Secretary of State the kind of functions exercised in England and Wales by the Secretary of State for the Home Department and the Ministers of Health, Education, Agriculture and Fisheries and Town and Country Planning. But the principle has been applied in the light of changing circumstances and of political necessities; and no one would contend that the division of responsibility between the Secretary of State and other Ministers with functions in relation to Scotland is either wholly logical or necessarily right. There are certain functions of government—for example defence, foreign affairs, trade—which must be dealt with on a Great Britain basis; but there are many others apart from those exercised by the Secretary of State which could be separately discharged in Scotland. The ultimate solution may be to have the Secretary of State for Scotland as an extra Departmental Minister responsible in the Cabinet for a group of Scottish functional Ministers looking after the present Secretary of State Departments and also some of these now organised on a Great Britain basis.

(2) The administrative organisation of the Secretary of State's own Departments was last reviewed in 1937 by the Gilmour Committee. The time is coming when a further review might perhaps be considered. The transfer of the Secretary of State's responsibilities for national health insurance and widows', orphans' and old age pensions; the new arrangements about public assistance; the enormous expansion of the Secretary of State's responsibility for town and

country planning and for economic development; the assumption by the State of the whole responsibility for the national health service including hospital service; the greater measure of government concern with agriculture, forestry and fisheries; these and other developments suggest that the present layout of the Departments should be impartially considered. Such a review might well confirm the suitability of the present arrangements; but it would help to answer those who argue that the Secretary of State has too many disparate responsibilities by demonstrating that he has at any rate the right kind of machine for dealing with them. [SRO, HH1/1231.]

A SCOTTISH ECONOMICS MINISTER AND THE STATUS OF BRITISH DEPARTMENTAL OFFICERS IN SCOTLAND, 1948

Following the publication of the White Paper on Scottish Affairs (see above), Arthur Woodburn agreed that the Scottish Office should pursue with British Departments the issue of increasing the status and responsibility of their Scottish officers. After some inter-departmental correspondence a meeting was held between the Scottish Office and these Departments. The first extract is from the minute of the meeting. The second extract is from the subsequent letter of Sir David Milne, the Scottish Office Permanent Under Secretary of State, to Thomas Padmore, Under Secretary at the Treasury.

Note of Meeting between the Treasury, Board of Trade, Ministry of Labour, Ministry of Works and Scottish Office, on Scottish Administration, 15 December 1948.

Sir David Milne recalled recent correspondence and discussions on this subject, and summarised the reasons which had led the Scottish Office to ask that further consideration should be given to these matters. Although the population of Scotland was less than one-tenth of her neighbour's, Scotland was a country more than half the size of England and Wales, with separate laws, traditions and a sense of nationhood. A separate system of administration existed in the spheres to which the Secretary of State for Scotland was by law responsible. As regards other spheres, particularly those of trade and industry, there was a widespread feeling that for the efficient handling of Scottish affairs a substantial measure of devolution to organisations and offices in Scotland was essential. It did not follow that machinery which was appropriate for the various regions of England and Wales was necessarily adequate in relation to Scotland, It was important not only that Scottish people who had business with Great Britain Departments should be able to transact as much as possible in Scotland, but also that machinery should be seen to exist whereby the Great Britain Department, in framing and executing policy, was fully informed of the Scottish situation and took full account of Scottish needs. It was in the light of such considerations that the Scottish Economic Conference had recently been established by the Secretary of State. The Conference was, however, a consultative not an executive body and Scottish feeling in favour of executive devolution remained strong in relation to the Economic Departments. It was not suggested that this could be met merely by altering the status of officers of those Departments in Scotland, but it was hoped that the Departments would lose no possible opportunity of delegating further responsibilities to those officers and so justifying an improvement in their status.

Mr Kendrew outlined the arrangements in the Ministry of Works. He pointed out that the Scottish Under Secretary of that Department was in effect in charge of a separate Headquarters Department with an Assistant Secretary and three principals to assist him. He considered questions of policy affecting Scotland and had direct access to the Treasury. He kept in close touch with the officers of the Department in London, who were concerned with similar problems in England and Wales and submitted questions requiring Ministerial consideration through the Permanent Secretary of the Ministry. He was in quite a different position from the officer in charge of the regional organisation of the Ministry of Works in the various regions of England and Wales.

Mr Neden said that the Ministry of Labour had considered very fully and sympathetically the possibility of delegating further powers to their Scottish Regional Controller but had found it impossible to do so. They were quite clear that no distinction could be drawn between the status and responsibility of the Scottish Controller and those of the Controllers in England and Wales.

Sir James Helmore analysed the functions of the Board of Trade and said that while the Board would be willing to consider at a later date whether some special delegation of responsibility could be made to their Scottish Controller in connection e.g. with the census of distribution, they too were quite clear that no further powers could be delegated at present. They did not consider that it would ever be possible to delegate powers connected with external trade; their functions in relation to retail trade would contract if rationing were abolished; and they were satisfied that in the case of distribution of industry everything that could properly be delegated had already been assigned to the Scottish and Regional Controllers.

It was reported by the Scottish Office representatives that the Ministries responsible for the socialised industries of coal, electricity, gas and transport proposed to review their organisations in Scotland after the arrangement for the conduct of those industries had settled down. It was hoped that the Board of Trade, the Ministry of Labour and the Ministry of Supply would also give special attention, as opportunity offered, to the possibility of further measures of devolution to their Scottish offices.

Reference was made to resolutions passed by Scottish Trade Union interests in favour of the appointment of an additional Minister or Ministers to deal with industrial and economic problems in Scotland. The question whether a single junior Minister might in effect act as a Scottish Parliamentary Secretary to a number of Great Britain Departments, e.g. the Board of Trade, the Ministry of Labour and possibly the Ministry of Supply, was discussed. It was felt, however, that it would be difficult for such a Minister to supervise effectively the work in Scotland of several major Great Britain Departments. Moreover, the appointment of such a Minister or Ministers would make it necessary to reconsider the question of a Minister for Wales, which, after careful consideration by the Government, the Lord President had dismissed as impracticable. [PRO, T 222/1048.]

Letter of Sir David Milne, Permanent Under Secretary of State, the Scottish Office, to Thomas Padmore, Under Secretary, the Treasury, on Scottish Administration, 20 January 1949.

I have since had some talk with my Secretary of State about this. He anticipates that the increased scope of Government activity will make further devolution to Scottish offices inevitable, but he does not wish to pursue this question for the time being and he will be content if the considerations to which we referred are noted in the appropriate quarters in relation to the statement on the subject in Command 7038.

As regards the Ministerial question to which reference was made at our meeting, Mr. Woodburn does not consider that the appointment of a Scottish Parliamentary Secretary to a number of Scottish Departments would afford a satisfactory solution. [PRO, T 222/1048.]

LABOUR AND THE DEMAND FOR AN ENQUIRY INTO SCOTTISH AFFAIRS, 1949

During 1949 the 'Covenant' movement renewed their campaign for Home Rule and began to collect signatures for a petition. In November the matter was brought to a head when the Conservatives published their own proposals aimed at increasing Scottish 'administrative autonomy'. The extract here is from the memorandum by Arthur Woodburn, the Scottish Secretary, to the Cabinet on the issue. The Cabinet 'endorsed' the memorandum but remitted to the Socialised Industries Committee a review of the nationalised industries in Scotland. In January the Committee agreed to retain the existing administration, largely on the basis that miners feared that an autonomous Scottish Board would lose British investment and English markets.

Memorandum by Arthur Woodburn, Secretary of State for Scotland, on Scottish Affairs, 12 December 1949.

I think it right to let my colleagues know that the protagonists of Parliamentary devolution are at present very active in Scotland; but for the moment my view is that no further action by the Government is called for.

2. There have, of course, been nationalist parties of various kinds in Scotland for a long time; so far none of them has achieved a large membership or any great influence. Within the last few years a new body, calling itself 'Scottish Convention' has come into being. It represents itself as all-party in character, although only the Liberal and Communist Parties are officially represented. Its object is to bring about a measure of Scottish Home Rule. Since 1947 it has convened a 'Nationalist Assembly', to which has been submitted a scheme of Parliamentary Home Rule based on the Northern Ireland model but going, in certain respects, beyond it. This year the Assembly adopted a 'covenant'—which it is claimed 500,000 people have already signed—pledging support for the policy of the Convention. The promoters no doubt intend to submit the covenant in due course with as many signatures as they can collect, and they will seek to time this so as to cause the maximum embarrassment before the General Election.

3. The Labour Party in Scotland has, on several occasions in the past, pledged itself on the question of a separate Parliament for Scottish domestic affairs; and, at the last General Election, by adopting the official model election address issued by the Scottish Council of the Labour Party, a number of the present members did so specifically. More recently there have been demands at the Annual Conference of the Scottish Labour Party, and from other quarters, for an enquiry into the possibilities of Parliamentary and administrative devolution to Scotland and into the financial and economic relationships between Scotland and the rest of Great Britain. At the Scottish Labour Party Conferences, 1945-7, resolutions in favour of such an enquiry were carried; but in 1948 the Conference decided that a fair trial should be given to the policy set out in the Government's White Paper on Scottish Affairs (Command 7308). At the Conference of this year the 1948 decision was endorsed and a further resolution in favour of an enquiry was overwhelmingly defeated because the Party were determined not to allow this issue to confuse the real conflict at the General Election.

4. On the main question of Scottish Home Rule, I have, since I became Secretary of State, taken and expressed strongly the view that the present time is not opportune for its consideration; and that indeed those who are pressing for it are doing Britain a dis-service abroad at the time when Britain's united influence is a vital factor in the safeguarding of world democracy. I have indicated that the Government are anxious to meet the reasonable desire of all

Parties in Scotland for a closer oversight of Scottish affairs. In pursuance of that policy, as set out in Command 7308, we have arranged for the Scottish Estimates to be debated in the Scottish Grand Committee, and for the second reading of certain Bills to be discussed there; and through the setting up of the Scottish Economic Conference representatives of all the main bodies concerned with the economic life of Scotland have been brought together under my chairmanship.

So far as they have gone, these arrangements are accepted as having worked well and fulfilled a need.

5. As regards the demand for an enquiry into the financial and economic position, I have so far resisted it on the ground that what factual information there is reasonably available at present is already published; that the investigation of the financial relations between Scotland and the rest of Great Britain would involve a serious diversion of effort and would produce results necessarily based, to some extent, on conjecture; and that any further factual information about industry north and south of the Border must await the results of the Census of Production and the Census of Distribution. In the meantime I have undertaken to publish annually—and have done so for each of the past three years—a White Paper about Scotland's economic position in which available statistics are set out; and we have also arranged to publish in the near future a handbook outlining the present administrative business in Scotland.

6. The position of the other political parties is that the Liberals are committed to Home Rule for Scotland and that the Conservatives are not. The Conservatives' position has just been explained in a document, obviously for use at the General Election. They reject the idea of a separate Scottish Parliament at present but promise to appoint a Royal Commission to review the whole position as between Scotland and England in the light of modern developments, and to make recommendations. What the recommendations are to be about is not clear; but the main campaign has been directed against the 'London' control of the nationalised industries and of former local authority undertakings. The Conservatives meanwhile propose a second Scottish Minister of Cabinet rank who would be mainly resident in Scotland and would act as the Secretary of State's Deputy over the whole field. They also want a third Parliamentary Under-secretary of State for Scotland—probably in the Lords. As regards the nationalised industries—the establishment of which on a Great Britain basis has been widely criticised in Scotland—they propose an all-Scottish Electricity Board answerable to the Secretary of State; a Gas Commission also answerable to the Secretary of State, which would supervise and co-ordinate the work of the various gas undertakings—over which local authorities would be allowed to resume responsibility if they wanted to; a Scottish Railways Board somehow integrated with the British Transport Commission; and an independent Scottish

Coal Board equal in status to the English Board. In the case of civil aviation they contemplate some restoration of private enterprise and promise an enquiry into the position including the question of the development of Prestwick as an international airport. Prestwick has all along been made a symbol of nationalist agitation.

7. The subjects of Scottish Home Rule and of a commission of enquiry are bound to be widely canvassed at the forthcoming General Election; and, while our MPs. have agreed to concentrate on the inter-party issues, I must report that in some cases I have persuaded them against their will and that some are genuinely apprehensive of this campaign. On the other hand, I anticipate that, with the Conservative declaration, the Press in Scotland will moderate their 'plugging' of devolution.

8. *Subject to the views of my colleagues, my intention is to stand on the line I have indicated in paragraphs 4 and 5 of this paper.*

9. These campaigns obtain their success because interest in the subject in Scotland is always present, widespread and sincere. It is accordingly essential that every support should be given to the great body of reasonable opinion in Scotland which does not support drastic changes but which is liable to be shaken by any action which can be represented as imposing on Scotland decisions in the making of which she appears to have had no real voice, or as being designed primarily to meet conditions south of the Border. I hope my colleagues will keep this danger in mind and be vigilant when they are dealing with matters affecting Scotland. I think it is also true to say that there have been occasions in which decisions concerning Scotland, which could not be questioned on merits, have been announced in a way which made it possible to misrepresent them. My own Department have a good deal of experience of the problem of presenting things to public opinion in Scotland in the best light; and they will, of course, be very ready to co-operate at any time in regard to the timing and form of announcements of Scottish interests. [PRO, CAB 129/37 CP (49) 251; SRO, HH41/454.]

LABOUR AND AN ENQUIRY INTO ANGLO-SCOTTISH FINANCIAL RELATIONSHIPS, 1950

Within a few days of becoming Scottish Secretary in March 1950, Hector McNeil met and agreed with his Scottish Ministers on the need for an enquiry into Anglo-Scottish financial relationships. At that time the 'Covenant' movement had obtained over a million signatures to a petition calling for legislative devolution. The first extract is from McNeil's letter to Sir Stafford Cripps, the Chancellor of the Exchequer, seeking his support for an enquiry. The second and third are their consequent replies. The fourth is from McNeil's Cabinet memorandum, adjusted after a meeting with Cripps who suggested the possibility of an enquiry into financial relationships. The fifth extract is from the subsequent Cabinet minute. After two further meetings the Cabinet decided that there was no case for legislative devolution, that the Covenant 'Commissioners' should see only the Scottish Secretary and not the Prime Minister, and approved the appointment of a Committee under the Chairmanship of Lord Catto, a former Governor of the Bank of England, to examine the practicability of producing a financial return on Anglo-Scottish financial relationships. The matter of the Electricity Board was included in the memorandum after some prompting from the Cabinet Office.

Letter of Hector McNeil, Secretary of State for Scotland, to Sir Stafford Cripps, Chancellor of the Exchequer, on Scottish Affairs, 29 March 1950.

I enclose a copy of a paper which I propose to circulate to the Cabinet as soon as is reasonable. It is for the publication of a statement of the relationship of Scottish revenue and expenditure to revenue and expenditure of the United Kingdom.

Although I gather that there has been some friendly discussion between your officials and the officials of the Scottish Office I understand that you still maintain the opposition which you indicated in a conversation with me. I take it that the basis of your opposition is that this involves a disproportionate amount of labour and that the results at any rate would not placate the Scottish population. On the first point, of course, I really can make no good judgement. I should be surprised if your Office found it at all an exacting task. On the second point, however, I am competent and I think in every respect you are wrong.

The vast majority of the Scottish people have always had a traditional respect for facts and if the enquiry displayed as I think no doubt it will display that the Scottish people were not being unfairly and perhaps even generously treated that would meet a great deal of criticism. It is not the extremists in Scotland who worry and who embarrass us politically, it is the impression among the population which the extremists have to some degree created precisely because there was a lack of information.

I therefore hope that you will be good enough to reconsider your position and at any rate I should be indebted if you permitted me an opportunity to come and talk to you before I circulate the paper. [SRO, HH41/454.]

Letter of Sir Stafford Cripps, Chancellor of the Exchequer, to Hector McNeil, Secretary of State for Scotland, on Scottish Affairs, 3 April 1950.

I have been into the question raised in your letter of March 29th and the draft paper you enclosed.

The 1935 paper was largely meaningless as it had no logical basis whatever. Fortunately in those days people were not so interested in the accuracy of Government as they are today!

We could get figures together on a similar basis with a tremendous expenditure of time and energy including the demand of certain statistics from Traders. Those used in 1935 were 31 years out of date and could hardly be used again!

I am advised that it would be quite impossible to defend the figures as anything but figures arrived at on a purely arbitrary basis.

The following methods were used for instance in arriving at different parts of Customs Revenue.

(1) For the major part, population proportions of the total were taken! That is it was assumed there was an equal incidence per head in the two countries.

(2) By revenue collected in Scotland, which may or may not have related to goods used in Scotland.

(3) For spirits only by reference to the quantities retained for consumption in each country.

(4) For Beer only by statistics collected from the Trade. (These were the ones then 31 years out of date!)

The I.R. figures are no more reliably based. You will readily see that such figures could not be defended for a moment as giving any worthwhile result. They would be shot down in flames!

I hope therefore you will desist from any further effort to get figures which must be completely valueless and which will nevertheless waste much valuable time and energy that might otherwise be used to increase the Revenue collected. [SRO, HH41/454.]

Letter of Hector McNeil, Secretary of State for Scotland, to Sir Stafford Cripps, Chancellor of the Exchequer, on Scottish Affairs, 6 April 1950.

I need hardly say that I am greatly disappointed by your letter of the 3rd April about the proposal to get out a return of Scottish revenue and expenditure.

I appreciate the trouble you have taken in going into the matter and I am not unmindful of the various difficulties you mention in your reply. I am deeply convinced, however, that the demands in Scotland for information of the kind I have suggested is so strong that we can no longer afford to disregard it. It is a demand which is being made by all shades of opinion and not least by those who have not yet committed themselves to the Scottish Covenant. As recent illustrations of the feeling on the matter I may refer to the speech made yesterday by the Lord Provost of Edinburgh to the annual meeting of the Convention of Royal Burghs in Edinburgh in which he went out of his way to emphasise the need for the fullest knowledge about Scotland's financial position before coming to any conclusion about the case for a Scottish Parliament on the model recommended by the Scottish Convention. In a supplementary Question in the House of Commons yesterday Henderson Stewart made the point that the demand for a financial return was universal in Scotland; and as you are perhaps aware all the Scottish Conservative members are trying to get a place in the ballot in the hope of being able to discuss the question of devolution later in the session. The Conservatives' official programme includes, of course, the proposal for the setting up of a Royal Commission to enquire into the whole relationship between England and Scotland with particular reference to finance.

I feel quite sure that against this background the Government cannot maintain the purely negative attitude we have hitherto adopted. If we do we must say in effect that the Government is unable to ascertain even approximately what Scotland is contributing to taxation and what Scottish services are costing the Exchequer. I have no doubt at all that to go on taking this line can do us nothing but harm in Scotland where it will be regarded by all moderate opinion as completely unreasonable. I am therefore very strongly in favour of proceeding with the preparation of a return on the best basis that we can devise. [SRO, HH41/454.]

Memorandum by Hector McNeil, Secretary of State for Scotland, on Scottish Affairs, 11 May 1950.

Apart from the 'Covenant' the Opposition are likely to press their own proposal in regard to Scottish Administration. Very briefly they want (a) to increase by two the number of Scottish Ministers, (b) to reorganise the nationalised industries and establish wherever possible separate and autonomous boards for Scotland, and (c) to set up a Royal Commission 'to review the whole situation between England and Scotland in the light of modern developments, and to make recommendations'.

So far as concerns the number of Ministers, I think we can take the line that the Government are keeping the position under review but that we are not convinced that there is any immediate necessity for an increase. As regards the nationalised industries, experience of the arrangements now in operation is still limited. In reply to criticism we have hitherto stressed the extent to which Scotland already has autonomous boards and the arrangements made in other cases to devolve responsibility to Scotland: and we have undertaken to keep careful watch on the way in which the arrangements so recently made are working in practice. But I have no doubt that feeling on this subject in Scotland is strong. I have been giving the whole position close consideration and I think we are particularly vulnerable in the case of electricity where responsibility is partly in the hands of an autonomous Scottish Board answerable to the Scottish Secretary and partly in the hands of the British Electricity Authority and two Area Boards responsible to the Minister of Fuel and Power. I propose to discuss this matter further with the Minister and if necessary to bring proposals before my colleagues for consideration.

It is when we come to the question of the financial and economic relations of Scotland to the rest of Great Britain, however, that I feel some immediate action is necessary. In the face of the 'Covenant' and in the circumstances of the new House of Commons I do not think we can continue to take a completely negative attitude in the Conservatives' proposal for a Royal Commission of Enquiry which is strongly supported by the Press and by moderate people who have not committed themselves to the Home Rule movement. However since we rejected this proposal before the Election I do not suggest that we should now accept it. But I think we must deal with the demand for up-to-date information showing how far in the matter of Government expenditure Scotland is standing on her own two feet. Information about this is clearly relevant to any examination of Home Rule proposals.

It seems to me practicable therefore that the least we do is to examine impartially the practicability of a financial return of the kind that is being asked for keeping in view the availability of information, the amount of work involved, and the value and reliability of any statistics obtained. [PRO, CAB 129/40 CP (50)101; SRO, HH41/454.]

Cabinet Conclusions on Scottish Affairs, 15 May 1950.

THE SECRETARY OF STATE FOR SCOTLAND said that the promoters of the Scottish 'Covenant' had asked the Prime Minister to receive a deputation of Commissioners from the 'Scottish National Assembly'. The resolution passed by the Assembly had referred to 'negotiations' between their Commissioners and the Government, and it should be made clear in any reply that the Government could not regard the Assembly as competent to 'negotiate' with the Government. The Opposition were not in favour of the Assembly's plan for a Scottish Parliament for domestic affairs, and it was understood that the Leader of the Opposition might be unwilling to meet the Commissioners. It was difficult to appraise the degree of public support behind the Covenant, notwithstanding the considerable number of signatures which had been secured. There was undoubtedly some restlessness in Scotland about the organisation of Government, but whether the Covenant represented a solution which would retain a substantial body of support in Scotland was a more debatable matter. The Scottish group of Labour Members of Parliament had recently asked that a Minister of State for Scottish Housing should be appointed, but he proposed to explain to them that he saw no advantage in dividing the present responsibilities of the Secretary of State, and that a multiplication of junior Ministers would not yield any satisfactory results.

In discussion it was pointed out that nationalist movements of the kind fostered by the Scottish National Assembly were out of accord with the current movement for increased integration in Europe. Moreover, any concession to a nationalist movement of this kind was likely to lead merely to further demands, both in Scotland and also Wales. At the same time it might be undesirable for the Government to appear to show discourtesy to the Commissioners, since this might cause resentment in Scotland. It might, therefore, be desirable for the Prime Minister to receive the Commissioners, though he would have to use the occasion to draw their attention to the weakness of their case and to the arguments against setting up a Scottish parliament for domestic affairs. It was felt, however, that it would be of assistance to the Cabinet to know whether the Scottish Members of Parliament who supported the Government were in favour of the Commissioners being received, either by the Prime Minister or by the Secretary of State.

The Cabinet agreed—(1) Invited the Secretary of State for Scotland to ascertain the views of Government supporters in the House of Commons on the manner in which the request of the Commissioners from the Scottish National Assembly for an interview with the Prime Minister should be handled. (2) Invited the Secretary of State for Scotland to submit a memorandum, showing the composition which he had in mind for the proposed committee to examine the practicability of producing a return of Scottish revenue and expenditure and an economic balance sheet for Scotland. (3) Agreed to resume their discussion of Scottish affairs at their next meeting. [PRO, CAB 128/17 CM 4(50)31.]

THE ORGANISATION OF ELECTRICITY SUPPLY IN SCOTLAND, 1952

The extract here is from the Memorandum by James Stuart, the Scottish Secretary, to the Cabinet's Home Affairs Committee on the issue of honouring the Conservative Party's Election commitment to re-organise the Scottish electricity industry. The Committee agreed that inter-departmental discussion could begin on introducing the necessary legislation. After nationalisation, consumers in the South-Eastern Area had had their tariffs increased to equalise them with rates in the North of England.

Memorandum by James Stuart, Secretary of State for Scotland, on the Organisation of Electricity Supply in Scotland, 8 February 1952.

I ask authority to frame proposals, in consultation with the Minister of Fuel and Power, for the reorganisation of electricity supply in Scotland. Broadly, what I should like to do is:-

(a) to transfer ministerial responsibility from the Minister to the Secretary of State;

(b) to make the three existing Scottish Electricity Boards 'all-purpose' electricity authorities;

(c) to set up a Scottish Electricity Council with limited powers to co-ordinate the work of the three Boards and settle points of difference between them.

Before submitting firm proposals for approval I should like, after any further interdepartmental consultations which may be required, to discuss the position in confidence, in conjunction with the Minister, with representatives of the British Electricity Authority and the three Scottish Boards.

At present the North of Scotland Hydro-Electric Board is responsible for the generation, transmission and distribution of electricity throughout the whole of the North of Scotland District. This District consists broadly of that part of Scotland lying to the north and north-west of a line drawn from Dumbarton to the Firth of Tay. The Board is appointed by the Minister and myself acting jointly but is in other respects responsible to me. Outside the North of Scotland District the responsibility for generating and transmitting electricity belongs to the British Electricity Authority as in England and Wales and the responsibility for distributing electricity belongs, subject to the general control of the British Electricity Authority, to the South-East and South-West Scotland Area Electricity Boards. The British Electricity Authority and the two Area Boards are appointed by the Minister and ministerial responsibility for them rests with him.

When the Bill for the Electricity Act of 1947 was before Parliament these arrangements were strongly criticised by the Conservative Opposition. It was argued that if Scottish Autonomy was possible in the North of Scotland District it should be possible in the whole country; and that it would be in accordance with Conservative policy and Scottish wishes to concede it. This argument seems to me irresistible; and it was in fact adopted in the statement of Conservative policy in relation to Scotland which was prepared in 1949 by a Committee, of which I was Chairman, and published under the title 'Scottish Control of Scottish Affairs'. This statement was explicitly endorsed in the general statement of Conservative and Unionist policy issued before the recent Election and has been widely publicised and welcomed in Scotland. I feel no doubt that its promise of legislation amending the Electricity Acts on the broad lines I am suggesting must be implemented.

In 1947 the inclusion of the southern half of Scotland in the area of the British Electricity Authority was defended on the ground that the supply of electricity and, in particular, the operation of the grid are of a nature which makes it unnecessary and indeed undesirable to recognise the Anglo-Scottish boundary. The position of the Highlands was distinguished partly on the ground that the Hydro-Electric Board had been recently established and ought to be allowed to prosecute the rather specialised work on which it had started and partly on the ground that in the Highlands the supply of electricity has social and economic significance different from that which it has in other parts of the country. While I regard it as important to maintain the special powers and responsibilities of the Hydro-Electric Board, I do not consider that the technical arguments for associating the rest of Scotland with England and Wales justify the political disadvantage of leaving the industry in Scotland under the control of the British Electricity Authority, whose major interests are necessarily in England and Wales and whose headquarters are in London. Difficulties between the Authority and the Hydro-Electric Board and between the Authority and the South-East Scotland Area Board have been considerable and the latter have given rise to much public criticism. There must obviously be close technical co-operation between the British Electricity Authority and the new Scottish Electricity Council which I propose should be set up, but I believe that this and any necessary transmission of electricity between one country and the other can be arranged by agreement between the two bodies whose interests need in no way conflict.

I have discussed these proposals with the Minister of Fuel and Power and he authorises me to say that he does not dissent from them. [PRO, CAB 134/909 HA(52)29.]

ADMINISTRATIVE DECENTRALISATION AND THE ROYAL COMMISSION ON SCOTTISH AFFAIRS, 1952

In June 1952 the Catto Committee on Anglo-Scottish financial relations reported and recommended that it was possible to produce a financial return on Scottish economic affairs. At the same time the Conservative Government, which had already appointed a Minister of State and a third Parliamentary Under-Secretary at the Scottish Office, felt obliged to continue its review of pre-election commitments. The following extract is from the Scottish Secretary's memorandum to the Cabinet on the issue. The Cabinet agreed with Stuart's proposal and Lord Balfour was subsequently appointed the Royal Commission's chairman.

Memorandum by James Stuart, Secretary of State for Scotland, on Scottish Affairs, 24 June 1952.

We undertook in our 1949 policy statement 'Scottish Control of Scottish Affairs' to set up a Royal Commission 'to review the whole situation between Scotland and England in the light of modern developments, and to make recommendations'. In our pre-election statement 'Britain Strong and Free' we reaffirmed the 1949 undertaking, saying that our policy included 'the appointment of a Royal Commission to review the economic relations between England and Scotland together with other important issues'. I have undertaken 'to consider the terms of reference of the Royal Commission as soon as the Report of the Catto Committee has been considered'. I am clear, therefore, that a Royal Commission must be appointed.

Terms of Reference

There are two questions which must be excluded. First, it would be inappropriate to ask a Royal Commission to consider the case for and against a Scottish Parliament and I have already said that this is a matter for Parliament itself. Secondly, in view of the findings of the Catto Committee there is now no point in asking the Commission to inquire further into the economic relationship between Scotland and England.

As regards the questions to be included, I think we must ask the Commission to consider the adequacy of the present machinery for exercising the Government's functions in relation to Scotland; and I propose that the Commission should be asked to review this against the general financial, economic and administrative background of the present day and in the light of such other considerations as may be put before it. The Commission will thus be able to consider whether or not any further administrative decentralisation is desirable and practicable, and in doing so to take full account of the considerations which have led to the demand for a Parliament as well as those which point in the opposite directions. This is necessary if the purpose of having a Commission is to be achieved. I would expect industrial and commercial interests, local authorities and trade unions, when giving evidence before and against the Commission, to come out strongly against any separatist ideas and against any proposal for change which would not lead to greater efficiency in the conduct of public administration.

It may be arguable as to whether to go further and ask the Commission to deal with the structure of nationalised industries. On the one hand there is no doubt that recent Scottish complaints of undue centralisation and London control are largely due to the organisation of the nationalised industries; and it may be argued that the Commission will be an ineffective answer to the criticisms if its terms of reference exclude some of the main subjects of criticism. On the other hand, it is difficult to see how the Commission could usefully examine the structure of nationalised industries at a time when surface transport and civil aviation policy is being modified, when steel is being restored to private enterprise and when legislation about Scottish electricity supply is in view. There is the further point that if the terms of reference cover nationalised industries we may be pressed to extend them further to include private industry. I shall be glad to have the guidance of my colleagues on this question. On the whole, I am in favour of limiting the Commission to consideration of the machinery of government. [PRO, CAB 129/53 C(52)212; SRO, HH41/1391.]

THE TREASURY, THE SCOTTISH OFFICE AND THE STATUS OF BRITISH DEPARTMENTAL OFFICERS, 1953

The following extract is from the evidence of Sir Edward Bridges, Permanent Secretary, the Treasury and Head of the Home Civil Service, to the Royal Commission on Scottish Affairs in 1953. Bridges gave the evidence, held in private before public examination, because of concern that the Commission had become overtly interested in questions of economic devolution. All witnesses received a note of the Commission's brief and its appreciation of Scottish administration in an appendix to their invitation.

Evidence (held in private) of Sir Edward Bridges, Permanent Secretary, the Treasury and Head of Home Civil Service, to the Royal Commission on Scottish Affairs, 8 July 1953.

Q. [Lord Balfour] It is fair to say that in our evidence there are no substantial criticisms of the organisation of the Secretary of State's departments. Nor have we found any substantial criticism of the working of the Scottish branches of the Great Britain departments other than the Ministry of Transport and the Trade and Industry departments, and to a less extent the Ministries of Civil Aviation and Fuel and Power. It is alleged in particular that the Scottish Controllers of these departments have insufficient executive authority within which they can authorise expenditure. Secondly, it is alleged that their duties are largely executive and advisory and that although they may be consulted on the Scottish aspects of policy they have little real share in its determination. It seems to us that measures to meet this criticism may be taken in two ways, one by providing for increased delegation to Scottish Controllers of Great Britain departments, or by transferring the particular functions in question to the Secretary of State. We have attempted to set out the arguments in principle in favour of either of these courses, and I think you have seen that.—A. I have been able to see them.

Q. We would be most grateful to have your reactions and comments on them.—A. First, if I may say so, I think it is significant that you feel that the area in which there is this criticism is limited to the trade and industry departments. That is the area of real difficulty, I think.

Q. And Transport.—A. Yes, I meant trade and industry in the widest sense. So far as transport is concerned I hope that the suggestion I made about roads will be of some help. But to come to the general problem ... there is one point I would like to comment on, and that is in 2(ii)(a) of the Appendix. You refer to the range of responsibilities and say:- 'While the range of [the Scottish Secretary's] responsibilities is extremely diverse, the volume of work involved in the exercise of any one function is small in comparison with that of the corresponding English ministry'. I am not sure whether 'volume of work' does not perhaps cover two different things. If you mean the volume of individual cases, obviously it is true, but when you come down to issues of policy I am not sure that the argument holds. If, for instance, you have to frame policy on rent restriction, or amend your policy on rent restriction, it is just as difficult in Scotland as in England, and the fact that you have a smaller country does not make it any easier. That brings me to this point. I rather feel—of course I am only speaking at second or third hand—that the burden on the Secretary of State is already a pretty heavy one, and his ultimate responsibility to Parliament and the Cabinet cannot be relieved beyond a certain point by further Ministerial assistance. I would myself doubt whether there is room for remedying the situation very much by further transfers to the Secretary of State. There may be a case for it in this particular instance or that, but I would not think that any really substantial transfer of additional powers to him was a feasible proposition. Then that brings one back to the first alternative—increased delegation to their Scottish officers by the Great Britain departments. That is certainly something which should be watched in any reviews of the regional system, and we should do what we can. But I am not quite sure that I feel there is not another alternative which in form is different from either of your two. I believe that there is room for making great progress, not so much by further formal devolution of powers, but by really making certain that the existing system works as well as it can be made to work. What I have in mind is that much more attention should be paid—this is mainly something for the Great Britain departments—to the personal factor, and we should make the most strenuous efforts to see that we send the best possible people to be Controllers in Scotland at the regional offices. I believe that a lot could be done in that way and one ought to have a concerted drive in all departments. What I would like to see is all departments making a point of sending up to Scotland to be their regional controllers some of the brightest and picked men of their young administrators, and that it ought to be very much a feather in the man's cap that he has been sent up here to be Scottish controller. At the present moment people feel rather flattered if they are chosen to be sent for a course at the Imperial Defence College and perhaps sometimes people have been pleased if they have been seconded to the Treasury for a period, but I want them to be jolly proud of being picked to come up to Scotland and do a tour of duty here. If you pick the most lively and alert administrators I think the first result would be that you would get people who are not merely interested in settling the day to day questions, but being people whose career will mostly be spent in policy questions they would naturally be interested to find out the Scottish reactions to the policy questions their departments were handling and they would also act as ambassadors or liaison officers, whatever you like to call it, to explain their departments' views to Scottish opinion. I believe that you would get much more life and vigour in the system.

Then also—greatly daring—I want to suggest this. Hitherto I think we have been rather too disposed to feel that when it is a question of choosing somebody to be controller in Scotland you first of all look for a Scotsman. I am not sure that is right. I think some of the trouble arises from the fact that people in Edinburgh and Glasgow feel they do not know the head people in Great Britain Departments, they do not know who they are, and they feel they are out of touch. But supposing after you had this system really working for some years you got the position where, say the Permanent Secretary of the Ministry of Fuel and Power had served a tour up here, I think it would have a very good effect on the department concerned and I think might have some effect on the people up here who would feel that they had a friend at court, somebody who understood their problems, and that is the sort of line on which I would like to see this tackled.... I believe that would bring more change and more rapidly than a formal devolution of powers. In this country we do not make progress by written constitutions, we gradually get the machine to work in the right way or in a different kind of way and we alter the constitutions to fit the facts afterwards.

Q. I do not know what the views of my fellow Commissioners on your suggestion would be but personally I find it an attractive one. There is the second point, that I think we have got to do something which will be recognised as giving Scotland, within the framework of the Great Britain Departments, a rather special position, because I think it is entitled to rather a special position. We are after all a little bit different from one of the English regions. We are a country, and we have sentiments, some of them regrettable perhaps just now, but I think something would have to be done to show that Parliament recognised that Scotland had a rather special position in this matter.

What would be your reaction to making the post of controller in Scotland slightly senior to the post of a regional controller in England? A. Here I am very glad that you have told me I can speak frankly and without being quoted. I discussed this recently with the Permanent Secretaries of a number of departments concerned, and all of them agreed to play on the suggestion which I have put ... But when I put to them the suggestion that a slightly higher status than Assistant Secretary might be called for, the general reaction was that they do not see the need for a higher status in Edinburgh than in some of the other regional capitals, if I may use the expression. That puts me in a very awkward position. The Treasury's duty is to sanction expenditure where necessary and where departments ask for it, but where departments do not ask for it, and where they say 'We cannot do something in Edinburgh without doing it in Manchester or Birmingham', you can see what a delicate and awkward position I am in.

MR GUILLEBAUD: As a matter of fact there are one or two departments at the present moment who have Under-Secretaries here in Scotland, although the great majority of them are of Assistant Secretary level. From the point of view of the Civil Service, one of the most important things is that the Scottish Controller shall have a real voice in questions of policy, major questions of policy, but is he not much more likely to have that if he has the status of Under-Secretary than if he has the status of Assistant Secretary? Is not the Under-Secretary's scope for taking part in policy decisions and policy questions greater than that of the Assistant Secretary?—A. I am afraid I have always felt that it really matters what the man is like, or whether he is determined to have his way. Perhaps that is because I was so very naughty when I was myself a junior officer. I do not really believe the rank matters as much as all that. What matters is to pick the really good man, the man who is a flier and is going far, but do not take it I am, so to speak, being sticky about this grading point, which is not an expensive one. I am in an awkward position.

SIR HUGH CHANCE: I would like to come back to the position of the Secretary of State. Sir Edward has made the point that submissions to the Secretary of State may not be large but many of them involve separate decisions on policy and they take a great deal of time. Does he think the Secretary of State is overloaded, and if he is, is it possible constitutionally to have another Minister not sitting in the Cabinet but with specific responsibilities allocated to him, perhaps with the Secretary of State keeping a general oversight of what happens in his department because he is recognised as the Cabinet Minister with a general over sight of Scottish affairs. Is that practical or desirable?—A. I would have thought that one of the linch-pins, so to speak, of our system is that you define the Ministers who are responsible for particular functions. I do not think you can have it both ways with one Minister who is responsible under the general supervision of another. I do not think that would work in Parliament. I think you either have the Secretary of State responsible for the lot, or you have a division and have, so to speak, the Secretary of State in duplicate.

Q. Would it be practicable to divide it up, for instance to have a Minister who is responsible for home affairs and agriculture, which you would remove from the Secretary of State? The Secretary of State would still have general oversight but there would be somebody of Ministerial status, though not within the Cabinet, who would have specific responsibility to Parliament for those sections at present under the Secretary of State, and so relieve the burden on the Secretary of State of the large number of individual questions for which he is responsible at present.—A. It is possible, but I should have thought you would have lost something. You have the advantage that you have one Minister who is responsible for the whole field, and once you put another Minister who is responsible alongside him you relieve the work but I think you lose something.

CHAIRMAN: You would weaken the Secretary of State's position as Scotland's Minister.—A. You would weaken his position as Scotland's Minister, and my feeling is that unless you are going to put a great deal more upon him which would make it essential to divide it you would lose more than you would gain by weakening his position by cutting him into two, but that is not a point for me. [SRO, HH41/690.]

THE STATUS OF SCOTTISH REPRESENTATIVES OF U.K. DEPARTMENTS, 1954

In March 1954 the Home Department received the draft report of the Royal Commission on Scottish Affairs. The report laid great stress on improving the status of British Departmental officers in Scotland. The first extract is from the minute of Sir Charles Cunningham, Secretary of the Department, on the issue. The second extract is from the Cabinet Memorandum by James Stuart, the Scottish Secretary, after he had received the final Report, which the Cabinet broadly accepted. The third is from a Board of Trade minute on what action it proposed to take to increase the status of its Scottish officers. Stuart accepted the proposal.

Minute of Sir Charles C. Cunningham, Secretary, the Scottish Home Department, on the Draft Report of the Royal Commission on Scottish Affairs, 19 March 1954.

Another general question which seems to me to raise itself again on reading the Report in this fairly comprehensive form is the position of the principal Scottish representatives of the Great Britain Departments. The Report brings out very properly that we want these people to be of good quality and status and to have as much delegated responsibility as possible. It emphasises, again very properly, that they have the duty not only of carrying on administration in Scotland but of keeping their Departments informed of Scottish needs and opinions. There is, however, some danger that critics may read into the Report a recommendation of a purely bureaucratic system of administration in Scotland in which all but the most major issues of policy are handled here by young Assistant Secretaries. It may be difficult to correct this impression without getting the emphasis wrong in other respects. I think, however, that Mr. Pottinger [the Commission's Secretary] might try to bring out more clearly that it is of cardinal importance that the Great Britain and U.K. Ministers concerned should accept the same personal responsibility for the Scottish business of their Departments as they do for the business relating to England and Wales. Accordingly, the problem is really to establish for each Department in Scotland an organisation capable of dealing with, so to speak, the Scottish customers of that Department; of disposing of as many administrative problems on the spot as the settled policy of the Department concerned allows; and, for the rest, of securing the necessary decisions quickly from the responsible Minister. If, for example, we take the parallel of an insurance company with its Headquarters in Edinburgh and a branch office in London, one would expect the branch office in London to be so organised that it could deal with all the business of the company which arises in London. It might well be that the branch office would from time to time have to take instructions from its Scottish Headquarters and its Scottish Headquarters would have to keep itself fully in touch with the London business; but these are really domestic matters. From the point of view of the customer, the relationship is in London with the branch office there.

The analogy cannot be complete because in the matter of central administration the personal responsibility of the Minister is more direct than that of the head of a business concern and the right of access to him is likely to be more continuously asserted. Nevertheless, I think we will all agree that the Great Britain Department should, to the fullest extent, have an organisation in Scotland accepting responsibility for the handling of all aspects of the Department's business, even if in a considerable number of individual cases a decision has to be obtained from the Headquarters, or from the Minister, of the Department in London. We ourselves have had some personal experience of this problem and its solution in the '30's when the Secretary of State's Edinburgh office was first opened. [SRO, HH41/853.]

Memorandum by James Stuart, Secretary of State for Scotland, on the Report of the Royal Commission on Scottish Affairs, 15 July 1954.

The main recommendations in their Report are that the Ministerial responsibility for the exercise of the following functions of government in relation to Scotland should be transferred to the Secretary of State:- (a) the responsibility of the Ministry of Transport and Civil Aviation for roads, including the construction, maintenance and classification of highways; (b) the Lord Chancellor's responsibility for the appointment of Justices of the Peace; (c) the responsibility of the Ministry of Agriculture and Fisheries for animal health.

The Committee also propose that the status of the Scottish representatives of U.K. Departments should be improved and their responsibilities increased. [PRO, CAB 129/69 C(54)223; SRO, HH41/860.]

Memorandum by Sir Frank Lee, Permanent Secretary, the Board of Trade, on Scottish Industrial Estates: Devolution of Authority to the Board of Trade Controller in Scotland, 15 November 1954.

The President will remember that, under pressure from the Treasury and the Scottish Office, he has reluctantly agreed that the Board of Trade Controller in Scotland should be given extended authority (not to be given, at any rate at the start, to Controllers elsewhere) in respect of (i) the allocation of existing factory space, and (ii) the approval of capital expenditure on extensions to factories.

The extended powers in respect of the allocation of existing factory space will enable the Controller to allocate to tenants on his own authority about two-thirds by number of the factories falling vacant in Scotland. It is right to say, however, that these will be the small factories, since he is *not* to have authority to allocate factories of more than 20,000 square feet. A good many standard factories in Scotland and elsewhere are more than 20,000 square feet in area, but it would be manifestly wrong *not* to bring such factories into the general picture so far as the choosing of tenants is concerned.

It is possible that critics will argue that we ought to go further into the devolution of authority in this field. But, in point of fact, our figures of 20,000 square feet as the limit compares with one of 5,000 square feet given in the report of the Royal Commission, so that we have a good answer.

As regards authority to approve capital expenditure, we propose to give the Controller authority to approve expenditure up to £20,000 on any extension to an individual factory. This compares with a 'nil' authority which existed at the time of the Commission's deliberations (and which is referred to in their Report), although at a later date we gave all Controllers authority up to £10,000.

We are confining the authority to expenditure on extensions and are *not* giving it in respect of expenditure on brand new factories. As the President will be aware, it is primarily in respect of new constructions that difficult policy issues (re-housing, etc.) arise, and we think it essential to keep central control in this field. [SRO, HH41/860.]

THE PRACTICABILITY OF CREATING A DEVELOPMENT DEPARTMENT, 1959

In October 1957, Sir David Milne, the Permanent Under Secretary of State, established a Committee of Heads of Department to review the functional responsibility and relationship of the Scottish Departments to each other. In particular the review was to assess the advantage of having the planning functions of the Health Department and the roads, industry and employment functions of the Home Department within one Department. The first extract is from a joint Memorandum by the Health and Home Departments, produced after objections from the Home Department on amalgamation. The second extract is from Milne's final Report. The Scottish Secretary, John Maclay, approved the Report and in April 1960 a limited redistribution of functions between Departments was implemented, including Fisheries and Highland matters from the Home Department to the Department of Agriculture.

Memorandum by the Scottish Department of Health and the Home Department, on the Administration of the Town and Country Planning, Highways and Industrial Functions of the Scottish Office, 5 June 1959.

In view of the cognate nature of the town and country planning, highways and industrial functions ... it is evidently desirable that there should be close and continuing co-operation between the administrative staffs [of the two Departments] concerned. This is particularly important in Scotland because there is unified Ministerial responsibility. The question therefore arises whether it would be desirable, if other considerations permit, to assign all three groups of functions to one Department. The following are the main arguments that have been put forward by those who see advantages in such an arrangement and by those who see disadvantages.

Advantages. On the one hand it is argued that assignment to one Department would, in the nature of things, facilitate the necessary co-operation. Moreover it would secure that a comprehensive view was obtained, and possible conflicts of interest focused, by the Head of Department whose responsibilities included the main Scottish Office aspects of the problems involved. This is held to be specially desirable in the industrial field at the present time, when a balance must be maintained between the claims of developing overspill areas on the one hand, and of existing depressed areas on the other, for new or transferred industry; and on this view the assignment of both interests to the same Department would make it more certain that the importance of this balance is recognised, both in general statements by or on behalf of the Secretary of State and in the handling of particular cases by his Departments.

The Department of Health is already responsible for administration of a number of services which are of importance from the land use standpoint—-

especially housing, water supplies, and (to a lesser extent) sewerage. Questions arising on the allocation of land for housing sites have for some years been dealt with, not by the Housing Division, but by the Town and Country Planning Divisions. The prospects of industrial employment and questions of highway development are even more vital factors in land use planning, and their assignment to the same Department as planning would, it is argued, be a further assurance that planning functions were discharged in a realistic manner having regard to the practical governing factors, rather than as a theoretical exercise in idealism.

If closer integration of responsibilities at a level below Head of Department proved practicable, it is held that this would enable duplication of paper work and dual representation at meetings to be reduced, and would help to ensure that opportunities were not lost in day-to-day administration because a matter came to be noticed in a particular context without its significance in an allied field being recognised. Thus, for example, it would be easier to avoid seeking to relocate in an overspill reception area a displaced industrial enterprise that happened to be particularly suitable for a depressed non-overspill area.

Disadvantages. On the other hand it is held that the possibility of overlapping or conflict between the Home Department and the Department of Health arises in only a very small part of the Home Department's industrial work, and that consultation between the Departments can ensure that the balance between the claims of overspill areas and existing depressed areas is properly maintained. The balance of the Home Department's industrial work consists essentially of displaying the Scottish flag and coping with the current industrial and economic crises that the Secretary of State has to concern himself with; this is regarded as by far the more important part of the work, and would not necessarily, it is held, be helped by association with planning. The expertise required and the wide range of contacts which have to be established with Government Departments and in other quarters could not be acquired, it is argued, by officers for whom the emergency operations in the Scottish interest would tend to be subordinate to a regular main interest such as planning.

The Board of Trade and other Whitehall Departments are used to pressure in the Scottish national interest from officers who do nothing else but assist the Secretary of State in his non-statutory functions as Scotland's Minister. These Departments might, it is suggested, be less tolerant of representations from the Planning Department in Scotland which went beyond contacts of the kind to which they are accustomed from planners in England or even Wales; they might feel that it was wrong that the officers who would have to hold the ring in the event of a dispute between a London Ministry and a Scottish local interest (e.g. about an airport development) should themselves have a nationalist axe to grind. It is thought to be relevant that the Minister of Housing seeks to an increasing extent to promote employment in Wales not as a Minister responsible for planning but as Minister for Welsh Affairs. [SRO, SOE1/170.]

Memorandum by Sir David Milne, Permanent Under Secretary of State, on the Review of the Distribution of Duties among the Scottish Departments, 21 July 1959.

We have given a good deal of thought to the question whether it would be desirable and practicable to arrange for the town and country planning functions of the Department of Health and the industry and roads functions of the Home Department to be carried out within one and the same department. These services (together with housing, water supply, sewerage and electricity) are the principal services in the Scottish Office affecting the physical and economic development of the country. Close co-operation between the officials concerned must be maintained at the points of contact in the administration of these services, e.g. because developing overspill areas and areas of high unemployment may have competing claims for new or transferred industries. While this can, of course, be secured under the present distribution of duties between Departments, it is arguable that it might be done more readily and more efficiently if the services were concentrated in one Department. Moreover, since in Scotland there is unified Ministerial responsibility for these services there is a prima facie attraction in assigning them to one department.

It would not, however, be possible to absorb industry and roads into the existing Department of Health, or planning into the existing Home Department, without completely upsetting the balance of the departments. Some more fundamental changes would therefore be necessary; and after examining a number of alternatives we have concluded that the only practicable method would be to re-arrange the functions of the existing Health and Home Departments between two new Departments, namely a Health and Home Affairs Department and a Local Government and Development Department.

Generally speaking, it can be said on the credit side that [this] alternative, in addition to achieving a union in one department of the services concerned with physical and economic development, would result in rather more uniformity of size and homogeneity of subject matter between the departments than there is at present. On the other hand, it is not without its own difficulties. First, under this alternative two of the present departments would completely lose their identity and two new ones would be created. Secondly, while there are arguments in favour of a Home and Health Department—both groups deal with individuals rather than environment, both have problems of institutional management, and there are increasingly recognised links between crime and ill health—the concept of a single Department for Health and Home Affairs is at first sight a novel one and might not be easy to present publicly. In particular there might be an unfavourable reaction from the medical and allied professions on the ground that the essentially medical aspects of the National Health Service might, in a joint Health and Home Department, become subordinated to the responsibilities transferred from the Home Department; and, although health would be as large an element in the new department as in the present Department of Health, comparisons might be drawn with England and Wales where the Ministry of Health devotes its whole time to health services. Thirdly, while ... the new Local Government and Development Department would only have one division fewer than the present Home Department (to relieve which was one of the main objects of this review), it would contain a high proportion of the subjects on which frequent reference to Ministers is necessary; and it would tend to grow in that it would contain those functions in relation to which the Secretary of State is most likely to acquire additional responsibilities.

Having regard to these considerations, most of us feel that, while a regrouping of the kind envisaged has certain attractive features, the advantages which it would give over what can be secured under the present arrangements are not of such weight as to lead us to recommend it at this point of time. In reaching this conclusion we have taken into account that interdepartmental co-operation is facilitated by the facts that the Departments are working under a single Ministerial head, the heads of the Departments meet regularly under the Chairmanship of the Permanent Under Secretary of State and the senior staffs are housed in the same building.

Economic Functions

We have reviewed the present arrangements for handling in the Scottish Departments general economic questions and detailed economic matters. In Scotland this work is facilitated by the existence of the Scottish Council (Development and Industry), an independent body which provides the Secretary of State with valuable advice on economic and industrial questions. Departmentally, the focal point for official consideration of such questions, especially those that come to the Secretary of State in his capacity as 'Scotland's Minister', is the industry division of the Home Department. This division provides the necessary liaison both with the trade and industry departments and with the Scottish Council, at whose meeting it is represented. It is also represented, along with the planning divisions of the Department of Health and the Great Britain production departments, on the Distribution of Industry panel which meets under the chairmanship of the Scottish Controller of the Board of Trade.

Economic questions often affect more than one of the Scottish Departments and in cases where major policy is involved or it is desirable to give the Secretary of State a general view of the proposals of all four Departments (e.g., investment programmes, Highland Development) they are brought before meetings of the Heads of Departments under the chairmanship of the Permanent Under

Secretary of State, who keeps in touch with, and is available to the Secretary of State and the Minister of State for consultation on, the major economic questions in which the Secretary of State is concerned as 'Scotland's Minister' (e.g., the large graving dock at Greenock, changes in distribution of industry policy).

Arrangements have also been made for the Minister of State to hold periodical meetings with the Scottish Controllers of the Board of Trade and the Ministry of Labour, in order to consider and discuss Scottish economic prospects and difficulties; and these meetings are widened from time to time to include representatives of other U.K. departments. [SRO, SOE1/170.]

Chapter Two
INDUSTRY AND EMPLOYMENT

THE STATE OF SCOTTISH TRADE, 1921

In August 1921 the Cabinet's Unemployment Committee invited the relevant Government Departments to submit reports on the effects of the economic slump on trade and employment. Robert Munro, the Scottish Secretary, remitted to the Board of Health the task of undertaking the necessary Scottish survey and the following is an extract from the subsequent Report of its Chief Intelligence Officer. Unemployment in Scotland stood at over 220,000, about 18 per cent of the insured workforce.

Memorandum by J.E. Highton, Chief Intelligence Officer, Scottish Board of Health, on the Inquiry into Industrial Unemployment and Distress in Scotland, 1 October 1921.

EXISTING TRADE POSITION. So far as industrial Scotland is concerned the position is one of almost unrelieved blackness. The purely agricultural areas are not yet affected appreciably, but in the coast strip which is dependent on the herring fishing, there is considerable stringency. The belt of serious unemployment follows that of densest population, but north of West Fife only a few towns are known to be badly hit, notably, Aberdeen, Brechin, Forfar, and Dundee. In the south-east the tweed towns make a pocket of serious unemployment, but otherwise this area is in comparatively good condition. The main belt of severe unemployment and accompanying distress runs through the mining, steel and shipbuilding areas of Fife, Edinburgh, Stirling, Linlithgow, Lanark, Dumbarton, Renfrew, and Ayr, and it runs practically continuously ... The importance of this latter point lies in its bearing upon (a) local resources available to relieve distress and (b) the possibilities of concerted action (i) in administration and (ii) in lawlessness should distress become more acute and widespread. South of Ayrshire the only place of serious unemployment known is Dumfries. Except from the point of view of numbers involved, it is difficult to pick out any industrial occupation as being principally affected by unemployment: almost all are in bad condition. Those concerned with food production and distribution and house-building are least affected. Of the others, those engaged in export trade and the means of export are worse than those engaged in home trade. Certain luxury services, such as sweet manufacture, pastry-baking, and amusement catering, are remarkably vigorous. Those perhaps do not involve a large number of employees, but the fact has significance, though not entirely a bad significance, in relation to the attitude of the people to the present crisis and also to the distribution of their burden within the community. Whole-time employment is seriously aggravated by partial unemployment. Practically the whole industrial population at present employed are working short-time. In duration and numbers, mining, steel and iron-working are the worst and the position is accentuated by the fact that in areas where these occupations are followed there are few other industries of substantial dimensions. The coal-mining areas come nearest to single occupation groups. Mr Matheson, general manager of the Caledonian Railway, which is mainly concerned with these industries, estimated that since December 1920, traffic receipts have fallen by 25%, taking 1913 as a standard, and by more than that in relation to the 1920 position. The figures of the Clyde Navigation Trust in Glasgow show that for the year ending 30th June, 1921, compared with the year ending 30th June, 1920, there was a decrease of 541,700 tons in imports and of 661,500 tons in exports or 15% and 19% respectively. The great bulk of the reduction in exports was due to coal and the great bulk of the reduction in imports was due to iron ore. There has already been a further decrease for the year beginning July 1921. In passing, it may be noted that while much of the past unemployment in coal mining has been voluntary and while flooded and otherwise damaged mines determine to a considerable extent the present distribution of unemployment, the present involuntary unemployment among coal miners would probably have been little, if any, less, and might indeed have been accelerated had no strike occurred, since the market is unable to absorb more than a proportion of the reduced amount of coal now produced—and, indeed, a considerable number of collieries which resumed after the strike have had to close down owing to the lack of orders. While the great bulk of general unemployment is simply one aspect of a world-wide depression, there is apparently a not inconsiderable part of it due to expansion in plant following upon the adjustment of industry to war needs. This is true particularly of the steel, engineering, coal-mining, chemical, and paper industries. Steel-makers state that to meet war production the normal expansion of plant was much accelerated and it is estimated that roundabout 25,000 men employed recently in coal-mining in Scotland are in excess of the capacity of the mines to absorb them for some years to come. This is not a matter peculiar to this country: it is part of the general problem of industrial readjustment throughout the industrial world ... but it aggravates appreciably the difficulty of solving the problem of local unemployment. Other factors tending to worsen the situation and complicate its solution are the movement towards industrial combination, both vertical and horizontal, following upon the war (though in operation before it) with consequential readjustment in local organisation and production (for example, the amalgamation of the coal, iron, shipbuilding, and shipping industries in the Clyde); the development of overseas competition in export trade (e.g. the increase in jute manufacturing plant in India in competition with Dundee for eastern markets, and of steel plant extensions in other countries—Sweden, America—and in particular the plant put down by the Germans in Lorraine and Luxemburg during the war and now in the hands of the French) and the extension of American shipping.

TRADE PROSPECTS. Almost all employers interviewed took a very pessimistic view of the future. Apart from the hosiery trade, which is not large ... few employers think that any substantial improvement of the trade position is probable before next spring. On the whole, the opinion is that things have reached about their worst. Engineering, shipbuilding, steel, shale-mining, and oil-refining, bleaching and dyeing, paper and cloth-weaving show few signs of revival. It is noteworthy that one or two shipbuilding firms prepared to accept contracts at a very small margin of profit have fair prospects. On the other hand, several large shipbuilders and engineers in the West of Scotland state that even with no margin of profit they cannot secure contracts and they are inclined to anticipate a worsening rather than a bettering of trade before the winter is through. The motor car industry, in particular, is very hopeless. The prospects of coal-mining are very uncertain. Winter household demands will improve the position somewhat, but there are large stocks on the market to be absorbed and the black outlook for other industries which take up coal are depressing factors. Some revival in export coal may be looked for, but, until the iron and steel industries show improvement and the Continental demand betters, the coal position must remain bad. The view of employers on the causes of depression and the hindrances to revival of trade differ little from those already much canvassed in the press during recent months. Reference was made on all hands to the depreciated exchanges on the one hand limiting the purchasing power of Continental countries and, on the other, enabling Continental products to under-cut home products in the world markets, the continued depression of the German mark at a greater rate externally and with the effect of widening the disparity between the exchange rate and the ratio of the levels of internal purchasing power of money in Germany and this country, must aggravate the influences of the bad exchange position. Engineers, shipbuilders, and dyers in the West viewed the Safeguarding of Industries Act as an unsettling factor in considering contracts. Several important firms thought that the Act would prejudice unfavourably a revival of their trade. The need for further wages cuts was much stressed and the present discussion on the withdrawal of the 12.5% bonus in the engineering and shipbuilding trades is affecting tenders for new work, and iron-fitters and founders in Stirlingshire are said to be retarding resumption of work until the first instalment of this bonus falls to be deducted from their men on the 1st October. There is little doubt ... that many large employers are pursuing a policy of great caution in the hope of a substantial fall in the costs of production within the next few months. While very resentful of the real or imagined use of economic power possessed by employers, trade unions are not likely, in view of their weakened resources and the circumstances of their members, to withstand successfully further considerable reductions in wages. It is very difficult to assess how far the pessimistic outlook of both employers and employees is fully justified; but while it is certain that there are substantial grounds for pessimism it is no less certain that hopelessness is a bad weapon with which to fight an economic crisis, and the present psychological state of employers will undoubtedly tend to retard trade recovery.

CONCLUSION. The position may be summed up in a very few words. The present condition of trade is almost uniformly bad and the prospects for the winter are little better. The relief available from private sources and co-operative societies for many workers has been considerable but is now largely exhausted. Distress is widespread and is especially marked throughout the steel and mining areas. As resources diminish and distress becomes more acute these particular areas will have to be very carefully watched. In them, and principally in Fifeshire, Lanarkshire, and Glasgow, there are very inflammable elements which, while subjected during ordinary times to damping down by the saner and much larger section of the community, will not improbably be fanned into activity as the endurance of that more sober section is broken by the continued tightening of waistbelts round empty bellies. [SRO, HH31/36.]

SKILLED WORKER UNEMPLOYMENT IN GLASGOW, 1923

In June 1923, with UK unemployment at 11 per cent, the Conservative Government asked the Minister of Labour for an assessment of its likely level during the coming winter. The Minister, Sir Arthur Montague-Barlow, projected an increase and recommended additional local authority relief work and measures to assist emigration. These proposals were remitted to the Cabinet's Unemployment Committee, which at the same time received a number of proposals for relief work from the Conservative MPs' Industrial Group. The following extract is from a memorandum on Clydeside unemployment subsequently submitted by Viscount Novar, the Scottish Secretary. The Cabinet took note of Novar's action.

Memorandum by Viscount Novar, the Secretary for Scotland, on Skilled Worker Unemployment to the Cabinet Committee on Unemployment, 31 July 1923.

I am gravely concerned at the present conditions prevailing in Glasgow and the other great industrial centres of the Clyde. To take one industry alone, viz., shipbuilding I find that in 1913, 37,000 and in 1920 43,000 were employed in this industry. In March of this year 19,000 only were employed in this industry. Speaking broadly there appears to be 24,000 of these workers unemployed on the Clyde at present. The present figures refer to journeymen and apprentices only. In addition there are the shipyard labourers, roughly about 35 per cent. more. For all classes the present unemployed figure on the Clyde shipyards may be put at 32,000. It is perhaps of interest to compare the shipbuilding position with that of industry generally: the percentage unemployed in all insured trades (Great Britain and Northern Ireland) in May, 1923, was 10.7. In shipbuilding (same area) it was 32.1, and in Scottish shipbuilding 39.4. It is further important to remember that the shipyard workers are only part of the mass of workers dependent on shipbuilding. To get a true view of the situation it is necessary to consider the ancillary trades, of which the principal are marine engineering and boilermaking. In Glasgow and the Clyde the number employed was in March, 1923, about 10,600 and 2,000 in these two trades as against 21,600, and 5,500 in 1920.

I give these figures ... to show the very serious position at present existing in this area. One of the serious aspects is that the majority of the men are skilled workers who when in employment were earning very good wages, to which the amount they now draw in unemployment benefit or from parish councils bears a very small proportion.

The not unnatural consequence is that there is at present existing in this area a spirit of hopelessness and sullen discontent which is very disquieting. This area as my colleagues know has always been one of the storm centres in the Kingdom, and unless some substantial contribution of work can be made to provide employment to a number of these men, I am very apprehensive as to what may happen in the coming winter.

Unfortunately the schemes of work suggested by the Industrial Group in their letter to the Prime Minister of 24th instant, a number of which were approved by the Committee on Unemployment on the 27th instant do not apply to Scotland, and accordingly Glasgow will not profit thereby except to a very limited extent, if orders for plant and material are placed there.

A suggestion is made in the letter that the schemes may include electrification of the railways round Glasgow, and I understand that this is to be considered.

The position is however in my opinion so serious that I think it is necessary to explore every avenue with the purpose of endeavouring to provide work for the unemployed skilled workmen in Glasgow and the Clyde area of a nature as near akin as possible to their own work, and I propose therefore to give instructions that enquiries should be made with this object in view.

I think it right to take this opportunity of warning my colleagues of the dangers of the present position in this area, and at the same time of indicating that if the enquiries I propose to make result in the framing of suitable schemes for providing work I shall ask the concurrence of my colleagues in adding these to the list of schemes already approved. [PRO, CAB 24/161 CP(23)366.]

UNEMPLOYMENT, RELIEF WORK AND THE SKILLED WORKER, GLASGOW, 1923

After the Cabinet's approval of Viscount Novar's memorandum (above) the Scottish Secretary instructed J. W. Peck, the Board's Chief Inspector, to conduct 'an inquiry into the possibility of framing further suitable schemes for providing the unemployed skilled workman with work' in Glasgow. The following is an extract from his interim report, which the Board and Viscount Novar accepted. His full report added that because of 'excess tonnage over freight requirements' employment in the Clyde yards would remain at 50 per cent of pre-war levels.

Report by J. W. Peck C.B. and D. Ronald, Intelligence Branch, the Scottish Board of Health, on Unemployment in Glasgow, 14 September 1923.

General Considerations. All the numerous persons whom we have consulted are fully impressed with the gravity of the problem and are only too anxious to co-operate in efforts towards a solution from whatever quarter. Neither in Glasgow nor in London did we find any impression that what has so far been done is really adequate to the volume of unemployment, or of jealousy or hostility to our investigations. The departments desire to co-operate and the local authority officials would welcome any help or leading from the Government. With 75 thousand unemployed in Glasgow and relief works stretched to the utmost providing only for 4 or 5 thousand, there is no temptation to take a complacent view of the problem.

Two difficulties appear to us to be outstanding: (a) the limited nature of relief works; (b) the exhaustion of finance.

As to the former, the types of work which are appropriate may be classified as follows:- road-making: Bridges: Public Buildings: Parks & Recreation Grounds: Reclamation of land: Gas extension: Water do.; Electricity Supply (Light & Power): Tramways: Docks, quays and harbours: Sewerage: Cemeteries. Under one or other of these twelve heads all the relief work at present being given falls. It was made clear to us that the bulk of the work of these types must necessarily be of the unskilled navvying kind though, of course, to a less degree in some than in others; and that in such work no real solution of the problem of the 15,000 unemployed shipyard workers and 20,000 engineers of Glasgow was to be found. Apart from the nature of relief work, the number of men absorbed is small in proportion to the volume of unemployment.

This consideration leads us to the second difficulty—finance. We were informed that within these types of relief work, a very large expansion upon the present proposals would be possible if money were available—and this in quite useful work of public value either immediate or future. For example, the Glasgow City Engineer thought he could formulate a very large new programme of road improvement and other public works and similarly the Electrical Engineer thought there were great possibilities in the way of extension of generating stations and laying of main cables to meet future requirements of the City. But in the case of the non-revenue producing undertakings the problem of the rates (already heavily burdened for these purposes) stands in the way. In the case of the revenue producing undertakings, extensions far ahead of what would be contemplated under normal conditions mean either an increase of charges (which might defeat their own purpose by reducing consumption and would in any case impose an additional burden on commercial users at a most unfortunate time): or a capital liability the interest and sinking fund charges for which would have to be financed out of the rates. Glasgow Corporation—fully alive though they are to the serious nature of the problem of the unemployed—feel they have gone as far as they can consistently with their responsibility for the rates of the City.

If, however, the terms could be made more generous, especially for the revenue-producing works (which are more likely to afford employment to skilled workmen than the non-revenue producing works), undoubtedly an extension of the efforts of local authorities and statutory public utility bodies would ensue. In particular, aid by way of substantial capital grants instead of interest charges would be fruitful. Here again the question of an exceptional scale for 'black spot' areas (which could be quite easily delimited through the current machinery of the Ministry of Labour's Unemployment Certificates) is worth considering. Special treatment of these areas appears to us to be justifiable having regard to the *national* character of the problem and the *organic* character of modern industry.

Investigations in Glasgow. We may now give in more detail a description of the results of our investigations in Glasgow so far as they have proceeded.

The total number of unemployed in Glasgow to-day is as follows:-

Men	60,609
Boys	2,596
Women	9,068
Girls	2,126
	74,399

The Ministry of Labour appreciate the serious position thus revealed but consider that the Corporation have done as much as they reasonably can in instituting new work, repairs etc. The Ministry recognise that these efforts affect only a small number of the unemployed work people in the city and that the schemes that so far have been put forward do not touch appreciably the large number of skilled artisans connected with shipbuilding and marine engineering. They have given instructions that no opportunity is to be lost of assisting in any scheme that would tend to reduce the number of employed work people.

Our inquiries meantime have been directed towards finding out what the Corporation, the Clyde Trust and the Railway Companies have done or are doing with a view to relieving the situation.

CORPORATION OF GLASGOW. Tramway Department.

The principal work in hand at present is the laying of a new tramway at Clydebank between Dumbarton Road and Duntocher via Kilbowie Road. There are about 120 men employed of whom 60 are unemployed tradesmen—engineers, carpenters, plumbers and the like. Boilermakers and platers have not been given any opportunity of working on this scheme as they are at present on strike. The permanent way engineer informs us that quite a number of these men have been on the unemployed gangs for the last twelve months and they have become quite efficient. They may now be said to have practically changed their occupations and wherever a man, who was a skilled tradesman in his regular employment, is on the unemployed gang, he is given skilled work to do so soon as he can make himself proficient under the new conditions. An instance of this was given where a foreman platelayer on this job who was at one time a ship's carpenter, is doing very satisfactory work.

The total number of unemployed in the service of the Tramway Department at present is 510. This will probably rise to 1,000 by the New Year. Owing, however, to the manner in which the tramway work is to be carried out, the number will diminish before the increase sets in.

Our enquiry was also directed towards finding out if in the matter of repairing motors, tramway cars or any other work upon which a skilled engineer could be put, full opportunity was given to the skilled unemployed. We were informed that all the necessary skilled men that could possibly be taken on were now installed in the Corporation car works at Coplawhill. The number of men employed on repairs at the present time is 604. These consist of engine fitters, blacksmiths, joiners, electricians, coach builders and painters.

City Engineer's Department: This is a department which employs the largest number of unskilled labourers. At present there is not a great number of men (only 269), but this will now rise rapidly towards the New Year, at which time it is estimated over 3,000 will be engaged. The work consists principally of roadmaking and excavation.

The City Engineer explained fully the position regarding the new road for which a contract was let the other day, amounting to £240,000. This is the new 100 foot road running between Anniesland Toll and Clydebank which passes through the Western Areas Town Planning Scheme. The Corporation in their conditions of contract have stipulated that machinery is not to be employed so as to afford the maximum opportunity for unskilled labour being engaged. The work is to be commenced at once.

A contract has been let for the construction of a new bridge over the Clyde between Oswald Street and the south side of the river. The amount of the contract is £100,000. We saw the plans of this structure. It is to be of ferro-concrete and so unfortunately from the unemployment point of view the skilled engineer will not be much required. A considerable quantity of steel work will be necessary but the placing of this material in position will be comparatively simple as compared with a girder bridge and will be done by men specially trained to this class of work and by semi-skilled labour. The remainder of the work consists in putting down the necessary piers and filling round the steel work with concrete. Most of the men employed will be of the navvy type. The bulk of the work consists of the mixing of concrete and the placing of it in position. No doubt some skilled men will be taken on but the number will be such as to have no appreciable effect on the total skilled unemployed.

Caledonian Railway: Mr Mathieson, General Manager of the Caledonian Railway, indicated to us that he considered the Company was not justified in using shareholders' money in carrying out work unless it was necessary. At the moment the Company had no more men employed on engine repairs than was necessary for the ordinary running of the railways, and the Company did not propose to employ more.

With regard to the electrification of railways, he considered that such a proposition was quite good for railways such as the London Underground where only passenger traffic was run; but that in the case of Glasgow it was a much more serious problem, where goods and passenger traffic were carried on the same lines. At the present time there was no proposal before his Company for electrification. He indicated that he had had several interviews with officials on this question, and he had asked them if the Government, in the event of the railways being electrified, would be prepared to meet the difference between the cost of electrification now and the 1913 cost. So far he said he had had no reply. He further indicated that in any case as far as his Company were concerned the only railway which could be electrified at the moment was the Cathcart line, and before the work could be put in hand it would be necessary to obtain Parliamentary powers. Mr Mathieson was formerly Chief Engineer to the Company, and he at once made the technical point that although electrification was undertaken to-morrow it would not employ many skilled men, except for the making of new motors for the cars which of itself would be a comparatively small item.

North British Railway: At an interview with the Assistant Manager we gathered that this Company are not at the moment contemplating the electrification of railways so far as Scotland is concerned. Their engine repairs are being carried on at the necessary rate to maintain the plant in efficient condition. He feels, as in the case of the Caledonian Company, that they are not justified in expending money on repairs other than those which are necessary at the moment.

In this interim report we have made a first review of the situation. In brief we find that while all the agencies are doing their utmost on the established relief work and Government grants are being given on a large scale, the combined effort is going to absorb only a small proportion of the unemployed of Glasgow—say five or six thousand—and that mainly on unskilled work. There are 75,000 unemployed in Glasgow of whom about 60,000 are men and it is estimated that including dependants about 200,000 persons are affected. None of the numerous administrative and technical experts and business men whom we have consulted could offer any hint of a solution of the larger problem—the great number still unemployed and the absence of opportunity for *skilled* labour.

We ourselves see little hope of a solution from any other quarter than the natural revival of world trade under free economic conditions. The causes of the present ills are not local though the effects are so exceptionally apparent on the Clyde. In the meantime we suggest the following points for immediate consideration.

(1) The possibility of making the Government Grants given through the Ministry of Transport and the Unemployment Grants Committee, on a more generous scale, especially to the revenue producing under-takings, so as to expand substantially the volume of relief work on present lines;

(2) The possibility of making these grants on an exceptional scale in the 'Black spot' areas such as Glasgow and the Clyde;

(3) The possibility of pressure from the highest quarter being brought to bear on the Railway Companies to undertake electrification of passenger suburban routes in Glasgow;

(4) The possibility of financial aids being given to the Railway Companies for the above purpose;

(5) The possibility of extending the operations of the Unemployment Grants Committee to Public Departments, Local Authorities and Statutory Bodies in the Irish Free State, the Colonies and India in respect of those parts of schemes of improvement and expansion which involve substantial orders for engineering plant and material, an essential condition of the grant being that the orders for the plant, material etc. must be placed in this country;

(6) The repeal of the 'direct labour' restriction in Section 3 (a) of the Local Authorities (Emergency Provisions) Act 1923. [SRO, DD10/363.]

GOVERNMENT ASSISTANCE FOR THE CLYDE SHIPBUILDING INDUSTRY, 1924-5

In October 1923 the Board of Health began a 'discreet enquiry' into the possibility of the Government providing a grant to Clydeside shipbuilders to develop the latest form of motor liner. This, it thought, would help reduce skilled worker unemployment. The first extract is from a draft memorandum prepared by Sir John Gilmour the following year for the Unemployment Grants Committee. The Committee's Chairman, Sir Laming Worthington-Evans, the Secretary of State for War, in fact refused to let it be discussed until it had been considered by the Board of Trade. The second extract is from the Board's reply, which Gilmour accepted.

Memorandum by Sir John Gilmour, Secretary for Scotland, on Government Assistance to the Shipbuilding Industry, 3 December 1924.

About a year ago my predecessor in office, Viscount Novar, obtained a Report upon the question of Government Assistance to shipbuilding from Mr. J.W. Peck, C.B., the Chief Inspector of the Scottish Board of Health. The Report approached the question from the standpoint (1) of encouraging research upon the problems of marine engineering involved in the most improved form of internal combustion engines at a time when they are in the experimental stage, and (2) providing a certain measure of skilled employment in the shipyards and engine shops during the present severe depression, especially on the Clyde.

Mr Peck's Report went into the matter carefully with reference to technical and other aspects. Some of his suggestions may have been superseded by the placing of orders for the large motor liners which have now been built or are under construction.

One suggestion, however, was the construction of one or two 20 knot, 28,000 horse-power liners of (say) 20,000 tons which would illustrate a remarkable advance in construction and offer a powerful demonstration of the resources of British engineering. So far as I am aware vessels of such a high speed and horse-power are not likely to be ordered in the near future unless some form of Government Assistance is offered.

Mr. Peck's Report was communicated to a number of Ministries concerned and I understand that it was briefly discussed at a meeting of the Unemployment Committee in January last near the end of the term of office of the Conservative Government. Nothing came of the matter at that time.

I suggest, however, that it might be worthwhile to review the matter now. The construction of ships of the high tonnage and horse-power mentioned above is apparently still in the experimental stage. A successful experiment with one or two ships carried out with any necessary assistance under the Trade Facilities Act or otherwise would be of value to the British shipbuilding and engineering industry. The construction of the initial ships would itself be of some advantage in providing employment in industries which are greatly depressed. If it led to the construction of further vessels of the same type the advantage would be even greater. [SRO, DD10/363.]

Letter of C. Hipwood, Assistant Private Secretary, Mercantile Marine Department, Board of Trade, 22 April 1925.

With reference to your letter of March 24th about a proposal to build high-powered motor liners in order to relieve unemployment on the Clyde and at the same time assist in the development of this form of propulsion, I am directed by the Board of Trade to state, that they regret they are unable to support this particular proposal.... The practical conclusion of the [Imperial Shipping Committee] report [Cmd. 1917] is that from the point of view of improving communication with Australia there is no case at present for spending public money on speeding up the ocean route between Suez and Fremantle. Improvement of communications can be put aside as a reason for giving assistance to shipbuilding, and it is also clear that if any such assistance is to be given in any form at the public expense, it would have to be general in character and could not be limited either to one portion of the United Kingdom, or to steamships in one particular trade, or to one form of propulsion.

A further consideration which the Board of Trade would regard as essential is that any subsidy or assistance given should aim at enabling shipbuilders to secure orders that are being placed in the ordinary course, and should in no case attempt to foster the building of ships that are not wanted. The tonnage afloat at present is in excess of the world's requirements, and to build unwanted ships with the assistance of public money is bad for shipping, and in the long run bad for shipbuilding also, for the unwanted ships can only run with the help of a heavy annual subsidy, and then it would run in competition with an established line and deter that line from placing fresh orders for ships with British shipyards. The Board's view is that any proposal for subsidy or assisting shipbuilding must be general in character and must be based on the principle that there is to be no arbitrary addition to the existing volume of tonnage, but an endeavour to secure for our shipbuilders a larger share in the normal tonnage orders. [SRO, DD10/363.]

THE ADMIRALTY AND THE WEST LOTHIAN SHALE OIL MINES, 1925

In March 1925 the Admiralty contract with Anglo-Persian Oil to buy West Lothian shale oil expired. The first extract is from a memorandum by the Cabinet Unemployment Committee explaining the circumstances of the issue. The second extract is from a memorandum by Sir P. Cunliffe-Lister, the President of the Board of Trade. The third is from a memorandum, subsequently presented, by the Scottish Secretary. The final extract is the Cabinet's decision on the issue. Later in the year 4,000 shale miners and 3,000 ancillary workers were sacked. The Unemployment Committee had Scottish Office representation.

Memorandum by the Cabinet Committee on Unemployment, Chairman, Sir L. Worthington-Evans, Secretary for War, on the Scottish Oil Shale Mines, 27 March 1925.

Shortly after the war, in response to the request of the Government, the Anglo-Persian Oil Company acquired a controlling interest in Scottish Oils Ltd., which Company controls and manages the properties of the individual Shale Companies which are situated in Linlithgowshire and Lanarkshire. At that time the Government were strongly of the opinion that the industry ought to be continued both on the ground that this home source of oil was an asset of real value in case of war and also because of the serious unemployment position in the locality and the absence of alternative work. Scottish Oils Ltd. have a contract with the Admiralty expiring on 31st March, 1925, to supply 30,000 tons of oil a year at £12 a ton. The total output of the mines is approximately 85,000 tons of fuel oil, 15,000 tons of lubricating oil, 36,000 tons of Kerosene and 20,000 tons of motor spirit a year in addition to certain by-products. The output of fuel could be increased by dropping one refining process. The number of men directly employed in the industry is about 8,200.

The total population of the area in which the industry is carried on is roughly 65,000 and it is estimated that 42 per cent of this population is directly dependent on the industry. In addition the cessation of the industry would mean throwing out of work about 2,000 coal miners producing coal used in the industry as well as a number of persons indirectly dependent on it. The area is already suffering acutely from unemployment due to the coal depression. As there is no alternative employment in the area the great majority of those employed in the industry will, if the industry is shut down, have to rely on Unemployment Benefit or Poor Law relief. If the mines are once closed they could only be re-opened at great expense which might in some cases be almost prohibitive.

In order to enable the industry to be maintained, Lord Bradbury and Sir Edward Packe, the Government Directors of the Anglo-Persian Oil Company have submitted a proposal that the Admiralty should enter into a contract with the Scottish Oil Ltd., to take the whole output of fuel oil, about 120,000 tons per annum, at a price of £7 per ton, which is equal to, say £7.11.0 per ton delivered. The £7.11.0 compares with £3.5.0 per ton, the cost of Texas Oil delivered ... While the Admiralty would regret the loss of the only home source of crude oil, having regard to the comparatively small present and prospective production, they do not attach the same importance to the maintenance of the supply as was the case in 1920. The Admiralty, moreover, consider that if the above proposal is adopted the increased cost £600,000 per annum should, for estimate purposes, be treated as a special Unemployment Service and should not ultimately fall to be charged against Navy Votes.

In favour of the proposal it is represented -

(1) that even if the output of oil is comparatively insignificant yet it is important to preserve the only home source of supply.

(2) that serious consequences must result from adding at least 10,200 men and their dependants to the ranks of the local unemployed. Assuming these men are all adults eligible for Unemployment Benefit the cost to the Unemployment Insurance Fund would not be less than £600,000 per annum. In addition of course large sums would have to be found locally for Poor Law Relief.

(3) that it may prove possible as a result of negotiations to persuade the Company to continue the industry on terms substantially more favourable to the Government than those contained in the present offer.

On the other hand it has been pointed out -

(1) that to assist the industry as proposed by means of a concealed subsidy involves a principle which is open to great extension and that it might be difficult to withhold similar benefits from other depressed industries, such as coal mining.

(2) that if the industry is really moribund as is said to be the case, the only effect will be to stereotype for an indefinite period a special form of State assistance of a highly uneconomical and unsatisfactory nature, and one particularly open to political criticism.

(3) that if once assistance is given political and other considerations will almost certainly compel its continuance.

(4) that having regard to the present views of the Admiralty it would not be easy to maintain the contention that the maintenance of the industry was desirable on defence grounds.

... The Committee are of the opinion that if the Industry is to be helped, assistance must be given by and through an Admiralty contract, justification for special treatment being based on the value of the home source of supply in time of war. In no other way could the case be successfully differentiated from other distressed industry cases. [PRO, CAB 24/172 CP(25)184.]

Memorandum by Sir P. Cunliffe-Lister, President of the Board of Trade, on the Scottish Shale Oil Industry, 3 June 1925.

The Company desire ... to be protected by Government assistance against losses on the shale oil part of their business, while retaining their other sources of profit, and they say that in the event of such assistance not being forthcoming they will close down part at any rate of the shale mines and works.

As the Admiralty are not anxious to obtain the Company's oil at present, and do not attach any considerable importance to keeping the mines in existence, the only ground for giving assistance is to prevent the serious unemployment which would be caused by the closing of the mines and works. I think however that it would be difficult to justify giving such assistance to companies in the comparatively satisfactory financial position of these undertakings as compared with that of undertakings in other industries, particularly the analogous case of coal mines. As I explained to the Cabinet, I feel the greatest difficulty in agreeing to any proposal upon which the coal-mining industry could found a claim to a subsidy. The only ground on which the Government could justify a subsidy to the Shale mines would be that the Government were using part of their profits in the successful Anglo-Persian venture to relieve distress in another undertaking in which they are also interested and which forms part of the larger enterprise. [PRO, CAB 24/173 CP(25)275.]

Memorandum by Sir John Gilmour, Secretary for Scotland, on the Shale Oil Industry, 8 June 1925.

The figures as to the number of persons indirectly dependent on the industry includes shopkeepers and their employees, railway workers, school teachers, tradesmen, etc., and their families—in other words, all persons who are dependent for their livelihood on the continued existence of the Oil Shale Industry.

It will be also observed that in 6 of the parishes, viz.: MidCalder, West Calder, Kirkliston, Kirknewton, Livingstone and Uphall, over 50 per cent of the population are dependent, directly or indirectly, on the Shale Industry. The collapse of that industry would be a severe blow to the whole district and would no doubt considerably affect the coal industry in the neighbouring coal fields. Apart from the Shale Industry there are (except in Bathgate) no industries of any magnitude except agriculture, and it is evident that, in the present state of employment, the men from the shale mines could not find employment either locally or in the neighbouring industrial areas of Lanarkshire and Midlothian. Should the mines close down, the Poor Law Authorities would be called on to assume an intolerable burden.

With regard to Uphall, which includes the large village of Broxburn, almost the entire community is dependent on the Oil Shale Industry. I understand, however, that a pipeline has been laid from Grangemouth to the Uphall Oil Works by means of which imported crude oil is conveyed to the works for refining, and I gather from the memorandum by the President of the Board of Trade that in any case this department of the industry would continue in operation. The number of men employed in the Oil Works, is however, said to be small in comparison with the number employed in the mines themselves. I suggest that before the question of assisting the Industry, whether by Admiralty contract or otherwise, is decided, an effort should be made to obtain further information as to which mines would probably be closed in the event of the Companies being left to their own resources, so that the full effect on the unemployment position can be measured. [PRO, CAB 24/173 CP(25)279.]

Minute of the Cabinet, the Scottish Oil Shale Mines, 1 July 1925.

The Cabinet resumed their consideration of the question of the Scottish Oil Shale Mines. In addition to the Papers [above] they had before them the Report of the Naval Programme Committee to the effect that their discussion on the general question of Admiralty oil fuel reserves in no way affected the question of whether or not assistance should be given by the Government to the Scottish Oil Shale industry as an unemployment measure.

The Cabinet were informed that it would be impossible for the Government to give any sort of special subsidy to the Scottish Oil Shale Mines without a perfectly good claim for corresponding treatment being made on behalf of coal mines which had already been closed down in very similar circumstances.

While recognising that their decision might give rise to claims for some special form of relief in the districts affected, the Cabinet agreed -That no special financial assistance could be given to the Scottish Oil Shale Mines. [PRO, CAB 23/50 CC 32(25)13.]

TRAINING CENTRES FOR THE SCOTTISH UNEMPLOYED, 1927

At the end of 1927 the Cabinet appointed a Committee of Ministers to review unemployment in the coal-mining industry. It reported on 5th December and recommended that special measures, including additional training centres and a Government sponsored 'transference' board, be established. The Cabinet accepted the report and the matter was remitted to the relevant Ministries to work out the details. However the Scottish Secretary had not been a member of the Committee and the first extract is from a letter of the Board of Health to the Scottish Secretary outlining its position. The letter was subsequently sent to the Ministry of Labour and the second extract is from its reply. A training centre for unemployed Scottish miners was later established in Glasgow.

Letter of J. Jeffrey, Secretary, Board of Health, on Industrial Transference, 9 December 1927.

(1) *Training Centres.* The [Cabinet] report does not mention where the 'further centre' for adults which has been authorised by the Treasury is to be located. Might I suggest that as the whole of the four existing centres are in England, arrangements might be made to have this fifth centre in Scotland? I understand that a number of Scotsmen have been sent to the existing English centres from time to time but this does not appear to be a sufficient and satisfactory provision. Our unemployment rate is still very high and every endeavour should be made to reduce it. Scotsmen would be much more likely to accept an offer of training if the centre were within reasonable distance of home than if it were in England. Establishment of a centre in Scotland would also have a good psychological effect especially in the Parish Councils some of whom are very pessimistic as to their future financial outlook. A Scottish centre would at least demonstrate that the Government were taking direct action to do something to relieve unemployment and incidentally the burden of Parish Councils even although the actual results might be slight. A colony in England, even if it took in Scotsmen, would not make the same appeal to our people.

(2) *Temporary Board.* Once the Board is established it will doubtless consult with the various Government Departments concerned (by the way, the Board of Health is not mentioned!) as to the best means by which it can work 'through the machinery' of these Departments.

The intention appears to be that the Temporary Board should concentrate its energies on mining areas which are to be scheduled [by the Ministry of Labour] and doubtless the problem of these areas will be sufficient at first to occupy the whole time of the Board. Besides mining areas there are, however, I need hardly remind you, other areas in Scotland with stagnant pools of labour where similar action for draining them might be taken with advantage. If, therefore, the Board succeeds as we hope it will, in draining the mining pool, I hope it may be found possible to extend its activities to these other pools. [SRO, DD10/194.]

Letter of F.N. Tribe, Principal Private Secretary, Ministry of Labour, on Industrial Transference, 26 January 1928.

We are opening one new Centre primarily for South Wales miners but not in Wales, for we find it better to take them out of the depressed areas and train them in a district where the chances of employment are good. That will make five Centres in all. They are still in an experimental stage and, as you know, it is difficult to get money for further extensions. If, however, it should be possible to open further Centres, my Minister will naturally consider the desirability of having one in Scotland. In the meantime, men from Scotland are eligible for training in the existing centres, and are in fact being taken for training there. As Sir John Gilmour knows, Sir Arthur [Steel-Maitland, the Minister of Labour] would be the last to under-rate the claims of Scotland.

As for the Industrial Transference Board, no decision has been reached about the source of any extra expenditure which its work may involve, but you can assure Jeffrey that the point he makes will not be overlooked. The Board will chiefly be concerned at first with unemployment in the coal industry, and at present that means chiefly South Wales and the Northern Coalfields, though it is recognised that in part of the Scottish Coalfield there is also a problem; it will, however, also have to tackle, probably the iron and steel trades. This again brings Scotland into the picture. [SRO, DD10/194.]

SURPLUS WORKERS AND INDUSTRIAL TRANSFERENCE, 1928

In the Autumn of 1928 the Cabinet established an Inter-Departmental Committee to review the operation of the newly established Industrial Transference Board. The first extract is taken from the Committee's report. Subsequently the Cabinet established a

Committee of Ministers to review the report and the second extract is taken from its conclusions. Amongst its members were the Chancellor of the Exchequer, Winston Churchill (Chairman), the Minister of Health, Neville Chamberlain, the Scottish Secretary, Sir John Gilmour, and the Minister of Labour, Sir Arthur Steel-Maitland. The Cabinet accepted the recommendations.

Report of the Inter-Departmental Committee on Unemployment, Chairman Sir Warren Fisher, Permanent Secretary, Treasury, 2 November 1928.

A brief survey shows that the problem of 'unemployment' lies less in the total volume of unemployment than its persistent density in a few industries and areas. The economic maladjustment, of which this unemployment in the basic industries of coal, iron and steel, shipbuilding and some textiles, is a symptom, is being slowly corrected, but at the best the existence of a surplus of labour in these industries must be faced, and no such improvement in trade can be looked for in the coming months as will have an appreciable effect upon the position. The urgent problem is that of dealing with a permanent surplus.* There is, for example, a surplus of not less than 200,000 workers in the coal industry, largely concentrated in South Wales, Durham, Northumberland, Lanarkshire and Fife. Apart from maintenance on the spot in idleness or on relief works, a course which perpetuates and intensifies the problem, the only method of dealing with the surplus is by a steady pursuit of the policy of transference. It is therefore from the point of view of facilitating *transfers* from depressed areas that we have considered a possible programme of works and development. Whatever policy is adopted it must be clearly a long range policy—the situation is not one which can be righted in a year.

* The permanent surplus has been variously estimated. There are indicators that there is a surplus in other basic industries other than coal, and the total ultimate surplus over peak requirements within the foreseeable period may prove to be in the neighbourhood of 300,000 rather than 200,000. These figures are of course exclusive of families and dependants. [PRO, CAB 24/198 CP(28)325: SRO, DD10/184.]

Report of the Cabinet Unemployment Policy Committee on Industrial Transference, 5 November 1928.

The most serious feature of the unemployment problem is the concentration in the depressed areas of large numbers of persons who are permanently surplus to the requirements of their industry. There is no ground for hoping that if these people remain where they are they will ever again obtain employment. Various remedies have been suggested, but they will bring no immediate help to the surplus population. The Industrial Transference Board, after considering the problem exhaustively came to the conclusion that the only thing to be done for this surplus population was to induce it to move elsewhere, and bring it back into the stream of living industry. The Government adopted this policy and in pursuance of it the Ministry of Labour are moving men and women and boys and girls from the desolation of the depressed areas to work elsewhere at the rate of six or seven hundred a week. The process of transfer is being facilitated by the provision of training centres where men unused to factory life can be fitted for new trades. These centres have already been expanded for the benefit primarily of men from the depressed areas. If the present rate of transfer can be continued, it means that in six months something like 15,000 persons will have been transferred from the depressed areas through the machinery of the Ministry of Labour.

The policy, if it is to succeed, must have the goodwill and co-operation of all classes of the community. It is not a question of asking for charity, or of asking employers to take on men whom they do not need. All that is asked is that of the large number of labour engagements which are made every week a relatively small proportion shall be given to these men, who include some of the cream of the industrial population.

In order to facilitate and further the Transference Scheme, it is proposed to reopen on more favourable terms the grants offered to Local Authorities through the St. David's [Unemployment Grants] Committee in respect of works financed out of loans in cases where Authorities in the more prosperous areas are prepared to employ a substantial proportion of persons from the distressed areas upon public works.

The offer of the improved terms will as a rule be conditional on the local authority drawing not less than 50 per cent of the Labour from the distressed areas, but the St. David's Committee will have the discretion to allow a lower percentage in special cases. [PRO, CAB 24/198 CP(28)334; SRO, DD10/184.]

THE CABINET AND THE SPECIAL AREAS, 1935

In the Autumn of 1935 the Cabinet established a Committee under the chairmanship of Neville Chamberlain, the Chancellor of the Exchequer, to examine the first annual reports of the two Special Areas Commissioners. Other Ministers on the Committee included the Scottish Secretary, the President of the Board of Trade, the Minister of Health, the Minister of Labour and the Minister of Agriculture. The following extract is from their Report to the Cabinet, prepared after they had received a report from a small group of ministers and officials on the work of the two Special Areas Commissioners. The Cabinet agreed with its comments, noting that there could be no 'sovereign remedy' for unemployment. The Scottish Special Area covered most of industrial Lanarkshire except Glasgow.

Cabinet Committee on the Reports of the Commissioners for the Special Areas, 18 October 1935.

An examination of this [report] shows conclusively the absurdity of the allegation that the Commissioners have failed. In any case it would, in our view, be premature to reach such a conclusion after the lapse of so short a time. The Commissioners are continually experimenting and their activities go on expanding with growing cumulative effect. This novel administrative venture has made an excellent start and the experiments which the Commissioners have been trying out are proving most valuable in showing the best ways for future advance and also those which should be avoided.

We do not believe that the introduction of new industries into the depressed areas is going to play any very large part in the near future in solving the problem of those areas. Speaking generally we doubt the feasibility of trying to persuade ordinary industry to go into the Special Areas. The influences telling in other directions seem to be strong. If it were possible to establish one or more Government factories in the areas—a matter which is under consideration—a useful lead would be given and in time private employers might also go there.

What policy should be adopted in the case of the unemployed in the Special Areas who cannot find work either in old or new industries in those areas?

In the first place we think that as many as possible of these people should be settled on the land. The Commissioners' Reports show that settlement can be effected in a great variety of ways—though not on a spectacular scale—and that in many of these ways a promising start has been made. Secondly, the younger men and women and the juveniles should be encouraged to transfer to more prosperous districts and any necessary extensions of the Ministry of Labour training schemes should be put in hand at once. In order that a transfer policy may be successful the country as a whole must be prosperous. In the view of the Chancellor of the Exchequer the financial position of the country is not at present unsatisfactory, and he has no reason to suppose that the present general prosperity will not continue. We attach great importance to the transfer policy. Finally there will remain those persons for whom there will be no employment and who cannot, for one reason or another, be moved out of the Special Areas. The Government's policy should be to make life for those people more tolerable, to keep them as contented and happy as circumstances permit, and to endeavour to ensure that this ultimate residuum is kept as small as possible. [PRO, CAB 27/257 CP(35)197; SRO, DD10/170.]

THE REARMAMENT PROGRAMME AND ECONOMIC DEVELOPMENT IN THE SPECIAL AREAS, 1936

In April 1936 the Cabinet agreed to a proposal for the relocation of a munitions factory from Waltham, London, to Bishopton, Renfrewshire, in the Scottish Development Area. However the Defence Policy and Requirements Committee, under pressure to economise on costs, agreed the following October to recommend Gretna and the Secretary of State for War, Duff Cooper, presented a memorandum outlining the reasons to the Cabinet. The following extract is from the memorandum by Walter Elliot, the Scottish Secretary, submitted in response. The Cabinet decided to adhere to its original decision. The Scottish Office was not a member of the Defence Committee.

Memorandum by Walter Elliot, Secretary of State for Scotland, on the Location of Proposed Cordite Factory at Gretna, 2 November 1936.

The proposal made in the memorandum by the Secretary of State for War (C.P. 262(36)) that the Cordite Factory should not be built at Bishopton in Renfrewshire (as sanctioned by the Cabinet on the 8th April, 1936), but on a site in Cumberland near Gretna or Longtown, raises a very serious question from the standpoint both of general principles and of the Government's position in the Special Areas in Scotland.

The Bishopton site was recommended by an Interdepartmental Committee who proceeded on the footing that it was desirable, if possible, to establish this Factory in the Scottish Special Areas. The Minister for Co-ordination of Defence [Sir Thomas Inskip] referred to the transfer of the existing Factory 'to a place in Scotland' in his speech in the House of Commons on the 20th July. The Lord President [Ramsay MacDonald] had previously said in his speech in the Debate on the Special Areas on the 2nd March that the Government themselves proposed to adopt the recommendations which they had been pressing upon private employers and to place important orders and plant new industries within those Areas in the course of the development of their rearmament scheme.

Although the Scottish Special Areas were not expressly mentioned, there is no doubt that the Government's general policy of stimulating economic development in the Special Areas, combined with the above-mentioned statements in connection with the defence programme, have aroused strong expectations in Scotland that the Cordite factory will be established within the Scottish Special Areas. The Scottish Development Council and the Economic Committee which it has set up, largely at the instance of my predecessor, to stimulate industrial revival, are closely interesting themselves in the question whether a due share of the rearmament programme is being allocated to Scotland.

There is no doubt that an announcement that the Cordite factory is not to be erected as hitherto announced in the Scottish Special Areas, would excite strong criticism in Scotland and that such a decision could only be defended in the coming Debates on the Special Areas and outside Parliament if it could be shown to be absolutely essential for over-riding reasons.

The reasons which are given in the Secretary of State's memorandum and in the Minutes and Conclusions of the D.P.R.C. do not appear to me on such examination as I have been able to give to furnish adequate justification for abandoning the Bishopton site. I should like to make comments on the following points:-

(i) *Labour supply and employment.*—I entirely agree with the Minister of Labour [Ernest Brown] that in these respects the Bishopton site has great advantages over the Gretna site. Moreover, the construction of a large Factory just outside the County of Dumfries will impose a heavy financial burden on the Local Authority of that County in respect of maintenance of roads, policing, &c., without any financial advantage, temporary or permanent.

(ii) *Water supply.*—I am informed that the Glasgow Corporation could spare without difficulty from their Milngavie reservoirs the estimated war requirement of 10 million gallons a day and could increase this to 12 million gallons a day by minor alterations and to at least 17 million gallons a day by laying additional mains to the reservoir.

In the case of the 'Gretna' site, if legislation is necessary to authorise abstraction of water from the River Esk, there may be serious risk of opposition and delay, especially in view of the fact that a proposal to abstract 2 million gallons a day from the Tweed for domestic purposes was held up by opposition for more than two years. In the circumstances, the anticipation that transfer to the 'Gretna' site would mean a saving of 6 or 7 months may require further examination. It should be remembered that the previous development of the 'Gretna' site was done in war and under D.O.R.A. powers.

(iii) *Facilities for factory expansion.*—This is mainly a technical matter, but it must be kept in mind that a large part of the site used by the Gretna Factory during the war has been developed for other purposes and is no longer available.

As for the final suggestion that the erection of a chemical factory is not in the long run a great asset to any district I think that this would prove a double-edged argument, and it would place any Government spokesman in a position of some difficulty if he attempted to use it as a reason why this factory, costing some £3.5 million, should not be constructed in an area containing 64,513 registered adult males unemployed to-day, where the Government has been using its utmost endeavours to get employers generally to undertake work of however temporary a character.

For these reasons I trust that the Bishopton site will be adhered to even if it involves somewhat greater cost than the proposed alternative site in Cumberland. [PRO, CAB 24/265 CP(36)300.]

THE SCOTTISH OFFICE AND ALTERATIONS IN THE SPECIAL AREAS SCHEDULE, 1937

At the end of 1936 the Cabinet remitted to an Inter-Departmental Committee composed of officials the issue of reviewing the Special Areas Act. The first extract is from the Committee's report, outlining its economic philosophy and its objection to extending the Special Areas boundaries in Scotland. The second extract is from the Scottish Office's reservation to the Committee's conclusions. The third extract is from subsequent discussion at the Cabinet's Ministerial Special Areas Committee. The Committee, whilst accepting that there should be only limited alteration to the boundaries of the Special Areas, did accept, on the recommendation of Neville Chamberlain, the Chancellor of the Exchequer, the establishment of trading estate public utility companies, part funded by the State.

Report of the Inter-Departmental Committee on the Special Areas, 11 January 1937.

The powers under the present Act plus the inducements which might be offered to industry can be broadly summarised as—

(a) Measures of social improvement plus measures of indirect economic development;

(b) Measures of direct economic development plus inducements to industry.

By measures of indirect economic development we mean measures for generally cleaning up the areas, certain public works (*e.g.*, sewerage schemes), assistance to Development Councils, etc. By measures of direct economic development we mean Trading Estates and site clearances mainly for industrial purposes.

The extent to which the former can be applied is largely a question of money. Many schemes initiated in the present Special Areas could be initiated in other areas. These schemes have, however, already proved very costly in the Special Areas and the cost would be increased, very roughly proportionately, as the areas were extended. Moreover, while in many cases of real benefit to the areas in which they have been applied, such schemes have been criticised as being palliatives and as making little contribution to the permanent re-establishment of better conditions.

The second class of powers is subject to different considerations. They are the powers to which most importance is attached at the present time and in the light of whose success or failure the future of the Act is likely to be judged. But the possibility of extension of these powers to other areas is not solely or even mainly to be decided in terms of money. The vital consideration is that there is only a limited aggregate amount of effect which they are capable of producing. These powers aim at the establishment within the Special Areas of industries not already there. But the total number of industrial undertakings which are looking for a home or which are ready to move from their present homes and which will be attracted to the Special Areas by any inducements which are within the sphere of practical politics is limited. Broadly speaking, therefore, the wider the areas are drawn, the smaller will be the effect of these measures in any particular place. More than this, the wider the range of attractiveness or repellency within the areas for which these measures are available, the less will be the chance of the worst spots deriving any benefit at all from them. Moreover, the wider the area, the greater the probability of opposition being raised to the policy of inducements from other parts of the country. For inducements are, after all, only the use of the taxpayer's money to bribe industry to go not where it is economic, but where it is uneconomic. Such a policy would probably command wide support if directed to the few areas for whose plight public sympathy is widespread. It might well excite opposition if applied over relatively wide areas.

... Reference has already been made to the relatively lower rate of unemployment in the Scottish Area as compared with the Special Areas in England and Wales [22% compared with 29%]. It will be seen that those of the areas [the Highlands, the Moray Firth] which, in fact, are suffering from prolonged and severe unemployment present in general special problems which cannot be adequately dealt with through the provisions of the Special Areas Act. As regards the remaining areas [West Lothian, Lennoxtown and Wanlockhead], the general level of recorded unemployment is not itself of such an order as specially to justify their inclusion within the Act. After a careful examination of all the relevant factors, it is considered that the balance of advantage lies in making no further extension of the Special Areas in Scotland and it is recommended accordingly.... As regards the claims of Glasgow, it will be observed that the unemployment position is more favourable than that recorded at Liverpool, Cardiff, Swansea, etc. but approximate to that at Middlesbrough. All the considerations enumerated ... in the case of Liverpool apply with added force to the case of Glasgow, since it possesses a much greater variety of industries than Liverpool and the improvement in the shipbuilding industry is likely to bring much greater relief, absolutely and relatively, to it. Moreover, it is likely, in view of its engineering and shipbuilding resources, to share to a far greater extent in the rearmament programme. It would be impracticable to bring in Glasgow with comparable degrees of unemployment, and it is recommended that it should not be included in the list of Special Areas. [PRO, CAB 27/577 DA(34)10, pp.5, 45, 4; SRO, DD10/170.]

Report of the Inter-Departmental Committee on the Special Areas, 11 January 1937; Alterations in the Special Areas, Scottish Office Reservation.

The unemployment situation in Scotland is still bad although recovery in iron, steel, shipbuilding, and engineering has caused some improvement in the West of Scotland. On the whole unemployment is much heavier in Scotland than in England and extends over a larger part of the country. The Unemployment Index (November, 1936) for Scotland is 19.1 as compared with 12.9 for Great Britain.

If the Special Areas were stereotyped on the restricted basis the proposed ... areas in which the existing severe unemployment becomes worse would be permanently shut out unless fresh legislation (involving renewed controversies) were introduced. The changes which have occurred during the past two years illustrate the disadvantages of such an inflexible system.

A more suitable method appears to be to avoid stereotyping the additional areas and to give the Commissioner discretion to exercise his powers in areas of high unemployment to be fixed from time to time by the Minister concerned acting with the advice of an informal Committee.

If, however, it should be decided as a question of policy to adopt [this alternative] the Scottish Office suggest that the scheduled areas should be readjusted ... This readjustment has been prepared after discussion with the Commissioner who attaches importance to having reasonably homogeneous and well-defined areas so as to avoid practical difficulties in administration which arise from the undue dissection of counties. A number of the areas omitted (*e.g.*, the Burghs of Lanark and Biggar) form pockets in an otherwise homogeneous area and, for administrative purposes, it might be more convenient to leave them in and to rely on discretion which the Commissioner has exercised in the past to exclude such places from assistance.

The additions proposed in Scotland ... are (1) Glasgow, (2) the Moray Firth Coastal district, (3) the part of Westlothian north of the railway line which is at present excluded, (4) small areas in Stirlingshire, including Lennoxtown, (5) a small area in Dumfriesshire including the lead mining village of Wanlockhead.

The proposed additions (3), (4), and (5) are small areas on the fringe of the present Areas in which depression exists in different forms of mining or in calico printing.

Glasgow has heavy and prolonged unemployment which persists in spite of increased activity in shipbuilding, etc. Both geographically and economically it is the centre of the existing Special Areas. Its economic interdependence with them was emphasised in the Final Report of Sir Arthur Rose who referred to the 'somewhat artificial nature' of the Scheduled Areas. The same point is brought out by the recent Report of the Departmental Committee on Gas Supplies in the West of Scotland which finds that modernisation of coke ovens and iron works is essential to the existence of the pig iron industry in Scotland and that the proposal to establish modern ovens in Lanarkshire is dependent on purchase of the oven gas by the Corporation of Glasgow. In these circumstances not only the Commissioner but other bodies, *e.g.*, the Nuffield Trust may be debarred from operations beneficial to the existing Special Areas if Glasgow is excluded. Glasgow is an integral part of the West of Scotland industrial district in a way which the relation of Liverpool to Lancashire offers no parallel.

The Moray Firth coastal district is suffering from severe and prolonged unemployment owing to depression in the Herring Industry. The assistance rendered by the Government to that industry by the Herring Industry Act has produced a little improvement. But the economic condition of the district remains very bad. Indeed a contraction of the herring industry was contemplated by the Act itself.

The establishment of other industries (such as exists in one or two of the herring ports) would be of great value as an auxiliary support to these communities.

The proposed additions do not include the Highlands and Islands. Most of the Highlands have a very high Unemployment Index. They might, however, be left out of the Schedule on the ground that the Commissioner's machinery is not suitable for dealing with them and that a Committee set up by the Scottish Economic Committee in consultation with the Secretary of State is at present considering the question of their economic development. [PRO, CAB 27/577 DA(34)10, pp. 54-5; SRO, DD10/170.]

Minute of the Cabinet's Depressed Areas Committee, on the Report of the Inter-Departmental Committee on the Special Areas, 10 February 1937.

THE SECRETARY OF STATE FOR SCOTLAND did not think that the formula was very well suited to Scotland. The Scottish picture was not one dotted with a number of black spots, but was a general grey throughout. The provision that only areas normally dependent mainly on a single industry were to be eligible would cut out some of the worst parts of Scotland, e.g. those where the three principal industries—fishing, agriculture and net-making—had simultaneously become depressed.

He thought that the formula would have to be varied in some way to meet the needs of Scotland. In addition, as he had said before, he thought that Glasgow ought to be included among the Special Areas. It was intimately connected with its very depressed hinterland in a way which Manchester, Liverpool, Cardiff, etc., were not.

Returning to the public utility company proposal, Mr. Elliot said that his suggestion would be that the proposal should be made applicable to the grey areas of Scotland, subject to a reasonable discretion to the authority running the scheme. It would be indefensible if the Government were to take no action to deal with the Scottish problem.

It was pointed out in reply that the logical conclusion of the Secretary of State's argument, and of the Scottish Office reservation [above], was that the whole of Scotland ought to be scheduled as a Special Area.

This, however, was out of the question. To schedule a whole country would be to stultify the term 'Special Area'.

In the case of Dundee, which was referred to in the discussion, it was shown that the unemployment figures had recently fallen from 29 per cent. to 21 per cent. Possibly the next return would show a still lower figure.

THE CHANCELLOR OF THE EXCHEQUER drew attention to the considerable financial benefit which Scotland was about to derive from the revision of the [local authority] block grant. In addition, very large armaments orders had lately been placed in Scotland.

It was agreed not to recommend the widening of the formula for the benefit of Scotland. [PRO, CAB 27/578 DA(34)11th.]

THE SCOTTISH OFFICE AND THE FUTURE OF THE SPECIAL AREAS, 1938

In June 1938 the Cabinet's Distressed Areas Committee received a report from its Inter-Departmental Committee recommending that the Special Areas Act should be allowed to lapse. This was supported by Ernest Brown, the Minister of Labour, but only if the financial provisions of the Special Areas Reconstruction Act, 1937 were allowed to continue. The following extract is from the memorandum by John Colville, the Scottish Secretary to the Committee. The Committee accepted Colville's proposal on housing and Brown's on the Special Areas Act, but delayed a final decision on the latter until the Autumn. In fact, because of rising unemployment, the imminence of the Barlow Commission report and the Government's political position since Munich, the Committee subsequently agreed, on the recommendation of Brown and Colville, to retain the Act until 1941.

Memorandum by John Colville, Secretary of State for Scotland, on the Future of the Special Areas Scheme, 17 June 1938.

Introductory.

There is no strong argument for continuing the powers of the Scottish Commissioner after March 1939 in so far as they relate to public works, social service and welfare schemes, and agricultural and related schemes. In all of these cases it should be possible to enter into appropriate commitments before that date. Similarly, in the case of housing in the Special Areas, appropriate commitments can be entered into to enable the Scottish Special Areas Housing Association to continue its work. On the industrial side the position is more difficult and certain doubts have been expressed by the Scottish Commissioner as to the proposed withdrawal of existing facilities.

Health and Housing.

Very considerable progress has been made in improving medical and allied services and the water supply, sewerage and sewage disposal services in the Scottish Special Areas. Numbers of grant-aided schemes have been completed or are in progress and others are in process of adjustment. Provided that the Commissioner is not restricted from considering on their merits all schemes which may come before him between now and March 1939, and provided that in necessitous cases meanwhile revision of the amount of assistance already offered is not ruled out, the position in the Special Areas will in most districts be not unsatisfactory.

With regard to housing, conditions in Scotland are admittedly much more serious than in England and Wales. In most areas throughout Scotland the solution of the housing problem at the present rate of progress will take at least 10 to 15 years. I am under considerable pressure from local authorities who represent that this work will involve them in an intolerable financial burden unless a very much greater proportion of the cost is borne by the Exchequer than at present. Progress has for the past two years been hampered by a shortage of bricklayers and materials, and, in order to improve the rate of progress and give financial relief to authorities in the Special Areas, the Special Areas Housing Association was set up towards the end of last year to undertake the building of houses by methods alternative to brick or stone. The Association's programme is intended to be supplementary to the local authorities' normal programmes. Up to the present the Association has been occupied with necessary preliminary work and is only now getting to the stage of placing contracts for the building of houses. By the 31st March, 1939, they will have placed contracts for perhaps 4,000 houses. The total number of new houses estimated to be required in the Special Areas to replace unfit houses and to put an end to overcrowding is about 50,000. Arrangements should therefore be made to allow the work of the Association to proceed after 31st March, 1939. Legislation for this purpose would not be required, provided the Commissioner can be authorised, before his office lapses, to enter into an agreement with the Association for the building of a specified number of houses. I suggest that this number should be 20,000, which would leave another 30,000 to be found by the local authorities, but the precise figure might be discussed with the Treasury in connection with the general examination of Scottish housing to which I refer below. At present costs this would involve an additional Exchequer commitment of about £3,000,000 to £4,000,000, of which £1,000,000 would be by way of loan.

The functions of the Special Areas Housing Association are at present confined to building houses to replace unfit houses and to relieve overcrowding. A special problem exists in some districts both within and outside the Special Areas of providing houses required to meet the needs of expanding or shifting industry. An examination of this problem is proceeding with a view to estimating the extent and to considering the possibilities of transfer of labour from the Special Areas. The Commissioner may be submitting proposals under this head shortly.

In the Special Areas in England and Wales a serious housing problem exists only in Durham and to a small extent in West Cumberland. In contrast, the problem is serious throughout the whole of the Special Areas in Scotland. Not only so, but it is at least as serious outside the Special Areas in Scotland as in them, and this has been recognised by the Inter-Departmental Committee of which Sir Horace Wilson was Chairman. This is a social question of first class importance, which has been specially examined by the Departments concerned, and I hope shortly to be able to submit the proposals shortly. Meantime, the machinery already exists for assisting the solution of the problem in the Scottish Special Areas.

Employment position.

In December 1934 the percentage of unemployment in the Scottish Special Areas was 28.9. The revised percentage in April 1938 was 16.9 and 17.0 in May 1938. The percentage decrease since December 1934 is about 37.0. This decrease is mostly in the heavy industries which show a fall of 55 per cent. as compared with 19 per cent. in the remaining industries. The heavy industries will no doubt continue to benefit from the rearmament programme, but unless a considerable diversity of industries can be attracted to the areas they will be liable during the next depression to be as hardly hit as before.

The decrease in the total numbers of unemployed in the Areas occurred mainly during 1935 and 1936. Since the beginning of 1937 the drop has been about 6 per cent. In general the unemployment position in the Areas is still serious, but only slightly more serious than Scotland as a whole. Scotland's general economic condition is reflected by an unemployment index of 16.3 (at the 16th May, 1938), compared with a figure for England of 11.6, that is to say notwithstanding the recent improvement in the position of the heavy industries, unemployment in Scotland is fully 40 per cent. more severe than in England. Before the 1929 depression the unemployment index for Scotland was 10.9, a figure which compared much less unfavourably with the then English figure of 9.0. Again since 1929 the rate of increase in the number of insured persons in England and Wales has been more than twice as rapid as that in Scotland (13.7 per cent. as against 6.4 per cent.).

Industrial development.

I attach ... for the information of my colleagues a note by the Scottish Commissioner in which he puts forward suggestions for the continuance of existing industrial inducements and for their application to necessitous areas irrespective of whether they are situated within the present Special Areas. In submitting these suggestions the Scottish Commissioner appreciates that they may involve an extension of the Special Areas Acts rather than of the Special Areas Reconstruction (Agreement) Act, under which the less comprehensive suggestions of the Minister of Labour might possibly be enacted. The Commissioner feels, however, that these more limited suggestions are inadequate for the needs of the present situation in Scotland and suggests that the difficulties involved in a more complete extension at this time merit the fullest consideration. With all due regard to the Commissioner's opinions, as expressed in the attached note, I concur in the view of the Minister of Labour and of the Inter-Departmental Committee that further legislation in terms of Special Areas with or without extension of the Areas is not desirable.

In reaching that conclusion I have had in mind principally the extreme difficulty of adhering to, or attempting to vary the present scheduled Areas. I am however, in entire agreement with the view of the Scottish Commissioner that, while every scheme designed to promote employment is of importance, the best security of the Areas against a relapse lies in the attraction to them of a considerable variety of industries, but that this process at present is only beginning. As the Commissioner points out, the value of the use of industrial inducements is unlikely to have been tested to the full by March 1939, both because of the short time during which they have been in operation, and because of the obscuring of normal trends by the rearmament programme. In the case of the new estates which the Commissioner has recently acquired in Lanarkshire termination of his power to offer inducements may cause serious difficulties, and if these cannot be removed under an agreement entered into before March 1939, special consideration may require to be given to the position of these estates.

The Report of the Royal Commission on the location of the industrial population may point the way to a more comprehensive solution of the problems of regional depression but it is clearly out of the question to attempt to formulate a permanent and comprehensive policy on the subject in anticipation of the findings of the Royal Commission.

Pending the submission of their report an interim and partial solution may be found as suggested by the Minister of Labour by legislation amending the Special Areas Reconstruction (Agreement) Act with the object of enabling financial assistance by way of loan to be provided for new undertakings in necessitous areas whether within or without the existing scheduled areas. But it would hardly be possible, at any rate in Scotland, to justify the termination next year of the financial provisions of the Act of 1937, pending a more comprehensive scheme, unless the new legislation which will probably be required for the provision of adequate loan capital for new undertakings is drawn in terms that are sufficiently wide.

I do not feel that the position in hard hit areas outside the Special Areas in Scotland can be held if the operations of the Reconstruction Association are to be confined to the present scheduled areas and to any areas certified before March 1939 under the Act of 1937. Such certification is dependent upon the formation of a site company which is prepared to raise 75 per cent. of the capital cost of development. No such company has been formed in Scotland, up to now, and it is doubtful if any will be formed there before the expiry of the Act of 1937 in March of next year. But there are a number of areas outside the Special Areas in Scotland which have been dependent on a few industries in which unemployment has been severe over a period of years. In such cases there is a real need for loan facilities to assist the promotion of new industries, and it is difficult to maintain that assistance should be withheld from a new undertaking in such cases solely because it has not been possible for a site company to be formed in the area by March 1939. Such a proposal would, in my view, perpetuate the difficulties which the arbitrary nature of the boundaries of the existing Special and Certified Areas have brought out. [PRO, CAB 27/578 DA(34)17; SRO, DD10/175.]

EMPLOYMENT PROSPECTS IN THE SCOTTISH DEVELOPMENT AREA, 1946-7

In December 1946 Tom Fraser, the Joint Scottish Office Under Secretary, presented a memorandum to the Distribution of Industry Committee forecasting an increase in Scottish Development Area unemployment and suggesting that 'if private enterprise proved backward in setting up industries the State should set up factories and run them there'. The first extract is from the Committee's minutes which concluded that Fraser should prepare a more detailed memorandum showing the measures taken to let factories and reporting any difficulties. The second extract is from the subsequent memorandum.

The Committee agreed that 'not enough was being done to solve the employment problem' and 'invited' Fraser to consult with regional officials on what further measures should be taken.

Minute of the Lord President's Committee: Distribution of Industry Sub-Committee, on Development Area Policy, 1 December 1946.

THE JOINT PARLIAMENTARY UNDER-SECRETARY OF STATE FOR SCOTLAND said the situation had caused him anxiety for some time. He has been assured during the summer that the future position would look better by the autumn, but he now feared that by mid-1948 there would be 60,000 unemployed males in the Scottish Development Area. Lanarkshire was the centre of this industrial illness in Scotland; the mining industry was petering out and he feared that fewer men would be employed in the iron and steel industry after the pending re-organisation. A large proportion of the factories being built by the Board of Trade were being built in advance of specific demand, and although as yet there had been no case of a factory standing unlet for want of an applicant firm who would employ predominantly male labour, there was no sign that such firms were applying in large numbers. It was necessary to establish in development areas under private or public enterprise industries which would take root and in due course attract ancillary industries round them. If old industries were dying, the State would either have to take the people out of the surrounding localities or provide fresh industries that would take root. He made no doctrinal plea for State activity in industry as such, although he felt there was a case for action to select the new industries which would replace dying ones. Industry needed planning; it was not sufficient merely to provide capacity. He suggested that it would prove necessary to invite private enterprise to use factories for a particular industry, with the warning that if they did not the State would enter the field. An example of an industry into which the State might find it necessary to enter was the heavy electrical engineering industry, which was not doing enough to meet demand. The Hydro-Electricity Board was having to place orders outside the United Kingdom. He believed that, with varying degrees of force, the same case held good in the other development areas.

THE MINISTER OF LABOUR AND NATIONAL SERVICE expressed a large measure of support for the point of view of the Joint Parliamentary Under-Secretary of State for Scotland. He felt that fresh treatment was needed. On the latest information the forecast of male unemployment in the Scottish Development Area by mid-1948 was 66,000. On the other hand, he pointed out that, if the Government entered the industrial field in the way proposed, this would do nothing to expedite factory building, which was the main instrument of development area policy. New methods, he suggested, would have to be tried since discontent was already growing. The need for legislation to implement the proposals before the Committee, which would be impracticable this session, would not be an obstacle to using firms as Government agencies in cases where factories under the programme were not taken up sufficiently quickly

THE PARLIAMENTARY SECRETARY TO THE BOARD OF TRADE doubted whether the picture was as black as had been painted by the Joint Parliamentary Under-Secretary of State for Scotland, although great energy in pushing on with factory building was plainly necessary. In addition to the normal programme, factories designed for heavy industry were being approved. The Board of Trade had innumerable applications from firms who wanted a mixed labour force, but it was true that this was not so as regards firms who would employ a predominantly male force. The former class of applicants were given a low place in the queue. He would not like to see the idea of State factories ruled out, and was attracted by the suggestion by the Minister of Labour and National Service that firms should be established in the development areas on agency work for the Government.

In discussion the following points were made:-

(a) The slowness of factory building was the root difficulty, and the proposals of the Joint Parliamentary Under-Secretary of State for Scotland would do nothing to meet it.

(b) No case had yet arisen where it had proved impracticable to let a new factory to a firm who would employ a predominantly male labour force. The fears expressed by the Joint Parliamentary Under-Secretary of State for Scotland would not be actualities until this occurred.

(c) The shortage of applications by firms who would employ a predominantly male labour force was, it was suggested, not very alarming in itself. Industrialists were backward in renting factories they had not seen, and the policy of advance factories, which created demand, had been framed with that in mind.

(d) The continuing labour shortage would compel firms to employ the labour they could get; thus, in the cotton and boot and shoe industries, men were being employed on what was traditionally women's work.

(e) It would be untidy to set up State factories in an industry which was not to be socialised.

(f) Plants of socialised industries could be directed to development areas, e.g. perhaps the Transport Commission might have rolling stock or bus bodies made in the Scottish Development Area.

(g) The heavy electrical engineering industry, quoted as an industry in which Government factories might be desirable, was not, it was argued, an appropriate field, since efficient and experienced firms already existed with whom a

Government factory would not be able to compete, as it would have to do, on level terms. [PRO, CAB 132/21 LP(DI)46 13th Meeting.]

Memorandum by Thomas Fraser, Joint Parliamentary Under Secretary of State for Scotland, on Employment Prospects in the Scottish Development Area, 21 April 1947.

The Board of Trade in planning additional sources of employment in the Scottish Development Area have hitherto worked on the assumption approved by the Lord President's (Industrial) Committee on 12th March, 1946, that it would be necessary to provide about 145,000 more factory jobs (85,000 men and 60,000 women) than were in existence in 1937.

If the assumptions on which these targets were based are still right it now appears desirable to increase the men's target to 95,000. At the time the original targets for the Development Areas were worked out it was not considered practicable to allow for jobs which had gone out of existence since 1937 or would go out of existence in the next few years, for example, from the closing of coal mines which became uneconomic. This factor is, however, known to be of special importance in the Scottish Development Area, and although a precise calculation of its effect is impossible I feel that some account must be taken of it. Equally, it is extremely difficult to make a precise allowance for certain factors on the credit side, such as the additional employment provided in small new developments, service industries, the substitution of men for women so far as women are scarce, and the transfer of redundant miners to Fife and the Lothians. In all the circumstances it is felt that the best approximation which can be made is to add 10,000 to the previous men's figure. Its rough and ready nature must however be emphasised.

Against the target of 95,000 men and 60,000 women it is estimated that additional sources of employment created or approved up to the end of January amounted to 49,900 men and 47,100 women. These totals are brought up to 54,500 men and 51,700 women if account is taken of the jobs which should be provided when the whole of the 'advance' factories are allocated.

The conclusion from the foregoing figures is that the problem of providing employment for women is substantially solved. The reasonably firm projects however still leave a surplus of 45,100 men. Allocation of the 'advance' factories should reduce this to 40,500 but this raises the whole problem of finding male employing concerns for existing or projected factories with which I deal in Part II.

PART II

The Board of Trade deserve high praise for the vigour and tenacity with which they have carried out [the Government's] policies and they have secured a substantial volume of male employment for Scotland. The measures all depend however on sufficient private firms of the right type coming forward and, as the figures I have quoted earlier show, this has not yet happened. The prospects will be improved by having factories of the right type already available or beginning under the 'Advance' factory programme to rise from the ground but meanwhile difficulties have occurred in letting factories to male employing firms of which specific instances are as follows:- (1) A block at Hillington was recently allocated to G.E.C. for a project employing 800 women and 200 men because no good male employing applicant was forthcoming. The Board of Trade quite rightly made great efforts to get G.E.C. to Scotland but it is a pity that the firm responded by bringing a female-employing project and that there was no better applicant for this particular factory. (2) Since the middle of October the Board of Trade have been making efforts to interest suitable firms in the fine Ministry of Supply factory of 900,000 square feet at Linwood. These efforts have now been rewarded by an application by the Pressed Steel Company and this project will be admirable if it comes off. The length of time which it has taken, however, and the absence of interest by any other good firms show how difficult the situation has been. (3) The Ministry of Supply factory of Germiston in the Glasgow area of 200,000 square feet is still without any satisfactory allocation. Half of it was allocated some time ago to the La Plante Choate Corporation who cannot commence operations for a long time owing to shortage of materials and accessories. The remainder of the factory has hitherto been occupied by the Ministry of Fuel on the repair of coal excavating machinery but this work is shortly coming to an end, so that the whole factory is likely to be idle in a month or two. (4) Similar difficulties have arisen with the Coltness Factory at Newmains, the Phoenix Works at Rutherglen and the Ministry of Supply store at Irvine, though in all these cases the premises are apparently not very suitable for ordinary industrial use, and there have been complications about making the Coltness factory available.

If satisfactory long-term uses were found for the above factories and the Blackburn Aircraft Factory at Dumbarton employment prospects might be increased by about 8,300 men and 2,400 women, thus reducing the surplus of men to 32,200 if all the 'advance' factories are satisfactorily disposed of. In view, however, of the history of efforts hitherto to let the factories mentioned above the prospects do not look very hopeful. There are various difficulties in finding sufficient of the right type of male employing firms, such as lack of scope for expansion in the heavy engineering industries following the war time expansion, the current lack of materials such as steel, and the individual problems involved in setting up new units in new areas, instead of expanding existing units.

Remedies for the lack of sufficient male employing projects might be sought in any of the following:-

(a) Measures to promote the prosperity of the basic industries of the area as suggested in the White Paper on Employment Policy (Cmd. 6527): This is obviously desirable but we must face the fact that in the Scottish Development Area coal-mining is diminishing: the major project for the steel industry involves a transfer from one part of the Development Area to another and no substantial increase in employment: and ship-building cannot be expected to continue indefinitely at its present high level of employment.

(b) A greater propensity to expand by native Scottish firms: Again there is nothing I should welcome more, but, apart from the problems of the basic industries to which I have referred, Scottish Engineering and other male employing firms suffer from the difficulties I have mentioned [above].

(c) More advance building of factories, particularly of the heavy type. This seems to me to offer the best prospect of attracting the right type of private firms and I am very glad that the present programme for the Scottish Development Area of over 2½ million square feet includes 840,000 square feet of a type suitable for heavy and medium engineering such as employs male labour. The employment programme of advance factory building has been taken account of in the figures given earlier in this paper.

Summary and Conclusion -

On the assumption that the targets set out in Part I of this memorandum are still the right ones.

(1) The firm projects for the Scottish Development Area still leave us short of employment for something like 45,100 men.

(2) The gap would be diminished to the extent of not more than 12,900 if the existing factories available and the advance factories now planned could be satisfactorily allocated to firms employing male labour.

(3) There, has, however, been great difficulty in securing such allocations so far.

The question which remains is whether in the circumstances we should continue to hope for a solution of the male unemployment problem from the existing policy, or supplement it by more direct Government production as I have suggested. I am convinced in my own mind that we should do the latter. [PRO, CAB 132/24 LP(DI)(47)41.]

BUILDING LABOUR, UNEMPLOYMENT AND THE SCOTTISH DEVELOPMENT AREA, 1947

In August 1947 the Government ran into severe balance of payments difficulties, largely over its trade with the USA. In response, to save dollars and boost exports, the Cabinet established an official Investment Programmes Committee to review and prioritise Departmental spending plans. The Cabinet also agreed that there should be some curtailment of the housing programme. The Investment Programmes Committee, after reviewing the supply of timber, subsequently agreed to impose a ceiling on the number of building workers and generally limit approval of new tenders to houses for mining and agricultural workers. By implication this also meant restrictions to the advance factory programme. The extract here is from the Scottish Office's observations to these proposals.

Letter of J.J.W. Handford, Assistant Under Secretary of State, the Scottish Office, on Building Labour, Unemployment and the Scottish Development Area, 11 September 1947.

We have been looking at I.P.C.(W.P.)(47) 19 and would like to make certain comments from the Scottish point of view. The Housing Departments have, of course, already made their position clear, and the following comments are made from a more general standpoint.

The paper argues very well the difficulty of converting a reduction of the building programme into a release of building labour for other work. It thinks, however, in terms of a shortage of manpower and it does not deal with the quite different problem which arises in many parts of Scotland, notably the industrial areas and possibly in the Development and other Areas in England as well, where there is unemployment and where a reduction in the building programme, in so far as it resulted in a release of workers and not merely in their absorption in maintenance work or the Black Market, would not make them available for other industry but simply make them unemployed.

One of the main purposes of reducing our building programme is presumably in the first place to make labour available for productive industry, notably the export industries. This whole concept is inapplicable to most of the industrial areas of Scotland especially the Development Area because:- (1) Productive industries are not held up for lack of labour. There is substantial unemployment in most of them. What prevents expansion of the productive industries is lack of raw materials and lack of factory space (vide in particular paragraph 8 of the White Paper on Industry and Employment in Scotland—Cmd. 7125). (2) In so far as raw materials, e.g. steel, are produced in Scotland the difficulty of increasing their output is not one of labour but of plant and more basic materials, e.g. coal. The difficulty of increasing coal output is partly one of labour, but this arises to some extent from shortage of houses in the new mining areas such as Fife. (3) There is thus not an overall shortage of manpower in Scotland but a surplus. If the building programme is reduced the surplus building labour will either go to the Black Market or become unemployed. The point is well brought out in the Ministry of Transport Paper I.P.C.(W.P.)(47) 14 in which they suggest that road schemes in the Development Areas and in the Scottish crofter counties should be treated on a different basis from those elsewhere. (4) Moreover the whole possibility of increasing output in Scotland and of enabling Scotland to make its maximum contribution to the export drive depends on maintaining a substantial building programme to provide houses for miners and to provide factories. If there are no more new factories Scottish labour will continue to be wasted.

We suggest, therefore that it would be desirable to cover these points in the Draft Report; and that it is for consideration whether there should be a further conclusion in I.P.C.(W.P.)(47)19 to make the points that a reduction in the building programme would have to be related to the labour supply situation in the building and other industries, in different parts of the country; and should not take place in areas where it would cause unemployment or where the building programme requires to be maintained if houses, factories and other things necessary to enable the local labour to contribute to the production drive are to be provided. [PRO, CAB 134/444 IPC(WP)(47)41.]

SCOTLAND AND THE DISTRIBUTION OF INDUSTRY PANEL, 1948

In May 1948 the Government's Inter-Departmental Committee on Building Controls agreed to recommend the relaxing of procedures for the extension or building of factories. In particular they proposed that the UK Distribution of Industry Committee Panel A should only deal with matters of general policy and not with individual applications from industrialists. They proposed, instead, that each Board of Trade Region should consider the applications and advise other Regions of any that might be suitable for their area. The first extract is from a Scottish Office letter to the Committee's chairman on the issue. The second is from a minute of the Permanent Under Secretary of State after he had spoken to Arthur Woodburn, the Scottish Secretary, and the third from a subsequent minute of the Home Department's Secretary. The Committee's proposals were later approved by the Government. The Scottish Departments were not represented on the Committee.

Letter of H.R. Smith, Assistant Under Secretary of State, the Scottish Office, on the Building Controls Committee Proposals, 11 June 1948.

In the very limited time available we have been able to study only the major recommendations contained in the Report, and we have discussed these with the Scottish Home Department. We are seriously concerned about the recommendations dealing with the future of Panel A. As we understand it Panel A was originally set up to enable the Departments concerned jointly to keep under review the development and execution of distribution of industry policy throughout the United Kingdom as a whole. It is in almost precisely this language that its functions are described in the White Paper on Employment Policy; and, so far as Scotland is concerned, the overall direction which Panel A has been able to secure has worked well. The effect of the Committee's recommendations, on the other hand, would be to convert the Panel from a body exercising these important directing functions into an appeal tribunal to settle differences between Regional Controllers, and seriously to disturb the machinery for the co-ordinated direction of the policy laid down in the White Paper. It is true that your Committee contemplates that the Panel will continue to deal with particular questions of location policy and the special problems and needs of particular areas; but in our view it will be difficult for the Panel to exercise these general functions which are mainly of an advisory nature if they have no executive power of decision over the location of major projects. The Panel at present provides the only machinery whereby location within Great Britain as a whole of important individual projects can be fully considered before final decisions are reached; and it seems to us essential that there should continue to be some machinery of this kind for dealing with major projects if distribution of industry policy is to be effectively directed on a national basis.

We agree that the present Panel A procedure can stand some over-hauling. But we suggest that the Panel should continue to exercise close supervision over the location of all major developments, say, over 100,000 square feet, and should continue to have as its special charge the scrutiny of all projects over 5,000 square feet in the Greater Birmingham and Greater London areas.... Naturally we have had no opportunity of consulting the Secretary of State at this stage; but in view of the very great value which is attached in Scotland to the present concerted examination by Panel A of major industrial projects, we think it likely that he will view with considerable concern the proposal that the Panel's functions should be substantially curtailed on the lines recommended in the Report. [SRO, DD10/560.]

Minute of Sir David Milne, Permanent Under Secretary of State for Scotland, on the Building Controls Committee Proposals, 17 June 1948.

On the understanding that there will be full consultation by the Scottish Regional Controller with us before he decided any individual case, and that we shall receive periodic reports showing all distribution of industry approvals given by the Board of Trade S of S does not wish to take any exception to the Committee's proposals. He is impressed by the need for reducing Committee work & by the fact that it will be up to the Board of Trade under the watchful eye of the Scottish Office the Ministry of Labour and Parliament to see that justice is done all round. [SRO, DD10/2.]

Minute of Charles C. Cunningham, Secretary, the Scottish Home Department, on the Building Controls Committee Proposals, 19 June 1948.

Mr Smith and I discussed this matter with the U.S. of S. to-day. So far as the Department are concerned there are two main difficulties.

1. Under the new procedure we shall have no advance information about new industrial enterprises which it is proposed to establish in England and Wales, and accordingly no opportunity of trying to divert to Scotland those which are particularly suitable for settlement in this country. U.S. of S assured us that the Secretary of State was fully aware of this when taking his decision to withdraw the representations made against the new Scheme.

2. The Ministry of Labour are very strongly opposed to the new Scheme for the same reasons as we have put forward. To some extent they were influenced in their attitude to it by the initiative taken by the Scottish Departments. They will, therefore, view with concern our defection at this stage in the argument. U.S. of S agreed that we should inform the Ministry of Labour that our change of attitude has resulted from a decision of the Secretary of State. [SRO, DD10/2.]

SCOTLAND, THE FORD MOTOR COMPANY AND THE DISTRIBUTION OF INDUSTRY, 1948

In July 1948 the Ford Motor Company informed the Government that it wished to expand its Dagenham works above the level it agreed in 1946. Almost immediately the Board of Trade tried to persuade the firm to expand in one of the development areas. However, Ford compiled its own report on relocation costs and insisted on remaining at Dagenham. The following extract is from the memorandum presented to the Distribution of Industry Committee by Tom Fraser, the Joint Parliamentary Under Secretary of State for Scotland. The Committee generally agreed that Ford's proposal should be refused, but referred the matter to the Production Committee for a decision. The

Committee took a similar view, but George Strauss, the Minister of Supply, and Harold Wilson, the President of the Board of Trade, decided to approve the proposal on the basis that refusal could adversely affect exports.

Memorandum by Thomas Fraser, Joint Parliamentary Under Secretary of State for Scotland, on Ford Motor Company's Proposals for Expansion, 10 December 1948.

I feel obliged to bring to the notice of my colleagues the Scottish point of view on the Ford Motor Company's proposals for expansion at Dagenham.

It seems to me that if we allow Fords to expand still further at Dagenham we are coming very near to abandoning the principles on which our distribution of industry policy is based. Fords were told in 1946 that their labour force would not be permitted to exceed 14,000 and this limit has already been substantially exceeded. I am afraid that if we do not draw a line now it will be impossible to resist any other manufacturer who wished to expand in the London area. Naturally any firm that has to disperse will be involved in expenditure, but the alternative is that the country should bear the cost involved in expansion in an already congested district through the inevitable increase in transport and housing difficulties, the strategic risk, and the loss involved to other parts of the country. It is because dispersal means a saving to the public in these and other respects that inducements are offered in the Development Areas, and this aspect of the matter should not be lost sight of.

Some of the objections to be raised by Fords against the Kirkby site, which is understood to be an inland site about 4½ miles distant from the nearest suitable berthage in Liverpool, would not appear to be applicable to a proposal to set up part of their production on Clydeside. Fords have been offered a riverside site on the Clyde comprising about 150 areas of dead flat serviced land with siding connections and trunk road access. The site immediately adjoins one of the biggest power stations in the West of Scotland and power supplies are already laid on to the site. As an inducement to the Ford Company the Clyde Navigation Trust are prepared to spend £750,000 on the provision of wharfage, including cargo sheds and railway tracks on the site to meet the Company's requirements and the general additional requirements of the Trust in the Clyde Area. The Scottish Office feel very strongly that this most generous offer by the Clyde Navigation Trust taken into conjunction with the financial facilities which could be made available by the Board of Trade under the Distribution of Industry Act, should go far to offset the financial disadvantages of the removal of this element in Fords production to Clydeside. Until such time as this berthage could be completed, ample dock facilities are available at a distance of about a mile.

As regards housing and other facilities for the workers on Clydeside, the site offered to Fords—and I understand very favourably considered by them—-

immediately adjoins a new housing estate under construction by the Renfrew Town Council, is readily accessible and is on a tram route from Glasgow (4½ miles distant). The new Ford development would also be closely adjacent to the larger new town development which has already been approved by the Lord President's Committee for the Houston Areas of Renfrewshire.

In specifying their requirements in the course of their investigations of the Clydeside facilities, Fords indicated that they would expect to build up to a labour force of upwards of 5,000 within three years. This labour force is readily obtainable in the Clydeside Area where the latest number of registered unemployed in Glasgow alone is 22,000, but it is difficult to see how it could be procured in that scale at Dagenham.

The Ford Company's report bases their objections to dispersal on financial grounds, but I am not convinced that the figures which they have produced do not require further examination. For instance, it would seem from the information obtained by the Department of Health for Scotland about the firm's requirements that the additional cost of power, estimated at £2. 4. 3d. per tractor in the report, could be reduced on Clydeside. The Company's very heavy demands for process water which seem to be a factor in their figures, could also be met very cheaply. Moreover, the firm's estimates for additional capital expenditure appear to take no account of assistance available under the Distribution of Industry Act, and it might well be that the cost of £8. 4. 2d. per tractor attributed to capital investment could be considerably reduced.

I therefore suggest that the Ford Company have by no means made their case for further expansion at Dagenham. The statement prepared by the Company on the cost of dispersal on a small scale, without reference to future expansion, must inevitably present a distorted picture of what might be involved. The Ministry of Supply are apparently willing to initiate discussions with the Company about their further programme, and my view is that the Committee can reach no decision until such discussions, at which the Board of Trade and the Scottish Office should be represented have taken place and complete information is available as to the possibilities of dispersal on a basis of expected future expansion. [PRO, CAB 134/130 DI(48)37.]

THE ADEQUACY OF FACTORY ACCOMMODATION IN SCOTLAND, 1949

In December 1948 Ness Edwards, the Parliamentary Under Secretary at the Ministry of Labour, informed Tom Fraser, the Joint Scottish Parliamentary Under Secretary, that he was disturbed by the low rate of factory building in the Development Areas and suggested that the Scottish Departments might like to undertake some inquiries. Fraser agreed and the Scottish Distribution of Industry Panel was instructed to prepare a memorandum for a meeting of the Scottish Economic Conference. The paper was initially drafted by Scottish officials of the Board of Trade, but was redrafted after the Home Department objected to a suggestion that Scottish industrialists lacked enterprise. The following is an extract from the finally agreed memorandum, which the Conference accepted.

Memorandum (SEC 27) by the Distribution of Industry Panel for Scotland on the Adequacy of Factory Accommodation in Scotland, May 1949.

Results Achieved so Far. The Distribution of Industry Policy reviewed today, four years after its adoption, appears, in conjunction with other developments since 1937, to have achieved substantial results. Projects in operation or planned for the Scottish Development Area produced 52,000 jobs between 1937 and February, 1949, and are expected eventually to offer 117,000 jobs which were not in existence in 1937. In addition to these new projects, existing concerns have contributed to the high level of employment during the post-war years in factories by employing more people than before the War. In general it may be said that the need for creating further new jobs for women will have disappeared in most places when the present programme has been completed. On the other hand new opportunities for employing men are still needed in a number of places.

The Distribution of Industry Act provides various forms of encouragement for the development of industry in the scheduled areas. Probably the most important has been the provision of new factories at favourable terms on Industrial Estates or on individual sites. In this connection the decision taken in 1946, to allow factories to be built in advance of approval of specific tenants, was of special advantage to Scotland. The earlier policy had been for factories to be built by the Estate Company only after their future tenants had definitely agreed to occupy them. Not many firms were prepared to commit themselves to occupy a factory which might not be available for two or more years. The construction of these 'advance' factories achieved a notable success. A programme of buildings covering two million square feet was put in hand, and most of the factories have already procured tenants.

Advantageous and disadvantageous factors arising from the general economic situation have recently affected the Scottish Development Area. Before the balance of payments crisis in the autumn of 1947 led to restriction being placed on capital investment and to the introduction of stricter 'essentiality' tests for new projects, the Scottish Development Area had profited from having a greater surplus of labour than the Midlands and South of England. This helped to offset the counter-attractions that much more Government war-time factory space was available in England than in Scotland, and together with the 'advance' factories was mainly responsible for the success which then attended the attraction of new projects to Scotland.

The economic measures adopted towards the end of 1947 had an important bearing on the distribution of industry policy. Since then firms applying for factories built under the Act have, before their application can be considered, had to pass quite severe tests of the capacity to contribute immediately and directly to the solution of our balance of payments problem. This policy has affected the Scottish Development Area in various ways:

(a) It has in many instances not been possible to prevent the expansion in London and the Midlands of firms whose production promised to make an early and substantial contribution to exports or import saving, but who were either unwilling or unable to carry out this expansion in the Scottish or any other Development Area;

(b) Less consideration has been given to preferential treatment in the supply of raw materials to new projects on the ground of their being in the Development Areas. They must also now contribute to the export drive:

(c) The establishment of consumer goods industries, in order to diversify the Scottish industrial structure, has received a set-back, because consumer goods industries tend to cater for the home market and, apart from food production, rarely satisfy the 'essentiality' tests.

(d) Authority for erecting further 'advance' factories has been withdrawn and other schemes have been deferred.

The part played by firms of Scottish origin in the progress of the Scottish Development Area naturally attracts public notice in Scotland. Because of the relatively small number of *major* expansion schemes initiated by firms of Scottish origin it has been suggested that Distribution of Industry policy has been applied in a way likely to offer more encouragement to firms outside Scotland than to native enterprises. This suggestion is not borne out by the facts.

As about two-thirds of the ... 338 acceptances [out of 397 applications] were Scottish, and the proportion of them rejected or deferred was about the same as for applications coming from elsewhere, the figures suggest that Scottish enterprise has done fairly well. In almost every case, moreover, the grounds for rejections have been that the production department concerned was unable to regard the firm's prospective output or export performance as of sufficient importance to justify the use of scarce resources at the present time.

Of all large industrial post-war projects (50,000 square feet and over) in the Scottish Development Area, including both those which are now in production and those which had still to reach that stage at February, 1949, 44 are by firms of Scottish origin (employment to be offered for 12,400 persons). 34 are from other parts of the United Kingdom (24,000), 7 are from United States or

Canadian firms (3,880), and 4 came from Europe (3,350). In addition four projects are accounted for by nationalised industries or Government Departments in the United Kingdom (2,360). It is true that only a small proportion of the major expansion schemes (12 over 100,000 square feet) are of Scottish origin, but projects of all sizes by firms of Scottish origin contribute about half the employment being provided by the new industrial developments in the Scottish Development Area.

Three outstanding Problems. The first outstanding problem in the Scottish Development Area is that of providing work for fit unemployed men. There are three men unemployed for every woman, but the new projects require only four men to three women.

This problem has several aspects. There is, for instance, the necessity for any large men-employing project attracted to the Development Area to be of sufficient importance in the current economic situation to obtain support on production and export grounds.

Comparatively few new projects wish to employ men exclusively. Accordingly a further obstacle is encountered in districts where women are available only in very small numbers.

The second outstanding problem arises from the substantial proportion of unemployed men in the Development Area who are elderly or less fit. New firms coming to a district show a tendency to recruit fit men, already in employment in other local factories, rather than to absorb the unemployed men. Accordingly a pool of less fit unemployed men persists.

A third outstanding problem arises from the over-dependence of some parts of the Development Area on a narrow range of industries. As was pointed out in the White Paper on the Distribution of Industry, the Scottish Development Area is still exceptionally dependent on the production of capital goods. The increased diversification which has been achieved in the last few years is gratifying, but considerably more is still desirable.

Conclusions.

In *West Dunbartonshire*, though much has been done to provide additional employment, a considerable residue of unemployment, mainly among men, is likely to persist. Factory building therefore is not yet adequate.

In *Lanarkshire* the situation is complicated by doubts as to the extent of migration out the county. If this migration attains the levels desired by the National Coal Board there will be no need for additional factory space. On the other hand, if migration falls short of the National Coal Board's expectations, additional factory space may be needed.

It is expected that there will be a moderate surplus of men in *Edinburgh and the Lothians*, (concentrated almost entirely in Edinburgh). Private development should be encouraged locally to absorb this surplus.

It is estimated that quite serious unemployment among fit men will persist in *Glasgow, Greenock and Port Glasgow*. Treatment of the problem in these areas is recommended as a matter of urgency.

In order to make an early contribution to this problem it is recommended that site preparation should be begun on a certain number of Estates already acquired in *Glasgow*, especially Balmore (North of City), Belvidere (South East of City), and Garscadden (West of City), where unemployment is substantial. [SRO, DD10/92/2.]

ADVANCE FACTORIES AND THE DEVELOPMENT OF EAST KILBRIDE, 1949-50

The first extract here is from a letter of the Home Department to the Board of Trade on the issue of building advance factories, sent after the discussion at the Scottish Economic Conference (see above). The Board, however, continued to maintain its stance of no relaxation in the test of export 'essentiality' and in the Autumn the East Kilbride Development Corporation also wrote to the Board on the issue. The second extract is from a letter of John Edwards, the Board's Parliamentary Secretary, to Arthur Woodburn, the Scottish Secretary, clarifying the position. The following spring, East Kilbride and Scottish Industrial Estates wrote again to the Board, and the third extract is a letter of support from Hector McNeil, the new Scottish Secretary, to Harold Wilson, President of the Board of Trade. The final extract is from a Board letter, sent after the Cabinet's Production Committee had met and agreed to modify the Government's policy. In March 1951 the Board and the Home Department agreed to rent the new advance factory to Rolls-Royce.

Letter of R.E.C. Johnson, Assistant Secretary, Scottish Home Department, on Advance Factory Building in Glasgow and East Kilbride, 23 June 1949.

There are three points that I should take up with you following the discussion about factory building at the Scottish Economic Conference on 20th May. Sir Steven Bilsland has also spoken about them informally to the Secretary of State. They concern: (1) site preparation on the Industrial Estates in Glasgow on which no work has yet been begun; (2) the building of nest factories in advance on some of the Glasgow estates; (3) advance building at East Kilbride.

On the first two points the paper for the Economic Conference (S.E.C. 27) pointed out that Glasgow was one of the areas where unemployment was most serious and recommended that site preparation be begun on a number of the Glasgow estates.... In brief—(1) Unemployment in Glasgow is very high and in particular large numbers of civil engineering workers of the type used in site preparation are available: (2) Scottish Industrial Estates' present programme is now well advanced and it is most desirable that some further work should replace, at least partially, that which is being completed; (3) (A point which Sir Steven Bilsland especially emphasised at the Conference) Glasgow has suffered more than most places from the restriction on factory building since 1947 as much of the ground acquired for industrial estate purposes was not available until after the restrictions were imposed.

As regards East Kilbride I understand that the acquisition of about 50 acres of land for an industrial estate has been authorised by the Board of Trade but that you have turned down a proposal to begin construction of four advance factories with the necessary roads. The point I am asked to put to you is that unless some early start is made with factory building the balanced development of this community will be seriously delayed. The Development Corporation expect to have 180 houses completed by the end of this year and 380 by the end of 1950. Even if factories are started now they will hardly be available before that time, and if there is any further delay, East Kilbride will develop as a dormitory for Glasgow, which is quite contrary to the intention of the new town.

We realise the difficulties involved in advance building at present. It is quite clear, however, from recent discussions at the Production and D.I. Committees, that Ministers desire a strengthening of distribution of industry policy and this desire is reflected in the decision to relax somewhat the standards of essentiality required for Development Area projects. It may be that there are now sufficient specific projects which you could approve as a result of this decision, and steer to Glasgow and East Kilbride, to meet in effect the proposals put forward by the Scottish Economic Conference and Scottish Industrial Estates. Even if this is not so, however, we would suggest that the proposals for advance site preparation and factory building are very modest and could be justified, in the local circumstances. At East Kilbride, in particular, it will be far easier to attract industrialists to the new town if prospective tenants can be shown at least one or two factories as well as houses on the ground. [SRO, DD10/91.]

Letter of John Edwards, Parliamentary Secretary, the Board of Trade, on Advance Factory Building at East Kilbride, 7 October 1949.

The President and I have received similar letters from Sir Patrick Dollan of the East Kilbride Development Corporation. We understand from the letter that you intend visiting East Kilbride on 10th October ... when the Corporation hope to discuss with you proposals to build their own factories. I was hoping to see you or Tom Fraser [Parliamentary Under Secretary] to let you know the Board of Trade's views, but as this was impossible I thought I should let you know in writing the general line we have been taking as I think it is important in this matter that the Government should speak with one voice.

I think the position is now accepted that advance factory building could not be justified while the present restrictions on Capital Investment are maintained. The Corporation are, however, anxious that we should make some start on the site development of the industrial area at East Kilbride so that it will be ready for factory building when suitable projects come along. Their wish for site development at East Kilbride links up with requests we have had from various sources to do at least some preliminary work on sites which we have in reserve in the Glasgow area but on which so far no work has been done. Our attitude to date has been that the expenditure of public money on the development of these sites would not be justified under present conditions so long as other estates exist in and around Glasgow which are already developed and which have room for a considerable degree of further factory building. For your own information, however, we are once again reviewing the possibility of doing at least some preparatory work on undeveloped estates and while it is by no means certain that such work will be finally agreed we feel at least that it is much less open to objection than any form of advance factory building. In the event of it being decided to proceed with work on the other sites held by the Board of Trade for future development by Scottish Industrial Estates Ltd., we shall certainly consider the claims of East Kilbride for initial site development at the same time. While I should not like any such assurance to be given to Dollan, I think there is no doubt that we should do at least some work at East Kilbride if the principle of further site development in the Glasgow area were accepted at all. All told, I think our line with Dollan should be that while we cannot commit ourselves to doing any work in the near future we are certainly prepared to review the whole position. [SRO, SEP 4/564.]

Letter of Hector McNeil, Secretary of State for Scotland, on Site Preparation at East Kilbride Industrial Estate, 10 March 1950.

Lord Bilsland and Sir Patrick Dollan, in their capacities as Chairman of Scottish Industrial Estates and Chairman of the East Kilbride Development Corporation, have sent me the enclosed letter proposing that a start should be made immediately on site preparation on the Nerston industrial estate at East Kilbride. I understand they have written to you in similar terms.

This question was, you will remember, raised with you by my predecessor and by both Bilsland and Dollan with John Edwards when you were up here last autumn and the general arguments in its favour are, I think, familiar to you. Briefly they are that housing development at East Kilbride is now proceeding at a pace which makes it essential, if the new town is to fulfil its purpose, to look ahead to employment opportunities for the population within about two years from now. The Corporation, for instance, finished 68 houses in 1949 (as compared with 97 for all the English new towns), 200 additional houses are under construction and have reached an advanced stage, and a further 200 are going out to tender shortly. We are therefore satisfied that the forecast enclosed with the joint letter by Bilsland and Dollan of the population build-up in the new town is realistic. Meanwhile unemployment is on the increase both in Glasgow and in the districts of North Lanarkshire which the new town of East Kilbride is designed to serve. For instance, in Blantyre-Cambuslang areas there are very few sites available for any further housing development and the Lanarkshire County Council look to East Kilbride to meet the bulk of the housing demand in these areas. The Scottish Industrial Estates Company have got an agreed plan with the Development Corporation, the boundaries of the Estate have been determined and both the Estates Company and the Corporation are simply waiting for the Board of Trade to acquire the ground in accordance with the previously agreed arrangements and to get ahead with preliminary development on the lines proposed. My Department have agreed to the County Council laying the main sewer to service the industrial estate and this work is in hand. Finally, the Development Corporation have already submitted to the Board of Trade a list of the firms who are anxious to take up space at East Kilbride and I understand that the issue of the first industrial development certificate is under consideration by your Department.

I therefore hope that it will be possible for you to agree to the request which Bilsland and Dollan have put forward but if you would like to discuss the matter first, at a meeting at which they might attend as you think fit, then perhaps we could have a talk about it. [SRO, DD10/91.]

Letter of J.L. Reading, Assistant Secretary, the Board of Trade, on the Production Committee's Modification of Industrial Building Policy, 25 August 1950.

Thank you for your letter of 22nd August [from R.E.C. Johnson] referring to Sir Patrick Dollan's letter to the Secretary of State about industrial development at East Kilbride and the subject of relaxation of the industrial building criteria. I regret that we have not previously told you what has been happening about the modification of industrial building policy and the commencement of a limited amount of advance factory building.

The Production Committee decisions of the 5th July were briefly:- (a) to relax restrictions on industrial building in the Development Areas and other areas of heavy unemployment in favour of those projects which would provide predominantly male employment, and (b) to embark upon a limited programme of advance factories to provide male employment in the Development Areas ...

Of the twelve advance factories to be built, the President decided [at the meeting] that eight should be started as soon as possible on land already acquired by the Board; four for Merseyside, two on the North East Coast, one in South Wales and one in Scotland; decisions in relation to the siting of the remaining four to be left until a little later on.

As far as East Kilbride is concerned, we have decided that we shall now seek Treasury authority to erect an advance factory there as soon as the state of site preparation work warrants this.

In regard to Balmore [Industrial Estate], we have always been under the impression, and Oakley [Scottish Regional Controller, Board of Trade] was consulted, that Balmore was the best site for an advance factory in Glasgow, provided we could get Treasury authority for the necessary site preparation work. The question of Balmore versus Garscadden to which you refer in your letter is one on which we ought to have the benefit of local knowledge and advice. I have, therefore, arranged with Oakley that he shall seek the advice of his Distribution of Industry Panel as to whether Balmore or Garscadden should be developed now to accommodate one of the advance factories in this new programme. In the meantime, in conversation with the Treasury, we understand that they agree with us in principle that it would be right to develop an estate in the North of Glasgow because hitherto most of the industrial development in Glasgow has been in other parts.

With regard to the letter which Sir Patrick Dollan has sent to the President, we propose to reply that in view of the modification of the industrial building criteria, we are going to press on with the initial development of the industrial estate at Nerston with a view to commencing the construction of a factory in advance of demand on it as soon as possible. We also propose to suggest that Sir Patrick Dollan should consult our Regional Controller about those concerns whose projects have been held up in the past owing to the capital investment restrictions but who are now prepared to go ahead and employ predominantly male labour. But I think we must stipulate that 'relaxation' can only be considered if they are firms new to Scotland or are existing Scottish firms which by expanding will provide worth-while additional employment. In other words, straightforward re-location of Glasgow industry must be ruled out under 'relaxation'. [SRO, SEP 4/565.]

THE CAIRNCROSS REPORT AND GOVERNMENT POLICY, 1952-3

In April 1952 the Local Development Committee of the Scottish Council (Development and Industry), under the chairmanship of Professor Alec Cairncross, reported that there were considerable prospects for industrial expansion outside existing Development Areas. As a result it recommended that the Government should change its priorities and take steps to stimulate industrial growth 'in promising locations', then make better use of existing 'man-power and natural resources', and finally assist any community suffering from industrial 'decline'. The first extract is from the letter of James Stuart, the Scottish Secretary, to Peter Thorneycroft, the President of the Board of Trade, inviting his views on a possible response to the proposals. The second is from the Board of Trade's reply, delayed partly because the Cabinet itself had undertaken a review of economic policy. The third is from the Ministry of Labour's observations on a draft letter of the Secretary of State for the Scottish Council (Development and Industry). Stuart's published response (July 1953) was on the lines suggested by the Board and the Ministry. IDCs were certificates issued by the Board authorising a new factory or extension of over 5,000 square feet.

Letter of James Stuart, Secretary of State for Scotland, on the Report of the Local Development Committee of the Scottish Council (Development and Industry), 24 June 1952.

The proposals are, briefly, that the Government should take powers to build factories in any part of the country, as they now can in Development Areas, and that they should also contribute in appropriate cases to the cost of factories built by local authorities for lease to industrialists.

These are obviously ambitious proposals and I do not think either the Council or the Cairncross Committee would expect that they can be put into effect in the near future. Indeed ... the report makes it clear that the Committee have been concerned mainly with long-term objectives. Nevertheless, they raise important issues to which we must presumably apply our minds.

I think myself that the Committee may have over-emphasised the rigidity of the present distribution of industry policy. The schedule of development areas can, of course, be changed to take in new areas of serious unemployment and, as I understand it, the chief obstacle to introducing new industrial development in the few black spots that remain today is not the inadequacy of statutory powers but the severe restrictions on capital investment and Government expenditure. Even so, you are at present considering the possibility of creating new development areas in the north-east of Scotland and in Lancashire and Yorkshire, and we have been discussing capital investment for industry at the Economic Policy Committee. On the other hand, the Distribution of Industry Act can, of course, deal only with areas where there is a 'special danger of unemployment' and it has always been held that it is only appropriate to schedule as development areas districts where the absolute number of unemployed persons is large. In small towns assistance can be provided in other ways, e.g. under the New Towns Act or by the building of factories by local authorities with Government assistance from the Development Fund. The Development Fund, however, can only assist individuals who contribute to the welfare of a rural community.

The Committee themselves point out the disadvantage of scheduling too many areas as development areas and the same might apply with even greater force to their proposal that the Government should take powers to build factories, or to assist the building of factories by local authorities, all over the country. [SRO, DD10/438.]

Letter of H.S. Gregory, Second Secretary, the Board of Trade, on the Report of the Local Development Committee of the Scottish Council (Development and Industry), 14 January 1953.

It can be said that Government policy is not to put obstacles in the way of development in promising localities (indeed I.D.C.s are issued for them). But at the moment positive Government action from public funds—omitting the defence factories—is restricted to the third of his objectives, and prima facie Cairncross would not inject public money into an area where the decline was approaching ruin. This may be right or wrong. But it is not the policy which the Secretary of State and the President are called upon to administer under the Distribution of Industry Acts. It might be argued that the sets of objectives are not utterly inconsistent and that the Government's general economic policy is sufficiently flexible to encourage the growth of industrial development alike in the developing areas and in the Development areas. But the Cairncross order of priority is certainly not consistent with the special Government assistance which is granted by the Distribution of Industry Acts and with the special responsibilities assigned to the President and the Secretary of State by these Acts.

... Professor Cairncross wants the Government to provide financial assistance for new factory building 'where conditions warrant this step' and he appears to have in mind that this assistance should be granted not only to bring new industrial development to those areas where there is a special danger of unemployment, but also, and as a first call on resources, to assist the growth of the developing areas. Such a policy would inevitably result in the Government being called to subsidise industrial development throughout the country, even in places where development is taking place without assistance. This would be a major change in economic policy in this field.

You will recall that in his memorandum on development area policy [November 1952] the President drew attention to the fact that proposals had been made for a fundamental change in the concept of development area policy and said that if such a change were made it would require legislation. He pointed out that this legislation might well prove to be of a controversial nature and he doubted whether it would be appropriate for the Government to contemplate such legislation in the near future. We suggest therefore that any expression of a general attitude to the Report should be that while it contains interesting and novel suggestions, they are matters for consideration in the longer term. In the meantime what lie on our hands are the existing Distribution of Industry Acts designed to assist in diversifying the industrial structure of those areas which are so heavily dependent on a narrow range of industries that they are liable to special danger of unemployment. My own feeling is that it would be wise if the Minister of State is able, to confine his remarks to such general expressions. [SRO, DD10/438.]

Letter of Mary Smieton, Under Secretary, Employment Policy Division, the Ministry of Labour, on the Report of the Local Development Committee of the Scottish Council (Development and Industry), 22 May 1953.

The draft makes clear that each of the various objectives set out in the Cairncross report has found a place in Government policy since the war, but it goes on to say that the relative priority suggested by Cairncross is novel. That last remark is true if we are thinking of that one point of Government policy which is represented by the President of the Board of Trade's powers under the Distribution of Industry Acts, but I suggest it is not true of Government policy as a whole. That policy puts right in the forefront the placing of our whole economy on a sound basis in which expansion of industry and trade can take place. The Chancellor's recent financial policy set out in the Budget is aimed precisely at making that expansion possible. The areas which will gain the main benefit from it are those set out in I of the Cairncross objectives, and objective No II will benefit also. Objective No III, arresting the decline of communities, is the object of the special piece of policy administered through the Distribution of Industry Acts.

I think that we ought to answer Cairncross in terms of Government policy as a whole, and that we ought not to put ourselves in the position of accepting an order of priorities in that context. [SRO, DD10/43.]

THE SCOTTISH SECRETARY AND RISING UNEMPLOYMENT, 1953

In January 1953 the Cabinet's Economic Policy Committee met to discuss approval of a new roads programme to alleviate unemployment in West South Wales and the first extract is from the note of reservation by James Stuart, the Scottish Secretary, on its proceedings. The meeting concluded by establishing an inter-departmental working party of officials, under the chairmanship of H.S. Gregory, the Board of Trade, to review what measures could be taken to improve Scotland's economic position. The Working Party reported in May and concluded that the Government's policy of relaxing controls over private manufacturing investment, whilst restraining the public sector, meant that there was scope for only limited action. The second extract is from the minutes of a later meeting of Ministers. In October the Government agreed to build the Clyde Tunnel and commit additional funds to improve Scottish roads.

Minute of Cabinet Economic Policy Committee, on the South Wales Steel Redundancies, 19 January 1953.

The Secretary of State for Scotland said that unemployment in Scotland had risen from 56,000 in November 1951 to 72,000 in November 1952. At 3.5 per cent., the Scottish percentage was by far the highest for any region and was nearly double the national average. In parts of Scotland, the percentage was very much greater. He was under strong pressure to improve the communications in the Glasgow area. In particular he recommended the construction of the Whiteinch/Linthouse Tunnel under the Clyde, a quarter of the cost of which would be borne by the Corporation, and the improvement of the Glasgow-Stirling Trunk Road and of communications in the Highlands. Unless some measures similar to those announced for Wales could also be announced for Scotland, his position would become very difficult.

In discussion the following points were made:-

The Parliamentary Secretary, Ministry of Labour [H. Watkinson], confirmed the seriousness of the unemployment position in Scotland, and suggested that the closing down of whole sections of industry provided a parallel with the situation in West South Wales. On the other hand, it was pointed out that the basis of the case for aiding West South Wales was that the Government was responsible for the modernisation of the tin plate industry which was causing the unemployment and therefore had a responsibility for its relief. If relief of unemployment for its own sake was made the basis for special measures, this would also have to be applied to other parts of the UK, and the commitment would be dangerously extended.

The Chancellor of the Exchequer [R.A. Butler] said that he fully appreciated the difficult position of the Secretary of State for Scotland. While it would not be possible, for the reasons which had been brought out in discussion, to hold out any hope that major improvements in communications could be undertaken, it was possible that a statement might be made on the relaxation of tax restrictions on capital investment and building and on the fuller implementation of the Government's powers under the Distribution of Industry Act. [PRO, CAB 134/846 EA(53) 1st Meeting; SRO, DD10/452.]

Note of Discussion at the Treasury on Measures for the Relief of Unemployment, 18 June 1953.

THE SECRETARY OF STATE began by recalling the decision taken in the Economic Policy Committee in January, that the three Ministers concerned should meet to discuss what measures for the relief of unemployment in Scotland and areas of England could be announced. This decision was related to the announcement made by the Home Secretary that a road scheme in Wales was to be given special priority, that consideration was to be given to other urgent road works in Wales and that other measures to improve the economic position of the area would be considered. The Secretary of State said that he was faced next month with a two-day debate on the Scottish Estimates, which the Opposition had chosen to devote to a review of Scottish industry and employment. Unemployment in Scotland was still dangerously high and he was most anxious to have some constructive statement to make. The most important measures seemed to him to be the improvement of roads in the Highlands, the construction of the Clyde tunnel and the improvement of the Glasgow/Stirling road. The Secretary of State also referred to the report of the Gregory Committee and said that he would like to see the distribution of industry policy modified in the sense suggested in paragraph 13(1) so as to allow factories to be built in appropriate cases for firms already in the development area who wished to expand their production; he also thought that, as suggested in paragraph 13(3), the Board of Trade should be authorised to discuss, in appropriate cases, the possibility of paying removal expenses.

THE PRESIDENT OF THE BOARD OF TRADE [Peter Thorneycroft] said it was clear that no public announcement could be made about any of the measures discussed in the Gregory report and he was afraid that the adoption of either of the suggestions put forward by the Secretary of State would be very expensive and would have only a negligible effect in improving the employment position in Scotland. His own feeling was that we should undertake a thorough review of the expenditure now being incurred in Scotland—he thought that the total would be quite impressive—and should concentrate on measures which were likely to produce lasting returns. He mentioned, as an example, the development of cattle rearing in the Highlands, of which he had heard glowing reports.

He did not think that large-scale road building would help on any significant scale to attract industry to Scotland or the Highlands.

THE CHANCELLOR OF THE EXCHEQUER thought that modification of the Distribution of Industry Act policy on the lines suggested would not produce a worth while return from the money expended. He was, however, anxious to help in some way and he was inclined to think that the most appropriate way of doing so would be by assisting road development. He would like to help with roads for the improvement of forestry and fishing, and he would also like to see some roads for general development proposes being proceeded with. He was not too impressed with the possibilities of developing tourism, although he agreed that the argument was one which could properly be used. The Chancellor proposed to discuss the whole matter with the Minister of Transport and to negotiate with him an annual programme on the basis of the list submitted. The Chancellor also thought that something could be done to speed up investment in the public sector (mainly in the nationalised industries) in areas of high unemployment. The Treasury would go into both these questions and would suggest a form of words which the Secretary of State could use in the Estimates debate. [SRO, DD12/555.]

BRITISH EUROPEAN AIRWAYS, RENFREW AIRPORT AND THE SCOTTISH AIRCRAFT INDUSTRY, 1954

In early 1954 British European Airways informed the Government that for economic reasons it wished to transfer its maintenance base at Renfrew airport to London. The Cabinet's Home Affairs Committee was unable to reach agreement on the proposal and the matter was referred to the Cabinet. The first extract here is from the memorandum by James Stuart, the Scottish Secretary on the matter. The second is from the subsequent Cabinet discussion. In April 1955 Scottish Aviation Ltd. secured a contract to maintain Royal Canadian Air Force Sabre aircraft at Renfrew and the Government accepted BEA's proposal.

Memorandum by James Stuart, Secretary of State for Scotland, on British European Airways: Maintenance Base at Renfrew, 15 November 1954.

As I made clear to the Home Affairs Committee, I do not dispute the case made on financial grounds by the Minister of Transport and Civil Aviation. I suggest, however, that, on the broadest social, economic and political grounds, we should not agree to the transfer of the British European Airways' (B.E.A.) maintenance work from Renfrew to London until alternative aircraft work has been found for Renfrew.

The B.E.A. base was established at Renfrew in 1949 with a flourish of trumpets; and great credit has since been taken for the major contribution it has made to the building up—belatedly—of an aircraft industry in Scotland. The fact that the aircraft industry has in the main established itself in England and Wales is a matter about which there is strong feeling in Scotland. Both parties have undertaken to do all they can to encourage development in Scotland; and we can claim that the recent assistance promised for the Prestwick Pioneer is an example of our good intentions. We shall, however, lose heavily in public estimation if we now allow the Renfrew base to close. As the Minister recognises, Scottish opinion in Parliament and outside, and irrespective of party, has shown itself solidly in favour of its retention.

I concede that B.E.A. have made out their case that over the next five years a transfer to London of the maintenance work now done at Renfrew will effect an average saving of about £160,000 a year.

But we must look at the other side of the case. We shall be accused of concurring in a transfer to London of aircraft work now done in a development area, of adding, to however small an extent, to the concentration of aircraft work in the most vulnerable parts of the country, and of dealing an unnecessary blow to the small and struggling industry in Scotland. We shall be told—not without justification—that it makes nonsense of our development area policy if we build factories at great expense in the development areas and then let a nationalised industry withdraw part of its work from a development area to London. The Opposition will point out that in the debates on the Civil Aviation Bill in 1946 they undertook that the Government would do all in its power to encourage the development of an aircraft industry in Scotland; that they were instrumental in establishing the Rolls Royce factory at East Kilbride; and that had they remained in office they would, in accordance with their undertaking, have seen that the Renfrew base would remained in use. I need not stress the political consequences of all of this.

It is true that only some 600 men are involved and that about half will be offered—though they may well decline to accept—employment in London. But the drain of skilled men to London will merely add to the strength of criticism; and the most will be made of the remaining redundancy, especially as the prospects of finding employment for the men in Scotland are not good. The demands for Scottish engineering workers are diminishing—in particular there is no demand for the aero-fitters who will comprise the bulk of the redundant skilled workers—and the semi-skilled and unskilled will also create a difficult problem. Rolls Royce are closing their factory at Larkhall and there is already grave concern about the possibility of maintaining employment in the Rolls Royce factories at East Kilbride and Hillington. In fact the firm are already allowing their labour force to run down. [PRO, CAB 129/71 C(54)347; SRO, DD17/917.]

Cabinet Conclusions, on British European Airways: Renfrew Maintenance Base, 24 November 1954.

The Minister of Transport said that, in view of the strength of local feeling on this matter, the Chairman of the Corporation had sought the Government's views on it. It was not a matter on which he could give formal direction to the Corporation, but he could hardly decline the request for an expression of the Government's views. It had been confirmed by an independent accountant that B.E.A. would stand to save at least £800,000 over the next five years by making this change in their arrangements; and that the Chairman had made it clear that, if the Corporation were required to keep the base open, they would expect the Government to recoup them financially for the additional costs involved. The Minister said that he was proposing to discuss the matter with representatives of the Scottish Trade Union Council and the Scottish Council (Development and Industry), when he met then later in the week: but, although he would announce no decision until after he had held those discussions, he considered that B.E.A. would have to be told that the Government did not wish to press them to cancel the proposed move. Until it was definitely known that the premises would be available on a known date, it was difficult to take effective steps to find alternative tenants for them.

The Secretary of State for Scotland said that opinion in the Home Affairs Committee had been evenly divided on this question. He recognised the force of the economic arguments for the course which the Minister recommended, but there was no doubt that a plan which involved moving work on aircraft from a Scottish development area to a populous part of London would provoke strong criticism on both sides of the House of Commons and from opinion in Scotland generally.

In discussion it was argued, on the one hand, that to compel B.E.A. to carry on activities which had been conclusively shown to be unjustified on commercial standards would be inconsistent with the Government's constant pressure on the nationalised industries to become self-supporting and to dispense with Exchequer subsidies. It was also pointed out that, if the Government were to recoup B.E.A. financially for the loss they would sustain by maintaining their base at Renfrew, they would find it difficult in future to resist demands for financial assistance from firms which they were seeking to persuade to establish factories in development areas.

The view was expressed, on the other hand, that the Government would be justified in taking a broader view of the matter. There were sound reasons for discouraging further concentration of industry in London. From the general employment point of view, moreover, B.E.A.'s proposal would involve, on the one hand, redundancy for at least 250 of their employees in an area where there was in any case an increasing degree of unemployment, and, on the other, an intensification of the labour demand in North-West London where there was already a shortage of skilled workmen.

It was the view of the Cabinet that no final decision could be taken on this question until the outcome of the Minister's discussions with representatives of both sides of Scottish industry was known, and until further information was available about the possibilities of providing continuing employment for B.E.A.'s employees at the Renfrew base.

The Cabinet—(1) Invited the Minister of Transport and Civil Aviation to make a further report on this matter in the light of his forthcoming discussions with the Scottish Trades Union Council and the Scottish Council (Development and Industry). (2) Invited the President of the Board of Trade and the Minister of Supply to report on the prospects of finding an alternative tenant for the Renfrew premises, who could provide alternative employment if the B.E.A., moved their maintenance base to London. [PRO, CAB 128/27 CC(54)78.]

THE SCOTTISH STEEL INDUSTRY AND THE FOURTH STRIP MILL, 1954-6

In August 1953 the STUC raised the issue of a steel strip mill for Scotland with Peter Thorneycroft, the President of the Board of Trade. The matter was remitted by Thorneycroft to his officials for a report. The first extract is from the minute of the Home Department's Secretary to Lord Home, the Scottish Office Minister of State, on the matter. The second is Home's minute. The third is his letter to Selwyn Lloyd, the Minister of Supply, sent after Thorneycroft had urged Lloyd (who held the steel industry brief) to review the situation. The fourth, from a Scottish Home Department minute, reviews the position in October 1955. After further Board of Trade pressure the Government's Iron and Steel Board persuaded the nationalised Welsh Company, Richard Thomas and Baldwins, to look at a number of UK sites, including Grangemouth. The fifth extract is from a Department of Health memorandum after the firm's visit and the sixth, seventh and eighth extracts are from minutes of Scottish Ministers. The final extract is from James Stuart's (the Scottish Secretary) subsequent letter to Thorneycroft. The Minister replied by saying that he appreciated the points made and would consult Stuart when the firm's position 'crystallised'.

Minute of Sir Charles C. Cunningham, Secretary, Scottish Home Department, on the Scottish Iron and Steel Industry, 30 July 1954.

You will remember that the Board of Trade's Scottish Controller recently completed a report on the Scottish Iron and Steel Industry. The outcome of this Report was that the President of the Board of Trade wrote to the Minister of Supply in general terms about the questions brought out in it.

The conclusions [of the Minister of Supply's reply] which seem to emerge are that (a) a very difficult situation will be created by the closure of the Hallside Works near Cambuslang, with the dismissal of 1,100 workers. As the Minister says, the Departments concerned should be considering how to deal with this when it arises; (b) the Iron and Steel Board think the Scottish steel industry should continue to concentrate on the production of plates and sections for heavy industry, and they see no prospect of a light strip mill in Scotland, though they do not rule out the possibility of some minor diversification of steel production; (c) further blast furnace capacity may be needed in Scotland, but this could most economically be sited at Motherwell rather than at Gartsherrie. [SRO, SEP4/17.]

Minute of Lord Home, Minister of State, Scottish Office, on the Iron and Steel Industry, 9 August 1954.

Yes. It might be that the employment prospects, as revealed by the enquiry we have asked the Ch. of Exchequer to promote will strengthen the case for a continuous hot strip-mill being placed in Scotland. [SRO, SEP4/17.]

Letter of Lord Home, Minister of State, Scottish Office, on the Scottish Iron and Steel Industry, 28 October 1954.

The immediate problems of redundancy at Dixons and Hallside can, I think, best be studied as part of the general enquiry into the prospects of employment and development in the Scottish Development Area which it has now been agreed should be undertaken by the Scottish Distribution of Industry Panel. I do, however, agree most thoroughly with Thorneycroft's suggestion that we should lose no opportunity of pressing on the Iron and Steel Board the need for some further diversification within the Scottish steel industry. It is true, as he points out, that the prosperity of the steel industry in Scotland is very largely bound up with that of shipbuilding; a marked decline in activity in the shipyards would react at once on employment in the steel works. Conversely, the establishment of a strip mill in Scotland would not only achieve a much-needed diversification within the steel industry itself, but would also make it easier to attract to Scotland the lighter industries consuming steel strip. I do hope that you will ask the Iron and Steel Board to keep this consideration in mind when they are considering the location of the new capacity. [SRO, SEP4/17.]

Minute of W. Russell, Principal, Scottish Home Department, on the Location of the Fourth Steel Strip Mill, October 1955.

The question of establishing strip mill capacity in Scotland was raised with the Minister of Supply by the President of the Board of Trade in 1954, following a survey of the Scottish Steel Industry undertaken for the President by the Board of Trade office in Glasgow. This report showed that the Scottish Steel Industry had fallen behind in re-equipment and modernisation, compared with the industry elsewhere, that it was unduly concentrated on the heavy side (production of steel plates, tubes, etc.) and that there was an urgent need for its diversification, particularly by the establishment of strip mill production at present lacking in Scotland. Lack of this type of production ruled out for practical purposes, the establishment of any industry requiring supplies of strip steel in quantity; it was, therefore, a substantial obstruction to the Government's distribution of industry policy.

The President's representations were referred to the Iron and Steel Board, and shortly afterwards the major redevelopment scheme at Colville's was announced. The Iron and Steel Board reported, however, that there was not at that time any question of substantial increase of strip steel capacity and that this was not likely to become active for a considerable time ahead.

Ministers agreed that the Scottish Distribution of Industry Panel, should, in the course of their survey of unemployment prospects in the Scottish Development Area, examine the repercussions of changes in the iron and steel industry. This was done, and in their Report the Panel confirmed the findings of the earlier Board of Trade report; the unbalance of the iron and steel industry was referred to, the heavy and narrow interdependence of the iron and steel, shipbuilding and heavy engineering industry in the main Scottish Development Areas was described.

If the Iron and Steel Board are now considering the establishment of a new continuous hot strip mill, we should, it is suggested, ensure that the claims of the Scottish Development Area, (which were pressed also by the President of the Board of Trade last year) should be fully considered.

The Scottish Council (Development and Industry) have also been undertaking a survey of the Scottish Steel Industry, and though they have not quite finished their enquiry, we understand that they are likely to draw attention to the present deficiency of the Scottish Iron and Steel industry and to represent that until a strip mill is built in Scotland there is little prospect of securing large scale industries requiring steel sheet or strip steel as a raw material. The Scottish T.U.C. are also interested in this matter and we understand that it is their intention to approach the Iron and Steel Board in the near future. Both the Scottish Council and the S.T.U.C. are, however, afraid that the Iron and Steel

Board will have taken committing decisions before the Scottish Council's enquiries have been completed. [SRO, SEP4/17.]

Memorandum by John Anderson, Secretary, Department of Health, and Sir Charles Cunningham, Secretary, the Scottish Home Department, on an Integrated Steel Strip Mill, 26 July 1956.

Nature of Project

This Company, which already operate large steel mills in South Wales, propose to erect a new integrated steel plant and rolling mill with a capacity of 3,000,000 ingot tons per annum. In the first stage the major production will be motor sheet with a little tinplate; the final percentage of production will be 50 per cent. motor sheet, 34 per cent. tinplate and 16 per cent. light steel plate. At present the main market for these products is in the Midlands and London: there will also be some export of sheet and tinplate.

Employment Required

The project would provide work for 6-7,000 persons mostly male of whom 40 per cent. would be skilled. A wide variety of skills is involved including fitters, electricians and chemicals as well as the skills more directly associated with steel-making, such as blast furnace operators and the like. If the plant is located in Scotland, a maximum of 800 key-workers would require to be imported the remainder of the labour being recruited locally.

Importance of project to Scottish economy

There is a shortage throughout the United Kingdom of steel sheet such as this project would produce. None is at present manufactured in Scotland and it has been represented that for this reason the shortage is more acutely felt by concerns here. It seems clear that although Scotland would not be capable at present of absorbing more than a slight proportion of the output from such a mill its location in this country would have a vitalising effect and help attract a range of industry which tends to congregate in the English Midlands. The point was expressed by the Scottish Controller, Board of Trade, in his evidence to the Select Committee on Estimates, when the Development Areas were under review. He suggested that a new strip mill in Scotland would do more to overcome the stubborn unemployment percentage in the Scottish development area than practically any other project. The Scottish Trade Union Congress have also pressed the Iron and Steel Board most strongly for a steel strip plant in Scotland. For these and other reasons the location of this present project is of direct concern to the Secretary of State. There is an added reason, now that a prima facie suitable site has been seen by the Company, for ensuring that full consideration is given to a Scottish location. This is that it is understood that the Company had tentatively selected a site in South Wales for the new mill and that it was only pressure from the Iron and Steel Board and the Board of Trade which induced them to look further afield before a final decision was reached. (The project will cost approximately £170,000,000 and the Government will have a considerable say and stake in the financial arrangements.)

Disadvantages of Scotland

The largest market for the strip mills final product is in the English Midlands so that sites for the project decrease in attractiveness in proportion to their distance from this market, because of the addition to selling prices made by transport costs (Grangemouth is approximately three times further from Birmingham than is Newport, Monmouthshire, the area the Company are thought to have in mind). Such disadvantages might be counterbalanced if other requirements were more easily met in the Scottish location. In this connection it must be pointed out that there is no foreseeable prospect on the present plan of meeting the Company's coking coal requirements from Scottish resources. The Scottish Coal Board's programme takes into account Bairds and Colvilles new requirements including the larger needs of Colville's present expansions at Motherwell but fresh plans to exploit deep-lying coking coal seams would require to be made now at considerable capital cost and considerable increase in mining manpower if the Scottish Division were to attempt to produce the total requirement. Although sufficient reserves of coking coal are known to exist under the Forth, the Coal Board have indicated that four new major collieries would be needed to meet the Steel Mills total demand. The coal position is mentioned at some length since it is our opinion one of the most important issues governing location and involves the higher programme policy of the National Coal Board. [SRO, SEP4/17.]

Minute of Lord Strathclyde, Minister of State, Scottish Office, on the Location of the 4th Steel Strip Mill, 31 July 1956.

A project of this size and nature might well have such favourable repercussion on Scottish Industry as to reduce any difficulties or disadvantages to minor proportion. I feel we should face the difficulties and do all we can to get the project for Scotland. [SRO, SEP4/17.]

Minute of J. Nixon Browne, Parliamentary Under Secretary of State, the Scottish Office, on the location of the Fourth Steel Strip Mill, 31 July 1956.

1. This is just what Scotland needs, we must not lose it.

2. The project is big enough for us to face the consequential problems of housing, etc. with equanimity.

3. Since the Scottish Trade and Industry debate this also has a political angle. The President of the Board of Trade took part in the debate—perhaps the Secretary of Scotland's letter to him should remind him of this point on two

counts;- (a) Both sides said Scotland needs a strip mill (b) Labour said Scotland's industrial advancement is far behind England's. [SRO, SEP4/17.]

Minute of N. MacPherson, Parliamentary Under Secretary of State, the Scottish Office, on the Location of the Fourth Steel Strip Mill, 31 July 1956.

Despite the sacrifice of good agricultural land, we should obviously go all out to get this for Scotland, provided the right type of coking coal is available. It would be folly to set up the mill unless it has access to raw materials on an economic basis. [SRO, SEP4/17.]

Letter of James Stuart, Secretary of State for Scotland to Peter Thorneycroft, President of the Board of Trade, on the Location of the Fourth Steel Strip Mill, 1 August 1956.

Our Departments have already been in consultation over the proposal by Messrs. Richard Thomas and Baldwins to build a new very large integrated steel mill and I have been kept in touch with the investigations made by the firm into the possibility of locating this plant in Scotland. A site has been examined in the Grangemouth area of East Stirlingshire and there are, I am informed, subject to more detailed investigation reasonable prospects of the firm's very difficult site requirements being met there.

You will readily understand that the importance of attracting this project to Scotland cannot be stressed too strongly in my view. There is no strip mill in Scotland at present and if the new one were established there it would give a much better balance to the Scottish steel industry. It would also make a notable contribution to the solution of our intractable unemployment problem—both in the labour it would itself employ and by giving the general Scottish economy a much needed shot in the arm. As you know, our unemployment percentage is 2.1 compared with 1.0 in England and Wales. In the Development Area it is 2.4.

I would suggest that to put the new enterprise in Scotland would also conform to good distribution of industry policy. Of the existing strip mills, two are in Wales and one on the North-East coast.* To put the other in Scotland would give us a good spread of this section of the industry. It would certainly be welcomed in Scotland as you will remember from taking part in our debate on Industry and Employment on Tues 26th; on the other hand a decision to put it in one of the areas which already have such a mill would cause widespread concern.

Perhaps when matters are further advanced we could, if any points of difficulty arise about siting the project in Scotland, have a discussion before a final decision is reached. I assume that on economic policy the location of this plant is a matter you will in due course be putting up to our colleagues.

* PS is asking PS to President to correct this. All 3 are in Wales. [SRO, SEP4/17.]

THE SCOTTISH FACTORY BUILDING PROGRAMME, 1954-5

The first extract here is from the note of a meeting of Ministers and Officials called in December 1954 by the Minister of State, Lord Home, to discuss Scotland's factory building programme. The second is from the Board of Trade letter of response to the issues the meeting had raised. The Journal of Scottish Political Economy *had just published an article indicating that Scottish factory building had fallen behind England's.*

Note of a Meeting of Ministers and Officials on Factory Building in Scotland, 7 December 1954.

The Minister of State said that he had been worried for some time about progress with the provision of new factory buildings in Scotland, both inside and outside the development areas. His anxiety had been strengthened by the figures which, at his request, Scottish Home Department had analysed in their Memorandum of 6th December. As regards the most important of the development areas, the Clyde valley, he had persuaded the Board of Trade and other U.K. Departments concerned that there should be a review of present and possible future trends which would have an effect on the employment position in the next few years, and the first draft of the report was expected to be ready at the end of January. In the meantime, however, he would like to discuss whether anything could be done elsewhere by bringing to the attention of local authorities outside the development areas their powers under the Planning Acts to provide sites for factories and even to erect factory buildings. He had read the D.H.S. memorandum on the subject, but pointed out that it assumed wrongly that his proposal was that local authorities should make such provision on speculation, instead of waiting, as he intended, until a suitable firm came along.

Sir Charles Cunningham [Secretary, Home Department] said that over the whole post-war period, even on the new basis of estimation by floor area, Scotland had had a reasonable percentage of new factory space. The greatest volume of this, however had been established in Scotland in the immediate post-war years, and Scotland's share had fallen off very sharply in the last two or three years. Paragraph 5 of his Department's memorandum showed that the only areas in which there had been any improvement had been in the eastern and south-eastern region of England—i.e. the area near London. Such evidence as could be got did not suggest that the provision of Government subsidised factories or the availability of housing had very much to do with it. The main factor was probably the convenience of proximity to London.

Commander Galbraith [Joint Parliamentary Under Secretary of State] said that, while it was difficult to see how the Board of Trade could be persuaded to improve their Distribution of Industry Policy, it discriminated unfairly against the firm like Templeton's [in Glasgow] who wanted to expand or move but could not qualify for assistance because they were within the Development Area already.

Mr Craig Mitchell [Deputy Secretary, Department of Health] said that he had no doubt that local authorities would at once consult his Department if they saw a chance of assisting a firm to come to their area. As the Planning Act powers were intended for use only in exceptional circumstances, this procedure was preferable to a circular.

After discussion it was agreed

(1) that S.H.D. would consider the best way of raising with the Board of Trade the concern of Scottish Ministers at the gravitation of Industry towards the Home Counties, and the possibility of reversing this trend;

(2) that S.H.D. would discuss with the Scottish Council (Development and Industry) whether they might be able to assist by identifying firms who were willing to expand but were in difficulties and by finding out the nature of their difficulties.

(3) that the Minister of State should discuss with an expert in Scottish banking the question of credit for the development of industries in this way. [SRO, DD10/401.]

Letter of Douglas Carter, Assistant Secretary, Industries and Manufactures Department, Board of Trade, on Scotland's share of Factory Building, 14 February 1955.

It seems to us, with respect, that it is not very profitable to discuss 'Scotland's share' on the basis of the industrial building statistics, and that if any note had to be prepared for Ministers, it should have a much wider context. The industrial building statistics show only what is going on in one part of the economy, viz. that part of manufacturing industry which is physically building units exceeding 5,000 sq. ft., and takes no account of investment in plant or machinery, or the many other factors of importance to Scotland's industrial future such as the huge investment in hydro-electricity or coalmining. Compared with its 'share' of insured population, Scotland has had rather less than its 'share' of industrial building recorded in our statistics, but the same is true of certain other parts of Great Britain. The East and West Ridings of Yorkshire have had much less than their 'share' of industrial buildings in all but two of the past ten years, and much is the same is true of the Northern Region and North West Region. Much of the industrial building in Greater London and the Midlands has been replacement, and much of it will mean less rather than more employment because the modern buildings will increase efficiency.

When one looks at Scotland's position absolutely instead of relatively, there are many encouraging points. For example:-

(a) The area of new industrial development approved in Scotland last year was higher than any year except 1946.

(b) Three of the five largest Government financed projects approved in 1954 were in Scotland. By the end of the financial year, we shall have approved expenditure of over £2½ million in Scotland, out of a total for all D.A.'s which may reach £6½ million. At the end of December, S.I.E. had under construction 180,000 sq. ft. of space. Within a few months, this is likely to become about 1 million sq. ft.

(c) Employment on the Industrial Estates in Scotland is at record level.

(d) Male unemployment in Scotland has fallen by 4,500 between 1948 and 1954, and although female unemployment has increased by 7,500, the number of women in work has grown considerably. Between 1948 and 1953, the female insured population in Scotland increased by over 33,000. In the Scottish D.A., unemployment has fallen by 4,000 (males only by 6,500) alongside a growth in the insured population of some 26,000. [SRO, DD10/401.]

PUBLIC EXPENDITURE AND NEW GOVERNMENT FACTORIES, 1957

In February 1956 as part of its economy drive the Government announced restrictions to its Development Area factory programme. The following January the Economics Ministers proposed to tighten this further by cutting the budget for assistance from £6½ million to £4½ million per annum. The extract here is from John Maclay's letter on the issue to Sir David Eccles, the President of the Board of Trade. Eccles replied by stating that the national interest required 'retrenchment' in Government expenditure, though 'the most deserving applications' for new factories and extensions would still be approved.

Letter of John Maclay, Secretary of State for Scotland, on the Effect of Economy Measures on Provision of Factories, 15 January 1957.

I am concerned at the effect which this suggestion would have in Scotland. I understand James Stuart did not object last spring when your Department's assistance for factory-building was restricted to projects of special importance and urgency because that formula made it possible to take into account the relatively greater unemployment of the black spots in the Scottish Development Area, and in the event four out of the eleven projects approved by your Department in 1956 were in Scotland. But a complete ban on assistance for new factories is a different matter. The only exceptions which you are proposing to make are for a few factory extensions presumably because of the moral commitment to allow firms which you have attracted to Industrial Estates to expand there. This will, however, mean that further assisted factory development will be confined to areas which have already benefited from your Industrial Estates, and that areas where there may now or in the future, be an urgent need for such development will be denied it. A case in point is the shale-mining area of West Lothian, where you have so far been prepared to face the decline in the Shale-mining industry because the Distribution of Industry Acts are available to attract new industry to it. But since the war only three small projects have been attracted to the area, one of these has not yet moved there, and the other two seem unlikely to yield any substantial extensions. For some times hopes have been held out of inducing Euclid Ltd. to establish itself in the area; but presumably these would be abandoned under your new proposals.

As you know, we are already having to face criticism—especially from the Scottish T.U.C.—that the relatively high rate of unemployment in Scotland—double that in England—is not receiving the special treatment it deserves under our distribution of industry policy, and odious comparisons are being drawn with the inducements offered to industry by Northern Ireland. It is also being pointed out that while Scotland may have had a substantial share of industrial development in the whole post-war period, her share of current development has declined. I appreciate that there is now a greater readiness to invest private capital in new development, but can we rely on this at a time when our policy is also directed towards limiting the total amount of industrial development?

In these circumstances, I feel that if your proposals are adopted, we must consider exempting the Scottish Development Area from this operation. There are other funds—such as housing subsidies—in which Scottish conditions have been accepted as justifying a different basis of assistance, even in the current atmosphere of retrenchment and I think that our high level of unemployment would be accepted as a justification for continuing to assist new factories for Scotland, at any rate in cases of special urgency and importance. [SRO, DD10/404.]

THE SCOTTISH SECRETARY AND THE NORTH AYRSHIRE DEVELOPMENT AREA, 1957

In 1956 the Select Committee on Estimates reported that the Government should initiate a review of Development Area policy to deschedule those areas no 'longer in special danger of unemployment'. However the Cabinet's Economic Policy Committee, although it accepted the principle of descheduling, agreed to delay any legislation until there had been fuller discussion on the matter between the Board of Trade, the Scottish

Office, Ministry of Labour and the Home Office. In February 1957, David Eccles, the President of the Board of Trade, reintroduced the proposal, arguing that in many of the Development Areas 'there had been overwhelming changes for the better'. The first extract is from the memorandum by John Maclay, the Scottish Secretary, on the issue. The Committee again agreed to delay any decision to allow for further inter-departmental discussions. The second extract is from the Committee's subsequent discussion. The Cabinet later decided, given rising unemployment, against amending legislation. Eccles wanted to deschedule the South Wales, Wrexham, South Lanarkshire, North Ayrshire and parts of the North Eastern and Cumberland Development Areas.

Memorandum by John Maclay, the Secretary of State for Scotland, on Development Areas, 25 February 1957.

In his memorandum (E.A. (57) 15) the President of the Board of Trade proposes the descheduling of a number of Development Areas, or parts thereof, including two areas in the Scottish industrial belt. My predecessor opposed this proposal when it first came before Ministers last June, and the arguments against it seem to me even stronger to-day.

As we [the Government] have pointed out in our reply to the Select Committee, they were mistaken in thinking that had certain parts of the Development Areas been descheduled more substantial results might have been achieved at less cost. Assistance has for some time been concentrated on those parts which have been in greatest need of it. More recently, as part of our economy measures, the President has felt obliged to discontinue all assistance for new factory-building (except in most unusual circumstances) and confined expenditure to necessary extensions of projects already assisted. This may cause particular difficulty in Scotland.

In these circumstances any alteration of the Development Area boundaries would not achieve anything. It would merely alter the map without in any way reducing our assistance. We have told the Select Committee that we will make proposals to Parliament when we consider the time appropriate. But this seems to me to be an inauspicious time for announcing such a proposal. Unemployment has risen, as the following table shows:-

	Percentage of Unemployment	
	January, 1956	*January, 1957*
	%	%
Great Britain	1.2	1.8
Scotland	2.7	3.0

The proposals for a free trade area have given rise to uncertainties in the minds of both employers and employees in certain sections of industry. Changes and economies in defence policy have led—to take Scotland alone—to the closing of the naval bases at Scapa Flow and Invergordon, the apparently inevitable abandonment of production at two Royal Ordnance factories, and several other minor closures.

De-scheduling would only increase anxiety and political discontent over these developments.

In all stages of the official discussions which followed the meeting of the Economic Policy Committee last June it has been made clear that the Scottish Office has been opposed to the principle of descheduling any area in present circumstances. My officials have pointed out that, even if a policy of descheduling were to be decided upon, it would be quite inappropriate to deschedule North Ayrshire, which is to be one of the main reception areas for the Glasgow overspill, just as the overspill operation from the largest pool of unemployment (outside London) is getting under way.

Under the Distribution of Industry Act, 1945, any descheduling in Scotland must be the joint action of the President and the Secretary of State for Scotland, and I must make it plain that I consider that any descheduling proposals are mistaken at the present time. In particular I could not agree to the descheduling of North Ayrshire. [PRO, CAB 134/1675 EA(57)17.]

Minute of the Cabinet Economic Policy Committee on Development Area Policy, 1 May 1957.

THE PRESIDENT OF THE BOARD OF TRADE [Sir David Eccles] recalled that, at their meeting on 27th February, the Committee had invited him to arrange for a further examination of certain aspects of development area policy. He was now able to make recommendations to the Committee on these points. First, he did not feel able to recommend the amendment of existing development area legislation in order to permit more flexible adjustments of policy. Public and Parliamentary interest in any such adjustments would remain keen, and it was thus unlikely that amending legislation on the lines originally suggested would yield any practical advantages. Second, he commended to the Committee the proposals to de-schedule certain development areas [East South Wales, Pembroke Dock, North Ayrshire].

He pointed out that the third special report of the Select Committee on Estimates had now been received; like earlier Reports of that Committee, it contained strong criticism of the continued inclusion in the schedule of such a large number of areas. There appeared to be a good case, on every ground, for now making substantial changes in the schedule: in addition to the continuing pressure from the Select Committee on Estimates, the climate of opinion in the country would favour such a change, and the probability that we were now on the verge of a renewed increase in economic activity made the present time propitious.

THE MINISTER OF LABOUR [Iain MacLeod] said that recent statistics showed that the development areas had fared better than Great Britain as a whole in recent months. In the period August 1956 to March 1957, unemployment in the development areas had increased by only 0.5 per cent against an increase of 0.6 per cent in Great Britain as a whole. He therefore saw no reason to dissent on employment grounds from the proposals of the President of the Board of Trade.

THE SECRETARY OF STATE FOR SCOTLAND said that there were powerful arguments against removing North Ayrshire from the schedule. The Royal Ordnance factory at Irvine was to be closed completely and an additional 650 people would be thrown out of employment as a result. Moreover, Glasgow contained a large number of unemployed, and it was physically impossible to provide new industry to give them work within the city. It was therefore important that power to attract industry should continue to be available in North Ayrshire, as this was an area to which the population of Glasgow was being transferred. If such power did not exist, the unemployment problem of Glasgow would simply be shifted to North Ayrshire. These areas should therefore be regarded as a single whole for employment purposes. As regards South Lanarkshire, he would be prepared, despite the difficulties involved, to see this area de-scheduled if it were essential that Scotland should make some sacrifice. Turning to more general arguments, he felt bound to point out that Scotland had a higher percentage of unemployment than England and Wales. The impending closure of two Royal Ordnance factories at Dalmuir and Irvine, the continuing difficulties of the shale oil industry, and the failure of hopes that a large new steel plant might be established in Scotland, made this a particularly inapposite time at which to remove Scottish areas from the schedule, particularly such an important one as North Ayrshire. The addition of the Buckie-Peterhead and Aberdeen areas to the schedule would not be regarded as yielding any off-setting advantages, and might only serve to raise false hopes; he did not therefore press this proposal.

The following points were made in discussion -

There was general recognition that there was a strong case against amending the present development area legislation along the lines which the Committee originally had in mind, and it was agreed that this proposal should not be pursued.

It was argued that the case for retaining North Ayrshire on the schedule was not as strong as appeared. One at least of the two Royal Ordnance factories would probably be turned over to civilian use, so that their closure would not necessarily add to the unemployment problem. Further, United States interests were showing interest in the area, influenced no doubt by the projected European industrial Free Trade Area. The most acute unemployment difficulties in Scotland were likely to arise in Dundee where the jute industry was in danger of extinction. It would be both sensible and realistic to adjust development area policy in Scotland so as to give more room for manoeuvre in providing assistance to those areas which would be in real need. It was also pointed out that it was not appropriate to use the powers of the Distribution of Industry Acts solely to facilitate the movement of population for planning purposes inside a development area. The point was also made that Scotland had been less affected than England by the increase in unemployment during the previous year: indeed, in North Ayrshire, unemployment had gone down during the period from August 1956 to March 1957 by 0.6 per cent.

Against this, it was argued that the difficulties in North Ayrshire were not solely due to the over-spill problem. There was an urgent need for more diversification of industry there. At present the area was much too dependent on heavy industry and it would accord with previous practice if industrial estates for Glasgow were established outside the city. Moreover, it might be unwise to invite the political difficulties which would follow the removal of North Ayrshire from the schedule when the result of this removal would have little practical effect in terms of reduction in expenditure.

The present moment was particularly propitious for making a large-scale alteration in development area policy; this could be presented as a sign of strength in the economy and a departure from the defeatist mentality which always looked back to pre-war days. An early announcement of an alteration in policy would be in harmony with the statement which the Minister of Labour proposed to make in the following week about the closure of a substantial number of employment exchanges.

Summing up the discussion, THE CHANCELLOR OF THE EXCHEQUER [Peter Thorneycroft] said that any amendment of development area policy would be politically contentious. But there was general agreement that this was a propitious moment at which to announce large-scale changes in policy. The sense of the Committee appeared to be that the existing legislation should not be amended: but that a major reduction in the existing extent of development areas should take place, accompanied however by some new additions to the schedule. He suggested that the President of the Board of Trade should circulate a memorandum to the Cabinet, for consideration during the following week, on this basis, and recommending that the areas listed ... should be removed from the schedule. The Secretary of State for Scotland would no doubt wish to make a separate submission to the Cabinet setting out the Scottish considerations and making his case for retaining North Ayrshire on the schedule. [PRO, CAB 134/1674 EA(57) 9th Meeting.]

THE SHALE OIL MINES, THE HOME DEPARTMENT AND PROVISION FOR FACTORY BUILDING, 1958

In the Summer of 1957 Scottish Shale Oils Ltd. informed the Government of its intention to close one of its mines at Niddry Castle. The Government arranged with the Company to postpone the redundancies (about 860 men) until its Economic Policy Committee had 'devised a scheme designed to secure the industry's planned contraction over a period of years'. A Working Party of officials, drawn from the Treasury, the Board of Trade, the Ministry of Power, the Ministry of Labour and the Scottish Home Department was established to review the situation and make recommendations. The following is an extract from its Report. At that time indigenous oils attracted a preferential rate of tax.

Report of the Inter-Departmental Working Party on the Scottish Shale Oil Industry, Chairman, M. Stevenson, Treasury, 5 February 1958.

The Scottish Home Department have expressed the view that the Working Party will have failed in the task entrusted to it if it does not devise a scheme which will provide for the transfer of workers rendered redundant to other work as and when they are rendered redundant, and that such assistance should be given as would keep the shale workers in employment until other work is available. They point out, in particular, that the closure of Niddry should increase the Customs revenue by about £350,000 [by the increased consumption of imported oil] and that if a small fraction could be devoted to meeting the annual deficit on operations at Westwood (at present £27,000 per annum), while part of the remainder were devoted to the attraction of new industry to the area, these measures would comprise a coherent scheme for preserving the strongest parts of the industry and for diversifying the resources of the area.

Two kinds of help have been suggested: the grant of some kind of subsidy or an increase in the preference in order to enable the remainder of the industry to keep going once Niddry has closed down, and special financial help to new industries establishing themselves in the area. The necessity for the first kind of help does not arise at the moment since the Company's plans do not extend beyond the closure of the Niddry group and, in view of the elimination of by far the larger part of the annual loss through this closure, it may keep Westwood in operation for several years.

Special provision of the second kind of help raises more complex questions. Since the end of 1955 the financial restrictions imposed on the Board of Trade have allowed factory building in the Development Areas only in cases of exceptional importance and urgency. It has also been the Treasury's policy to consider recommendations for loans, on the advice of the Development Areas Treasury Advisory Committee, only in the most exceptional cases. Present financial policy envisages the continuation of these severe limits on the scope of the Board of Trade's operations under the Distribution of Industry Acts. In principle the possibility remains of recommending more liberal provision for factory building in the Development Areas as a whole which would facilitate action by the Board in those parts of the Areas suffering most from unemployment. This, however, would not necessarily mean that the Board of Trade were justified, if suitable projects came forward, in incurring expenditure on factory building in the shale oil district. From the standpoint of priorities based on the state of unemployment, it is to be noted that, even if the whole shale area closed down, the level of unemployment there would still be lower than might arise in West South Wales or Dundee. For West South Wales the Board is doing what it can to interest in the area industrialists contemplating building factories for such projects in appropriate cases. This clearly falls short of the proposal for assistance to the shale oil area. As regards Dundee, the President of the Board of Trade stated in Parliament on the 17th July, 1957, that 'the Board of Trade will meet any reasonable request to provide additional factory space for leasing to firms already established and to others coming into the area for the first time, and in appropriate cases, Treasury loans to such firms will be available under the Distribution of Industry Acts'. Proposals for Dundee are coming forward slowly but in so far as these, together with proposals in respect of other needy areas, become firm projects, they are likely to be difficult to meet within the financial limits imposed on the Board of Trade for new projects for 1958. Even so only a token contribution to unemployment in the problem areas would have been made. This, however, in the view of the Scottish Home Department, is an additional argument for the provision of more funds for factory building in Development Areas.

Secondly, the Board of Trade's ability to give financial help towards factory building in a Development Area does not by itself mean that new project will, in fact, be attracted to a particular place within such an Area. The Government have no power to direct firms to particular places, and a firm's decision to establish a new factory in one place rather than another depends to a large extent on the conditions and general facilities for industrial development in the place itself and on the firm's judgement of the suitability of the location for its project. While the provision of a Government-financed factory on favourable terms can go a considerable way to offsetting the disadvantages of certain parts of the Development Areas and may act as a positive attraction to firms with insufficient ready capital and without any very strong geographical ties, they may prefer nevertheless to build their own factory, or use an existing factory in a more central location.

The prospects of new industries being attracted to the shale oil area are quite uncertain. The Board's experience has not been very encouraging and it is clear that the area suffers the disadvantages attaching to any area in which mining has been carried out for many years. One illustration of this lack of attractiveness is the lack of success of Scottish Oils Ltd. in disposing of the site of their closed works at Addiewell, even though it is near the main railway line and is equipped with sidings and a modern power station. The Scottish Council [(Development and Industry)] take a more optimistic view of the possibilities of the area but feel that the relative lack of success so far has to be ascribed to the counter-attractions of New Towns and trading estates. Whether or not this view is justified, the fact remains that the New Towns and trading estates exist and will no doubt continue to exercise that counter-attraction.

Finally, it would be a quite new departure to earmark any funds voted for assistance to Development Areas for an individual Area. The Board of Trade would not agree to the establishment of any such lien on part of the funds to be administered under this part of the Vote, while any such earmarking of the whole or part of a particular item of revenue for a specific purpose would be equally repugnant to the normal principles of the management of the Exchequer.

We have been unable to reach agreed conclusions. For the reasons given [above], the Departments represented on the Working Party, other than the Scottish Home Department, have not felt able to recommend that special measures, of a different order from those contemplated in similar situations elsewhere should be taken to transfer redundant workers to other employment. They do not consider, in fact, that the shale oil area can make a special claim for help. They realise the resentment which the closure of the industry will arouse, especially since the product is taxed (even though the effect of the tax arrangement is to afford a very large degree of protection to the industry) but do not consider that this in itself justifies such special treatment.

The Scottish Home Department, on the other hand, are of the opinion that the possibility of a male unemployment rate of 8.5% arising if the whole of the shale oil industry should close down and the risk of its persisting in this area, which offers very restricted opportunities of other employment, is so serious as to justify using a small part of the extra revenue which will accrue annually to the Exchequer as a result of the closing of Niddry to give additional financial help to the industry for a number of years in order to keep it in being while renewed efforts are made to introduce new industry to the area. At the same time they would urge that the difficulties of this area emphasise the need, which is frequently stressed in Scotland, for more generous financial provision for the building of factories in Development Areas. They are more optimistic than other Departments as to the prospect of results if more money were available for this purpose and some preference given to the shale oil area, as to Dundee and Greenock, in spending it. [SRO, SEP4/1669.]

THE CABINET, SHALE OIL AND THE RELUCTANCE OF INDUSTRY TO MOVE TO SCOTLAND, 1958

The following is an extract from the Cabinet's Economic Policy Committee minutes on its consideration of the Shale Oil Industry Report (see above). The Chancellor of the Exchequer, Derick Heathcoat Amory, had already indicated his acceptance of the Report's Majority view.

Minute of the Cabinet Economic Policy Committee, on the Future of the Shale Oil Industry, 19 February 1958.

The SECRETARY OF STATE FOR SCOTLAND said that, while he accepted that no steps should be taken to prevent the Niddry closure, he was very concerned by the position which would arise if there was yet a further contraction of the industry. Government action in relation, for example, to the jute industry and to the closing of Service establishments, was already leading to a marked rise in unemployment in Scotland. Great political difficulties would follow a general contraction of the shale oil industry unless the Government were able to state that a long-term plan existed under which the process would be a gradual one and would be coupled with special measures to attract new industries to the area. The closing of the Niddry Castle section would reduce the Company's operating loss to insignificant proportions and would also benefit the Exchequer. Advantage should be taken of this to formulate a paper, and measures, on the lines which he had suggested.

In discussion, it was generally agreed that the Government should not attempt to persuade Scottish Oils Limited to keep open the Niddry Castle section of the industry; but it would be important to secure an assurance from the Company that before any further closures were decided upon, they would consult with the Government.

In further discussion, it was argued that it would be impracticable to attempt to link any further contraction of the shale industry with the planned development of new industries to take its place. It was impossible to forecast with any accuracy whether, and at what rate, firms might be attracted to those areas in Scotland where there was extensive unemployment; some new factories were in prospect, for example in Dundee and Greenock, but there was a marked reluctance on the part of industry generally to undertake new projects in Scotland. This was no doubt due, in part, to the difficulty of persuading key personnel to move there. The situation might however, be alleviated if Scottish workers were prepared to make longer daily journeys from their homes to their places of employment. On the other hand, it was recognised that, while employment prospects in and around the major centres in the Midlands and the South of England remained reasonably good, there was an increasing tendency for pockets of comparatively severe unemployment to develop elsewhere, for example, in such regions as Merseyside, Wales and Scotland. It might be useful to put in hand a re-examination of existing policy with a view to ensuring that speedy remedial action could be taken to assist such areas. In this connection a study might be made of the possible extent to which the nationalised industries, over whose activities and purchasing power the government exercised a measure of influence might be of assistance. While there were clear limitations on what might be done in this regard, in view particularly of the reductions which had been made in the capital investment programmes of the nationalised industries, it was the case that the possibilities of inducing private industry to site their factories in these areas solely by means of persuasion were now virtually exhausted. [PRO, CAB 134/1678 EA(58) 2nd Meeting; SRO, DD10/413.]

THE FOURTH STRIP MILL AND BROADENING SCOTLAND'S ECONOMIC BASE, 1957-8

In October 1957, the Minister of Power, Lord Mills, whose brief at that time included the steel industry, and the Chancellor of the Exchequer, Derick Heathcoat Amory, submitted a memorandum to the Cabinet's Economic Policy Committee in favour of siting a new integrated steel strip mill at Newport in South Wales, largely for economic and technical reasons. The first extract is from a memorandum from John Maclay, the Scottish Secretary, on the matter. Although the Committee agreed that steel capacity should be expanded, it decided to defer a decision until the 1958/9 investment review. The second extract is from a memorandum submitted by Maclay the following March which included a report by the Scottish Council (Development and Industry) that the running costs of a site at Grangemouth were only marginally above that at Newport. He was supported by Sir David Eccles, the President of the Board of Trade, and Iain MacLeod, the Minister of Labour. In the event the Committee could not reach agreement and the matter was referred for Cabinet discussion. The next extract is from the Cabinet's minutes, after which Maclay asked his officials for further advice, the fourth extract. The next two extracts are taken from subsequent Cabinet meetings, between which Maclay had visited Sir Andrew McCance, Colvilles' Managing Director.

McCance authorised Maclay to say that his firm would be interested in assisting the management of any consortium formed to build a mill. At the end of May the Minister of Power advised the Government's Iron and Steel Board that siting all the capacity at Newport was 'not acceptable' and that there should be some sheet capacity in Scotland. In September the Board reached agreement with the private firm Colvilles to extend its operation at Ravenscraig. The final extract is from the Cabinet's minutes on hearing the Minister of Power's recommendation that one third of the public investment (£50 million) should go to Colvilles. The Scottish Secretary had earlier told the Minister that he thought the proposal gave Scotland 'a fair deal'.

Memorandum by John Maclay, Secretary of State for Scotland, on Steel: Location of Proposed New Strip Mill, 18 October 1957.

I strongly support the arguments in favour of locating the proposed strip mill at Grangemouth put forward by the President of the Board of Trade in his paper (E.A.(57)109).

The new strip mill gives an opportunity, which may not recur for a generation, to apply a significant correction to the present unbalance of industrial distribution in Great Britain and to create a new growing point for industry in central Scotland. Wherever it is located, the mill will tend to attract steel-consuming industries to its vicinity. Investigations which the Scottish Council (Development and Industry) have made on Scottish Industrial Estates even now reveal that, of the 100 firms wishing to expand, 83 are users of sheet steel: they have also made enquiries in the Midlands which suggest that, although the motor body firms would not shift, there are others who are worried about the labour situation there and would willingly consider a move to Northern England or Scotland, where they could be more readily supplied from Grangemouth than from Wales. All this could be done without damaging the existing Scottish heavy steel industry and the consuming industries based on it.

At the same time Grangemouth offers the attraction of a considerable pool of labour available to man a new industry; indeed the labour build-up of the project would fit in excellently and economically with the provision of overspill arrangements for Glasgow. All this is in contrast to Newport where a new mill must inevitably draw off labour from existing industry and increase existing congestion, and to Immingham where, broadly speaking, the labour would have to be brought in from other areas altogether.

I do not dispute the Minister's estimates of the costs of production at Grangemouth as an evaluation of the situation as it would exist in the short term. I think, however, that in the long term the position might well be modified.

I endorse the President's observation that the cost of measures which will otherwise be necessary to prop up the Scottish economy, especially in the shale and Glasgow overspill areas, must be brought into the balance sheet. As these measures would succeed in maintaining employment only in part, we should also take account of the cost to local authority and Government services in the south of the increased congestion caused by the drift south from Scotland which the new strip mill could check.

The point made [above] leads to a consideration of the wider background of the general economic situation in Scotland. The Scottish percentage of unemployment has persistently remained at about twice the percentage for Great Britain and at a meeting only this week the Scottish T.U.C. strongly represented to me that this disparity was indefensible and urged the need for doing as much as is now being done in Northern Ireland. Moreover, both the S.T.U.C. and the Scottish Council (Development and Industry) have expressed grave concern about the effect of the defence cuts and have suggested that Scotland is being called on to bear a disproportionate share of the resulting reduction in employment. I do not myself see how we can continue to defend a situation in which nothing is done to remedy the disparity in the unemployment figures, particularly when as a result of the defence cuts, the run-down of the shale industry and the doubtful prospects of the jute industry there is good reason to fear that the position will worsen. [PRO, CAB 134/1677 EA(57)112.]

Memorandum by John Maclay, Secretary of State for Scotland, on the Provision of a Fourth Strip Mill, 13 March 1958.

... I recognise that West South Wales has a serious unemployment problem. But, Newport, which is itself acutely short of labour, is not within easy reach of this area, whereas there is already a considerable pool of labour within daily travelling distance of Grangemouth. In West Lothian and the Falkirk-Stirling district there are now 3,500 unemployed as a result of the decline in the shale oil and light castings industries; this figure will be substantially increased this year as a result of the recent decision to close down a further section of the Shale industry. At the technologist level too there is real need to arrest the export of scientists and engineers from Scotland who cannot find appropriate employment north of the border.

The main argument for locating the strip mill at Grangemouth is not merely the relief of unemployment but the opportunity it would give to broaden the whole basis of the Scottish economy. Unemployment in Scotland, even at the best of times, tends to be roughly double that in the whole country (the latest figure is 3.6% for Scotland and 1.9% for Great Britain) and it would be even higher if it were not for the persistent net migration of about 24,000 people a year. Events of the last few months have also shown that any tendency towards recession still hits the Scottish economy more severely than the rest of Great Britain. Both these factors are evidence of the persistent imbalance in the Scottish economy. In addition, the recent decision to close T.E.E. in Greenock and Donibristle, to reduce the mark-up in jute, and to refuse further assistance to the West Lothian shale industry have caused serious local difficulties, for which no solution is in sight.

In circumstances like these the Government will undoubtedly be forced to resort to special measures, at unknown cost, to protect particular industries to relieve local unemployment; however necessary these may be in the short term, they are unlikely to lead to a permanent solution. The location of a strip mill in Scotland presents an opportunity to establish a long-term balance of industry in Scotland which may not arise again in the foreseeable future. It would also contribute to a more rational distribution of steel production in the United Kingdom, by avoiding the concentration in Wales of the country's entire production of strip steel. [PRO, CAB 134/1679 EA(58)21; SRO, SEP4/2089.]

Cabinet Conclusions, on the Location of the Fourth Strip Mill, 29 April 1958.

In discussion it was suggested that since the exports of metal-using industries were likely to encounter increasingly strong competition, the choice of the site for the new strip mill should be determined primarily by reference to the economic implications of operation at each of the possible sites ... The costings put forward by the Scottish Council in relation to Grangemouth [on imported coking coal and transport of finished steel to the Midlands] had been rejected by the Ministry of Power; and it seemed clear that, on economic grounds, the Newport site enjoyed an advantage which would become even more significant if production was increased beyond the assumed initial level. On the other hand, it could be argued that this advantage was not so substantial as to outweigh the consideration of social policy which the Government were statutorily bound to take into account in seeking to effect a balanced distribution of industry. From this point of view there were strong arguments for the Grangemouth site. Unemployment at Newport was negligible; but at Grangemouth it was already high and was tending to increase as the result of the Government's own action in closing Service establishments and promoting a contraction of the shale oil industry. The migration of skilled labour from Scotland was a matter of increasing concern, and Scottish opinion regarded the Government's decision on the location of the new strip mill as a critical test of their willingness to take bold and imaginative action in order to secure a greater diversification of industry in Scotland where no steel strip mill capacity existed at present. The choice of Grangemouth as the site for the new mill should therefore do much to reduce local unemployment by attracting related industries to the industrial area of Scotland, whereas a decision in favour of a Welsh site would merely intensify the concentration of steel strip production in Wales contrary to any sound policy for the distribution of industry.

[However], local feeling on the location of the new mill was no less strong in Wales than in Scotland, particularly since it was widely known that Richard Thomas and Baldwin's, Ltd., had declared themselves in favour of the Newport site. If the Government now preferred Grangemouth, their decision would be interpreted by the Welsh nationalist sentiment as deliberate discrimination against Wales. [PRO, CAB 128/32 CC 35(58)4.]

Memorandum of Sir W.S. Murrie, Secretary, Scottish Home Department, 30 April 1958.

Who would build the Mill?

Richard, Thomas and Baldwin's wish to build the mill at Newport so that it can be associated with their Ebbw Vale works, and would no doubt be reluctant to establish themselves in Scotland. But we have taken it that, as the firm is still nationalised, it could be directed to establish the mill in Scotland. It has also been assumed that it would be difficult to find a Scottish firm or consortium (e.g., of Colvilles or Stewart's & Lloyd's) to build the mill in Scotland because Colvilles are not interested and Sir Andrew McCance [Colvilles' Managing Director] believes that a fourth strip mill is not required at this stage. Nevertheless, in para 3 of his paper E.A. (58)21 of the 13th March the Secretary of State expressed the view that if the Government were to come to a firm decision that it should be sited at Grangemouth and were finding the money for this, he could not believe that a consortium could not be persuaded to build there in the national interest, and that it seems reasonable to suppose that in such circumstances Scottish Steel Masters would get together and offer to build it, perhaps on a smaller scale than is now contemplated, rather than see a Welsh firm establish in Scotland. The detailed questions of how a consortium could be formed seems to be one that the Secretary of State might well discuss with Lord Bilsland [a Director of Colvilles and past chairman of SC(DI)] tomorrow.

The promotion of ancillary industry

The Scottish Council discussed the effect on other industries of locating the strip mill in Scotland in ... their memorandum which the Secretary of State circulated [to the Cabinet]. We understand that their confidence that the establishment of the mill would lead to a growth of user industries is based on informal discussions with concerns producing motor-cars, refrigerators, washing machines and other consumer goods. The Minister of Power does not accept this; in so far as his argument is based on the Iron and Steel Charges Scheme the Scottish Council reply that industries can have no confidence that steel charges will continue to be equalised under the charges scheme and that, in practice, whenever particular kinds of steel are in short supply, consumers at a distance from the steel works either go without or pay the transport cost over and above the legal charge; the consumer industries will therefore be discouraged from developing in Scotland until we have a strip mill. [SRO, SEP4/2090.]

Cabinet Conclusions, on the Location of the Fourth Strip Mill, 2 May 1958.

In discussion there was considerable support for the proposal that Grangemouth, rather than Newport, should be selected as the site of the proposed new steel strip mill. No other industry would be granted an Industrial Development Certificate for the construction of a plant at Newport, where unemployment was negligible; and the Government would invite well-founded criticism if in the case of a project which they themselves were financing, they deliberately ignored the criteria which, in the interests of ensuring a balanced distribution of industry, they compelled private enterprise to observe. The progressive deterioration of the central belt in Scotland made it increasingly urgent on social grounds to provide alternative employment in that area, and the location of the new mill at Grangemouth would be advantageous from this point of view. Any decision to reject a Scottish site and so deprive Scotland of any strip mill capacity would be regarded as evidence that the Government were not sincere in their recent declarations that they intended to take effective measures to anticipate the development of local unemployment; and it would subject the relations between England and Scotland to a new and severe strain.

... It would also be reasonable to assume that the erection of a strip mill at Grangemouth would attract industries to establish themselves in Scotland; and the social benefits which should flow from the reduction in unemployment would be re-inforced by the economic advantages implicit in the expansion and diversification of Scottish industry in general.

On purely economic grounds, however, Newport should clearly be chosen as the site of the new mill; and in the case of a commodity which played so vital a part in our economy and faced such intensive competition as steel, it would be unwise not to allow the location of new capacity to be decided mainly on economic considerations. An effective distribution of industry policy could not afford wholly to set aside such considerations in favour of social arguments; and if we were to remain a competitive trading nation, our economic policy must be flexible to recognise and encourage the development of industries in the areas to which they were naturally attracted by the play of economic forces. Moreover the success of the new mill would be considerably affected by the quality of its management. No Scottish steel-making firm was prepared to undertake the management of a strip mill at Grangemouth and, if the mill was constructed on that site, it would probably be necessary to direct Richard Thomas and Baldwin's, Limited, to accept responsibility for its operation. There could be no assurance that in these circumstances the project would be easily or satisfactorily established. [PRO, CAB 128/32 CC 37(58)1.]

Cabinet Conclusions, on the Location of Fourth Strip Mill, 21 May 1958.

The Prime Minister said the arguments which had been advanced in support of the various possible sites during the Cabinet's earlier discussions were very evenly balanced. A decision was not urgent, and it might therefore be desirable to defer discussion for a short time during which members of the Cabinet might reflect further on the issues involved. In doing so, however, they should distinguish between the various considerations that were relevant. It was possible, for example, to regard the question as primarily one of broad national policy, involving not merely economic factors but also social and political issues, including sensitive questions of Scottish and Welsh sentiment. It was also necessary, however, to have regard to the considerations, in terms of the distribution of industry policy, which the Government were bound to take into account in granting an Industrial Development Certificate for the construction of a major industrial plant, and to enquire how far these considerations might properly be affected by the fact that the Exchequer would have to provide practically the whole of the capital expenditure involved. Moreover, the decision must inevitably be affected by the extent to which it was reasonable to suppose that the effective management of the new plant could be secured irrespective of its site. [PRO, CAB 128/32 CC 44(58)6.]

Cabinet Conclusions, on the Location of Fourth Strip Mill, 23 October 1958.

In discussion a general welcome was extended to these proposals, which struck a fair balance between the claims of Scotland and those of Wales and between the interests of private enterprise and those of public ownership. The decision would not receive unqualified approval in Scotland, where organised labour would still press for the whole of the additional capacity to be located at Grangemouth. Scottish public opinion would probably be reconciled to the new proposals, however, when it was realised that the Ravenscraig project would increase the capacity of Colville's by 340,000 tons of other products as well as by 250,000 tons of sheet steel and would be so planned as to allow further expansion in the future. [PRO, CAB 128/32 CC 77(58)3.]

SCOTTISH AVIATION AND AIRCRAFT PRODUCTION IN SCOTLAND, 1958

In the autumn of 1958 Scottish Aviation, Scotland's only aircraft manufacturer, ran into financial difficulties and announced a programme of redundancies. The first extract is from the joint memorandum by John Maclay, the Scottish Secretary, and Aubrey Jones, the Minister of Supply, to the Cabinet's Economic Policy Committee on the issue. The second extract is from the Committee's subsequent minutes. However, a month after the Committee's meeting, with the Company having finance available only until the end of January, Harold Macmillan, the Prime Minister, 'directed' Maclay 'to place the affairs of Scottish Aviation before the Cabinet'. The final extract is from his Memorandum. The Cabinet agreed to the proposal, but warned the Company that there could be 'no indefinite support' and that it should seek to merge with English Electric.

Memorandum by John Maclay, the Secretary of State for Scotland and Aubrey Jones, the Minister of Supply, on Scottish Aviation Limited, 17 November 1958.

We wish to draw the attention of the Committee to a crisis which has been reached in the affairs of Scottish Aviation Limited, Prestwick.

This Company manufactures at Prestwick the Twin Pioneer, a short-range light passenger/freighter aircraft particularly adapted for operation from short landing strips in undeveloped country. This aircraft succeeds the single-engined Pioneer of which there has been a production for nearly a year. Thirty-two are on order for the R.A.F., and twenty-eight have been ordered by civil customers. All these orders are due to be completed by February, 1959. Further R.A.F. requirements are unlikely to exceed a few for wastage and may be nil. There are a number of outstanding civil enquiries and, in the expectation of further sales, Scottish Aviation Ltd. have planned to continue building aircraft at the rate of two per month until the middle of 1959. However, prospects of further large commercial orders are not promising. They have no other major activity at Prestwick.

The Company dismissed some 200 men from Prestwick at the end of September, and now employ about 2,300 there. They foresee a further redundancy of about 750 during the winter if no new orders are received.

The Finance Corporation for Industry have lent a total of about £3¾ millions to Scottish Aviation, and have made various efforts during the past year to persuade one or other of the larger aircraft companies to take them into partnership. These efforts have so far met with no success, and in view of the Company's lack of prospects F.C.I. have now decided that a further advance of £50,000 next week must be their last. They are not making this decision known to the Company for the time being, pending a reply to questions which Lord

Weekes (the Chairman of F.C.I.) has addressed to de Havillands, Hawker-Siddeley, and Vickers as a final effort to raise their interest in Scottish Aviation. If, as is expected, these Companies declare no interest, F.C.I. intend to announce their decision at the meeting of the Board of Scottish Aviation on xth November.

Economic and Political Consequences

The total insured population in the Prestwick area is about 40,000 and unemployment is 1,723 or 4.3%. In the metal-using industries in Prestwick, where labour is about 7,000, there are about 180 unemployed and only 30 vacancies. The prospects of quickly absorbing a large number of men from Scottish Aviation Ltd. into other employment are poor.

The Secretary of State considers that this situation may well have serious economic and political consequences, to which he wishes to draw the Committee's attention. Any action which resulted in the closure or contraction of the works of Scottish Aviation Ltd. at Prestwick would indeed be very serious, particularly at the present juncture, when there is so much anxiety about unemployment in Scotland. The firm are the only airframe makers in Scotland, and the cessation altogether of this modern industry would be severely criticised as contrary to the Government's declared policy of diversifying Scottish industry. Further, the development of the Twin Pioneer is regarded in Scotland as an outstanding achievement of individual enterprise.

The dismissal in September of about 200 of the 2,500 employees at Prestwick was the subject of much public agitation and Press comment, and at meetings of employees and members of the local Trades Council, a call has been made for Government intervention. The transfer of the work being carried out at Prestwick, and of the labour force engaged on it, to another aircraft factory in the south would be regarded as hardly less disastrous than simple closure, with its resultant unemployment at Prestwick. The level of unemployment in Scotland is consistently about twice as high as in Great Britain as a whole, and it is regularly argued that it would be higher still if it were not for emigration, and that the only cure lies in the creation of a proper diversification of industry.

While it was known that F.C.I. were concerned about the position of Scottish Aviation and that they had been considering the possibilities of merger, sudden intimation of the drastic action they propose to take at such short notice has left insufficient time for consideration of the acute problem which the situation presents. In view of the very serious consequences of the possible close down at Prestwick we feel bound to bring the matter to the attention of our colleagues, and the Secretary of State feels:- (a) efforts should be made to explore every possibility of merger which would leave the firm at Prestwick (the Minister of Supply considers that, in view of the [lack of interest by other companies] there is virtually no hope of this) (b) pending such exploration, F.C.I. should be urged to postpone action which would result in the precarious position of the Company becoming public knowledge. [PRO, CAB 134/1680 EA(58)87.]

Minute of the Cabinet Economic Policy Committee, on Scottish Aviation Ltd., 19 November 1958.

THE SECRETARY OF STATE FOR SCOTLAND said that the serious position outlined in the memorandum had only emerged during the last few days when he and the Minister of Supply had been informed by the Finance Corporation for Industry (F.C.I.), which had already invested £3¾ millions in the company, that the Corporation were prepared to make one further advance of £50,000 but that this would be the last. The company had been in difficulties earlier in the year but it had then been thought that these would be surmounted. They now had orders for sixty Twin Pioneers which would last them until February, 1959, but they needed to sell 100 if they were to show any profit. Apart from two more aircraft for the Royal Air Force there were no firm future orders in view. On the other hand, many experts were convinced that the Twin Pioneers had considerable potentialities because of its unique performance: some shortcomings had still be rectified, but once this had been done the aircraft might well command a ready market. He wished to emphasise the psychological importance to Scotland of keeping the only air frame firm in the country in production: failure to do so would create doubts about the sincerity of the Government's declarations that they were seeking to bring about the diversification of industry in Scotland. There would undoubtedly be a considerable outcry if the firm went into liquidation and caused heavy unemployment in Prestwick. The Prime Minister had already been approached by local interests about the far less serious problems which were in any event going to arise as a result of some redundancies among the 2,300 men employed by the firm. In view of the firm's short order book and their financial position the only practical course seemed to be to seek to secure a postponement of the F.C.I.'s announcement to the company that only one more advance would be made, in order to explore whether a merger with a larger aircraft firm would be possible: if a merger were arranged it was most important that the factory at Prestwick should remain in operation.

In discussion the following points were made -

Unless further orders were received the factory at Prestwick (employing 2,300) would have to close down within six months. The prospects for additional orders were not good, and in the long-term the outlook for the company was bleak. In the firm's other factory at Renfrew, which worked on repair and maintenance contracts for the Royal Canadian Air Force, there was sufficient work for three years and it might be possible to find work at Renfrew for some 250 men from Prestwick.

The performance of the aircraft was not yet fully satisfactory. It was under-powered and its 'one-engine out' performance was unsatisfactory. This meant that under international standards it could not at present take a full pay load. Moreover, it had not yet been fitted with tested de-icing equipment, and its range was restricted. These factors had made it unattractive to British European Airways as a machine for use on the Scottish Island services. The company were however making a determined, and successful effort to overcome these faults. It has indeed been suggested that they should be awarded a development contract in order to assist them in their current efforts: this course would not, however, accord with current policy and would not in any case offer any lasting solution to their difficulties.

The late point in time at which the problem had been reported to Ministers placed them in a difficult position. They should in general be very cautious about considering steps which would in effect mean putting Government monies, whether directly or by subsidised orders, into failing companies; particularly since it was probable that in a contracting industry other undertakings would find themselves in similar difficulties.

The general problem of unemployment in Scotland was a serious one. The unemployment level there, already high, was rising even faster. Prestwick was not at present on the list for special treatment under the Distribution of Industry Acts (indeed it was not as yet a borderline case), but the failure of Scottish Aviation would bring unemployment there well over the level of 4 per cent which was used as a criterion. The political and social consequences of the company's being forced into liquidation should not be under-rated.

By its nature air-frame work was not perhaps altogether suitable for Scotland since the aircraft industry generally was concentrated in the Midlands and South of England. It might therefore be worth considering whether the Prestwick factory could be converted for other light engineering uses.

THE CHANCELLOR OF THE EXCHEQUER, summing up, said that it seemed evident that the only way of keeping Scottish Aviation in production would be either by the provision of new capital or by means of a merger. It was clear that F.C.I. would not consider investing any further substantial sums in the undertaking. What was needed therefore was more time in order to explore the possibilities of a merger; while F.C.I. were an independent body, it would be useful for the Secretary of State for Scotland to see the Chairman in order to establish the prospects of F.C.I. postponing any final action until the question of possible mergers had been further explored. [PRO, CAB 134/1678 EA(58) 26th Meeting.]

Memorandum by John Maclay, Secretary of State for Scotland, on Scottish Aviation Ltd., 23 December 1958.

Scottish Aviation Ltd. manufacture at Prestwick Airport the Twin Pioneer, a short-range light passenger freight aircraft, particularly adapted for operating from short landing strips in undeveloped countries. About sixty Twin Pioneers have so far been completed or ordered, including thirty-six for the Royal Air Force, and the Company are reasonably optimistic about obtaining further orders, particularly from overseas. The Company employs some 1,950 men at Prestwick, having dismissed some 400 men during the last three months.

The Finance Corporation for Industry (F.C.I.) have lent Scottish Aviation a total of £3¾ mls. and have made various efforts during the past year to persuade one or other of the larger aircraft companies to take them into partnership; as a result there is a possibility of merger with the English Electric Company, but they cannot be expected to reach a decision on this for a month or two. In the meantime F.C.I. decided at the end of November that they could make no further advance to the Company, which will accordingly have no money with which to pay wages after the first week in January. If they could be enabled to survive until February payments will accrue from the Minister of Supply and from commercial sources which would keep them going until the end of March by which time a decision should be reached on the question of merger and further overseas orders may have been obtained. The immediate problem is therefore to find about £100,000 in order to keep the Company in production through January while the possibilities of a merger can be further explored.

Unemployment in the Prestwick area at Mid-November was 1,255 or 3.2 per cent., and the prospects of absorbing a large number of men into other local employment if Scottish Aviation closed down are poor. About 100 of the men already discharged have been offered employment at St. Albans by Handley Page, but such a transfer of skilled men from Scotland to the South arouses fierce political criticism. The general anxiety about unemployment in Scotland is of course acute and the closing down of the only firm in Scotland making air frames would produce a first class row. On the other hand the Minister of Supply feels that Government financial assistance to maintain Scottish Aviation Ltd. as an isolated unit would not accord with present policy for the aircraft industry, which seeks to encourage the industry to concentrate into stronger groups. The Company themselves fully appreciate that in the longer term they cannot survive unless they amalgamate with a larger undertaking.

Since unemployment at Prestwick has not been sufficiently severe to bring it into the list of places eligible for assistance under the Distribution of Industry Acts, threatened unemployment cannot be taken into the reckoning by the

Development Areas (Treasury Advisory) Committee even if the Company could be satisfied about their prospects of viability.

As a result of discussion, the Chancellor of the Exchequer has agreed that the Minister of Supply should be authorised exceptionally to make a specific payment to the Company of £50,000 in respect of the four aircraft which are at present being constructed for the Royal Air Force, on condition that the F.C.I. provide a similar sum. I have put this solution to Lord Weekes, the Chairman of F.C.I. and hope to have his answer before the Cabinet meets. If these arrangements are made, the Company should be enabled to bridge the gap until they receive the further payments due to them in February, and this will give vital time for pursuing the possibilities of merger and of obtaining further orders from overseas. [PRO, CAB 129/95 C(58)263.]

RISING UNEMPLOYMENT AND INDUCEMENTS FOR SCOTTISH INDUSTRY, 1958

In November 1958 Harold Macmillan, the Prime Minister, established a special Cabinet Committee on Employment to review what measures the Government might take to alleviate rising unemployment 'without imposing too great an additional strain on the balance of payments or inflation'. He subsequently allocated the meeting on 22 December for a discussion on Scotland. The first extract is from the memorandum submitted by John Maclay, the Scottish Secretary. The second is from the Committee's discussion, after which the Ministers agreed to speed up the leasing of the Greenock torpedo factory and the plans for a Clyde graving dock. They also agreed, without commitment, to arrange for the planning of a Tay road bridge and that the Board of Trade should re-examine the desirability of constructing advance factories in Scotland. The Government had recently announced a £3¾ million grant for Scottish Local Authorities to undertake additional capital investment.

Memorandum by John Maclay, Secretary of State for Scotland, on Unemployment in Scotland, 18 December 1958.

Level of Unemployment. Unemployment has always been at a higher rate in Scotland than in Great Britain as a whole. This was so before the war and it has continued to be so even during the recent years of prosperity, although the absolute level was then very small. In the last few years, however, the difference has become serious:-

Total unemployment as at Mid-November

1955	1956	1957	1958
Scotland			
48,700	50,800	56,400	94,800
(2.2%)	(2.3%)	(2.6%)	(4.4%)
Great Britain			
225,900	264,600	316,500	536,000
(1.0%)	(1.2%)	(1.5%)	(2.4%)

The rate of increase is getting faster in Scotland:-

Scotland

July	August	September	October	November
75,400	79,400	79,800	85,800	94,800
(3.5%)	(3.7%)	(3.7%)	(4.0%)	(4.4%)

At the same time there is regular emigration from Scotland, both overseas and to England, which is not off-set by immigration into the country. Over the past five years the net annual emigration from Scotland is estimated at 24,000; in 1957 it was 35,500. There seems to be no doubt that if it were not for this movement out of Scotland the disparity between the unemployment rate in Scotland and England would be much greater than it is.

Causes. The causes of the high level of unemployment in Scotland include (a) general factors and (b) the special difficulties of individual industries and areas. In general, Scotland inevitably suffers from an 'end of the railway line' economy and transport costs enter into the discussion of almost all our industrial problems. A continuous effort is necessary to offset the distance of Scottish industry from its markets and sources of supply and the gravitational pull of the richer industrial centres in the south. In the second place, Scotland still has too few baskets for her eggs. It is true that many new industries have been introduced since the war, and that our traditional heavy industries have maintained a consistently high level of production until the recent recession in steel. Nevertheless, we still need greater diversification, especially in the electronics and chemical fields and in the production of consumer goods for the mass market. Because Scottish industry is concentrated on too few lines a general recession tends to hit Scotland harder than the rest of the country. In addition, there are particular factors like the age of many Scottish coal mines, the difficulties of the herring fishing, the decline of the jute industry and the peculiar difficulties of terrain, transport and lack of population in the Highlands, all of which have a greater impact when the economy is in general difficulties.

The Areas where unemployment is persistently high or there is a chronic lack of employment opportunities include the following:-

Dundee. At the present time unemployment in Dundee is not much above the Scottish average. But the problem of the jute and allied industries which still employ 19,000 people out of the city's insured population of 86,500, remains intractable. We do not know how much of the industry can be expected to survive the economic changes of the next ten years or so, and we do not therefore know on what scale to plan for the introduction of other enterprises in its place. It is clear that Government expenditure will continue to be required in Dundee on a substantial scale.

Greenock. Employment opportunities in Greenock and Port Glasgow are restricted by geography. The situation has been aggravated this year by the decision to transfer the Torpedo Experimental Establishment (T.E.E.) to Portland.

North Lanarkshire. This area is at present hard hit by the recession in steel. (There is 8.5 per cent. unemployment in 'metal manufacture' in Scotland.) Unemployment in the area is 3,466 as against 544 a year ago. Employment opportunities will be further reduced by the closure of uneconomic and exhausted pits.

West Lothian. The employment provided by the shale industry has declined from 4,043 to 2,651 over the past ten years. This has not resulted in any substantial increase in local unemployment [because of Edinburgh], but represents a permanent decline in Scottish employment opportunities in an area to which it has proved very difficult to attract new industry. The shale industry seems bound to cease production altogether within 25 years as a result of the exhaustion of the shale reserves.

Fife and Midlothian. Decline of some older industries, such as shale, could be accepted if it were accompanied by the natural growth elsewhere. One of our Scottish problems is that it has proved very difficult to stimulate the growth of balancing industries in the developing coal area of Fife and Midlothian; this has added to the difficulty of transferring miners and their families from the declining pits in Lanarkshire.

Current Difficulties. Twenty of the 36 pits which are to be closed as a result of the recent decision are in Scotland and it has just been announced that 10 more pits are to be closed during 1959 because they are worked out. I understand that the operation will be phased so as to minimise the unemployment created in the long term but the immediate effect will be to rob several communities of their economic basis. In all, 5,650 jobs now provided by the National Coal Board will cease to exist.

Action Already Taken. The diversification of industry in areas of high employment has been one of the objects of the distribution of industry policy since the war. Thirty-five per cent. of Board of Trade expenditure on factory building under the Distribution of Industry Act, 1945, has been in Scotland, and 47,600 jobs have been created in Government factories built since the war, with a further 4,000 to come from factories still to be completed. A remarkable contribution to new developments in Scotland has been made by American and Canadian firms, but there have been comparatively few immigrants from England and Wales and new Scottish developments have been disappointing.

The recent decision to provide Government finance to assist the creation of steel sheet capacity at Colvilles is one of the most important steps taken by any Government to further the diversification of industry in Scotland. It will be essential that no opportunity should be lost of attracting to Scotland consumer goods industries which will use the new output of steel sheet which will become available in a few years' time.

The issues which call for special attention at the present time include the following:-

Factory Building. The Board of Trade will need to maintain the high level of their expenditure in Scotland. It seems to me to be of the highest importance that the available funds should be used to increase the inducements to industrialists to set up production in areas of high unemployment. The case of Acme Wringers, who are looking urgently for existing premises for a new line of production and are interested in the T.E.E. suggests that our special needs in Scotland might well be met by one or two factories built in advance of demand and strategically placed. There is a strong psychological advantage in being able to take an enquirer to an actual brand new building and tell him that he can have it tomorrow. For this reason I think the experiment should be made, on a limited scale. In any case, it would help to relieve unemployment in the building industry.

Capital Investment Short Term—If Scottish local authorities should come forward with additional schemes which can be completed quickly and will provide employment in black areas I may require to ask the Chancellor of the Exchequer to authorise further allocations of capital investments for this purpose to my Departments.

Long Term—In general public works are not large employers of labour. But the improvement of communications is of great importance to industrial efficiency. The road programme on which I am engaged [£40ml for the four years 1958-62] is largely devoted to the improvement of commercial arteries.

Exports. I welcome the steps being taken to promote exports by means of short-term loans to overseas Governments under the Export Guarantees Act. Full consideration should be given to the particular circumstances of any orders which could be promoted by this means.

Office Building. We should also try to get more office work, i.e., Government offices, insurance companies, etc. into Scotland especially into towns where the opening for female labour has been reduced as a result of the decline in jute, linen and other textile industries.

Summary. To sum up, the persistently high level of unemployment in Scotland calls for continuous efforts on the part of the Government Departments to encourage the establishment of new industrial enterprises, especially in fields, e.g., chemicals, precision engineering, electronics and consumer goods, in which the economy is weak. Such efforts are bound to involve Government expenditure, and from time to time co-ordinated emergency action may be necessary in order to secure some particularly valuable new industry or to prevent the loss of a long-established concern. The problems of several difficult areas in Scotland (e.g. Greenock and the shale area) can only be solved by long-term action on these lines to create diversification of industry; in others (e.g. Dundee and the Highlands) special action is also necessary to strengthen the existing local economy. At the present juncture, when unemployment over the whole of Scotland has reached 4.4 per cent. and is still increasing, I think we should be justified in building one or two advance factories in black spots. [PRO, CAB 134/1734 ED(58)28; SRO, DD10/110/2.]

Minute of the Cabinet Committee on Unemployment, on Unemployment in Scotland, 22 December 1958.

In discussion it was suggested that the high and persistent level of unemployment in certain parts of Scotland indicated that it was inappropriate to suppose that a solution of Scottish unemployment could be achieved by means of short-term measures which would be completed by the end of 1959. There might be a case for some extension of this date on a selective basis in order to enable more far-reaching projects to be launched in certain areas. On the other hand, the additional investment which had been authorised in Great Britain as a whole in an endeavour to reduce the level of unemployment had now reached a very substantial total; and, if we were not to provoke a revival of inflationary pressure by committing ourselves to an investment programme which would exceed the genuine savings likely to be available to finance it, any additional investment authorised for Scotland would need to be offset by corresponding reductions in England and Wales. There was a limit however, to the amount of industrial investment which could usefully be made in Scotland; for the Highlands in particular the right solution of the problem of unemployment in the long-term might well be either an increase in emigration or the acceptance of a rather lower standard of living than obtained elsewhere in the United Kingdom. It was, however, generally agreed that the further stimulation of investment in Scotland must be approached with some caution; and, although projects extending beyond 1959 need not be debarred from examination, the

Government should not be committed in any way to endorsing them until it was possible to form a more accurate estimate of the extent to which they were likely to be financed by genuine savings. [PRO, CAB 134/1734 ED(58) 4th Meeting.]

INVESTMENT ALLOWANCES AND SCOTLAND'S EMPLOYMENT NEEDS, 1959

In February 1959 John Maclay, the Scottish Secretary, wrote two letters to Derick Heathcoat Amory, the Chancellor of the Exchequer, on additional Government investment to assist the reduction of unemployment and on a proposal by the Scottish Council (Development and Industry) on the introduction of a special Scottish investment allowance. In the event the Chancellor introduced investment allowances in his Budget and agreed a package of additional public expenditure for the period 1959-60. The following extracts are from letters between Maclay and Amory on both these subjects once the Budget had been announced. In July the Cabinet agreed with the Chancellor against the introduction of regional investment allowances.

Letter of Derick Heathcoat Amory, Chancellor of the Exchequer, on the Scottish Investment Programme, 1959-61, 16 April 1959.

Turning to your proposals for additional investment in 1960-1 over and above such of the programmes as have already been approved (and not all have) I have this to say in general. I appreciate your concern about the level of unemployment in Scotland and the need for planning works ahead for achieving the maximum effect on employment and securing that money is wisely spent. Apart from my earlier remarks about the inevitable time lag in the effects of our reflation exercise which, in my opinion, makes it difficult to assess now what the final effect will be on the unemployment level in 1960-1, I do not at present feel convinced that the general recovery may not effectively reduce Scottish unemployment in 1960-1 to an acceptable level if, by that latter phrase you mean its customary level over the past few years. The recent fall in unemployment in Scotland from the January peak of 5.4% to the March figure of 4.8% is large absolutely, and the same relatively, as the fall for Great Britain as a whole. The fall in Scotland is indeed better than the experience of Wales, where the level has not improved to the same degree and now not far short of that in Scotland (4.6% in Wales against 4.8% in Scotland). I could not therefore now accept your contention without also accepting that it applies to Wales (and possibly to the Northern and North-Western Regions of England to a lesser extent). [SRO, DD10/121.]

Letter of John Maclay, Secretary of State for Scotland, on the Scottish Investment Programme, 1959-61, 14 May 1959.

I feel ... that I must comment on the implications of what you say in ... your letter, which seems to suggest that so long as there is some improvement in the Scottish unemployment figures we can be content with a percentage that is twice as high as that for Great Britain as a whole. The fact that Scotland has always had a much higher percentage than England was serious enough even in the days of over-full employment (in 1951 Great Britain 1.2%, Scotland 2.5%) but the disparity has now been brought forcibly to everyone's attention and we really cannot be content with measures which, while enabling Scotland to share in a general improvement cannot be expected to correct this disparity. Thus the Budget concession with regard to investment allowances, welcome as it is, is not regarded as having met Scotland's special needs in the way that the differential allowances proposed by the Scottish Council would have done.

Clearly anything that can be done to increase investment in the public sector is useful, and I wonder whether more might not be done by Great Britain Departments such as the Post Office and the nationalised industries, to steer orders in the direction of Scotland, but by far the most important task must be to stimulate the development of private industry. I hope that some useful suggestions may come out of the discussions on distribution of industry policy that are now in progress under the aegis of the Board of Trade. But I gather that the proposals that may emerge from these talks are likely to involve legislation and it would therefore be some time before they could be implemented. They may not therefore be an answer to the special criticism which we are facing in Scotland and which is bound to be pressed during the next few months.

I need not say that two steps that would greatly help would be favourable decisions on the proposed orders for new Cunarders and on the Greenock graving dock project. But apart from these specific schemes we must I am convinced find some general way of doing something more to reduce Scotland's disparity in the field of employment. [SRO, DD10/121.]

Letter of Derick Heathcoat Amory, Chancellor of the Exchequer, on the proposal of the Scottish Council (Development and Industry) for a Special Scottish Investment Allowance, 21 May 1959.

Since the Scottish Council submitted this memorandum I have, as you know, proposed a general restoration of investment allowances for capital expenditure on new industrial assets becoming due and payable after Budget day. The rates of investment allowances for the main classes of assets will be 20 per cent. for new plant and machinery and 10 per cent. for expenditure on the construction of industrial buildings.

These measures are in line with the general intention of my Budget proposals to stimulate the economy and in the process to stimulate investment, and their main object is to encourage firms who are planning either extension or modernisation schemes to put them in hand now. They will of course benefit industries in Scotland equally with industries in the remainder of the United Kingdom and will go a long way towards meeting the Scottish Council's proposal for the institution of an investment allowance in Scotland at a 25 per cent. rate.

There are, I fear, serious objections of principle and practice in the way of the suggestions that there should be discriminatory investment allowances in favour of Scotland, or specified areas of Scotland. Any proposal to discriminate in taxation matters in favour of parts of the country would be open to the most serious objections of principle; and it could not fail to bring up claims for preferential treatment over a wide field. A system of discrimination based upon designated areas would, moreover, give rise to particularly formidable practical difficulties which could hardly be met even if any concessions were extended to Scotland as a whole. I am afraid therefore that I cannot see my way to accept the proposal for specially favourable investment allowances for Scotland. [SRO, DD10/417.]

Letter of John Maclay, Secretary of State for Scotland, on the proposal of the Scottish Council (Development and Industry) for a Special Scottish Investment Allowance, 27 May 1959.

I entirely agree that your budget proposals for the restoration of investment allowances for capital expenditure on industrial assets should encourage firms who are considering extension of modernisation schemes to put them in hand at an earlier date.

I am afraid, however, that we cannot expect the Scottish Council to accept the view that some kind of discrimination of investment allowances on a geographical basis is unacceptable in principle. In this I am sure that they would now have widespread support. You will have noticed, for instance, that in the debate on development areas on the 14th May Priscilla Tweedsmuir said that Scotland's problems are always twice as difficult as the problems south of the Border and that inducements for industry must therefore be specially favourable to Scotland as a whole. Similarly, John George said that the object of the Unionist Party should be to bring the unemployment figures of Scotland down to the national average within ten years; he felt that the measures already taken had proved to be a palliative rather than a cure.

I am sure that these arguments will be repeated in the two-day debate which we are to have on industry and employment in Scotland on the floor of the House this year. At present I understand that the working party of officials under the Board of Trade chairmanship on distribution of industry policy is considering, among other things, the possibility of investment allowances on a geographical basis. It seems to me that if we intend to do something effective to remedy the longstanding disparity between the Scottish and English unemployment figures we shall have to examine a remedy on these lines very seriously when we receive the working party's report. [SRO, DD10/417.]

Chapter Three
HOUSING AND URBAN DEVELOPMENT

HOUSING THE WORKING CLASSES AFTER THE WAR, 1918

In early 1918 the Coalition Cabinet began a review of its post-war plans for housing. The following extract is from the memorandum submitted by Robert Munro, the Scottish Secretary. The Cabinet agreed with the proposal and remitted to the relevant Ministers the task of preparing the necessary legislation.

Memorandum by Robert Munro, Secretary for Scotland, on Housing of the Working Classes after the War, 19 February 1918.

I concur generally in the view of my colleague, the President of the Local Government Board, as to the importance of pressing forward without delay the preparation of schemes for the provision of houses for the working classes at the end of the War. The Report of the Royal Commission on Housing in Scotland, the issue of which last year gave a great impetus to the discussion of the question, showed that the urgency of the Scottish problem is at least equal to that of the English problem.

Following upon the decision of the War Cabinet on 24th July, 1917, a circular similar to that issued in England and Wales was issued by my direction to Local Authorities in Scotland by the Scottish Local Government Board. The returns received from 297 out of 311 Local Authorities show a need for approximately 110,000 houses, and a willingness on the part of these Authorities to erect about 99,000 houses, provided satisfactory financial assistance is received from the Exchequer.

I have been in frequent conference with the President of the Local Government Board and my other Ministerial Colleagues interested in the subject as to the basis on which financial assistance should be given towards housing schemes in view of the exceptional conditions arising out of the War. I have also had an opportunity of considering the proposals of the President of the Local Government Board in process of their adjustment with the Treasury. While these proposals differ from the recommendations of the Royal Commission on

Housing in Scotland in respect that under them a proportion of the estimated annual deficit in connection with housing schemes will fall to be met by Local Authorities, the proportion suggested,—viz: one-fourth of the deficit, which in no case is to exceed the equivalent of one penny per £ in the district of the Local Authority—seems to me in the circumstances reasonable. Such an arrangement, conducive as it will be to economy in carrying out housing schemes, appears to be conceived on sound lines. [PRO, CAB 24/12 GT 3665.]

HOUSING LIABILITIES AND THE SCOTTISH PROGRAMME, 1920

In June 1920 Government proposals to introduce 50,000 ex-servicemen into the building trade to boost its flagging housing programme ran into considerable trade union opposition. The Cabinet initated a general review of the position and the extract here is taken from the memorandum by Robert Munro, the Scottish Secretary. In the event the Cabinet appointed a special Committe (with Munro as a member) to review the position and suggest ways 'to hasten the erection of houses'. It reported the following month and recommended offering a guaranteed week in exchange for 'dilution'.

Memorandum by Robert Munro, Secretary for Scotland, on Housing Liabilities, 9 June 1920.

With reference to the memorandum by the Chancellor of the Exchequer regarding Housing Liabilities [CP 1330], I have to say that I can confirm from the Scottish point of view the case presented by him. In view of the increase in wages, past and prospective, and the increase in the cost of materials for house building, the seriousness of the financial position cannot well be exaggerated. Unless some very drastic measures are taken, the Government will be faced with a huge annual financial deficit. So far as Scotland is concerned, the deficit per house in future is likely to exceed £60 per annum unless costs are reduced.

INCREASE IN COST PER HOUSE In illustration it may be pointed out that since November last the estimated average increase in the cost of houses is over £200 per house. The following table shows how the estimated costs, as shown by tenders submitted, have steadily risen during the past six months.

TYPE OF HOUSE.	ESTIMATED COST IN NOVEMBER 1919.	ESTIMATED COST ACCORDING TO MOST RECENT FIGURES.
	£	£
3 apartment cottage	709	936
3 apartment Flatted house	633	850
4 apartment Cottage	800	1,035
5 apartment Cottage	887	1,190

These figures cover only increases in wages and materials to date. Any subsequent increases will fall to be reimbursed to the contractors, and to that extent the cost per house will be enhanced.

WAGES Since last Autumn, wages in the building trade have advanced approximately from 1/6 to 2/- per hour, and even at the latter figure negotiations and strikes are on foot for higher rates. Wages in the building trade in Scotland to-day run from 1/10¾ to 2/- per hour. Although joiners only are actually on strike there is a movement to bring up the wages of all branches in the building trade to 2/6 per hour—an increase equivalent to 25% on existing rates.

EFFECT ON GOVERNMENT SUBSIDY OF INCREASE IN WAGES It is estimated that the average cost per house is made up of 45% of labour and 55% of materials. Taking the average cost per house at £1000, an advance of 6d. per hour in wages would amount to an increase of not less than £112 per house. Under the rules for fixing rents the capital cost of a house does not fall to be considered, and consequently all increases fall on the Exchequer, the contribution by Local Authorities being limited by statute. Economic rents at the prices now ruling average from £90 to £100 per annum, and as the average rental is between £20 and £25 per annum, the loss per house exceeds £60 yearly.

Taking 10% as a fair rate to cover loan charges, repairs, insurance and supervision, the extra annual charges if an increase of 6d. per house were granted on current rates will amount to £11 per house. On the Scottish programme of 60,000 houses during the subsidy period, the annual contribution by the State would be increased by £660,000.

LIMITATION OF DEFICIT The suggestion in paragraph 6 of the Chancellor of the Exchequer's memorandum that 'no housing contracts shall be concluded which will impose more than a stated amount of deficit', is, I am advised, not practicable. I am informed that no local authority in Scotland would proceed with housing under these conditions, and that any proposal to increase their statutory liability would be resented and opposed. At the present moment, it is impossible to get contractors to enter into fixed contracts, and, so long as this state of affairs continues, it is not feasible to put as limit to the amount of deficit.

SUPPLY OF LABOUR The supply of labour in Scotland is hopelessly deficient. In the Glasgow Kennyhill scheme, only bricklayers were available for 316 houses. The completion of houses for occupation in Edinburgh and Glasgow for the May term has also been delayed on account of the Joiners' strike.

The following table shows (a) the present amount of labour engaged at the moment on schemes being carried out in Scotland (the number of houses for which tenders have been accepted being 7,693) and (b) the amount of labour that should be engaged on these schemes at the moment to enable the above number of houses to be completed by the end of the present year:-

Number of men at present employed.

Brick-layers.	Joiners.	Other trades.	Total.
601	110	1751	2462

No. of men who should be employed at present if houses to be completed by 31.12.20.

Brick-layers.	Joiners.	Other trades.	Total.
2726	2575	12079	17380

The estimated deficiency is therefore 14,918 men.

The above calculation is made on the assumption that two men per house per annum is required to ensure the completion of the houses tendered for by the date mentioned.

COST AND SUPPLY OF MATERIAL (a) As regards the cost and supply of material, the situation would appear to be equally critical. If possible, the Profiteering Committee's Report should be issued at an early date, to enable the Government to consider whether a case has been satisfied for legislative action. It is estimated that in Scotland, the price of building materials since last Autumn has increased by 50%, and this of course adds considerably to the cost of the houses.

(b) As regards the supply of building materials, it has transpired within the last few days that a shortage of bricks is inevitable, although the Department of Building Material Supply repeatedly assured the Scottish Board of Health that for the next year at least a sufficiency of all kinds of material had been arranged for. The difficulty of obtaining supplies has already been brought to the notice of the Scottish Board of Health by different local authorities. It is possible, however, that that difficulty at the moment is due more to the lack of adequate transport than to lack of materials.

RECOMMENDATIONS To ease the situation many suggestions have been made. It has for example been suggested that legislative action should be taken to control wages and to prevent the indiscriminate raising of the same on private contracts, whereby labour is enticed from housing and an artificial district rate of wages is set up.

To control the price of building through existing agencies or by means of legislative action. The difficulties in the way of this course seem to me to be insuperable.

It is, however, I think urgently necessary to take measures to secure

(a) Dilution of Labour.

Trades Unions have already made it clear that they are opposed to dilution, until it can be proved that building trade operatives now engaged in other occupations have been drawn back to their ordinary occupation. To bring this about operatives would require to be assured of equally good conditions to those obtaining in the employment to which they have gone. That would include broken time, which would of course inevitably increase the cost of housing.

(b) Increased output.

(c) Additional power to local authorities to control the erection of buildings of less public importance than housing.

In this connection the action of the Scottish Appeal Tribunal appointed to deal with appeals in regard to Local Authority orders prohibiting the erection of buildings of less public importance then housing has been such as to indicate that no material help is to be expected from provisions of the Housing (Additional Powers) Act of last year. [PRO, CAB 24/107 CP(20)1437.]

THE CABINET AND SCOTTISH HOUSING POLICY, 1921

In July 1921 members of the Cabinet's Finance Committee met with Sir Alfred Mond, the Minister of Health, and agreed that with the onslaught of an 'unparalleled depression' Government expenditure should be reviewed. In particular they agreed that the Government's subsidy under the 1919 Housing Act should be withdrawn. The Scottish Secretary was not invited to attend and was absent introducing the Government's Railway Bill when the matter was raised at a larger conference of Ministers on 12 July. The following extract is his statement to a meeting of Ministers the following day. No subsidy was to be paid for any contract not already agreed.

Cabinet Conclusions: Statement of Robert Munro, Secretary for Scotland, to Conference of Ministers on Housing Policy, 13 July 1921.

The Secretary for Scotland stated that he had been unable until now to raise the Scottish aspect of the housing question, since he had been engaged on other business which he had undertaken at the request of the Cabinet. He agreed that it would be impossible to have a policy in Scotland different from that in England, but there were special aspects of the Scottish housing problem which he would have to deal with. These were the fact that the problem in Scotland was much more acute than in England and that a Bill affecting Housing in Scotland was still before the House of Lords and had not yet become Law. He wished to know what line he should take in regard to this Bill. His position was a difficult one because he would now be obliged to make a statement completely divergent from the policy which he had advocated only three or four weeks ago. At that time he had been in complete ignorance of the proposed change in housing policy and he had informed the House of Commons that the measure was an urgent one. As regards one special point he presumed that if the Crofters' Housing Scheme could be saved, a question on which he would consult the Treasury, the Conference would raise no objections.

The Secretary for Scotland then stated that the change in policy set forth in the Statement by the Minister of Health rendered nugatory the policy of his Bill. The difficulty had been brought to a head by reason of an amendment to reject the Bill. Some statement on this amendment would have to be made. He wished to make the strongest protest against his not having been summoned to the meeting of the Finance Committee of the Cabinet on which the Housing Policy of the country was revised, and he desired his protest to be placed on record.

The Conference took note of the Statement by the Secretary for Scotland. [PRO, CAB 23/26 CC(21)60th Appendix IV.]

PRIVATE ENTERPRISE, RENT RESTRICTION AND HOUSING POLICY, 1922

In December 1922 the new Conservative Government remitted a review of housing policy to a special Cabinet Committee under the Chairmanship of Lord Cave, the Lord Chancellor. The Committee were specially requested to review the issue of State assistance for new working class housing. The following is an extract from the memorandum by Lord Novar, the Scottish Secretary. In the event, Arthur Boscawen, the Minister of Health, advised the Committee that as the Government was to continue the Rent Restriction Act some State assistance to alleviate the shortage of houses was 'unavoidable'. Novar 'reluctantly concurred' with the recommendation.

Memorandum by Viscount Novar, Secretary for Scotland, on the Rent Restriction and Addison Acts, 29 December 1922.

Experience of the Addison Act warns us that the great consideration in dealing with the housing shortage is to avoid interference with private enterprise. The Rent Restriction Act having stopped building, the Addison Act was adopted as a palliative, and it is the ending of that Act that can alone restore initiative and activity to the building trade. The only justification, therefore, for any further Government intervention is to regard it as work given under unemployment schemes except as regards the smallest house, construction of which will not be renewed without a substantial bonus.

It is to be recognised that under the Mond or any other form of subsidy the number of houses built will be very small, while the negative results of checking the building trade may be serious.

To my mind the least harmful of such devices is to grant a bonus for the building of the smallest class of house, either directly to the builder or through the Local Authority, such house to be completed within a definite period.

If the Rent Restriction Act is to be extended, then it should be for the shortest possible period, and with an absolute certainty of that limit being respected, while under no circumstances should it be extended at all without far-reaching limitations.

(a) It should be limited to the smallest class of house.

(b) Houses whose owners require them for business or the personal residence of themselves or families should be exempted.

(c) All premises used as boarding houses should be excluded.

Finally, the arbitrary transfer of property right without compensation under the Rent Restriction Act must have a bad moral effect on the community and is a dangerous precedent in a non-socialist state. Moreover, it destroys the security of a form of property which has hitherto been a very favoured subject for investment. [PRO, CAB 27/208 H(22)9.]

LORD NOVAR AND A DIFFERENTIAL HOUSING SUBSIDY FOR SCOTLAND, 1923

Following the discussion of the Housing Policy Committee (see above) the Minister of Health presented a Bill to the Cabinet which included a Government subsidy of £6 for twenty years towards the building cost of each house. Scottish Local Authorities immediately objected and argued that the subsidy was insufficient given higher Scottish building specifications. The first extract is from Lord Novar's memorandum to the Cabinet's Home Affairs Committee, submitted after he had met representatives from a number of Local Authorities. The second extract is from the subsequent Committee meeting.

Memorandum by Viscount Novar, Secretary for Scotland, on Housing: Proposed Subsidy to Local Authorities in Scotland, 22 March 1923.

Scottish Local Authorities have strongly represented that in fixing the amount of subsidy which the Government may undertake to pay under any future State-assisted housing scheme, regard must be had to the extra cost of building obtaining in Scotland.

The Secretary for Scotland received a deputation composed of representatives of Scottish Local Authorities, large and small, burghal and county, at which the foregoing view was strongly pressed, the Local Authorities taking up the position that both from custom and for climatic reasons it was necessary to build a house superior both in accommodation and construction to that being built in England. The Secretary for Scotland was not satisfied that apart from the considerations mentioned with regard to superior accommodation and construction there was justification for the assertion generally made that the cost of building per se must necessarily be greater in Scotland than in England, and he arranged that the expert officers representing Local Authorities should meet expert officers representing the Board of Health in Edinburgh and go into the question of comparative costs in the two countries.

That meeting has since taken place and the Local Authorities' representatives submitted thereat figures showing that the type of four apartment house generally being erected in Scotland under the 1919 scheme would at present day prices cost £530 or £115 in excess of the estimate of the Ministry of Health for their A3 type of house, namely £415.

That difference they accounted for as follows:-

Increased accommodation	£ 51.17.-.
Sarking and felt	8. -.-.
Heavier roof timbering, hatchways, etc	9. 3.-.
Three coats plaster instead of two coats	6. -.-.
Roughcasting	12. -.-.
Extra plumber work	25. -.-.
Plastering of scullery	3. -.-.
	£115. -.-.

It will be seen that nearly half of the excess in cost is due to what is termed 'increased accommodation', by which is meant greater superficial area, and greater cubic capacity.

The Board have used every endeavour to reduce the cost of building in Scotland and for that purpose have prepared plans of houses which conform more nearly with the English A3 type, and have urged Local Authorities to adopt them, so far without success.

It was felt by the Board of Health Officers that the type hitherto adopted in Scotland did not offer the best common basis for comparative purposes, and the cost of erecting in Scotland an A3 type house of the same size and construction and having the same fittings as in England was gone into. The Local Authority expert officers brought out the cost at £453.10/-. being £38.10/- in excess of the Ministry estimate of £415. The difference in cost was accounted for as follows:-

Sarking and felt	£ 8. -.-.
Roughcasting	12. -.-.
Three coats plaster instead of two coats	6. -.-.
Heavier timbering on roof	6. -.-.

Extra external plumbing	3.10.-.
Plastering walls of scullery	3. -.-.
	£38.10.-.

The Local Authority officials claimed that in fixing the amount of the subsidy Scotland is entitled to claim an extra amount in respect of the whole of the expenditure.

The Secretary for Scotland is advised that, making full allowance for differences of climatic and other conditions, the whole of this extra expenditure claimed by the Local Authority officers is not warranted and that the most that can be justified in respect of the differences referred to is the sum of £23, made up of cost of:-

Sarking and felt	£ 8. -.-.
Roughcasting	12. -.-.
Plastering walls of scullery	3. -.-.
	£23. -.-.

With regard to the extra cost of three coats of plaster, this addition is one which is insisted upon by the operatives in Scotland who decline to put on two coats. The Secretary for Scotland is advised that there is no reason why the extra cost of plaster should be provided.

The Secretary for Scotland is of opinion having regard to the facts and figures set out above:

(1) That no case can be made for asking for a larger subsidy for Scottish Local Authorities in respect of any excess of cost due to the 'increased accommodation' in type of house at present being erected in Scotland.

(2) That the Scottish Local Authorities have a case in so far as the increased cost is rendered necessary by climatic conditions. In a type of house comparable with the English A3 type that increased cost amounts to £23.

The estimated deficit in respect of that sum equated over twenty years is 38/-, and assuming that a flat rate of subsidy were fixed for England it would appear that an additional sum of £1 should be added to that flat rate of subsidy as a fair division of the additional annual burden which will be thrown on Scottish Local Authorities in consequence of what appears to be necessary additional capital expenditure.

As an alternative method of producing the same result it is suggested that, instead of this additional sum per year being added, the same rate of subsidy should be paid in both countries, but in Scotland it would be paid for a period of 25 years instead of 20. The financial benefit is practically the same under both alternatives. [PRO, CAB 24/159 CP(23)163; SRO, DD 6/682.]

Cabinet Home Affairs Committee, on the Scottish Housing Subsidy, 27 March 1923.

The *Secretary for Scotland* informed the Committee that he had reluctantly come to the conclusion that a higher rate of subsidy would be necessary in Scotland if full advantage of the Act was to be obtained. After careful consideration he was convinced that owing to climatic conditions the irreducible increased cost of erecting an A-3 type house in Scotland was £23, and he proposed that an additional sum of £1 should be added to the flat rate of subsidy, or, in the alternative, that the £6 subsidy should be paid in Scotland for a period of twenty-five years instead of twenty years.

The Committee were generally of opinion that if the more favourable terms proposed for Scotland were inserted in the Bill it would be impracticable to withhold these terms from England and Wales.

The Committee agreed to recommend to the Cabinet—That as regards the subsidy there should be no differentiation in favour of Scotland and that accordingly the terms of Clause 1 of the Bill fixing the maximum subsidy at £6 per house per annum for not more than twenty years should be applicable to Scotland. [PRO, CAB 26/5 HAC(23)7th:4.]

THE SCOTTISH HOUSING SHORTAGE, 1924

On the day the minority 1924 Labour Government was formed, a special housing committee was established to review housing need and proposals for an increased subsidy. The Scottish Office immediately asked the Board of Health for information on 'the annual provision required given the present shortage over a seven, ten and fourteen year programme', and an estimate of the necessary skilled labour and materials. The first extract is from the Board's reply. The second extract is from the subsequent Committee minutes, which at a later meeting noted that Scotland had made 'small progress under the Chamberlain scheme'.

Letter of J.L. Jack, Director of Housing, the Scottish Board of Health, to F.O. Stewart, Principal, the Scottish Office, on the Scottish Housing Shortage, 25 January 1924.

Letter and enclosure received. Question one: assuming a present shortage of 100,000 houses and normal annual requirements at 7,500 there would require to be provided in Scotland in seven years 152,500 or say 22,000, 17,500 and 14,000 per annum respectively. Question two: on basis of 1.5 men per house foregoing programme would require 33,000, 26,000 and 21,000 men respectively. Estimated that there are employed on state assisted housing schemes in Scotland at present 4,500 men of all trades. Difference between that figure and preceding figure is measure of increase required but there should be deducted 9,550 men registered at present as unemployed in Scotland. Impossible on such short notice to differentiate between individual trades. Question four: Board informed that total annual output of bricks in Scotland is 144 millions sufficient for 7,200 houses if whole output available for that purpose. Board also understand that Scottish cement works can produce 100 thousand tons. Particulars as to other materials including timber not available at present. [PRO, CAB 27/201.]

Cabinet Housing Policy Committee, on the Scottish Housing Shortage, 29 January 1924.

The Committee was informed that in Scotland the total output of bricks was 144,000 per annum, which would be sufficient for 7,200 houses if the whole output were available for this purpose, and that the cost of transport was a factor preventing the conveyance of bricks from a distance. The cost of stone houses was £25 to £30 more than brick houses. Scottish cement workers could produce 100,000 tons per annum. Five to eight tons of cement were required for a brick house, and fifteen to twenty for a concrete house. As regards light castings the plant was sufficient for the programme suggested.

The Committee agreed that the Scottish Board of Health should prepare an estimate of the actual cost of house production in Scotland. [PRO, CAB 27/201 H(24)1st.]

HOUSING IN SCOTLAND: THE NEED FOR SPECIAL EFFORT, 1925

In 1925 the Scottish programme of house building ran into difficulty, largely through a failure of the local authorities to agree with the trade unions a scheme to overcome the shortage of skilled workers. At the same time a proposal by Lord Weir to introduce steel housing to reduce unemployment amongst shipyard workers (but at lower shipyard rates of pay) also raised the prospect of industrial action. The first extract is from a letter of Sir John Gilmour, the Scottish Secretary, to Stanley Baldwin, the Prime Minister, on the subject. The second is from the minutes of a subsequent special conference of Ministers. Amongst those attending were Stanley Baldwin, Sir John Gilmour, Neville Chamberlain, the Minister of Health, and Sir Arthur Steel-Maitland, the Minister of Labour. The third and fourth extracts are from further letters of Gilmour to Baldwin. In December the local authorities refused the subsidy offer and Baldwin announced the establishment of a Scottish National Housing Company to build 2,000 steel houses.

Letter of Sir John Gilmour, Secretary for Scotland, to Stanley Baldwin, the Prime Minister, on the Proposed Scottish Housing Subsidy, 12 September 1925.

You will remember that we were to have a discussion on the problem of Housing when you came back from the Continent. I should very much like to have an opportunity of discussing this with you before you make your speech in Glasgow on October 1st.

I am trying to arrange a meeting with Winston Churchill on the 22nd September, when I shall be in London, and if it was possible for me to see you about that time perhaps your Secretary could let me know.

I have discussed this matter with Steel-Maitland [the Minister of Labour] from the point of view of unemployment, and we think that we should make an effort to provide work on the production of supplementary houses through the medium of something in the nature of a Public Utility Company.

... I am having a meeting with all the Local Authorities on the subject of Housing in Edinburgh on the 13th October, but I am afraid they are only pursuing dilatory methods and that if any progress is to be made in this question, the Government will have to take a hand. [University of Cambridge Library, Baldwin Papers Vol. 24.]

Minute of a Conference of Ministers on the Housing Situation in Scotland, 22 September 1925.

The Minister of Health compared the general position in regard to housing in England and Scotland, and emphasised the need for special effort to be made in Scotland, to promote the building of Steel Houses. At the present time, Local Authorities in Scotland, as in England, were not embarking on this form of construction to any material extent, partly owing to fear of trouble with the building operatives, and partly on financial grounds. But whereas in England steady progress was now being made with brick construction, in overtaking the arrears of housing, in Scotland, the situation was becoming worse. After discussion with the Secretary for Scotland, he proposed that a special subsidy of £40 a house over and above the Wheatley Subsidy (which in capital value represents about £160) should be offered to Local Authorities in Scotland for the first 4,000 steel houses to be erected under the Scheme within a limited time. The additional subsidy should not be restricted to any particular form of steel houses but it should be conditional on a low price being obtained, and in order to secure this, it was essential that the manufacturers of any one type of house should be able to count on orders of not less than 1,000 houses. It was generally recognised that Local Authorities might still be unwilling to endanger their relations with the building operatives by accepting these terms, and that the Government might feel bound to go further and embark on a scheme of construction independent of Local Authorities, either through the medium of an *ad hoc* Public Utility Society, or otherwise.

It was decided—that the broad outline of the proposals of the Minister of Health and the Secretary for Scotland be approved and that the representatives of the Departments concerned should meet under the Chairmanship of Sir George Barstow to work out the details of the scheme and to prepare a statement which the Prime Minister might embody in his speech at Glasgow on the 1st October. [PRO, CAB 24/175 CP(25)411.]

Letter of Sir John Gilmour, Secretary for Scotland, to Stanley Baldwin, the Prime Minister, on the Proposed Scottish Housing Subsidy, 25 September 1925.

After our recent meeting the representatives who met with Sir George Barstow had considerable discussion on the detail of the schemes for alternative methods of construction. I saw Elliot [Parliamentary Under Secretary for Health] and Jack, of the Scottish Board of Health, in the evening, and was rather disturbed to hear that in their opinion, the £40 subsidy, which Chamberlain suggested, would be so unattractive to the local authorities in Scotland that they had proposed to the Treasury that there should be a £50 subsidy and that the houses should be limited to 3,000. I feel myself very strongly that the number of houses to be supplied under this proposal should in any case not be less that 4,000, and while I do not wish to press for any great extravagance, I think that it would be desirable to give even the terms of £50 per house to the 4,000 if it is going to result in the local authorities taking a favourable view of our suggestions. I say this because I am clearly of opinion that if we fail to obtain the necessary co-operation of the local authorities and have to proceed with a scheme on other lines, we will have the entire contribution from the rates, which amounts to £80 per house.

I am awaiting a statement which is being compiled by the Treasury for the purposes of your speech, and which will be sent to you, I understand, direct. All I am anxious, however, about is that we should keep to the figure of 4,000 houses, and that you should make it clear in your speech that you are asking for the co-operation of the local authorities in putting through this scheme mainly on the grounds of the rapidity of construction and of mass production.

Winston Churchill asked me to make it clear that the Government intended to proceed with the construction of the houses even if the local authorities did not support it. I think it might be injudicious to make a statement of this kind at the present moment in view of the fact that if the local authorities thought that the Government were going to proceed in any case they would be less anxious to co-operate because they would have to contribute so much out of the rates: and in the second place I am meeting a committee which has been formed at my request to discuss how we can meet the housing shortage in

Scotland by just these alternative methods, on October 13th. I think, therefore, that the wise policy to pursue would be to announce the Government's intention of proceeding with the scheme which we decided on, emphasising the serious shortage of houses in Scotland, the lack of operatives, and the larger number of single and two roomed houses in Scotland. If, as a result of your statement of policy, it becomes clear at a late date that the local authorities are not going to assist, it will then commit the Government to greater expenditure when you speak at Stirling in November.

Your attention will no doubt have been called to the report of the Building Trades Conference, presided by Mr. Barron of Glasgow, in the 'Times' of September 23rd, in which it is stated that 'the whole question of housing would soon reach a critical stage and already there are rumblings of the coming storm. Inability of the country to meet the cost would be the rallying cry for every selfish interest among the people, They must take care that they are blameless in giving any real ground for the cry by doing their bit etc.' [University of Cambridge Library, Baldwin Papers Vol. 186.]

Letter of Sir John Gilmour, Secretary for Scotland, to Stanley Baldwin, the Prime Minister, on the Proposed Scottish Housing Subsidy, 13 October 1925.

... In the afternoon I met representatives of the local authorities, following on the meeting which I had with them last July. I think it is quite clear that they are attracted by the terms of the announcement which you made at Glasgow and I am hopeful that they may make use of this opportunity: but the meeting made it clear that they realised that the conditions with which the added subsidy is linked up, that orders should be given to the number of 1000 houses, and that skilled [building] labour should be limited to 10 per cent., will in practice exclude nearly every one of the alternative methods except the Weir house and it is also clear both from what has appeared in the press and from the statements made at this meeting by Labour representatives that in the event of a local authority giving an order to Weir, there will be a building strike.

I asked that they should give me definite replies by November 15th as to their intentions, but in view of what they said I have extended the period to the end of November. I think that this concession, while it will delay matters somewhat, is necessary if we are to avoid having to at once decide to erect houses without the assistance of the local authorities. [University of Cambridge Library, Baldwin Papers Vol. 24.]

THE HOUSING SUBSIDY AND THE SPECIAL POSITION OF SCOTLAND, 1926

In the summer of 1926 Neville Chamberlain, the Minister of Health, submitted a memorandum to the Cabinet in which he recommended the gradual withdrawal of subsidies for local authority housing. He argued that since 1919 in England there had been substantial progress towards reducing the housing shortage and that private enterprise had become sufficiently organised to meet any remaining deficit. The continuation of the subsidy, he also argued, would raise house prices, increase Government expenditure and have a 'crippling effect' on his plans for the Health Service. The following extract is from the memorandum submitted in response by Sir John Gilmour, the Scottish Secretary. The Cabinet agreed to reduce the subsidy for England, but retain it in full for Scotland.

Memorandum by Sir John Gilmour, Secretary of State for Scotland, on Housing, Reconsideration of Subsidy, 30 July 1926.

Production. The number of houses erected in Scotland with State assistance during the last 3.5 years is as follows:-

1923	6,618 houses
1924	4,382 "
1925	8,201 "
1926 (6 months)	5,459 "

In addition it is estimated that there are being erected without State assistance some 1,000 to 1,500 houses annually—a very small contribution.

The largest number per annum built in Scotland since the War is 10,505 houses in 1922. As something like 10,000 houses are required to meet the normal annual needs in Scotland it will be seen that the shortage has been increasing. It is hoped this year to get at least 12,000 houses apart from steel houses under the Government's special scheme.

Cost of building. As in England there has been a slight rise during the past two years. A 3 apartment flat inclusive of roads, sewers, etc., costs at present about £450. That figure is somewhat higher than in England.

Financial Burden of Housing Subsidies in Scotland on Exchequer. The Board of Health Estimates for the year 1926/7 include £1,072,306 for housing subsidies. This includes £977,926 for the Addison [1919 Act] Scheme which will probably be somewhat increased next year and thereafter may be expected to be constant for a long time.

An output of 10,000 to 12,000 houses per annum would add approximately £100,000 annually to the above subsidies. A cut of £1 per house would thus save only some £20,000 in all in the next two years.

The Scottish local authorities take up practically the same position as the English authorities and in addition contend that owing to the special efforts recommended to them by the Government in the last twelve months there should not at present be any alteration of policy.

As regards the provision of houses for the poorest inhabitants, the greater proportion of the Scottish State-assisted houses have been houses of 3-apartments (living room and two bedrooms with scullery, bathroom and other conveniences). A considerable number of 2-apartment houses (living room, bedroom, scullery, bathroom and other conveniences) have also been provided by local authorities.

While I am in complete agreement with the Minister of Health as to the policy of a gradual abandonment of the subsidies for building, the seriousness of their burden and their crippling effect on other developments, I feel that the conditions in Scotland are such as to warrant special treatment. The special position of Scotland is recognised by the Minister of Health in ... his Memorandum, and I am clearly of opinion that a continuance of the present subsidy until October 1928, is necessary if the present improved rate of progress in house building in Scotland is to be maintained. [PRO, CAB 24/180 CP(26)300.]

REDUCING HOUSING SUBSIDIES: SCOTLAND'S OPTIONS, 1928

In Spring 1928 Neville Chamberlain, the Minister of Health, submitted a memorandum to the Cabinet on the issue of further reductions in housing subsidies for England and of concentrating any further state-assisted housing on the 'least well paid worker'. The extract here is from the memorandum submitted in response by Sir John Gilmour, the Scottish Secretary. The Cabinet approved both Ministers' proposals.

Memorandum by Sir John Gilmour, Secretary of State for Scotland, on Reconsideration of Housing Subsidy, 5 March 1928.

The situation in Scotland has improved considerably since this matter was under consideration in 1926 in respect that since then the annual output of houses has increased very materially. But the state of matters is still very unsatisfactory. The shortage of houses to-day is probably not any less than it was in 1919 when the local authorities estimated it at 131,000. The output of houses since that date has been insufficient to permit of any reduction in the shortage. Indeed for the period up to the end of 1925, the number of houses provided was not sufficient to meet the ordinary normal demands (except in the year 1922 when a small number over the estimated normal annual requirement of 10,000 houses was available towards a reduction in shortage). In 1926, however, matters had definitely begun to improve, and in that year nearly 15,000 houses were provided with and without assistance, 5,000 therefore being available towards reduction of shortage. In 1927, 22,000 were similarly provided, giving 12,000 towards reduction of shortage. If the output of 1927 can be maintained for a few years, the housing situation will be considerably relieved, and I am anxious that as far as reasonably practicable, with due regard to the needs of the Exchequer, nothing should be done which will have the effect of diminishing this output.

I am, however, of opinion that a reduction in the present rates of subsidy payable in Scotland can be justified when the revision is due in October next. Since October, 1926, there has been a steady fall in building costs, and the following table of prices may, for the purpose of comparing the fall in prices, be contrasted with the table given in ... the Memorandum of the Minister of Health. In this connection I should explain that the description 'parlour' and 'non-parlour' does not obtain in Scotland, the houses being graded according to the number of apartments and type, i.e., flatted, cottage, or bungalow:-

Average Price of 3-apartment flatted house

3 months to	31st December, 1926	£388
do.	31st March, 1927,	£378
do.	30th June, 1927,	£384
do.	30th September, 1927	£382
do.	31st December, 1927	£361

It seems clear, therefore, that a reduction in subsidy in Scotland can be justified on the basis of a fall in building costs, provided always that no increase in prices takes place between now and 1st October, 1928, when the costs for the two years preceding that date and the anticipated costs for the following two years fall to be reviewed by the Minister of Health and the Scottish Board of Health. Everything meantime points to a continuation of the downward trend of prices.

In view of the fall in building costs and in the hope that that will continue, I would propose, when the revision takes place after 1st October, 1928, that, so far as Scotland is concerned, reductions in subsidy equivalent to those already imposed in England should take effect as from the date to be fixed in the Order to be then issued. These reductions are from £6 to £4 per house per annum for 20 years in the case of the Act of 1923 and from £9 to £7:10/- (in rural areas from £12:10/- to £11) in the case of the Act of 1924.

These reduced subsidies would therefore be payable until the next review comes to be made after 1st October, 1930, and, as regards the reduction for England and Wales now proposed by the Minister of Health of £50 in all subsidies, I should like to enter a caveat that, when the next revision period (after 1st October, 1930) arrives, my acceptance at this time of reductions similar to those imposed upon England and Wales at the last revision period shall not be held to involve an automatic acceptance of reductions similar to those now proposed by the Minister of Health for England and Wales. In view of the statutory provisions as to revision of subsidy, it is perhaps unnecessary to enter such caveat, but in view of the difficulties and peculiarities of Scottish housing, I feel bound to indicate that it might be impossible to impose in Scotland in 1930 such reductions, and I desire to keep the position open. [PRO, CAB 24/193 CP(28)68.]

SLUM CLEARANCE, AFFORDABLE RENTS AND THE HOUSING GRANT, 1929

In July 1929 the new Labour Government reversed the previous Government's proposal to reduce housing subsidies (see above), but delayed consideration of further measures on slum clearance until the relevant Ministers had consulted with the local authorities. In November the Minister of Health submitted a memorandum to the Cabinet proposing to increase the rate of subsidy for slum clearance. The following extract is from the subsequent memorandum by William Adamson, the Scottish Secretary. The Cabinet agreed to a slum clearance bill, subject to further consultation between Adamson, the Chancellor of the Exchequer and the Minister of Health on the unit basis of the grant. Clearance schemes cost more than 'green field' sites because of the necessity to compensate existing owners for the loss of property.

Memorandum by William Adamson, Secretary of State for Scotland, on Slum Clearance, 4 November 1929.

Need for increased grant. The proposals in the memorandum of the Minister of Health ... appear to contemplate Exchequer assistance on a more generous scale than at present, in order to stimulate Local Authorities to greater activity in dealing with the slum problem. As to this Scottish Local Authorities have expressed the view that they will be financially unable to proceed much further with slum clearance schemes unless the present 50% grant is materially increased, the average deficit falling on the rates at present being about £8.10s.0d. per house as compared with the £4.10s.0d. which they have to pay under the Wheatley Act. The grant which they are asking for the future is a 75% grant.

Amount of Rent payable by slum Dweller. I note that in England it is estimated that about 50% of the inhabitants of slums may be able to pay the rent of a Wheatley Act house (say 10/- to 10/6 a week inclusive of rates) and that the remainder may be able to pay 7/6 per week (inclusive of rates). Information before me shows that only a comparatively small proportion of the occupants of Scottish slums could pay the Wheatley rents.

It has to be borne in mind that in contrast to England where the proportion of one and two apartment houses is small, over half of the houses in Scotland are of one and two rooms and these types of houses preponderate in the congested areas of the large towns. The rents paid for these old houses vary in different places. Information obtained in connection with Improvement Schemes shows that the average rent (inclusive of rates) paid by tenants of old houses may vary from an average of 1/6 in one area to 3/5 in another for a one apartment house; from 2/- to 5/4 for a two apartment house; and from 2/6.5 to 7/1 for a three apartment house.

What the Scottish Slum Dweller can Pay. It appears to me that even a rent of 7/6 per week (i.e. £19.10.0d. per annum) is more than most of the Scottish slum dwellers can afford and that they are still less able to afford the rent of a Wheatley house. In my view a rent of about 4/- per week (inclusive of rates) is as much as can be expected from the majority. Even this rent is materially higher than the rents paid for the old houses—especially for the single apartment houses, the tenants of which, when moved have to pay for a two apartment house. The great demand from Scottish Local Authorities at the moment is for two apartment houses but it is clear that this demand is based not so much on the accommodation required by the families who are to occupy the houses as on the rent which they can afford to pay. The rent of a two apartment house under the Slum Clearance Rehousing Scheme is generally about £12 per annum (exclusive of rates) or £15 (inclusive of rates) i.e. about 6/- per week as compared with the 7/6 per week suggested for England.

Conclusions. In my view therefore a larger grant must be available for Scotland if we are to provide houses that the poorer persons can afford to occupy. If the Unit Grant were fixed for Scotland so that in effect the Local Authorities' share of the loss would be the equivalent of the sum which the Wheatley Act contemplated they would bear, viz., £4. 10s. 0d., there would be every incentive to the Local Authorities to proceed actively with slum clearance. The necessity for a larger grant in Scotland per unit arises partly from the fact that building costs are generally dearer in Scotland, owing principally to the different methods of construction followed for climatic reasons; that the special circumstances obtaining in Scotland have been recognised by the continuance by successive Governments of the Wheatley Act subsidy for a longer period; that the ratio of increase in rent that would fall to be paid by the slum tenant for his new house would from the figures given by the Minister of Health and this memorandum, be greater in Scotland than in England; and that in recent years there has been a greater ratio of unemployment in Scotland.

For the reasons given, I consider that the Unit of Grant should be greater in Scotland than in England and that in any negotiation with Scottish Local

Authorities I should be authorised to deal with them on the understanding that I would make the best possible bargain with them but would not be limited to the amount that may be determined for England.

As an indication of the additional cost to the Exchequer of an increased grant, I might point out that during 1926, 1927 and 1928, the number of houses completed under Slum Clearance Schemes in Scotland averaged a little over 2,000 per annum. If as a result of an increased grant equivalent to what the Local Authorities desire, viz., 75% of the loss instead of 50%, this number could be increased to 5,000 houses per annum, the increased annual Exchequer Contribution for Scotland would be roughly about £21,000 on a total housing vote for Scotland of over £1,500,000. [PRO, CAB 24/206 CP (29)29.]

WORKING-CLASS WAGES, HOUSING SUBSIDIES AND NATIONAL EXPENDITURE, 1931

In February 1931 the Labour Government, in an effort to overcome its 'unbalanced' budget, established a Committee under Sir George May to review public expenditure and suggest possible economies. Amongst its recommendations the Committee suggested a reduction in the subsidy provided by the 1924 and 1930 Housing Acts. The extract is from the Department of Health submission to a subsequent Cabinet Committee on the proposal. In the event the Cabinet could not agree on what 'cuts' to make and on 24 August Ramsay MacDonald, the Prime Minister, formed a National Government.

Report of the Cabinet Committee on the Report of the Committee on National Expenditure, Observations by the Department of Health for Scotland, 10 August 1931.

Proportion of Cost of House Represented by Subsidy. It should be pointed out that the grant under the Act of 1924 is not a percentage grant on the cost of the house but a grant per house irrespective of cost and size, that the English non-parlour house, used for comparison, is one of four apartments, whereas the Scottish figures apply to all types of houses—two, three and four apartment houses; that only a comparatively small proportion of the houses built in Scotland in the years shown ... was of four apartments, the majority being two and three apartments, and that these were built chiefly in the flatted tenement type which is a cheaper type than the four apartment-non-parlour cottage type. If the average cost in Scotland of the four-apartment cottage type be taken for the year 1930, viz £449, it would be found that the proportion of the cost represented by subsidy is only 34.5% as against 31% in England for the same type of house.

The Department have had the utmost difficulty in persuading Local Authorities to build the larger type of house. A serious reduction in the amount of subsidy would probably have the effect of still further strengthening the demand for smaller houses.

Fall in Costs and Reduction in Subsidy Under 1924 Act. When the Act of 1924 was passed, it was contemplated that an annual Exchequer subsidy of £9 per house, plus an annual rate contribution of £4:10/- would enable new and up to date houses to be let at rents corresponding to those charged for houses built pre-war which might not have the modern conveniences provided in the new houses. During the early years of the Act, building costs were such that in many cases a rate contribution much in excess of £4:10/- had to be made, having regard to the rents which could reasonably be obtained for the houses. The lower costs in later years have enabled the local authorities to reduce the rate burden, but in comparatively few cases is it even yet as low as £4:10/- per house.

The most common type of house now being provided is the three-apartment flat. The average price of this type for the first six months of 1931 has been £357 [including land]. With a contribution from the State of £9, a rate contribution of £4:10/-, interest at 4½ per cent., and owners rates at 5/- per £, and a sum of £6 per house to cover repairs, management, unlets, arrears, and insurance, the rent per annum that would require to be charged for this house would be £15, exclusive of occupiers rates. If occupiers rates at 5/4^{d} per £ (the average for Scotland) be added, the total inclusive rent would be £19.... This latter figure of rent [£28 inclusive of occupiers rates for houses completed after October 1932] will it is suggested, be beyond the capacity of the working class to pay on present wages, and unless the opinion of the [Committee] is justified that a reduction in subsidy will result in appreciable reduction in costs of building (a very problematical assumption), rents suitable to the economic needs of the persons concerned would be obtainable only by an increase in the local rating burden, i.e. a transference of burden from the Exchequer to the local rates. Such a result would, it is feared, mean the erection of fewer houses.

In considering the date from which any reduction in subsidy is to take place it should be noted that proposals approved are now proceeding on the understanding that the present rates of subsidy will be paid if the houses are completed before the next review period at October 1933. Any reduction prior to October 1933 in respect of these houses could not be made without a clear breach of faith with the local authorities and private builders concerned.

1930 Act—Reduction of Subsidy. This would obviously mean a serious curtailment of slum clearance work in Scotland and of the rehousing of slum dwellers who can least afford to pay high rents. Local authorities, on the faith of the promises given, are busily engaged in making preliminary arrangements for such rehousing and in some cases have already entered into commitments in respect of schemes which cannot be completed by April next. At the end of July, tenders had been approved for the erection of 3,352 houses under the 1930 Act. The rehousing programmes of local authorities, however, contemplate the erection, by the time the statistical review in 1933 is due to take place, of 25,412 houses to replace uninhabitable houses and 12,698 to relieve overcrowding, a total of 38,110 houses. Obviously, any proposal to alter the rate of subsidy determined by Parliament only a year ago would seriously affect these proposals. It has not yet been found in the light of experience that the subsidy proposed is excessive.

Summary. Broadly speaking the effect of reducing the housing subsidies under the 1924 and 1930 Acts will be as follows:-

(1) Local Authorities will immediately concentrate on the completion of houses before the date when the reduced subsidies are to take effect. There will be a spurt at first, but later there will be fewer houses under construction. The experience in connection with the 1928 cut clearly showed this. The effect of the threatened reduction in subsidy in 1928 was shown by the big fall in 1930 in the number of houses completed, only 11,056 as compared with 18,240 in 1929, 17,772 in 1928, and 19,048 in 1927.

(2) Unemployment in the building industry will be increased. At the end of June 1929 when local authorities were making special efforts in house building in order to get the benefit of the larger subsidy (the reduced subsidy was to apply to houses completed after 30th September 1929) there were only 7,482 persons unemployed in the building industry in Scotland: at the end of June 1931 there were 15,840.

(3) The houses provided will either have to be let at higher rents—probably beyond the means of those for whom they are intended, or alternatively, the burden falling on the rates will have to be increased. The alternative would thus be merely a transfer of burden from the Exchequer to the local rates.

In conclusion it must be borne in mind that, so far as Scotland is concerned, the building efforts since 1919 have only kept pace with the annual normal needs and have not made any inroad into the huge shortage that existed in 1919. [SRO, HH45/114.]

THE SCOTTISH HOUSING SUBSIDY, 1932

In November 1932, Sir E. Hilton Young, the Minister of Health, submitted a memorandum to the Cabinet on the 'desirability of withdrawing' housing subsidies in England and Wales. He argued that as building costs had fallen there was no financial reason for the Government to subsidise a local authority building programme, except for slum clearance. The following extract is from the memorandum by Sir Godfrey Collins, the Scottish Secretary. The Cabinet agreed to withdraw the English subsidy, but retain a subsidy of £3 for two years in Scotland.

Memorandum by Sir Godfrey Collins, Secretary of State for Scotland, on Housing Policy—Scotland, 24 November 1932.

I have been in consultation with the Minister of Health on the subject of housing policy, and am generally in agreement with his views as to the desirability of withdrawing subsidies whenever it is possible to do so, as expressed in his Memorandum, dated 17th November, 1932. The modifications which I have to suggest in his proposals are dictated by the special circumstances of Scotland in regard to housing.

In spite of all our efforts since 1919, the housing shortage in Scotland is still acute. According to statements received from local authorities in 1930 it was estimated that, apart from the houses required to meet the annual normal needs of the population, 67,464 houses were required to replace houses unfit for human habitation, to abate overcrowding, and for other miscellaneous reasons. The clearance or improvement of slum areas and the abatement of overcrowding are therefore matters which still demand unremitting attention. The recent Census reports show that, while there has been considerable improvement since 1921, overcrowding is still very prevalent. For example, in Glasgow, 58.1 per cent. of the houses are of one and two rooms, while 55.4 per cent. of the total population live in houses of these sizes; of one-roomed houses, 12,930 are occupied by 4 persons and over; and of these houses, 1,598 had 7 occupants and over. The corresponding figures for the other three large cities show that conditions in Dundee are slightly worse, and in Edinburgh and Aberdeen somewhat better, than Glasgow. These four cities comprise 38.6 per cent. of the whole population of Scotland.

At present the subsidy under the 1924 Act stands at its original figure of £9 for Scotland, whereas in England it has been reduced to £7 10s. Total abolition would, therefore, mean a larger step in Scotland than it would in England and from investigations which I have made I am satisfied that it would be unsafe to withdraw immediately and at one stroke the whole of the subsidy payable under the 1924 Act.

Whatever may be the cause, it is a fact that private enterprise has not functioned to anything like the same extent in Scotland as it has done in England. For example, I find that of the total houses erected since 1919 in England, private enterprise has produced about 69 per cent., whereas of the total houses erected in Scotland during the same period, private enterprise has produced only 31 per cent. The difference is even more pronounced when the figures for the year ending 31st March, 1931, are compared. In that year private enterprise in England erected 128,728 houses without State assistance, whereas the corresponding figure for Scotland was only 1,408. These figures represent approximately 41 per cent. and 11 per cent. respectively of the total number of houses erected in the two countries during that year.

It is obvious, therefore, that, if subsidy were wholly withdrawn, private enterprise would have to fill a much wider gap in Scotland than in England, and for that reason it would take a longer time to get into its full stride. In the interval some subsidised provision will, I am convinced, require to be made in respect of houses erected to abate overcrowding and to meet the case of the low wage earner who cannot afford to pay an economic rent for a house erected at present-day building costs. In contradistinction to the situation in England, there is little immediate prospect of Scottish local authorities erecting houses without State assistance at a time when they are being urged to cut down their expenditure, because, after allowance is made for the fall which has taken place in building costs and in the rate of interest, these authorities are still unable to provide houses to let at a reasonable rent, especially at a rent within the means of the low wage earner, without charge to the local rates.

The Building Societies, as in the case of England, have submitted proposals to me whereby their funds would be made available, on terms, for the provision of new houses for sale or for letting to working class occupiers. These proposals are being examined. They involve negotiations with the local authorities. I am also conferring with representatives of the building trades. As regards the proposals, it has to be borne in mind that the Building Society movement is much less strong in Scotland than it is in England. Until three or four years ago, when a number of English Societies opened branches in Scotland (mainly in Edinburgh), the extent of the Building Societies' operations was extremely limited. Under the stimulus of competition their business is steadily increasing, but further time is required in order to see how far the Societies will be able to assist in the provision of houses for the working classes, and the extent to which private builders will produce such houses with or without the aid of financial facilities offered by the Societies. Meanwhile, we must continue to rely on the provision of houses by local authorities.

I submit for the consideration of my colleagues, therefore, that the 1924 Act subsidy should be continued in Scotland, but at a reduced rate and for a limited period—say 2 years—the subsidy to be restricted to houses which are erected by local authorities—

(1) For the abatement of overcrowding; and

(2) For the accommodation of low wage earners.

As regards (2), it is difficult to frame a statutory definition of a low-wage earner, but the end in view might be secured administratively by confining approval of schemes to cases where the houses are to be occupied by persons unable to pay a rent of more than, say 6s. per week. With occupiers' rates added, this would mean an inclusive rent of about 8s. per week.

Looking to present-day building costs and rates of interest, a State subsidy of £9 could not be defended and I would propose, therefore, that the subsidy should be of an amount sufficient only to enable the houses to be let at the rent indicated in the preceding paragraph.

The average cost of a 3-apartment (I.e., kitchen and two bedrooms) flatted house (the most common type of house) erected by local authorities in Scotland during the first nine months of this year was £355. More recent information would appear to indicate that similar houses might now, or in the near future, be produced at a figure ranging from £300 to £325. Assuming the lower figure of £300 and interest on the loan (spread over 60 years) at 3.5 per cent., it would, I find, require a State subsidy of £3 17s 8d. and a local rate contribution of £1 18s 10d. for 40 years to enable the houses to be let at the rent which I have suggested. With money at 4 per cent. the corresponding figures would be £4 15s. 4d. and £2 7s. 8d. As I am exceedingly anxious to use every endeavour to reduce building costs because it is only in this way that we can hope to return to the position where houses will be produced to be let at an economic rent, I would be prepared to restrict the State subsidy to £4—leaving the local authority to find the balance of the deficiency. [PRO, CAB 24/235 CP(32)411.]

SCOTTISH HOUSING AND STATE ASSISTANCE, 1934

In January 1934 Sir E. Hilton Young, the Minister of Health, submitted a memorandum to the Cabinet on future English housing policy, laying special emphasis on Government assistance for schemes of slum clearance and for the provision of housing for those overcrowded. The following extract is from the memorandum submitted in response by Sir Godfrey Collins, the Scottish Secretary. The Cabinet agreed that the matter in both countries was 'one of urgency' and remitted it to a Ministerial Committee to consider what legislation should follow.

Memorandum by Sir Godfrey Collins, Secretary of State for Scotland, on Housing (Scotland), 2 February 1934.

I lay before my colleagues a brief Note on Scottish Housing policy.

My purpose is to let them know that I shall, at an early date, submit proposals for dealing with the Housing problem in Scotland and that in many particulars they will be based upon the same considerations as are set forth in the memorandum of the Minister of Health. For instance, with regard to slum clearance, the policy I am pursuing is similar to that indicated in the memorandum. There remain (1) overcrowding, (2) the provision of houses to meet the ordinary needs of increased population, (3) reconditioning.

The situation in Scotland as regards overcrowding is very much worse than in England. 14.9% of the Scottish population is living more than 3 to a room as compared with 1.49% of the English. This situation was recognised last year when the Cabinet, and subsequently Parliament (in the Housing (Scotland) Act, 1933), approved the proposal to give a special subsidy of £3 a house for dealing with low-paid wage earners living in overcrowded conditions, while no similar subsidy was provided in England.

So far local authorities have not availed themselves to any appreciable extent of the £3 subsidy and they have very generally represented that they find themselves unable to provide houses, even with its assistance, without making rate contributions which impose an undue burden on the locality.

I am satisfied, therefore, that only really generous assistance on the part of the State will secure early and effective dealing with overcrowding in Scotland. The object of the proposals I shall submit will be to ensure that the assistance to be given by the State for overcrowding will provide a stimulus sufficient to ensure that the problem of overcrowding will be dealt with as effectively as that of slum clearance.

In Scotland, as in England, the Local Authority is under the statutory obligation, if necessary, to provide houses. The Minister of Health and the Secretary of State for Scotland are also given statutory powers to compel the local authorities to fulfil that obligation. I am satisfied, however, that it is impracticable to use any such powers against local authorities as a whole. They are only servicable if the assistance of the State is such as to secure the willing co-operation of the great body of Local Authorities, in which case they can effectively be used to deal with a small recalcitrant minority.

With regard to the provision by unassisted private enterprise of the ordinary houses required for the working classes, I desire at present only to say that unfortunately in Scotland there seems little prospect of private enterprise functioning effectively. In my view, however, the importance of this consideration in connection with the matters dealt with in the Memorandum is that it makes it all the more essential that the provisions we make to deal with overcrowding should be fully effective.

There remains the question of reconditioning. My colleagues will remember that a Committee similar to the Moyne Committee was appointed by me to deal with that question in Scotland. The recommendations vary in certain important respects. But I do not think it is necessary at this stage to enter into this question further than to say that in this matter we may find it necessary in

Scotland to proceed along somewhat different lines than those suggested in the Memorandum of the Minister of Health. [PRO, CAB 24/247 CP(34)34.]

SCOTLAND'S SPECIAL HOUSING CIRCUMSTANCES, 1934

In November 1934, after considerable inter-departmental discussion, the Cabinet's Housing Committee resumed consideration of the Housing Bill. The first extract is from a discussion at its fourth meeting, after the Bill's general principles, a subsidy to assist slum clearance and the relief of overcrowding, had been agreed. The Committee had previously agreed that each local authority should survey the extent of its housing need before embarking on any detailed plan. The second extract is from the subsequent memorandum by Sir Godfrey Collins to the Cabinet on the Scottish Bill, which the Cabinet accepted. The Cabinet agreed a basic English subsidy of £3 for twenty years.

Cabinet Housing Policy Committee, on the Housing Bill, 20 November 1934.

Political issues raised by the Bill. THE SECRETARY OF STATE FOR DOMINION AFFAIRS [J.H. Thomas] said, that, as the Committee was aware, the Government were introducing no new Bills in the new Session likely to secure for it any great political popularity. On the assumption that the Government would run its normal course, with a general Election taking place in the middle or latter part of 1936, he saw at present no Bill, except the present one, which was likely to gain for them any great popular support.

If the Minister of Health were to allow it to be known that under the new Housing Bill it was proposed to spend eighteen months on the survey before work could be commenced, it might make a very unsatisfactory press. If, however, the Government were to rely on what the Bill was going to accomplish after it was passed, they must expect to be faced repeatedly with the question, how many new houses had been built under its provisions? They were thus left with the conclusion that the one value of the Bill politically was the fact that it was going to facilitate the building of new houses. It was most important, therefore, that the Government should endeavour at all times to stress the point that the encouragement and acceleration of the house building programme was the Bill's primary object, and that any local authority which, in reliance upon the Bill, commenced to accelerate its building work would not suffer for doing so.

THE MINISTER OF HEALTH replied that he quite followed the contentions that had been put forward. First, he would like to make clear what the programme was, as it was envisaged by himself. The Bill would be introduced at once, and it was hoped that it would be passed by June. From that time forward the Department would be in a position to encourage housing authorities to start building on a large scale, leaving only a reasonable margin on what their needs in respect of slum clearance and overcrowding were likely to be.

THE SECRETARY OF STATE FOR SCOTLAND said that with slum clearance on their hands, local authorities would be very heavily pressed already, and would in many cases have to consider the reorganisation of their staffs to enable them in addition to deal with the new problem of overcrowding. Local authorities might thus be very slow in tackling the new task.

THE MINISTER OF HEALTH said that this was not the position in England and Wales. The scheme was already exciting a great deal of interest and a good deal of work could be put into effect at very short notice.

THE POSTMASTER GENERAL [Sir Kingsley Wood] enquired whether the financial conditions as laid down in the Bill were at present sufficient to enable the local authorities to get on at once with the actual work of house building.

THE CHANCELLOR OF THE EXCHEQUER [Neville Chamberlain] said that he had given consideration to this point, and was proposing the addition of certain words which were being worked out by the Treasury and the Ministry of Health to make the position perfectly clear. The wording he had in mind would be in the form of a proviso that nothing would prevent the Minister paying a subsidy in respect of houses and flats under the Bill, as soon as the Bill was passed.

THE SECRETARY OF STATE FOR SCOTLAND said that he doubted whether this would be sufficient, at any rate in Scotland, to stimulate building. He feared that in the case of many local authorities political considerations were given precedence over the public interest in such matters, and local authorities with a large Labour majority might be expected to be extremely slow in taking up the new scheme.

THE SECRETARY OF STATE FOR DOMINION AFFAIRS replied that, whilst they might offer some opposition for a time, such an attitude would enable the Government in the long run to turn the tables upon them very effectively. The local authorities in question would be on very weak ground if they sought to postpone indefinitely such good causes as the relief of overcrowding and slum clearance.

THE POSTMASTER GENERAL thought that Councils with Labour majorities might well try to put off building, at any rate until, January 1936. They could then say that very little had been done under the new Act to the time of the General Election.

THE SECRETARY OF STATE FOR SCOTLAND emphasised that such an attitude was likely to be widespread in Scotland.

THE MINISTER OF HEALTH replied that, on the other hand, it was certainly not the attitude of English authorities. They were eager to start work, and the terms offered under the Bill were likely to be sufficient to encourage them to go ahead. A representative of the London County Council had, of course, been present during the discussion on the Bill, and he had raised no objections to the general proposals.

THE SECRETARY OF STATE FOR SCOTLAND said that so far as Scotland was concerned the political factor was disturbing. [PRO, CAB 27/565 HA(34)4th.]

Memorandum by Sir Godfrey Collins, Secretary of State for Scotland, on the Housing (Scotland) Bill, 8 December 1934.

At their meeting on the 21st February last ... the Cabinet, who had before them memoranda on Housing Policy by the Minister of Health and myself, together with the Report of a Cabinet Committee ... recognised that some modification of the Minister of Health's proposal would be necessary to meet the special housing circumstances in Scotland, and authorised the opening of negotiations with the local authorities in England and Scotland on the basis of the proposals approved by the Cabinet.

Since then I have had meetings and correspondence with the Chancellor of the Exchequer and the Minister of Health with regard to the provisions of the Scottish scheme, and agreement has been reached on the following basis:- (a) a uniform subsidy of £6.15.0. per house for forty years subject to a contribution of £3.5.0. per house from the rates; (b) additional special housing assistance not exceeding £4 per house subject to a contribution from the rates for authorities in large burghs who are obliged to undertake an extensive amount of redevelopment work in central areas at a necessarily high cost, regard being had by the Department and the Treasury, in determining the special assistance, to the loss falling on the authority by reason of their decrowding operations as a whole; and (c) subject to consultation with the Treasury in individual cases, additional special assistance for local authorities in remote areas where the provision of the accommodation required would impose a substantial burden on the local rates, regard again being had, in calculating the special assistance, to the loss falling on the authority by reason of their decrowding operations as a whole.

As to rents it is proposed to include provisions in the Bill in order to secure that houses built for slum clearance and decrowding purposes will be reserved for persons who cannot be expected to pay more than a maximum rent to be determined by the Department of Health, having regard to the circumstances of the particular district. [PRO, CAB 24/251 CP(34)294.]

NEW SUBSIDIES FOR SCOTLAND'S HOUSING, 1938

In 1938 the housing subsidy payable to local authorities came under statutory review. However local authorities complained that with building costs rising the existing subsidy of £6 15s. was inadequate if they were to maintain an output of 20,000 houses per annum. The Government agreed to continue the subsidy until the end of the year but invited Walter Elliot, the Scottish Secretary, to discuss the matter with local authorities. The first extract is from Departmental discussions with the Treasury on the subsidy and related matters. The second is from John Colville's (Elliot's successor) Cabinet memorandum, submitted after discussion with Sir John Simon, the Chancellor of the Exchequer. The third is from the minute of a further Departmental meeting with the Treasury to clarify the Housing Board's programme. The Department accepted the Treasury's proposal.

Minute of the Meeting of the Department of Health and the Treasury, on Housing Subsidies, 7 October 1938.

At the meeting on the 5th October the Sub-Committee [of the Scottish Local Authorities Association] had suggested Exchequer contributions of £11, £12 and £13 and rate contributions of £4, £4,10/- and £5, for three-, four- and five-apartment houses respectively.

The Department's alternative proposals were Exchequer contributions of £10.10/-, £11.15/- and £13, and rate contributions of £4.10/-, £4.15/- and £5 for three-, four- and five-apartment houses respectively.

Mr. Tribe [Under Secretary, Treasury] referred to the Sub-Committee's attitude with regard to the rent factor in the calculation of the proposed subsidies. *Mr. Henderson* [Under Secretary, Department of Health] said that the Department were in a somewhat weak position in suggesting 6/9d. as the average rent. The subsidies under the Act of 1935 had been fixed on the basis of an average rent of 6/-, and Local Authorities knew of this. They could argue that if 6/- was the appropriate figure in 1935 it was still the appropriate figure to take as wages had not risen. He felt, however, that the Local Authorities were likely to accept 6/9d. for the purpose of negotiation.

Mr. Henderson said that the Sub-Committee also disputed the Repairs etc. Allowance of £5.10/-. They said that while this was the figure generally taken the cost of repairs had increased. They had not, however, pursued this particular argument.

Mr. Tribe then explained that the main point was the preservation of a ratio of 2:1 between the State and rate contributions. He recalled that Local Authorities had readily accepted what was virtually a 2:1 ratio under the Act of 1935. The Ministry of Health had indicated that they would feel particularly embarrassed if there was a general departure from this ratio on the present occasion, and the Treasury took the view that they should 'die in the last ditch' in resisting such a departure. *Mr. Henderson* reminded Mr. Tribe that what had enabled Local Authorities to accept the 1935 settlement was that at that time they were making substantial profit out of the 1930 Act subsidies. *Mr. Tribe* countered by pointing out that the present enormous Exchequer commitments for Defence must have a bearing on this matter. The state of public finances was far worse now than in 1935. *The Secretary* [W.S. Douglas] explained, however, that there was really very little difference in money between the Treasury proposals and the Department's new proposals. On the basis of an annual programme of 20,000 houses the additional burden on the Exchequer would be only £15,000 to £20,000. Were the Treasury to die in the last ditch for £20,000?

With regard to the fact that Scotland's housing needs are relatively greater than those on England, *Mr. Usher* [Assistant Secretary, Treasury] suggested that while a heavier programme justified a larger Exchequer subsidy it did not necessarily affect the ratio between the State and rate contributions. *Mr. Henderson* could not agree. The heavier programme would undoubtedly result in a heavier rate burden. Moreover, if as the Sub-Committee contended, Local Authorities could not get an average rent of 6/9d. their contribution would in fact be more than half the Exchequer contribution. In addition, Local Authorities expected interest rates to rise against them and so increase their burden still further.

At this point, Mr. Tribe indicated that the matter would have to be referred to Sir Alan Barlow [Under Secretary, Treasury] for decision.

Grant for Reconditioning.

Mr. Henderson said that he had consulted Mr. Wrigley of the Ministry of Health, who had indicated that if a reconditioning grant in Scotland were confined to Local Authorities with a contribution from the rates he would not feel embarrassed with regard to possible repercussions in England. Mr. Wrigley would, however, strongly oppose any proposal to give private owners a grant for reconditioning, or to give Local Authorities a subsidy without requiring them to make a rate contribution.

Mr. Tribe drew attention to the fact that the Sub-Committee had not met the point that reconditioning would actually decrease the amount of available accommodation at a time of clamant shortage. Apart from this, it seemed to him that reconditioning amounted to a proposal to improve accommodation for the general population, and as such should be resisted.

The Secretary explained that there were many properties which, if not reconditioned, would very soon have to be dealt with as slums. The work of reconditioning could not be begun immediately, and the Department would retain full power of approval of schemes. *Mr. Usher*, however, emphasised the view that reconditioning would not be slum clearance work in the usual sense; it more closely resembled a scheme for the improvement of general housing conditions.

After further discussion *the Secretary* suggested as a compromise that reconditioning should be carried out neither by Local Authorities nor by private owners but through the proposed Housing Board. This would remove the political objections to (i) increasing Local Authority ownership of house property and (ii) the subsidising of private enterprise.

Mr. Tribe agreed that the objections against bringing Local Authorities into the reconditioning field were weighty but felt that the principle of a reconditioning grant required careful consideration.

Mr. Henderson reminded the meeting that the Government would be strongly pressed to make a reconditioning grant available. While the matter could not be dealt with in the forthcoming Bill the Secretary of State would be pressed to make an announcement and it was essential that the principle involved should be decided very quickly.

Housing Board.

Mr. Tribe said that Sir A. Barlow felt that the next step with regard to the setting up of a Housing Board was for the Secretary of State to see the Chancellor. It did not seem possible to carry the matter further by discussions between officials.

Consolidated Subsidies (Continued)

The discussion on this point was continued later with Sir Alan Barlow, who finally agreed, with some hesitation, to the Department's compromise proposals, namely:-

	3 Apt.	*4 Apt.*	*5 Apt.*
State Contribution	£10.10/-	£11.15/-	£13
Rate Contribution	£4.10/-	£4.15/-	£5

In doing so, however, Sir Alan Barlow said that the Department must make it clear to Local Authorities that the normal ratio between State and rate contribution must be 2:1: that the present departure from that ratio was to be regarded as a 'bonus' to Local Authorities in respect of special Scottish difficulties and was to be confined to the first subsidy period commencing with the passing of the forthcoming Bill; and that the concession was not to be founded upon as a precedent for future subsidy periods.

Sir Alan Barlow felt that it was only on such a basis that the concession of a more favourable ratio than 2:1 to Scottish Local Authorities could be justified in relation to the position in England. [SRO, DD6/1599.]

Memorandum by John Colville, Secretary of State for Scotland, on Housing Subsidies: Scotland, 19 October 1938.

The rates of housing subsidies payable to Scottish local authorities for slum clearance and decrowding operations prior to 1st April, 1938, were continued for a further period from that date by the Housing (Scotland) Acts (Continuance of Contributions) Order, 1938. My predecessor explained, that while for technical reasons the order then made had to relate to a period of three years, it was the Government's intention to continue discussions that were then taking place with local authorities; and it was implied, though not expressly stated, that if as a result of these discussions any alteration in the rates of subsidy were found to be necessary, provision would be made for the alteration to take effect from 1st January, 1939.

Discussions with local authorities have continued since then and general agreement has been reached with them that the two separate subsidies under the Housing (Scotland) Act, 1930, and the Housing (Scotland) Act, 1935, relating to slum clearance and decrowding respectively should be consolidated into one subsidy for those two purposes.

Building costs have risen appreciably and in view of the urgency and magnitude of the Scottish housing problem, I propose that there should be a certain increase in the average rates of subsidy. On a programme of 20,000 houses a year it is estimated that the additional cost to the Exchequer will be of the average order of £20,000 in respect of each year of the next subsidy period, which will last until 30th September, 1942. The additional cost will remain a charge on the Exchequer for 40 years, the period over which housing subsidies are spread.

I am convinced that this additional expenditure is necessary to enable the attack on Scotland's deplorable housing conditions to be maintained. For some time local authorities have strongly represented that the subsidy under the 1935 Act, which was based on building costs about 30 per cent. less than present costs, is wholly inadequate and it was with some difficulty that they were persuaded to accept the proposal to postpone consideration in the beginning of the year.

I propose also to make arrangements under which the Scottish Special Areas Housing Association will be authorised to build 20,000 houses after March 1939 in the Special Areas under the same general procedure as they are operating at present. For this purpose the Association will be reconstructed. In addition, I propose that either the reconstructed Association or one of the existing Scottish National Housing Companies should carry out a number of demonstration schemes by alternative methods of construction in selected districts outside the Special Areas with a view to stimulating local authorities to attack the grave Scottish housing problem in new ways.

I have been in consultation with the Chancellor of the Exchequer in regard to my proposals and have obtained his agreement to the terms of this Memorandum. I should be glad to have authority to prepare and submit to the Home Affairs Committee the necessary Bill, which must be passed before the Christmas recess. [PRO, CAB 24/279 CP(38)221.]

Minute of the Meeting of the Department of Health and the Treasury, on the Proposed Housing Board, 26 October 1938.

Mr. Tribe referred to the draft provisions prepared by the Department for inclusion in the forthcoming Bill with regard to the setting up of a Housing Board and said that the Chancellor of the Exchequer was opposed to the establishment of a new statutory body. The Treasury had contemplated that the constitution of the existing Special Areas Housing Association should be amended to enable them to build the demonstration houses which the Treasury had agreed should be provided outside the Special Areas. *Mr. Douglas* indicated that his recollection was that the Chancellor had said that he could not agree that the Exchequer should take over what was properly a local authority obligation to build outside the Special Areas but that he was prepared to approve of houses being built outside these areas to demonstrate speed, costs, alternative construction, etc., provided that these houses were not to be regarded as a contribution to the housing needs of the localities in which they were built. *Mr. Douglas* did not think that the Chancellor had condescended on the details referred to by Mr. Tribe. *Mr. Henderson* outlined the existing statutory provisions with regard to Housing Associations and explained that in connection with their present operations the Special Areas Housing Association were dependent on the co-operation of local authorities. If the Authorities were to operate outside the Special Areas and if the Government desired the Association to be freer from statutory control by local authorities than it is at present, the new body would have to be something else than a Housing Association. It could not be a hybrid body and the Department had suggested that it should be a Housing Board. *Mr. Tribe* agreed that the Association could not continue to be called the Special Areas Housing Association but it ought to continue to depend on co-operation with local authorities. He saw no reason why, even although local authorities would make no contribution to the cost of the proposed new houses, they should not hand over the Exchequer contributions to the new body. *Mr. Douglas* said that it was no part of the Department's proposals that the new body should operate in any area without the fullest co-operation of the local authority. This could, however, be achieved administratively: whether there should be a statutory requirement in the matter raised other questions. It seemed to him that to provide for the payment of Exchequer contributions through local authorities was to choose a long way round. Moreover, the

Department had hoped that the new body would be able to facilitate the housing of the population who moved from one area to another, not only inside the Special Areas, but from these areas to other areas outside. Besides, the Secretary of State thought that the new body should undertake a limited amount of experimental reconditioning. All of this carried the proposal beyond the scope of the Special Areas Housing Assocation. *Mr. Valentine* [Secretary to the Commissioner of the Special Areas in Scotland], supporting the general argument, explained that the Commissioner for the Special Areas attached great importance to the desirability of getting away from the 'local authority' tie.

Mr. Tribe, however, held strongly that the new body must operate on the basis of receiving the normal Exchequer subsidies through the local authority. The less to be included in the new Bill the better. All that would be necessary in his view would be a provision enabling the Department to pay to the new body direct the equivalent of the local rate contributions for the houses which they would build and empowering them to build a limited number of demonstration houses outside the Special Areas with Treasury consent. His idea was that the Special Areas Housing Association should be left to complete their existing programme, deriving their authority to do so from the Special Areas Act, but the Association's memorandum and articles of association should be amended to give them the power to build the proposed demonstration houses outside the Special Areas. The Treasury felt that the new body should be set up administratively. To establish anything of the nature of a National Association by Statute would be to suggest that the new body was to take over the housing functions of local authorities—a proposal to which the Treasury were definitely opposed. The Treasury were, however, prepared to make the concession that whereas the North-eastern Special Areas Housing Association in England received from the Exchequer only such part of the rate contribution equivalent as was proved to be necessary on each individual scheme, the equivalent of the full rate contribution would be given to the Scottish body in order to enable them to build up a reserve. [SRO, DD6/1599.]

THE POST-WAR SCOTTISH HOUSING PROGRAMME, 1944

In October 1944 the Government's Reconstruction Committee ran into difficulty over the date to begin the post-war housing programme and Winston Churchill, the Prime Minister, established a special Cabinet Committee to review the situation. (Ernest Bevin, the Minister of Labour, had been particularly concerned about its impact on war production.) The following extract is from the memorandum subsequently presented to the Committee by Thomas Johnston, the Scottish Secretary. The Committee took note of its contents and after reviewing a similar memorandum from the Minister of Health agreed that a limited programme could begin in May 1945.

Memorandum by Thomas Johnston, Secretary of State for Scotland, on Permanent Housing in Scotland, 25 November 1944.

Needs and Programme.

It is estimated that Scotland requires at least 500,000 additional houses to replace slums, to relieve overcrowding and to meet the needs of persons having no homes of their own.

The target programme contemplates that these houses will be provided over a period of ten or twelve years after the war. As an instalment of this programme it is the aim to have 20,000 houses built or building at the end of the first year in the transitional period and 30,000 additional houses at the end of the second year.

(This is, of course, additional to the temporary housing programme out of which it is estimated that Scotland will get in the two years about 40,000 houses. That is a total figure of 90,000 houses in the two years. This compares with a total production of houses in the two years 1937 to 1938, including private enterprise, of 47,000 houses.)

Local authorities were asked on the 19th October to submit proposals showing the sites which they intend to develop first and the order of their development; these proposals are just beginning to come in.

Acquisition of Housing Sites.

Scottish Local Authorities already own sufficient land for 56,000 houses and are in process of acquiring sites for 35,500 additional houses. All of these sites have been approved from the planning point of view and are widely distributed over the country. This figure is being constantly and progressively added to.

Layout and Type Plans.

Layout plans, including plans prepared before the war, have been received for 25,000 houses.

Local Authorities have been told that for houses to be built during the transitional period they may use pre-war type plans suitably adapted to include additional fitments.

Arrangements have been made with the Royal Incorporation of Architects in Scotland for the preparation of standard type plans which will be made available to Local Authorities who desire to use them. The use of these plans will expedite the preparation of housing proposals by Local Authorities.

Preparation of Housing Sites.

Sites capable of taking some 9,000 houses were serviced with roads and sewers before the war and are available for immediate development. In addition, arrangements are already in hand for servicing within the next six months sites for about 37,000 houses.

Local Authorities are being urged to make the utmost progress in the servicing of housing land.

Houses under Construction.

Local Authorities have been gradually completing houses on which work was temporarily suspended at the outbreak of war. The houses completed since the war began number 35,000. In addition, authority was given for a programme of 2,000 new houses in 1943 and 1944. The number of houses at present under construction in these categories is 3,219.

Scottish Special Housing Association.

The Housing (Scotland) Act, 1944, contains provisions enabling the Scottish Special Housing Association to undertake a vastly enlarged Housing Programme after the war in areas where the need is greatest.

This Association, which is a limited company incorporated under the Companies Act, was set up originally in 1937 to build houses in the special areas of Scotland. It is a non-profit making organisation and its Council of Management contains representatives of all political parties. Its activities will be financed wholly from the Exchequer.

The association has been entrusted with a target programme of 100,000 houses to be built over a period of 10 or 12 years in supplementation of the programmes of Local Authorities. These houses will form part of the total programme of 500,000 houses to be built in Scotland in that period. A list of the areas of 'greatest need' where the Association is to build has been adjusted with the Treasury. These areas are mainly in the industrial belt and the Association is in touch with the Local Authorities concerned for the acquisition of sites and the preparation of plans.

It is an essential feature of this arrangement that the Association will help Local Authorities who help themselves. No Local Authority will be permitted to lie back and allow the Association to do their housing work for them. On the other hand, co-operation between the association and Local Authorities will secure that housing arrears in the hardest hit areas will be overtaken more rapidly than would otherwise be possible.

Supply of Building Labour.

The position in regard to the supply of building labour will be particularly difficult in Scotland in the immediate post-war years. Whereas the Scottish building programme in the first two years represents 1/6th of the total programme for Great Britain (50,000 out of 300,000) the Scottish labour force before the war was only 1/10th of the total force in Great Britain. Special arrangements will therefore be necessary if the Scottish programme is to be carried out as planned.

Apart from any steps that may be practicable to increase the proportion of building labour in Scotland, it will be of the greatest importance that alternative methods of construction which make a minimum demand on the services of building craftsmen should be used to the fullest possible extent. Before the war numbers of steel and timber houses were built in Scotland and the resumption of these and other forms of building on a substantial scale is essential. A start has already been made with 100 experimental Weir steel houses as a preliminary to a mass production programme of 10,000 steel houses in the first five years. I am anxious that this should be supplemented by the importation from abroad of prefabricated timber houses. [PRO, CAB 124/460 GEN 51/4.]

RISING COSTS AND THE HOUSING SUBSIDY, 1946

In October 1945 the Labour Government remitted to the Lord President's Committee consideration of its prospective housing legislation. The extract here is from the memorandum by Joseph Westwood, the Scottish Secretary, outlining details of the Housing (Financial Provisions) (Scotland) Bill, which the Committee accepted.

Memorandum by Joseph Westwood, the Secretary of State for Scotland, on Revision of Housing Subsidies, 16 January 1946.

I should like to have the approval of my colleagues to the proposals contained in the Appendix to this paper with regard to the Exchequer and local contributions to be paid for houses completed in Scotland by local authorities and the Scottish Special Housing Association between 8th March 1944 and 30th June, 1947. I have confidentially consulted the appropriate associations of local authorities who have accepted the proposals.

The total of the Exchequer and local contributions represents the estimated deficit on the Housing account after making provision for an average rent of 10/- per week, exclusive of rates. The estimated deficit has been calculated on the same basis as under the Housing (Financial Provision) (Scotland) Act 1938 but, mainly because of the much greater cost of building at present, it is substantially higher than in 1938. For example, the estimated deficit on a typical house of four rooms (living room and three bedrooms) has increased from £16.10/- for 40 years to £30 for 60 years. Comparative building costs are £530 in 1938 and £1,140 to-day.

Hitherto the ratio between the Exchequer and local rate contributions in Scotland has been about 2.5:1. My present proposals provide for a ratio of rather more than 3:1. I am quite satisfied that during a period of exceptionally high prices we cannot fairly treat local authorities any less generously than that. Even the ratio which I propose involves an average rate contribution of about £7 per house as compared with £4.15/- under the 1938 Act. I have, however, warned the local authorities that when costs finally settle to a normal post-war level, it is intended that the rates shall revert to the original 2.5:1.

The subsidies proposed will be payable for houses completed between 8th March, 1944 and 30th June, 1947. 8th March, 1944 was the date on which the then Minister of Health announced in the House of Commons that while it was not yet possible to say what the amount of subsidies would be they would be applied retrospectively when finally fixed. As regards the terminal date, I had originally thought of a longer subsidy period with a falling rate of subsidy, but the local authorities represented that the trend of prices was so uncertain that it might be unfair to them to fix the subsidy too far ahead. For periods subsequent to 30th June, 1947 I suggest that the subsidies should be fixed by Order.

I would propose to provide for two new additional subsidies to meet special circumstances.

(a) In mining areas the expenditure of local authorities in providing housing accommodation is frequently abnormally heavy because of the payment of compensation to secure mineral support and so protect the houses from the effects of mining subsidence. This is a matter on which the local authorities concerned have made strong representations from time to time. I therefore propose that I should have discretionary power to pay an additional Exchequer subsidy up to £2 per house for sixty years, subject to the payment of a rate contribution of one half of the Exchequer subsidy, where I am satisfied that a local authority have to use a particular site which necessitates substantial additional expenditure on this account.

(b) In a few urban areas, for example Glasgow, where housing land is becoming scarce, I propose to approve the erection of blocks of flats of more than four storeys and, where necessary, the provision of lifts. I am advised that the cost involved in the provision of lifts would justify an additional Exchequer contribution of £7 per house for 60 years with a contribution from the rates of half that amount, and I would accordingly propose to make assistance of this order available in suitable cases.

I propose to extend the scope of the work of the Scottish Special Housing Association and am in process of strengthening its organisation for this purpose. At present the Association receive grants and loans from the Exchequer to enable them to build houses in supplementation of the housing operations of local authorities in districts where the housing needs are greatest. My proposal is that the Association should now develop a strong direct labour force and undertake house building in any part of Scotland where this appears necessary or desirable. For example, the Association would build as contractors for the local authority who could not obtain satisfactory tenders, either because the tenders received were too high or showed evidence of a price ring; it would build where it is difficult to get tenders at all or where, because of shortage of labour, the local authority find it impossible to make satisfactory progress. The Association could also be used to build as contractors for the Secretary of State in any case where a local authority defaults in the exercise of their housing powers and it becomes necessary to build houses for them. In all these cases the cost of the houses would ultimately be borne by the local authority but the Association would require to be financed while carrying out the work and I would therefore propose to make loans available to them for this purpose. [PRO, CAB 132/2 LP(46)10; SRO, DD 6/503 (part).]

NEW TOWNS FOR SCOTLAND, 1946

In March 1946 the Labour Cabinet formally approved a bill to establish a number of new towns in Britain and remitted detailed consideration of the matter to its Distribution of Industry Sub-Committee. The following extract is from the memorandum by Joseph Westwood, the Scottish Secretary, seeking permission to establish six such towns in Scotland. The Committee agreed to East Kilbride but invited Westwood to have further discussions with all those concerned about new towns for Fife.

Memorandum by Joseph Westwood, Secretary of State for Scotland, on New Towns in Scotland, 13 May 1946.

I have been considering the extent to which it will be necessary to provide new towns in Scotland in furtherance of the Government's policy of planned decentralisation of population and industry and to meet the need for the creation of new communities to serve areas of large scale industrial development: and I am submitting in this memorandum a general appreciation of the long term problem and of my proposals for meeting immediate needs.

New towns will be required in two main areas of central Scotland—first, in the Clyde valley (which embraces the greater part of the Scottish Development Area) to cope with the overspill resulting from the planned decongestion of the City of Glasgow and other large towns and to provide new housing and industrial facilities as an integral part of the Government's development area policy: and secondly in the County of Fife and in the Lothians south of Edinburgh to meet the needs of the new coalfields in those areas.

Proposals for the Clyde Valley Area

My proposals for the establishment of new towns in the Clyde Valley area arise out of recommendations recently made in the report prepared for the Clyde Valley Regional Planning Advisory Committee by their consultant, Sir Patrick Abercrombie. The Committee carried out a most comprehensive survey of the whole Clyde Valley region with particular emphasis on the problems arising from the appalling housing and industrial congestion in Glasgow. The Planning consultant's report stresses especially the following facts. Glasgow with a population of about 1,100,000 is one of the most congested areas in Great Britain—700,000 people being huddled together in and around the City centre within a space of three square miles, and in these congested central areas housing densities range up to 127 houses to the acre. The houses are mainly of the 1 and 2 room type, and in some of the central wards the percentage of houses of two rooms or less is as high as 93%.

Industrial congestion in the central areas of Glasgow is no less acute. Housing and industry are inextricably mixed up and industrial concerns have no room to expand. There is an urgent need for re-locating in better surroundings and for introducing new industries on a substantial scale to secure a properly balanced industrial structure. The Board of Trade estimate that to remedy unemployment in Glasgow about six million square feet of new factory accommodation is required. This figure takes no account of the need for re-locating industries at present accommodated in unsatisfactory premises.

Glasgow cannot go on expanding outwards as this would lead to the City and the surrounding towns becoming one large urban sprawl. A planned policy of decongestion and decentralisation is urgently needed.

Similar problems of housing and industrial congestion exist on a smaller scale in other towns in the region such as Greenock and Clydebank.

Against this background the Clyde Valley Committee recommend the establishment of four new towns in the area—at East Kilbride in North Lanarkshire (about seven miles from the centre of Glasgow, at Bishopton in Renfrewshire (about ten miles from the centre of Glasgow), at Houston in Renfrewshire (about twelve miles from the centre of Glasgow), and at Cumbernauld in Dumbartonshire (about twelve miles from the centre of Glasgow).... In addition the Committee recommend the extension of a number of existing towns elsewhere in the region.

Each of these four new towns would ultimately have a population of between 50,000 and 60,000 and would provide for an over-spill from Glasgow and other areas (e.g. Greenock) of 200,000 to 250,000 people.

I accept in principle the Committee's basic recommendation that the provision of new towns in the Clyde Valley area is essential for securing the decongestion of Glasgow and the properly balanced provision of the new housing and industrial facilities that are so urgently needed in this part of the Scottish Development Area.

I am also in broad agreement with the Clyde Valley Committee as to the areas in which the new towns should be developed and I am satisfied that the establishment of a new town at East Kilbride should be regarded as a project of first priority. The County Council of Lanarkshire are anxious to make an immediate start with the building of a substantial number of houses at East Kilbride and it is clear that these houses must be planned as part of the new town. I should, therefore, like the authority of my colleagues for the initiation of early discussion with all the local authorities concerned on the basis that the Clyde Valley Committee's proposals are accepted in principle by the Government and that the establishment of a new town at East Kilbride will be put in hand as a priority project.

Proposals for Fife and the Lothians.

Substantial developments of new coalfields in the County of Fife and the Lothians are now beginning and in the next decade or so these areas will become the principal coal-mining areas in Scotland. In the next few years sinkings will take place in three main areas in the County of Fife and two areas in the Lothians. The workings of these new pits will involve the rapid build-up of an additional labour force of 10,000 to 15,000 mineworkers, the majority of whom will be drawn from other parts of the country, and new housing accommodation for these workers will have to be provided. I am anxious to ensure that these houses are built in the right places as part of properly planned communities constituting a complete break from the out-moded conception of the mining town. In some cases it will be appropriate to provide the necessary housing and other facilities by expanding some of the existing towns; in other cases it will be necessary to develop new towns with populations ranging from 10,000 to 15,000. I propose to consider with the Minister of Fuel and Power and the local authorities concerned the precise areas in which new communities should be established and I hope to submit specific proposals at an early date. [PRO, CAB 132/22 LP(DI)(46)13.]

NEW TOWNS FOR RENFREWSHIRE AND FIFE, 1946

The extract here is from the memorandum by Joseph Westwood, the Scottish Secretary, to the Distribution of Industry Sub-Committee again raising the issue of establishing new towns in Scotland. During discussion Hugh Dalton, the Chancellor of the Exchequer, argued that Westwood's proposal would give Scotland 'a disproportionate share of the initial programme' and the Committee accepted the recommendation of Tom Fraser, the Joint Parliamentary Under Secretary of State, that the Lochgelly-

Cowdenbeath proposal was the most urgent. At that stage four English new towns had been approved.

Memorandum by Joseph Westwood, Secretary of State for Scotland, on New Towns in Scotland, 26 July 1946.

Clyde Valley Area

The Sub-Committee, at their meeting on 23rd May ... approved in principle the proposal to develop a new town at East Kilbride in the Clyde valley area. I have had a meeting with the local authorities primarily concerned, who welcomed the proposal, and preliminary work in connection with the planning of the town is now in hand. The Ordnance Survey have completed an aerial survey of the proposed site and are at present engaged in preparing a map of the contours. Concurrently with this work my Department are pressing on with the preparation of the outline plan of the town so that the site may be designated under the provisions of the New Towns Bill as soon as possible after it becomes law. Discussions have also taken place with the Board of Trade about the development of an industrial estate and the site of the industrial zone in which this estate will be situated has been provisionally agreed. It is proposed that the industrial estate should form one of the first developments in the new town.

The case for the development of the [other] towns is set out in my memorandum L.P.(D.I.)(46) 13. Briefly, housing and industrial congestion in Glasgow and other towns in the region is so acute that there is an urgent need for a planned policy of decongestion and decentralisation of population and industry. It is equally necessary to introduce new industries into the area on a substantial scale to secure a properly balanced industrial structure. For example, the Board of Trade estimate that to remedy unemployment in the Glasgow area alone, up to six million square feet of new factory accommodation may be required. If this accommodation is to be made available within a reasonable time, it is necessary to reach decisions now about the areas in which it is to be provided.

There is a particular need to provide new industrial facilities to the west of Glasgow to relieve unemployment in the city itself and to meet the needs of the Greenock area. There is considerable housing and industrial congestion in Greenock and as the topographical features limit the extent to which new building can take place in the town itself, a substantial decentralisation of population and industry will be necessary. In addition, new industries are required to provide the necessary industrial diversification. As a solution to these problems the Clyde Valley Committee proposed the establishment of two new towns—one at Bishopton in Renfrewshire (about ten miles from the centre of Glasgow and 9 miles from the centre of Greenock) and the other at Houston in Renfrewshire (about 12 miles from the centre of Glasgow and about 11 miles from Greenock). After studying the Committee's report I have come to the conclusion that the proposal for a new town in the Bishopton area should be accepted and I understand that the President of the Board of Trade agrees with this view. Considerable detailed field survey work will be necessary before the precise site of the new town can be determined and I am therefore anxious to have the approval of my colleagues to the proposal for a new town so that this detailed work may be carried through immediately in association with the local authorities concerned.

Central Fife Area

At the meeting of the Sub-Committee on 23rd May I was authorised, in consultation with the President of the Board of Trade and the Minister of Fuel and Power to work out with the local authorities in Fife and the Lothians, detailed proposals for the creation of new towns to serve the new coalfields areas. Since then, I have had a meeting with representatives of the Central and South East Scotland Regional Planning Advisory Committee and the local authorities concerned about the extent to which new townships should be provided in central Fife. Substantial new mining developments will take place in this area within the next few years and additional man-power will require to be imported for the purpose. In addition a very substantial amount of new housing will be needed to replace unfit houses in the existing mining villages which are typical of the worst kind of mining establishments. I have now reached the conclusion, with which the Minister of Fuel and Power and the President of the Board of Trade agree, that in addition to the considerable housing developments which will be carried out by local authorities in the Kirkcaldy and Buckhaven-Leven districts two new townships should be developed in central Fife as soon as possible. One of these towns would be in the Lochgelly-Cowdenbeath area and the other in the Markinch-Leslie area. Each of the towns would cater for an additional population of the order of 20,000 people and they would be planned so as to provide ample facilities for new industrial development in order to ensure a properly balanced industrial structure. The new townships would be centrally situated near the main railway lines and the proposed new trunk road running through Fife from the north to the south via the Forth road bridge. The Planning Consultant to the Central and South East Scotland Regional Planning Advisory Committee is recommending the development of new towns in these areas in his report which will shortly be issued to the local planning authorities in the region and to the Government Departments concerned.

I accordingly ask the approval of my colleagues to my proposal for the development of these new towns and to my proceeding immediately with the preliminary work involved. [PRO, CAB 132/22 LP(DI)(46)45.]

NEW TOWNS FOR MINING AREAS, 1946

The extract here is from the memorandum by Joseph Westwood, the Scottish Secretary, to the Distribution of Industry Sub-Committee again raising the issue of establishing new towns in mining areas (see above). The Committee agreed to Westwood's proposals.

Memorandum by Joseph Westwood, Secretary of State for Scotland, on New Towns in Mining Areas, 4 November 1946.

In consultation with the Minister of Fuel and Power I have been considering the extent to which it will be necessary to provide new townships in these areas in which large new mining developments are to be carried out, and I am setting out in this memorandum a statement of the long term problem and of my proposals for meeting immediate needs.

The future of coal mining in Scotland was exhaustively examined by the Scottish Coalfields Committee whose report was published in 1944 (Cmd. 6575). Briefly, the Committee recommended that if the pre-war Scottish output of 30 million tons of coal per annum was to be maintained substantial new developments, including major new sinkings, would be necessary in the counties of Fife, Clackmannan, Stirling and the Lothians and in central Ayrshire. Investigations have shown that these counties will, as a result of the progressive decline in the output of the central Lanarkshire coalfields, become responsible within the next twenty years for about 80 per cent. of Scottish coal production as compared with 60 per cent. at present.

These new developments will necessitate the provision of new housing accommodation on a very substantial scale for the miners and their families and it is essential to ensure that plans for the provision of this housing accommodation are made sufficiently far ahead to enable the new pits to come into operation at the earliest possible date. In some cases the new housing accommodation will have to be provided by adding to existing villages; but to meet the major requirements it will be necessary to establish entirely new communities. These should be of a balanced character providing employment for members of the miners' families and with social amenities and facilities up to modern standards.

The areas in which large numbers of new houses are most urgently required are—Leslie and Markinch in East Fife, and Sinclairston in Central Ayrshire; and I am anxious to have the authority of the Sub-Committee to the establishment of one new town in each of these areas.

My proposals for the establishment of the new town at Leslie-Markinch have already been before the Sub-Committee ... and I should like very briefly to recapitulate the arguments in support of this project. Two new pits are to be sunk near this area, the first of which will come into production by 1951 and will ultimately provide employment for about 2,300 miners. The second pit will start production by about 1957 and will employ about 2,000 additional miners, making a total employment figure for the two pits of 4,300. In addition, accommodation is required now for several hundred miners who are at present living in unfit or overcrowded houses in the vicinity. To accommodate a mining population of the order of 4,500 in a properly balanced community the total population will have to be about 30,000 people, and I propose therefore the establishment of a new community on this scale adjoining the existing small towns of Leslie and Markinch. The site of the new town has been selected after full consultation with the Ministry of Fuel and Power, the Board of Trade, the Ministry of Labour, the Ministry of Transport and the local authorities concerned; it is centrally situated near the main railway lines and proposed new trunk road running through Fife from the North to the South via the Forth Road Bridge, and is capable of rapid development. I am being strongly pressed by the County Council of Fife to make an early start with preliminary work on this project so that housing developments which are about to be carried out by the Council may be planned as part of the new town.

Two new sinkings are planned for the Sinclairston area of Central Ayrshire, the first providing employment for upwards of 2,000 miners and the other employment for about 500 miners. These new pits will not come into production until 1953-1957 but there is at present an urgent need in this area for about 500 houses to replace unfit and overcrowded houses in the surrounding mining villages which are reaching the obsolescent stage. In addition, nearly 500 new houses are required for additional miners who could be employed to increase production at existing pits. The County Council of Ayrshire are pressing for a first development of 500 houses in the area and it is essential that this development should be planned as part of the new township. Taking into account the labour requirements of the proposed new sinkings, of expanded production at existing collieries, and of the needs of general industry to secure a properly balanced industrial structure in this expanding mining area, the new town should ultimately have a population of about 30,000 people. The site at Sinclairston, which is 6½ miles due East of the town of Ayr, has been selected after consultation with the Ministry of Fuel and Power, the Board of Trade, the Ministry of Labour and the Country Council. Rail facilities are available direct to the site and road communications are excellent. [PRO, CAB 132/22 LP(DI)(46)94.]

AFFORDABLE RENTS, HOUSING NEED AND SUBSIDIES, 1947

In March 1947 Hugh Dalton, the Chancellor of the Exchequer, wrote to John Edwards, Parliamentary Under Secretary of State at the Ministry of Health, indicating that with the reduction in interest rates he intended to reduce the housing subsidy. The first extract is from a letter of Joseph Westwood, the Scottish Secretary, to Dalton, on the issue. Aneurin Bevan, the Minister of Health, replied on similar lines for England and Wales. The second is from Dalton's reply to Westwood.

Letter of Joseph Westwood, Secretary of State for Scotland, to Hugh Dalton, Chancellor of the Exchequer, on the Scottish Housing Subsidy, 14 April 1947.

Thank you for sending me a copy of your letter of the 31st March addressed to Edwards about the revision of housing subsidies. I note that in your view we should now expect the rents of local authority houses to be increased and the rate of Exchequer contributions to come down.

Let me say at once that I fully appreciate your difficulties and the importance of securing economies wherever practicable. So far as housing subsidies are concerned I am anxious to effect a reduction as soon as this is possible.

At the moment, however, I am confronted with a general demand that the subsidy should be increased. At their Annual Conference last week the Convention of Royal Burghs of Scotland passed a resolution requesting me to increase 'financial assistance to the local authorities concerned so as to free them from continually requiring to meet the losses involved by increasing rents and local rates'. The Association of City Councils have made similar representations, and I am being pressed in the same direction by individual local authorities, particularly County Councils.

In the face of this pressure I would have considerable difficulty in maintaining the subsidies at their existing level for another year which is the proposal already submitted to you. My case vis-a-vis local authorities for continuance of the existing rates is in fact somewhat vulnerable. As the figures which I have submitted show, it is based on the increase in the average cost of a four-apartment house from £1,130 in November 1945 to £1,286 being roughly balanced by the reduction in the rate of interest. But local authorities will almost certainly point out that the figure of £1,286 is the average for 1946 and that the corresponding figure today is higher, and that the reduction in the rate of interest did not take effect until mid 1946—after the loans for many of the houses covered by the revision of subsidies had been negotiated at the higher rate of 3⅛%. These seem to me to be formidable criticisms which I shall have to face, and even if the subsidies remain as they are, there will inevitably be a deficit which local authorities will have to meet either from the local rates or out of increased rents.

I am bound to say that I see no hope whatever in getting authorities, on top of all of this, to accept a reduction of subsidies, involving a further deficit to be met out of local rates or rents, and in my view it would be a bad move politically to impose a reduction. My reasons are these:-

(i) The rent factor in the calculation of subsidies was increased in Scotland when the existing rates were fixed in 1945 from 7/- to 10/- a week or by 43% and I consider that it would be difficult to justify raising it still further after so recent and substantial an increase.

(ii) Moreover, in Scotland, 10/- is the factor taken for urban and rural districts alike since our local government system makes it impracticable to distinguish between areas for this purpose.

(iii) Generally, if rents are forced up, local authorities would be obliged to give rebates from rent in an increased number of cases or in increased amounts, or both. Alternatively local authorities would tend to let their houses to tenants who can afford to pay the increased rents and this would involve an unfortunate departure from the principle that need should be the primary criterion in the selection of tenants. The Acts require authorities to give a reasonable preference to persons who are occupying insanitary or overcrowded houses, have large families or are otherwise living in unsatisfactory housing conditions, and these are usually the persons who are least able to pay high rents.

(iv) The Acts also require authorities in fixing rents to take into consideration the rents ordinarily payable by persons of the working classes in the locality. While admittedly this provision is merely a guide to authorities we should not, while the provision stands, take action which might in any particular case tempt an authority to forget it altogether.

For these reasons I consider that a rent factor of 10/- is as much as we can justify in Scotland in present circumstances. I hope, therefore, you will see your way to agree to our proposal that we should adhere to this figure and approach authorities on the basis of the continuance of the subsidies at the existing rates. To my mind the most satisfactory method of effecting a reduction in subsidies would be to secure a reduction in costs as soon as possible, and I have already made preliminary arrangements to appoint a Committee to go into this question. As housing costs come down—and the fact that we are at present restricting new approvals may encourage an early movement in this direction—we would seek to retain the existing rent factor of 10/- so that the broad effect would be merely a postponement of what you are now suggesting. [SRO, DD6/1602.]

Letter of Hugh Dalton, Chancellor of the Exchequer, to Joseph Westwood, Secretary of State for Scotland, on the Scottish Housing Subsidy, 10 May 1947.

I have carefully studied your arguments with sympathy for your difficulties. I can, reluctantly, agree that subsidies should continue at their present level for a further period of one year from the 1st July next. But there can, of course, be no question of increasing them. And if, before the end of the year, there has not been a substantial reduction in building costs, we shall, of course, have to re-examine the whole basis of housing finance if we are to carry through the sort of programme we have in mind without imposing an intolerable burden on the taxpayer and the ratepayer.

I hope that you will be very firm with the local authorities on this question of housing finance. They are going to benefit very considerably from the new block grant—I look forward to hearing how they will receive this good news when you open negotiations with them, as I hope you will quickly—and they must realise that the Exchequer cannot carry all their burden for them. To continue the existing housing subsidies for one more year is the very limit to which I can go. [SRO, DD6/1602.]

THE DOLLAR CRISIS AND THE SCOTTISH HOUSING PROGRAMME, 1947

In August 1947 the Government ran into severe balance of payments difficulties, largely over its trade with the USA. In response, to save dollars and boost exports, the Cabinet established an official Investment Programmes Committee to review and prioritise public expenditure. The Committee, after reviewing the housing programme and the supply of timber, subsequently agreed to impose a ceiling on the number of building workers and generally limit tenders to housing for mining and agricultural workers. The extract here is from the Department of Health's observations to these proposals. In October the Cabinet agreed to a UK programme of 140,000 houses per annum and to review the situation in June 1948.

Review of Investment Programme, Observations by the Department of Health for Scotland, 27 August 1947.

Housing.

The labour ceiling for housing was restricted earlier in the year to 582,000. The Investment Programme Committee now suggest that this figure should be reduced by a further cut of 92,000 to 490,000 at June 1948. These are Great Britain figures and the Scottish breakdown is not available. It is estimated, however, that on the assumption that part of any reduction would be borne by repairs and maintenance and conversions and adaptations, the existing labour force on new housing construction in Scotland might fall by about 20 per cent.

Such a reduction between now and June 1948 would have a most serious effect on the completion of houses now under construction. The completion rate is already far behind schedule. Whereas it was originally estimated that it might be possible to complete a total of 24,000 houses in Scotland during 1947, the number actually completed up to the end of July was only 5,600. It was hoped that as the temporary house scheme came to an end in the early part of 1948, additional labour would progressively be released for employment on permanent house schemes in order to expedite the rate of completion and restore the balance of the programme as a whole. But if a cut of 20 per cent. in the labour force were imposed this would become impossible.

In accordance with declared Government policy and under Government pressure the local authorities of almost every county and burgh in Scotland have entered into definite contractual arrangements for the erection of houses in their districts. House building is widespread and does not lend itself to reduction by a concentration of effort on a 'smaller number of projects'. Indeed, the Lord President's Committee agreed at their meeting on 12th August, 1947, that work should proceed on houses under construction and in approved tenders. At that date there were 37,800 houses under construction in Scotland, and 24,100 additional houses were in approved contracts but had not been begun. It seems essential to take account of these commitments and to implement the decision of the Lord President's Committee by arranging for sufficient supply of labour and materials to finish these houses as soon as possible.

The Department are particularly concerned lest any reduction in permanent housing, in the absence of any effective means of direction, may merely lead to an augmentation of labour for less essential building work and black market operations. In their view, it is of the utmost importance that licensing work should be severely cut and all non-essential projects eliminated.

So far as new contracts are concerned, pending the results of the present review the Department have already taken steps, in accordance with the decision of the Lord President's Committee, to restrict approvals of new tenders to those required for the construction of houses in rural and mining areas. [PRO, CAB 134/444 IPC(WP)(47)4; SRO, DD10/117.]

A NEW TOWN FOR RENFREWSHIRE, 1948

The following is an extract from the memorandum by Arthur Woodburn, the Scottish Secretary, to the Lord President's Committee on establishing a new town at Bishopton-Houston, Renfrewshire. Although Woodburn indicated that the Government had, since 1946, approved additional towns for England, the Committee was informed that Hector McNeil, the Foreign Office Minister of State and MP for Greenock, had indicated his objection, largely on the grounds that it would be better to develop the Kip Valley. The Comittee agreed the proposal in principle, but invited Woodburn to re-examine whether or not the Kip Valley could be developed. In December 1949 Woodburn resubmitted the proposal and secured the Committee's approval, but the devaluation crisis and McNeil's appointment as Scottish Secretary subsequently meant the project's abandonment.

Memorandum by Arthur Woodburn, Secretary of State for Scotland, on New Towns in Scotland, 20 April 1948.

The problems which the proposed new town is intended to solve are as follows:-

(a) The Burgh of Greenock, which at present has a population of about 80,000 has almost completely exhausted all the immediately available sites within the present burgh boundary both for new housing and for industrial development. The town, which was grossly congested before the war, suffered more extensive war damage than any other town in Scotland except Clydebank and in fact about 1,000 houses were destroyed. The total number of houses required amounts to 13,500; 5,000 of these can be built within the present burgh boundaries but only as part of a long-term programme for the redevelopment of the central town area. The balance of 8,000 houses, including houses immediately required, will have to be located outside the present burgh boundary. The town is very closely hemmed in topographically and a properly planned extension to secure accommodation for all these houses is ruled out.

The shortage of industrial sites is equally acute and the current employment situation in Greenock presents grave and urgent problems. The total number of unemployed at the end of March was 2,000 or about 6 per cent. of the population—the highest total number of unemployed in any town in Scotland except Glasgow. Moreover Greenock, with the immediately adjoining burgh of Port Glasgow, has a very ill-balanced industrial structure, 45 per cent. of the insured population being dependent upon ship-building and marine engineering.

It is therefore essential to find additional land for housing and industrial development and the bulk of the requirements can only be met outside the limits of the present burgh, after taking full account of the long-term possibilities of redevelopment. One possible solution—proposed by the Corporation of Greenock—would be to permit the town to straggle south-westwards in the only direction open to expansion along the line of a relatively narrow valley—the Kip Valley—in such a way that isolated housing schemes would be built up to a distance as far away as five miles from the present town centre. Such a solution would, however, create a continuous elongated ribbon of development from Port Glasgow through Greenock to the head of the valley of about 12 miles and would locate the bulk of the new houses required in a situation relatively very remote from the main centres of existing and future employment to the east of Port Glasgow. Even this solution, however, would produce little additional land suitable for industrial development for Greenock itself and is not a solution which, as Planning Minister, I could approve. The alternative scheme—and it is the only possible alternative—for securing a grouped development with an ultimate target population of about 40-45,000 in the Bishopton-Houston area, which is recommended in Professor Abercrombie's report to the Clyde Valley Regional Planning Committee, is one which, on the advice of the Scottish Physical Planning Committee, I feel is the only acceptable one.

This solution would also have the advantage of providing a grouped centre to serve the equally pressing needs of Renfrew Burgh—to which nearly 15,000 people travel to work every day and for two-thirds of whom no housing accommodation can be made available in or near Renfrew itself—and would assist in dealing with the overspill problem from Glasgow. The precise site of the new town has not yet been delimited but the area provisionally selected is one which in the opinion of the Board of Trade is likely to be more attractive to industrialists than any other area in this part of Scotland. Moreover, this area is particularly convenient to serve the general requirements of East Renfrewshire where it is anticipated that there will continue to be a need for additional labour in existing enterprises, including in particular the Linwood factory recently taken over by the Pressed Steel Company. Any shipyard workers who move to the new town and wish to continue in their employment in Greenock and Port Glasgow would, of course, have to travel back to those towns but the journey to the shipyards from the new town would be little greater than from the alternative housing sites in the Kip Valley while other workers in the new town area would have employment facilities at hand which cannot possibly be made available in the Kip Valley.

The Bishopton-Houston area lies about 9 miles east of Greenock, about 12 miles west of Glasgow, about 4 miles west of Renfrew. It is therefore ideally situated to provide a combined solution for both the housing and industrial needs of each of these three towns, but it would be impossible for these local authorities, singly or in combination, to undertake a grouped development on the lines proposed; indeed it is just this type of development for which the machinery of the New Towns Act was designed. [PRO, CAB 132/10 LP(48)35.]

THE SCOTTISH HOUSING PROGRAMME, 1948

In April 1948 the Department of Health submitted a plan to the Investment Programmes Committee for a balanced programme of house building through the increased allocation of basic materials. The Department's aim was to achieve an output of about 30,000 houses per annum by 1952. The following is an extract from the Committee's minutes when Craig Mitchell, the Department's Deputy Secretary, was called for discussion. Later the Government agreed to maintain output for 1949 at its 1948 level of 20,000 houses. No decision was reached over subsequent years.

Minute of the Investment Programmes Committee, on the Scottish Housing Programme, 1948-52, 12 May 1948.

MR. CRAIG MITCHELL said that housing need in Scotland was even more acute than in England but the programme was much more seriously out of balance. There had been a drastic cut in new approvals from some 51,000 in 1946 to 18,500 in 1947 and it was proposed to approve only 5,000 more in 1948, 4,500 of which would for miners and agricultural workers. Even so to achieve a balance by 1950 it would be necessary to complete 20,000 houses in 1948 and 20,000 more in 1949. This could not be done on the present timber allocation and the Department were pressing hard for the allocation to be increased. The lack of balance was worst in non-traditional houses of which it had been necessary to approve a large number because of the preliminary constructional work already done in the factories. The programme now submitted made no provision at all for the replacement of unfit houses or the relief of overcrowding as such.

The completion of 20,000 houses in 1948 was thought by the Department to be feasible in the light of progress so far. The average rate of completions at present was 1,260 a month compared with 1,800 a month needed to reach 20,000 in the year, but the rate was increasing and more completions normally occurred during the latter part of the year than during the early months. The Ministry of Works had estimated that sufficient labour and materials, other than timber, would be available.

It was suggested that even on a completion rate of 20,000 a year the programme was so seriously overloaded in the initial stages that some proportion of houses already started but not yet up to damp course level ought to be stopped. Against this it was pointed out that a large number of the houses in the early stages were of the non-traditional type which passed through the succeeding stages very quickly and that the lack of balance in traditional houses was less serious. Indeed, in traditional houses the chief hold-up was in the plastering stage because of shortage of plaster. In any case the Department were anxious to avoid giving definite instructions for the cancellation of contracts in view of the claims for compensation which would result. Nor was it desirable to start in 1948 less than 13,000 for which provision was made in the programme, since the majority of houses approved but not started were again of the non-traditional type and must be carried through because of factory commitments. 5,000 of them were to be erected by the Scottish Special Housing Association, chiefly for miners and agricultural workers. The programme for Weir and Atholl non-traditional houses, which were of steel construction, had already been revised and it had been made clear that it could only be continued on a basis of an altered specification economising in steel and that the houses must compete in price with traditional houses. The Department were concentrating on the building of non-traditional houses for miners and agricultural workers because they needed less skilled labour and could therefore supplement provision in remote and already heavily committed areas.

It was also suggested that timber and steel requirements for 1948 and 1949 had been over-estimated in view of the pattern of the programme and the number of houses whose requirements were already incorporated in the structures. The Ministry of Work's estimate was that 36,000 standards would be needed in each of these 2 years as opposed to 40,000 standards and 39,000 standards respectively estimated by the Department of Health.

MR. CRAIG MITCHELL said, however, that his Department's estimates were based on the calculations of their technical advisers and he did not think it would be safe to budget for less. It had always been recognised that houses in Scotland required more timber than English houses because a heavier type of construction was need to withstand against the severer weather. The amount allowed per house had already been reduced from 2.5 to 2 standards and any further reduction would run counter to established building practice in Scotland and arouse strong opposition in the industry.

The Committee then discussed the programme submitted for 1952, when it was hoped to complete 31,000 houses. It was suggested that this would be beyond the capacity of the building labour force, unless it was increased above the pre-war level, in view of the many other new buildings e.g. factories, schools, hospitals, which would be required.

MR. CRAIG MITCHELL thought that the estimate was optimistic but not impossible of achievement. Prospects would have been much more promising if the training schemes for the building industry could have been continued in Scotland, where there was a continuing need for it. At present, however, the Department were chiefly concerned with the programme for 1948/1949 and urged that enough timber should be allocated to enable 20,000 houses to be completed in each of these two years so that a balanced programme could be achieved by 1950. [PRO, CAB 134/438 IPC(48)22nd:2.]

TUBERCULOSIS AND THE SCOTTISH HOUSING PROGRAMME, 1948

In October 1948 the Investment Programmes Committee agreed a Department of Health request for 1,000 Swedish timber houses, but rejected a request for 5,000 additional 'prefabs'. The extract here is from the subsequent letter of Arthur Woodburn, the Scottish Secretary, to Sir Stafford Cripps, the Chancellor of the Exchequer, on the issue. Cripps minuted 'that the people should not die if it was possible to save them' and the issue was remitted back to the Committee, which agreed an additional 4,000 'Blackburn' houses, to be completed by June 1950, mainly for those suffering from TB.

Letter of Arthur Woodburn, Secretary of State for Scotland, to Sir Stafford Cripps, the Chancellor of the Exchequer, on the Scottish Housing Programme, 26 November 1948.

I am very concerned about the present and future housing position in Scotland. I should like agreement to build more houses next year, and to foresee, if possible, a programme for some years ahead. My reasons fall into a few different categories.

In some cases, for example Glasgow, existing houses are deteriorating so rapidly that there is danger of considerable chaos in the foreseeable future. Apart altogether from overcrowding, since the war over 1,300 houses in Glasgow alone have physically reached the stage when the owners have abandoned them and left them 'in the lap' of the Corporation. Further, 30,000 more are reported by the Property Owners, and this estimate is not disputed by the Corporation, as progressively reaching the point when they also will be abandoned. A few of these houses in Glasgow are actually falling to pieces, and in quite recent weeks in tenement property, we have had the collapse of a complete inside stone staircase which left the tenants marooned in the top floors. Within the last few weeks too, John Rankin of Tradeston has raised a case where the whole wall of a tenement is bulging outwards, and the stones are falling in the people's flats. The new Gorbals M.P. has reported in discussion in the Scots Labour Group that families are taking it in turns sitting up though the night to keep rats off the families and that in other cases the inhabitants require to use umbrellas inside the homes during wet weather. In another part of the West of Scotland, houses have been abandoned to the tenants, and the local authority can no longer recover owners' rates since even the rents fail to maintain the houses. In many cases renovation cannot help.

In the last survey the overcrowding in England was 3.8% while in Scotland it was 22.6% six times as bad. But in Coatbridge the overcrowding is 44.8% and in Glasgow 29.1%.

The increase in deaths from Tuberculosis

A serious situation is developing with the rising rate of deaths from tuberculosis. Unless this is checked, it is likely to become cumulatively worse. I am grateful for the authority to produce a further 1,000 houses as an immediate contribution to checking the worse contacts. These are already on the production line and will be erected by the end of March. I am sure some benefits will arise. One could have understood a rising rate of detected cases because of the better methods of diagnosis, but at the same time one would have expected a fall in the death rate. This is so in England and Wales, but in Scotland the deaths have risen since 1938 by 31% in 1947—2,581 in 1938 and 3,390 in 1947. A great deal of publicity has been given to the terrible conditions in the Gorbals, Glasgow, but few people realise that there are six wards of Glasgow, where the conditions are much worse. The tuberculosis rate for England and Wales has come down from 62 per 100,000 in 1938 to 55 in 1947. In Scotland as a whole the figure has risen from 69 in 1938 to 80 in 1947, but in Glasgow the figure is 126 for the City as a whole. When we come to the wards of Glasgow, in 1947 Mile End had 241, Blythswood had 176, Provan 172, Parkhead 170, Woodside 158, Dalmarnock 159, and only then the Gorbals with 151. Only Lisbon, Berlin and Vienna can surpass the Glasgow figure.

The Scottish Health Services Council has appointed, at my request, a Committee to advise on steps which can be taken, but it needs no Committee to confirm that the miserable overcrowding in tenements in these congested towns is a prime cause. The report of the National Association for the Prevention of Tuberculosis states:- 'The Scottish Health Services Council have appointed a Committee to advise on tuberculosis, but it is obvious that something much more than advice will be necessary. Scotland is behind England in the number of houses that have been built.'

We don't agree with this but the Press, of course, make the most of it.

It is extremely gratifying that the Minister of Health in England and Wales can claim such progress towards his objective but his success makes the contrast in Scotland appear relatively black indeed. I recognise, of course, that we have done a good job in Scotland in many ways, judging on an absolute basis, but relatively comparing the progress and the need, the outlook seems to many local authorities a slow long and tragic progress towards overtaking their targets. My drastic refusal to permit new tenders has removed from local authorities even the symbol or pretence that they are doing anything at all. This combined with the conditions is creating a feeling of despair and the silent pressure of the moment may soon burst out in public denunciation. We cannot plead in Scotland that our target has been met.

While it is true that the building programme in Scotland was completely out of balance the severe restriction on any new building is in some cases going to lead to unbalance in another direction. The decision of the Planning Committee was absolutely right in requiring the Housing programme to be brought into balance. This has been successful to an extent that went beyond even their calculations. They reckoned that Scotland could not complete 20,000 permanent houses this year. Already the numbers are about 17,300 with seven weeks to go. I am confident that we will complete 20,000 by the end of the year which, along with some 7,500 temporary houses will bring the total up to about 28,000. I am confident also that next year the figure of 20,000 permanent houses will be exceeded, others things being equal.

Alongside our urgent need for more accommodation we are informed that there is prospect that unless further housing work is forthcoming unemployment will develop during 1949. In the building industry proper, this applies ... mainly to bricklayers in certain districts. But the trouble does not end there because labour is being discharged from factories engaged in house production which will have to close down altogether when their current programmes come to an end. The most pressing example is Blackburn's factory at Dumbarton whose programme of permanent aluminium bungalows is phased to finish in March, 1949. Already the labour force at this factory has fallen from some 3,600 at 6th January, 1948 to 1,700 at the end of October. It is expected that 300—350 more will be discharged during December. The employees affected are mainly semi-skilled or unskilled men and women whose prospects of being absorbed into other industries are reported by the Ministry of Labour to be poor.

I am most anxious to have your authority to place new contracts for some 4,000 additional houses to meet these difficulties. I appreciate, as Sir Edwin Plowden has pointed out, that the Government are pledged in the submission to Q.E.E.C. to observe the principle that aggregate expenditure on social investment should not rise above the level recently approved, and that any additional resources should be concentrated on directly productive industrial investment. But this applies to Great Britain as a whole and does not necessarily preclude Scotland from getting a larger share of the approved total. [PRO, T 229/344.]

DEVALUATION AND THE SCOTTISH HOUSING PROGRAMME, 1949

In response to economic difficulties the Government devalued sterling in September 1949 and immediately instituted a review of expenditure plans. The following month the Cabinet agreed to reduce the housing programme for 1950 by about 10 per cent. The following is an extract from a subsequent Department of Health memorandum to the Investment Programmes Committee. In the event, the Cabinet, after the General Election, agreed to continue the reduced programme for 1951 and 1952.

Memorandum by the Department of Health for Scotland, on Scottish Housing: Investment Review, 1951-52, 29 December 1949.

Progress in 1949.

The approved estimate of £38 million for 1949 was broken down as to £36 million for new construction and £2 million for prefabricated temporary houses and permanent aluminium bungalows.... the actual expenditure closely approximated to this estimate, being (£36.9 million) for new construction and £1.7 million for prefabrication, or a new excess of (£.5 million) over the total estimate. In terms of houses completed, the estimate was 25,000 and actual performance (25,500).

The number of houses under construction at the end of the year was (31,000) compared with 38,500 at the end of 1948. The average time taken to complete a house improved from about 25 months at the end of 1948 to about 15 months at the end of 1949.

In considering the speed of building in Scotland account must be taken of certain limiting factors which affect progress. First, contracting by separate trades as contrasted with the single or main contractor system more prevalent in England and Wales, makes co-ordination of the work on the site more difficult. Next, the industry is not well distributed in Scotland, e.g. there has always been a shortage of plasterers for housing work and in some districts the number of bricklayers is below scale. Further, in some respects construction is heavy in Scotland e.g. in the roofs and the walls. Lastly, outside the industrial belt, sites tend to be remotely situated and schemes small. The Department will, of course, do all they can to secure a further reduction in the time taken to build houses, but in the light of these considerations the speed of building in Scotland is likely to remain somewhat slower than that prevailing in England and Wales.

Programme for 1950.

The memorandum submitted to the Committee in October 1949 indicated that the Department had agreed with the Ministry of Health that Scotland's share of the total reduction of £35 million in housing expenditure should be £3.5 million, and explained that apart from a reduction in the number of houses to be licensed for building by private enterprise, this reduction of expenditure would be absorbed in economies to be effected in the price of houses built by local authorities for letting. These proposals were approved by Ministers and the following steps have since been taken to put them into operation:- (a) The rate of approving licences for private building has been reduced from about 1,000 houses a year to about 500. The Department estimate that this will effect a saving of £.75 million in 1950. (b) Local authorities have been told that 50% of the houses in their schemes may now be of the smaller sizes, mainly of three apartments. This decision, which modifies the requirement previously in operation that schemes should contain a substantial preponderance of houses of four or more apartments, has been widely welcomed by local authorities whose anxiety to modify even current schemes may indeed temporarily check continuity of progress. The Department estimate that under this head about £1 million will be saved in 1950. (c) In addition, local authorities have been asked to reduce prices by at least £50 a house through building economies which can be effected without detriment to standards of construction or accommodation. Examples of these economies were given in the memorandum submitted to the Committee in October, 1949. In the main they will affect the earlier stages of building and the Department estimate that the consequent saving will amount to at least £.25 million in 1950.

The total estimated reduction of housing expenditure in 1950 to be achieved by these means is therefore about £2 million which will bring down investment on new houses from the approved level of £38 million to £36 million in that year. The number of houses to be completed in 1950 is estimated at 25,000: this allows for a reduction of about 500 in the number to be built privately.

Programmes for 1951 and 1952.

If programmes of 1951 and 1952 are to be kept within the diminished rate of capital investment ... expenditure on new construction would have to fall from the present approved level of £38 million to £34.5 million in order that the agreed reduction of £3.5 million a year to be obtained from economies might be fully operative in these years. The number of houses to be completed would, however, remain at the level of 25,000 as proposed for 1950.

The Department consider that in view of the general housing position in Scotland larger programmes would be fully justified in 1951 and 1952. The Committee have on previous occasions been told of the deplorable housing conditions that exist throughout the country and particularly in the large towns. The situation is specially bad in Glasgow where a large mass of house property is unfit to live in and beyond repair. Owners have for long protested that the restriction of rents, rising rates and rising costs of repairs have left them in deficit and some have abandoned their property. Alongside this, local authorities have been able to do virtually nothing to clear the slums during the past 10 years, and with the reduced rate of building during the war and after, overcrowding which existed in 22.6% of all Scottish working-class houses in 1935, can hardly have diminished much and in some districts is probably more acute. The 100,000 permanent, temporary and emergency dwellings provided since the war have only partially met the quantitative demands of families without separate homes. On top of all this, increasing demands are expected from the Services, from industry, the Police and various Government Departments.

Against this background the Department are anxious that the Scottish housing programme should be expanded at the earliest possible moment. As indicated in I.P.C.(49)3 they have previously suggested that the programmes for 1951 and 1952 should provide for the completion of 27,000 and 30,000 houses respectively. They appreciate the immediate need for restraining investment expenditure and realise that an expansion of this order might not now be fully practicable. But as a first step, [the Department] suggest that the reduction of housing expenditure now being effected should be partially restored in 1951 and fully restored in 1952. This would involve an expenditure of £37 million on new construction in 1951 permitting the building of 26,600 houses, and of £38 million (the present approved level) in 1952 permitting the building of about 27,300 houses. In both cases these figures are calculated at present prices and on the basis of maintaining the new proportion of 50% of small houses and the other building economies also referred to. [PRO, CAB 134/452 IPC(WP)(49)110.]

SCOTTISH RENTS AND THE NEW HOUSING SUBSIDY, 1952

At the end of January 1952 R.A. Butler, the Chancellor of the Exchequer, informed the Cabinet's Home Affairs Committee that he intended to raise interest rates to 4.5% and was prepared to increase the housing subsidy. The Committee accepted his proposal and increased the English 'notional' rent by two shillings to 18s per week. However, T.D. Galbraith, the Scottish Joint Parliamentary Under Secretary, indicated that the Treasury's formula would mean Scottish rents rising substantially more, from 11s 4d per week to 16s 2d, and claimed that it would be 'difficult to explain'. The first extract is from the memorandum the Scottish Secretary was asked to submit for the Committee's next meeting. The second extract is taken from its minutes which concluded by agreeing that Galbraith should discuss with the Treasury a comparable Scottish figure before his next meeting with local authorities. In late February Stuart announced a 'notional' rent of 16s 2d, a subsidy of £42 for a 4-apartment house and moves to cut production costs. The English subsidy for a comparable house was set at £26 10s.

Memorandum by James Stuart, the Secretary of State for Scotland, on the Review of Housing Subsidies, 30 January 1952.

The elements of the Scottish subsidy calculation are generally the same as in England; the outgoings on the housing revenue account in respect of the average house are set against the income from rent, Exchequer and rate contributions. The Scottish calculation has however to take account of one factor not applicable to England and Wales viz:- the burden of owner's rates, which increase proportionately with the rent.

Cost of the house. We propose to take £1,575 as the cost of a house, including land and site servicing. This is based on the latest available average of tender prices with a deduction of £100 in respect of the adoption of 'low-cost' principles. The Scottish local authorities are unlikely to accept this figure. They dispute our method of calculation and put forward figures of the order of £1,700.

Maintenance and management. We have agreed with the local authorities on £11 as a reasonable figure.

Owner's rates. The latest available figure is 5/7d. in the £. This means a burden of 5/7d. for each £ of rent.

Rent. We propose a notional rent of £40 (15/5d. a week). This compares with the rent of £26 (10/- a week) assumed when the subsidies were fixed in 1945, and £29.9.4d (11/4d. a week) when they were adjusted in 1950. This falls short of the rent of 18/- a week (£46.16s.- a year) proposed for England. But conditions are different in the two countries. There is a long established tradition of low rents in Scotland, and local authorities have difficulty in bringing their rents into reasonable relationship with current costs. In 1949 the average rent for all post-war houses was £28.4.- a year (10/10d. a week) compared with 14/3d. a week (£37.1.s- a year) in England, and there has been little advance since then. The local authority associations are unwilling to agree to a higher figure than £33 as the notional rent, but some authorities are charging rents of about £40. We shall probably have to impose our figures.

Calculation of the Deficit. On the basis of these figures the deficit to be shared between the Exchequer and the rates is £55. If the deficit is shared in the ratio of 3:1 (which is somewhat more favourable to the Exchequer than the present 3.3:1) the Exchequer would pay £41.5.- and the local authority £13.15.-. [PRO, CAB 134/909 HA(52)25; SRO, DD6/1613.]

Cabinet Home Affairs Committee, on the Scottish Housing Subsidy, 1 February 1952.

The Joint Parliamentary Under-Secretary of State for Scotland said that the system of housing subsidy in Scotland was similar to that in England and Wales with which the Committee were familiar: but the figures were different. Agreement with the Scottish local authorities was improbable. They had agreed with the Secretary of State's suggestion that the cost of maintenance and management should be £11 a year. But they had countered his suggestion of a figure of £1,575 for the cost of a house with one of £1,700, and they had refused to accept a notional rent of £40, suggesting instead £33. If the deficit resulting from the Secretary of State's assumptions was divided between the Exchequer and the local authority on the same basis as in England and Wales, the cost in subsidy would be £41. 5s. 0d a year to the Exchequer and £13 5s. 0d to the authority.

The Minister of Housing and Local Government recalled that the proposal in England and Wales was to accept a notional rent of 18/- or 19/-. though he remained worried about the large contribution in both England and Wales and in Scotland which the rest of the community was being required to make for the benefit of those who lived in subsidised houses. He proposed nevertheless to raise at Cabinet the question of stabilising for a period the rate of interest charged on housing loans; but since it was essential that he should continue his discussion with the local authority without delay he was prepared to negotiate with them on the basis of a notional rent of 19/-.

The Financial Secretary of the Treasury said that in the Treasury's view a notional rent in Scotland of £42 a year corresponded to a rent in England and Wales of 19/- a week, taking into account the differences in conditions between England and Wales and Scotland. It was the Treasury view that £42 should be the figure used in Scottish negotiations.

The Joint Parliamentary Under-Secretary of State for Scotland said that the Scottish Secretary required a decision in order to continue his negotiations with the local authorities on the 4th February. He was not satisfied that the figure of £42 was comparable with the English figure and the increase in the notional rent proposed in Scotland would be difficult to justify as it was much greater proportionately than the increase in England. [PRO, CAB 134/908 HA(52)4th:2.]

SCOTLAND'S REQUIREMENT FOR MORE ASSISTANCE IN HOUSING, 1952

In August 1952 Harold Macmillan, the Minister of Housing and Local Government, prepared a memorandum for the Cabinet's Committee on Development Charges, laying great stress on home ownership, charging economic rents for council housing and renovating the private tenanted sector. The following extract is from a subsequent memorandum by James Stuart, the Scottish Secretary, of which the Committee took note.

Memorandum by James Stuart, Secretary of State for Scotland, on Housing Policy, 15 September 1952.

I agree generally with the Minister of Housing and Local Government's statement of our long-term objectives in housing policy: (1) that the great majority must buy their own houses at cost or pay an economic rent for them; (2) that we must, in due time, make local authorities concentrate their efforts on overcrowding and slum clearance; (3) that we must start to close the gap between rents and costs.

I must, however, make it clear that to attain these objectives in Scotland will take much longer than in England and Wales and will require more assistance, for the following reasons.

General Housing Conditions

The 1951 Census has again emphasised how much worse the housing situation is in Scotland than in other parts of the United Kingdom. More than 15 per cent. of the Scottish people live with more than two persons per room, as against 2 per cent. in England and Wales, where even in 1931 it was less than 7 per cent. By that standard Scotland is more than 20 years behind. The two worst areas in England are Tyneside and Merseyside where the figure is between 5 per cent. and 6 per cent. For Clydeside it is 23 per cent. For Greater London the figure is 1.7 per cent.

In framing housing policy in the past these vastly different circumstances have been recognised and on more than one occasion a subsidy has been continued longer in Scotland than in England and Wales.

Private Enterprise

Between the wars private enterprise made a relatively small contribution to the building of new houses in Scotland. In England and Wales the private builder built for sale or let almost three times as many houses as the local authorities. In Scotland he built only half as many as the local authorities.

Under existing conditions I can see no prospect of private enterprise in Scotland making a greater contribution than pre-war. It is from the middle classes that most owner-occupiers come, but middle class incomes (in Scotland) have not kept in step with the increase in the general level of costs, and certainly not with building costs, which are considerably higher than in England. Few if any will build houses to let in view of the financial uncertainties involved (see paragraph on Rating below).

The Rating System

In Scotland rates are levied on owners as well as on occupiers. Any increase in rates therefore imposes an additional burden on the owner who is unable to recoup himself because of the Rent Restriction Acts. The effect in Glasgow has been to reduce the 47.5 per cent. increase over the 1914 rent granted in 1921 to 22 per cent. over 1914.

As the actual rent paid is the valuation on which rates are levied, any increase in the rent results in an increase in the amount of rates payable by both owner and occupier. For example, in Glasgow where the owners' rates are 7s.9d per £, it would be necessary to give the owner a net increase of £10.

If the law of rating in Scotland is not altered, and if Scottish owners are to be put into the same position as English owners, it will be necessary to allow an increase of rent, to make good the existing financial disadvantage of Scottish owners; to meet the increased cost of repairs, and to cover the increase in owners rates which will arise from an increase in rent (valuation). This would mean a very great increase in controlled rents in Scotland, and considerably more than the Minister of Housing's proposals would call for in England.

Maintenance and Repair of Existing Houses

As a result of the operation of the Scottish rating system the net rental received by Scottish owners, and therefore the amount available for repairs, has over a long period of years, fallen far short of that available to English owners. This is reflected in the present state of Scottish housing property. While I am in agreement with the Minister of Housing's proposal that an increase in rent should be conditional on the property being in a proper state of repair, I doubt the ability of many owners of tenement property in industrial Scotland to meet the cost that this would involve, or if able, their willingness to do so. The situation is causing me some anxiety and I am at present having it examined in detail as a matter of urgency. I hope shortly to submit the result of that examination together with proposals for the consideration of my colleagues. [PRO, CAB 134/807 DC(52)13; SRO, DD6/1567.]

SCOTTISH HOUSING, RENT AND REPAIRS, 1953

In January 1953 Harold Macmillan, the Minister for Housing and Local Government, submitted a memorandum to the Cabinet on future housing policy towards the privately rented sector. The extract here is from the memorandum by James Stuart, the Scottish Secretary, outlining the Scottish position. In the event the Cabinet broadly accepted the principle of 'economic rents' and remitted detailed discussion of the legislation to a small ministerial committee.

Memorandum by James Stuart, Secretary of State for Scotland, on Housing Policy: Rent and Repairs, 30 January 1953.

1. I am in complete agreement with the Minister of Housing and Local Government about the need for finding an early solution of the rent restriction problem. Discussions which I have had with him have shown, however, that conditions in Scotland are so different from those in England and Wales that a separate Scottish solution, to be embodied in separate legislation, is required.

2. Rent control has operated in Scotland in much the same lines as in England and Wales. In Scotland, however, there are no great variations between 'old controlled' rents (i.e. those continuously controlled since 1914) and 'new controlled' rents (i.e. those which first came under control or were re-controlled in 1939); and I am satisfied that the fairest way of enabling Scottish landlords to put their houses into repair and keep them in repair is to increase all rents by a flat rate percentage.

3. The Scottish system of valuation and rating differs in its essential features from that in England and Wales. In Scotland, it is the rent actually paid which determines the gross annual value; unless that rent can be shown not to be a *bona fide* one. Rates on houses are paid on the gross annual value, and payable not only by occupiers, but also by owners, and the owner's share of any increase in the rate poundage has to be met out of the rents.

4. Scottish landlords have been faced not only with a very substantial rise in the cost of repairs, but also with a large and progressive rise in the amount of owner's rates. They have therefore been at a serious disadvantage as compared with English landlords, and having experienced even greater deterioration of Scottish house property, it will be necessary to increase rents to reflect the higher cost of repairs and to take steps to ensure that this increase is not whittled away by further increases in the amount of owner's rates.

5. It is possible to ascertain with a fair degree of accuracy the proportion of the gross rent of controlled houses which Scottish landlords were spending, or ought to have been spending, on repairs in 1939. The figure is roughly 21 per cent. A committee which I set up recently to investigate and report on the increase in the cost of repairs of house property since 1939 has now advised that the cost of repairs of house property generally has risen by 174 per cent since that date; and that as it is more costly to repair old houses (which form the bulk of controlled houses) there may well be a case for taking 200 per cent as the increase. If the latter figure is accepted, landlords who were spending 21 per cent of the gross rent on repairs in 1939 would have to spend 63 per cent to carry out the same amount of work today—an increase of 42 per cent of the gross rent. On these figures there is a strong case for increasing the rents of all controlled houses in Scotland by about 40 per cent. For a typical Glasgow two-roomed house this would mean an increase in rent of less than 2/6d. a

week. I propose, however, to have further discussions with the Minister of Housing and Local Government to see how far an increase of this order would compare with the increase of rent which he is now proposing for England and Wales. It is clear that the increases for the two countries should be broadly comparable.

6. Since the present level of controlled rents has proved insufficient to enable landlords to keep their houses in repair, and since the whole object of increasing rents is to encourage landlords to put their houses into good repair and thereafter maintain them in repair, there are very strong arguments for giving landlords an immediate increase of rent. It would, of course, be necessary to provide that, if after a reasonable period any landlord had failed to carry out the repairs necessary to put the house in good tenantable condition, the tenant should be able to withhold the increase of rent, in addition to any sums which he may already be entitled to withhold under the Rent Restriction Acts.

7. Any increase of rent would, under the present Scottish rating system, attract both owners' and occupiers' rates. It is, however, essential to avoid this result. Otherwise the increase of rent would be reduced by the amount of owners' rates and would be quite insufficient to enable landlords to keep their houses in repair, and Scottish tenants (unlike those in England and Wales) would incur a substantially increased liability for rates in addition to their increased liability for rent. I propose therefore that the increase of rent, which would be represented as an additional payment by the tenant towards the cost of repairing and maintaining the house, should not be taken into account in fixing the rateable value of a controlled house, and should not therefore attract either owners' or occupiers' rates.

8. In addition, and to prevent any diminution in the sum payable to the landlord for repairs, as a result of increases in rate poundage, I propose that owners' rates for all rent-controlled houses should be stabilised at their present level.

9. Action on these lines would, I think, meet the immediate difficulties of Scottish landlords. But a long-term solution must be found if the difficulties inherent in the Scottish rating system, under which any increase of rent attracts owners' rates, are to be overcome. I propose therefore to appoint a committee to examine the Scottish rating problem in all its aspects, including the practicability of abolishing owners' rates. [PRO, CAB 129/58 C(53)33.]

PROSPECTS FOR SCOTTISH NEW TOWNS, 1953

In October 1953 Harold Macmillan, the Minister of Housing and Local Government, presented a memorandum to the Cabinet's Economic Policy Committee suggesting that new town development should be 'accelerated'—'to secure a return on the investment already made'. But he also suggested that local authorities should contribute more towards development costs and that private sector involvement should be increased. Peter Thorneycroft, the President of the Board of Trade, also presented a memorandum in which he indicated that attracting employment to new towns might conflict with attracting employment to the development areas. The extract here is from the memorandum by James Stuart, the Scottish Secretary, outlining the Scottish position. The Committee agreed that no new legislation was required, but that the Minister for Housing and Local Government should co-ordinate a review of new town housing and employment costs.

Memorandum by James Stuart, Secretary of State for Scotland, on New Towns in Scotland, 6 October 1953.

The general policy considerations covered by the Minister's paper also arise on the Scottish new towns subject to the following differences in detail:-

(a) The Scottish local authorities have from the beginning co-operated fully as partners in the development of the Scottish new towns and have agreed to provide at their own cost the basic services of water, drainage and highways (other than pure development roads) in the new town areas subject only to some limited and largely recoverable financial aid from the Corporations during the early and 'lean' years before the rateable value has built-up sufficiently to secure the local authorities an adequate return. The Scottish local authorities have spent or are committed to spend about £5 million on these services in the two new towns. The assumption by the Scottish local authorities of these responsibilities has, of course, relieved the Development Corporations and the Exchequer *pro tanto* of substantial liabilities but has imposed a corresponding strain on local rate-borne resources. I am in a position to say that the local authorities could not do more and that to ask them to assume total responsibility for the new towns at the present time would be out of the question.

(b) As in the case of the English New Towns the full development value of these projects has yet to mature and it is only now that the real sources of revenue to the Corporations, namely, rents from commercial and other remunerative premises, are beginning to build up.

(c) The Scottish rating system under which the Development Corporations as landlords are saddled with substantial rate burdens in the form of owners' rates substantially affects the picture in Scotland. For instance, in East Kilbride out of every £1 of rent received by the New Town Development Corporation they hand over to the local authority not less than 12s. 5d. in the form of owners' rates and in the case of house property, to recover this liability from the tenant would mean driving the rents up to impracticable levels. This is a fundamental and serious problem affecting the whole field of rateable property throughout Scotland and it is now being considered by a committee which I have appointed under Lord Sorn.

(d) The attraction of new industrial enterprise to the Scottish new towns is, of course, essential to their success. East Kilbride enjoys the advantage of being in the Scottish Development Area and, thanks to the efforts of the President of the Board of Trade and the Minister of Supply, excellent progress has been made. There have also been established there the Mechanical Engineering Research Laboratory and other research sub-stations of the Department of Scientific and Industrial research giving employment to scientific and laboratory staff and skilled craftsmen. As a result, the provision of jobs at East Kilbride is actually running ahead of the provision of homes. At Glenrothes less progress has been made but there a slower build-up was in any case expected since this scheme will grown into full maturity only after the new pits and the large new colliery sinkings are in full production (which will not be for some years). I should like to be confident that sufficient industry will be attracted to Glenrothes to provide a balanced employment for the population as it builds up. This problem was brought to the notice of the President of the Board of Trade when he recently visited Scotland, and he and I both have it in mind, though it is not an immediate one.

Future prospects

(i) For broadly the same reasons as are set out by the Minister in his paper there is no prospect of stopping the two new town projects now in progress in Scotland or of transferring the total liability to the local authorities. There is moreover less likelihood in Scotland of a substantial measure of the liability being assumed by private enterprise. Both schemes are designed to fulfil national purposes which cannot except to a limited extent be achieved by any local or private interest. East Kilbride, for example, although designed largely to cater for overspill from Glasgow, is also a project which will help to fulfil development area policy on the industrial side and Glenrothes will draw its new population from widely scattered communities and is part and parcel of an overall plan to develop the national asset represented by the substantial resources of unworked coal in East Fife. (ii) In the Glasgow area further decentralisation will undoubtedly be necessary. Glasgow, despite the substantial progress made with new housebuilding, is still the most congested city in the United Kingdom. About 700,000 people in the city are living in a limited area of 1,800 acres and there are districts where the density reaches the fantastic level of 700 persons per acre.

In one particular black spot there are no fewer than 12,000 people living in a cramped area of 18 acres. It is unthinkable that we should attempt to reproduce these densities on redevelopment and when the time comes for extensive slum clearance and rebuilding it will be possible to re-settle only about 30 per cent of the original population of those congested districts. It is clear that about 100,000 houses will have to be found outside the present city limits. The problem is one of considerable urgency since all the available housing sites within the city of Glasgow are now being developed and there is no more scope for peripheral expansion without encroaching on land which is either of the highest agricultural value or minerally unstable or is at such altitudes that it is not suitable for building. The problem of how these houses are to be provided is being examined at present by the local authorities who are to furnish me with a report on the whole situation towards the end of this year; and I must warn my colleagues that further new town developments may well prove to be the only practicable solution. (iii) I am of course considering what contribution the local authorities themselves can make in these matters and we shall take into account the possibility of getting contributions from Glasgow towards re-housing costs in East Kilbride or in other new towns which it may be decided to build to relieve the Glasgow problem and this will form part of the submission which I shall be making to my colleagues in due course. [PRO, CAB 134/849 EA(53)122.]

THE CABINET AND CUMBERNAULD NEW TOWN, 1955

In March 1955 the Scottish Office secured Glasgow's participation in a scheme to build Cumbernauld New Town. Shortly afterwards James Stuart, the Scottish Secretary, submitted a memorandum to the Cabinet's Economic Policy Committee seeking approval for the scheme. The first extract is taken from the memorandum and the second from the subsequent Committee minute.

Memorandum by James Stuart, Secretary of State for Scotland, on Glasgow Housing—Proposed New Town at Cumbernauld, 23 April 1955.

Glasgow needs at least 100,000 new houses to replace slums, to relieve overcrowding and to provide each family with a house if its own. Over 40,000 families in the city are still living at more than two persons per room compared with about 13,000 in the whole of the L.C.C. area which has four times the population of Glasgow. About 37 per cent of all houses in the city have no separate w.cs. and 50.1 per cent have no baths; the corresponding London figures are 2.6 and 14.4 per cent respectively.

In slum areas like the Gorbals, congestion is almost unbelievably high—densities range from 400 to 700 persons per acre—and redevelopment cannot be tackled on any substantial scale unless land can be found for the surplus population who cannot be resettled when slum clearance takes place. The Corporation in fact calculate—and I agree with them—that it will be possible to put back into the congested areas only about 50 per cent of the people living there at present, even if the cleared sites are rebuilt with high flats.

The burden of housing provision in the city has so far fallen on the Corporation who have been building about 5,000 houses a year within the last few years and have in fact built 34,000 houses since the war. The Corporation cannot maintain this programme since all vacant sites in the city will be fully built up by 1957/8. Straightforward boundary extensions of the city are ruled out by topography, mineral subsidence and the need for preserving what is left of the very inadequate green belt, the greater part of which consists of agricultural land of high quality.

It is therefore a matter of great urgency to get new developments started outside the city, unless the housing programme is to come to a dead stop.

A Joint Committee of all the local authorities in the Clyde Valley Area have had the problem under review for the past two years. A complete scheme for dealing with the whole of Glasgow's overspill will take time to work out, will involve detailed discussions between the Glasgow Corporation and the potential receiving authorities, and probably new legislation on the lines of the Town Development Act which at present applies to England and Wales only. Meantime the Joint Committee have recommended as a first step that a new community should be developed at Cumbernauld, about 13 miles north east of Glasgow in the County of Dunbarton. The Committee emphasise that if this new community is not started soon the building of houses for Glasgow families will come to a halt by 1957/8. The Committee have recommended that this new development should be carried out under the New Towns Act and this proposal has been strongly pressed on me by the Glasgow Corporation, the local authorities represented on the Committee and in the House. Preliminary technical investigations carried out by my Department show that the Cumbernauld area could accommodate about 14,000 houses giving an ultimate population of about 50,000 people with some scope for expansion beyond that figure. It would be eighteen months to two years before houses could come 'off the line' at Cumbernauld; an immediate decision is therefore required.

The capital cost of the project under the New Towns Act, spread over 12-13 years of development would be about £31m. Of this total, about £27m. would be spent on housing: and most of the balance on commercial and industrial development, showing a profit. The money would be advanced to the New

Town Corporation from the Consolidated Fund on the usual repayment terms. The only direct Exchequer grant—non-recoverable—to the New Town Corporation would be Exchequer subsidy under the Housing Acts. As the great bulk of the houses would be allocated to Glasgow's nominees this subsidy would consist of the normal Exchequer contribution but for houses not allocated to Glasgow nominees there would be an additional subsidy representing the equivalent of the local authority statutory rate contribution.

Since this proposal was first put forward by the Clyde Valley Joint Committee a year ago, I have been in negotiation with Glasgow Corporation with a view to getting them to participate financially and administratively in the scheme. This has not been easy. Glasgow say—and they have received considerable support in the House—that their problem is proportionately four times as great as that of the L.C.C. and that, as the previous Government agreed to the development of 8 new towns to deal with London overspill and one new town at East Kilbride, which was partly intended to help Glasgow, there is no good reason why the present Government should not assume full responsibility for a new town at Cumbernauld to cater exclusively for Glasgow.

I proposed to the Corporation that if the Cumbernauld scheme were launched under the New Towns Act they should contribute the statutory rate contribution in respect of every house built there for a Glasgow family and should also share with me and the local authority for the Cumbernauld area—the County Council of Dunbarton—the deficit arising on the new town undertaking as a whole. This deficit will in any case arise largely on the Housing Account because under the present Scottish Rating System it is impossible, with the prevailing level of rents, for rent income plus subsidy to balance annual charges plus the burden of owner's rates payable by the new town development corporation.

I have now reached the stage in my negotiations when Glasgow Corporation have agreed to pay the appropriate statutory rate contribution for ten years (average £14 per house) in respect of families nominated by them for housing accommodation at Cumbernauld.... I am clear that the local authorities receiving Glasgow's overspill will require the Corporation to make very substantial contributions over and above the rate contribution for ten years towards the cost of housing Glasgow's nominees, since they will be most reluctant to accept any burden which would impose any substantial charge on their ratepayers. I have also explained to Dunbarton County Council that in so far as the increase in their rate income from the Cumbernauld development exceeds the loan charges and other annual expenditure on services provided there by the County Council, they will be expected to contribute from this rate income surplus towards the deficit on the New Town undertaking.

While I have made it clear to Glasgow Corporation and Dunbarton County Council that these arrangements are subject to the approval of my colleagues, I am satisfied, after many months of difficult negotiation, that they represent the best possible bargain to the Exchequer. They will ensure a community of interest between the Government, Glasgow Corporation and Dunbarton County Council to secure the best possible return from rents and rates on the project and so keep the deficit on the project down to a minimum. I am indeed hopeful that by relating the ultimate Cumbernauld settlement to the arrangements for dealing with Glasgow overspill generally we can hope to get the economics of costs and rents for Glasgow housing into better balance.

I have emphasised in this paper the urgent need for getting ahead with the proposed New Town project and I consider it essential to make an announcement on the matter before the General Election. I should, therefore, like to have the approval of my colleagues to my announcement now that, should the present Government be returned to power, they will immediately put in hand the development of the project under the New Towns Act on the basis of the financial arrangement described in this Memorandum. [PRO, CAB 134/1227 EP(55)3.]

Cabinet Economic Policy Committee, on the Establishment of Cumbernauld New Town, 28 April 1955.

The Secretary of State for Scotland said that Glasgow's housing problem was the worst in the United Kingdom, and the Corporation had been very slow in making plans for a new town. They had missed the opportunity when most of the English new towns were being planned. The density of population in Glasgow was such that it would be impossible to re-house those living in slums on the present site. The proposed new town would only deal with part of the overspill. The Glasgow Corporation had eventually agreed to pay the statutory rate contribution for houses at Cumbernauld let to their nominees, and an additional payment, to be negotiated, if other local authorities catering for Glasgow's overspill demanded such a payment.

The Chancellor of the Exchequer said that he agreed with the proposal of the Secretary of State and the draft Press announcement. However, he would wish the financial situation of the Corporation of the new town to be reviewed periodically by the Secretary of State and himself in order to keep the Exchequer's liability to a minimum. In particular, rents payable for the houses would have to be reviewed if the Scottish rating system were reformed. The structure of the Corporation would have to be watched in the light of the experience gained at East Kilbride and Glenrothes, which had not been wholly satisfactory.

The following points were raised in discussion:-

(a) The establishment of a new town at Cumbernauld would increase the pressure for other new towns to reduce the pressure of population in Manchester and possibly Birmingham. So far most new towns had been established near London.

(b) The building of new towns was a very expensive method of rehousing. The Minister of Works calculated some time ago that the total cost amounted to about £6,000 for each family. It would be useful if the development of new towns could be linked with slum clearance schemes, so that the population of a slum area could be temporarily housed in the new town while that area was rebuilt with tall buildings to a high density. There was a danger that city centres would never be properly rebuilt. However, in Glasgow the density of population in certain areas was far too high to be maintained in the rebuilding plans, and it must not be forgotten that the subsidy payments on blocks of flats were very high.

(c) Although Cumbernauld was in a development area the Board of Trade would not wish to provide factories there at uneconomic rents for re-housing of Glasgow firms. If they did so their efforts in other Scottish development areas, such as Northern Lanarkshire, would inevitably be reduced.

(d) Cumbernauld was near enough to Glasgow to become a dormitory satellite rather than a proper new town. This would help to avoid the problem of re-housing Glasgow industry, much of which could not be moved, but it was an unfortunate precedent, which was contrary to the principle of the development of new towns.

The Committee—(1) Approved the proposal for establishing a new town at Cumbernauld set out in E.P.(55)3. (2) Invited the Secretary of State for Scotland, in consultation with the Chancellor of the Exchequer to review the financial situation of the Cumbernauld Corporation periodically in order to keep the cost to the Exchequer to a minimum. (3) Invited the Secretary of State for Scotland and the President of the Board of Trade to consider further the industrial development of Cumbernauld. [PRO, CAB 134/1226 EP(55)1st:3.]

HOUSING SUBSIDIES AND GLASGOW'S OVERSPILL PROBLEM, 1956

In 1955 the Government announced reduced subsidies for council housing in England. Although a subsidy of £22 1s was to be paid for slum clearance, only £10 was to be offered for such 'general needs' as the relief of overcrowding and housing the homeless. At the same time the Government also proposed to offer additional grants for the development of English new towns. The following extract is from the Scottish Secretary's memorandum to the Cabinet's Home Affairs Committee on the Scottish housing bill. Rents, exclusive of rates, then averaged £16 per annum, well under half the English amount. The Committee approved Stuart's proposals.

Memorandum by James Stuart, Secretary of State for Scotland, on Housing and Town Development (Scotland), 17 July 1956.

Housing Subsidies

In arriving at the new rates of subsidy, I have assumed a very substantial increase over the next few years in the level of the rents now being charged for local authority houses. The present rents are too low; I have assumed that they will be more than doubled. To this end, I have already sent out a circular to local authorities in strong terms calling for a comprehensive review of rent policy. With enlarged rent income from existing houses local authorities should be able to build the new houses still required with subsidies much lower than the current costs of the new houses would otherwise justify.

A Working Party, consisting of officials of the local authorities and of my Department which I appointed to ascertain the facts on which the review of the housing subsidies should be based, have confirmed that the numbers of houses still needed in Scotland to relieve overcrowding and to house those without homes of their own are greater than the number required to replace the unfit houses, large as this is. I feel obliged, therefore, to continue to pay a subsidy for some time yet for houses built for all these needs.

I propose that the new rates of subsidy should be these:-

(a) A basic flat rate of subsidy of £24 a year for 60 years for approved needs. This compares with the present rates of £39 15s. (for three-apartment houses), £43 5s. (four apartments) and £46 15s. (five apartments).

(b) A rate of £30 for houses required to meet the urgent needs of industry which are built for incoming people under approved arrangements.

(c) A rate of £42 for houses provided under an approved scheme of town development to house 'overspill' from Glasgow Corporation and possibly one or two areas on Clydeside. (I shall expect Glasgow Corporation and any other sending authorities to pay to the local authority or new town development corporation which builds the houses a contribution of £14 per house for at least the first ten years.)

(d) For houses provided in multi-storey buildings, the basic subsidy rate of £24 should be supplemented by an additional contribution calculated in each case to cover two-thirds of the amount by which the approved costs of these houses exceeds the cost of ordinary houses. (This will apply normally to buildings of six and seven storeys).

The existing statutory obligations on local authorities to contribute fixed contributions from the rates should be abolished. My subsidy proposals, however, assume that local authorities will still meet their fair share of the burden of subsidised housing: at reasonable rents they will still have to make from the rates contributions amounting to about one-third of the Exchequer's contributions: and to the extent that they are unwilling, or unable, to increase rents to the figure assumed in the calculations, the balance will have to be met from rates.

I propose that in place of making an additional subsidy available (as has been done in England and Wales) to local authorities who can show that even with reasonable rents the reduced rates of subsidy will impose an undue financial burden on the rates, the Scottish Special Housing Association will assist these authorities by building some of the houses still required. The Association will also be used to assist in building houses to take 'overspill' from Glasgow.

These proposals, which have been agreed with the Chancellor of the Exchequer, will produce a substantial reduction in Exchequer expenditure on housing in Scotland as compared with the present subsidies. The saving, of course, emerges only as the new houses are built, but I estimate that over the next five years it will amount to over £3 million.

Town Development

I also propose to include in the Bill provisions substantially on the lines of the Town Development Act, 1952, which applies only to England and Wales. Under that Act local authorities with overspill problems are empowered to enter into agreement with other authorities to receive their overspill and to make financial contributions in respect of their receptions. Exchequer grant is also provided for expenditure by authorities receiving overspill on a limited range of basic services.

The Clyde Valley Planning Advisory Committee have represented to me that legislation on these lines, with minor adaptation to fit Scottish local authority conditions, is necessary as one of the instruments for dealing with Glasgow's overspill problem. Put briefly, the facts are that by the end of 1958 the City will have no more building sites for housing available and must rely, for securing the rehousing of something over 100,000 families and, more importantly, progress in its slum clearance and redevelopment schemes, on the receptions of this overspill outside the City.

The City's annual provision for their waiting list of 5,000 houses will therefore rapidly fall if this reception at a fairly high rate cannot be arranged. Two new towns, East Kilbride and Cumbernauld, already exist to cater for Glasgow overspill, but between them are incapable of maintaining the City's output. I do not rule out the possibility that the designation of a further new town may be required at some future stage; meantime, and as a continuing resource, further aids to the reception of overspill are required.

The Clyde Valley Planning Authority Advisory Committee have made a survey of areas suitable for the first phase of reception of overspill and have sounded the local authorities of these areas on their willingness to receive population from Glasgow. A reasonably encouraging response has been secured. Inevitably, these authorities are concerned about the financial terms for such receptions; the first ingredient is the overspill subsidy set out ... above which should be attractive coupled with the exporting authority's basic contributions of £14. The Committee have made recommendations to me on the scale of Exchequer grant for other services which should in their view be made available. Discussions on this and other financial aspects of town development will be initiated shortly at official level with the Treasury and other interested Departments and thereafter the local authority associations.

I regard legislation on the lines of the Town Development Act, 1952 as essential if progress with Glasgow's overspill problem and the redevelopment of her central and slum areas is to gain momentum and if the scheme of subsidies set out above is to work to full advantage. Scotland's only major overspill problem is Glasgow's; there are, however, other areas on Clydeside with comparatively minor problems who might at a later stage wish to take advantage of the legislation. [PRO, CAB 134/1255 HP(56)83; SRO, DD6/2591.]

CONTROLLING THE SCOTTISH HOUSING PROGRAMME, 1956

In October 1955, as part of an emergency Budget, the Cabinet agreed to reduce the house building programme by about 10 per cent. However, the following January Harold Macmillan, the Chancellor of the Exchequer, wrote to Duncan Sandys, the Minister of Housing, and James Stuart, the Scottish Secretary, indicating that 'in view of the gravity of the economic situation' he might have to ask for a further reduction. The first extract here is from his letters to Sandys and Stuart asking them to implement a reduction. The third, fourth and fifth extracts are from subsequent letters between Stuart and Macmillan.

Letter of Harold Macmillan, Chancellor of the Exchequer, to Duncan Sandys, Minister for Housing and Local Government, on the Housing Programme, 5 September 1956.

I am afraid that we must intensify still further our disinflation policy this autumn. You will have seen the truly alarming August figures of the reserves. Then there is Suez and all that Suez means.

There was an understanding between yourself and Rab Butler [last year] that we should work to a total of 270,000 houses of all kinds and 120,000 local authority houses in England and Wales. But we must think again. I would urge you most strongly to agree to limit local authority houses in England and Wales to a maximum of 100,000 starts this year. I shall ask James Stuart to ensure that the Scottish element in the total of 270,000 houses is reduced by the same proportion. The credit squeeze has been slow to bite on private housing but the latest figures show a 10% reduction on last years rate of starts and this downward movement may go further. [SRO, DD6/1565.]

Letter of Harold Macmillan, Chancellor of the Exchequer, to James Stuart, Secretary of State for Scotland, on the Scottish Housing Programme, 5 September 1956.

I enclose a copy of a letter I have sent to Duncan Sandys.

I hope you will be willing to take whatever steps are required to bring your proprortion of the 270,000 figure down proportionately. This means that your total should not exceed 24,000 including private construction. This is on the basis that your share of the 270,000 is the same proportion as you had of 1955 completions. [SRO, DD6/1565.]

Letter of James Stuart, Secretary of State for Scotland, to Harold Macmillan, Chancellor of the Exchequer, on the Scottish Housing Programme, 26 September 1956.

As I pointed out in my letter of 19th January, we have passed the peak of the Scottish programme, and the estimates which I then gave for the two financial years showed a considerable drop of about 16 per cent. in the two years 1955/56 and 1956/57.

You will appreciate that we cannot control the completions to ensure that, year by year, the downward trend should follow precisely the pattern in England and Wales. The circumstances are different—for example the different timing of subsidy changes because of the impact of the Rating and Valuation (Scotland) Act, 1956. Thus for the first part of 1957/8—for which the tenders are already approved—completions may not differ much from those of the previous year. On the other hand, with my announcement that the new reduced rates in Scotland will apply as from August 1st, and the local authorities strongly expressed views that they will very seriously affect the rate of building, I think there is no doubt that next Autumn will see the commencement of another substantial drop in the completion of local authority houses. The credit squeeze does not appear to have affected private housing in Scotland yet, but in view of its small proportion, any slight trend one way or the other is not likely to influence the total housing figures.

In all the circumstances, and in view of the assurances which I have given in the course of the subsidy review, that the special needs in Scotland, where as you know there is still a serious leeway to make good, would be fully taken into account, I think that it is preferable to leave the recently announced reduction in subsidies and the increased interest rates to work out their impact on the Scottish housing programme before considering what alternative steps might be taken. I fully expect that the subsidy changes will result in a substantial drop in the rate of submission of tenders in the near future, but it is too early yet to attempt to gauge its extent. [SRO, DD6/1565.]

Letter of Harold Macmillan, Chancellor of the Exchequer, to James Stuart, Secretary of State for Scotland, on the Scottish Housing Programme, 8 October 1956.

Thank you for your letter of the 21st September about the housing programme.

I am content for the time being to wait and see what the effect of the new housing subsidies will be upon the Scottish programme. But it is becoming so important to relieve the economy of the burden of house-building that I am reluctant to take any risks, and would like to be sure that, if we have to do something more, there are means of doing it ready at hand. That is why I have suggested, as you will see from ... my letter to Duncan Sandys, that our officials look for some suitable administrative brakes. May I take it that you will agree to your officials taking part? [SRO, DD6/1565.]

Letter of James Stuart, Secretary of State for Scotland, to Harold Macmillan, Chancellor of the Exchequer, on the Scottish Housing Programme, 24 October 1956.

Thank you for your letter of the 8th October about the control of the housing programme.

My officials will, of course, be ready to take part in any discussion which may be arranged on this subject.

As I indicated to you, however, in my letter of 19th January last, the size of the Scottish programme has been falling of its own accord for some time. The number of subsidised houses completed by local authorities, the Scottish Special Housing Association and the New Town Corporations fell from 34,000 in the financial year 1954/55 to 27,600 in 1955/56—a drop of about 19 per cent—and present indications are that the number will be down still further in 1956/7. This drop has occurred quite apart from the proposed reduction of the housing subsidies. Although the downward trend in the number of houses in new contracts approved was slightly checked in August, when it became known that the subsidies were to be cut, I expect this to be only a temporary check and that, in fact, the figures may fall rather more sharply as the cut takes effect. If this proves to be the case, no question of deliberately pruning back the programme in Scotland may arise.

I have not taken into account the contribution of private enterprise to the Scottish programme which, as you know, is relatively very small. Earlier in the year it seemed that private house-building was going to show some greater increase, but the figures for the quarter ended in September reveal a sharp decline in the number of houses completed. It may be that this was partly due to bad weather, but I imagine that the credit squeeze is also telling against expansion.

It is a pity that private building should show a drop but if the 'squeeze' proves to be the main cause of this decline, I don't see what can be done. [SRO, DD6/1565.]

SCOTTISH HOUSING AND PUBLIC EXPENDITURE, 1957

In autumn 1957 the Government agreed to further reductions in the housing programme. The extract here is from a letter of John Maclay, the Scottish Secretary, to Peter Thorneycroft, the Chancellor of the Exchequer, on the issue. Thorneycroft agreed that Maclay could use administrative action to keep the programme to 19,800 but asked that he first consult Henry Brooke, the Minister of Housing. The second extract is Maclay's letter to Brooke and the third, Brooke's reply.

Letter of John Maclay, Secretary of State for Scotland, to Peter Thorneycroft, Chancellor of the Exchequer, on Housing Expenditure in Scotland, 25 September 1957.

I understand that in the course of a recent talk at official level about capital expenditure on Scottish housing, the Treasury suggested that the Estimate submitted by my Department of 19,800 houses to be completed by public authorities in 1959/60 should be reduced by about 17 per cent. to 16,500, and that the rate of approvals should be at once cut back to secure this result.

I gather that this proposal derives from Henry Brooke's offer to make a reduction of 17 per cent. from the 1959/60 Estimate for England and Wales: but I am afraid that it does not take sufficiently into account the very different circumstances in the two countries as reflected in the estimates for 1959/60, which I mentioned in Cabinet.

For public housing alone, England and Wales originally produced a run-down of 4 per cent. in 1959/60 against the level of the programme in the present year. Scotland, on the other hand, proposed a run-down of 26 per cent. The revised programme for England and Wales now involves a reduction of 20 per cent. from the present level, which is also less than Scotland's 26 per cent.

Acceptance of the Treasury suggestion for a revision of the Scottish estimate for 1959/60 would widen the gap, since the Scottish reduction would become one, not of 26 per cent., but of 38 per cent.

But one cannot look at public housing alone: a proper comparison should embrace the activities of all housing agencies, including private enterprise, and is best appreciated if the peak years of 1953 and 1954 are taken as the base line. Assuming that private enterprise output remains at its present level in both countries, such a comparison shows an estimated run-down in England and Wales, on the revised 1959/60 figure, of about 26 per cent., and in Scotland of about 38 per cent. as the 1959/60 Estimate stands, and 46 per cent. if it were reduced as proposed by the Treasury.

A cut of this order would, in my view, fall much more hardly on Scotland than on England and Wales, particularly since the housing conditions in the two countries are so very different. As the differences have on more than one occasion been described in correspondence between ourselves and between our respective predecessors, I need not go into the details here. The essential fact is that housing conditions in Scotland are very much worse than in England and Wales: the Census shows that overcrowding is about eight times greater; and the special problem of Glasgow and the Clyde Valley, involving the rehousing of an overspill of about 300,000 people, has no parallel elsewhere in the country.

On top of this, whereas in England and Wales private enterprise at present builds about one-half of the total programme and may shortly do more, in Scotland the great bulk of the houses are built by public authorities and the contribution of private enterprise is very small and not likely to increase appreciably. For this reason a cut in public housing in Scotland would be an absolute cut not likely to be compensated for by private building and would be much more serious than such a cut in England and Wales.

I am naturally anxious that Scotland should make its due contribution to economy in public expenditure at the present time, but I hope that what I have said will persuade you that housing is not the place for a deliberate cut. The programme is running down of its own accord and I should judge that the increased difficulties which local authorities will be faced with in financing further development may accelerate the decline, so that by 1959/60 it is probable that actual housing output may not reach the level we have forecast.

I should prefer any cut to come about this way, and I would ask you therefore not to press that we should take deliberate steps now to effect the proposed reduction in 1959/60. [SRO, DD6/1565.]

Letter of John Maclay, Secretary of State for Scotland, to Henry Brooke, Minister of Housing and Local Government, on the Scottish Housing Programme, 10 October 1957.

I have been having talks with the Chancellor, as you have also, about cuts in expenditure on public housing, and I think I should let you know my position so far as Scotland is concerned.

As you know, we reduced our subsidies considerably in our recent Act, and this reduction, together with the fact that some Scottish counties and small burghs are nearing the end of their housing programmes, has allowed us to forecast a substantial rundown in our estimates for the next two years. The figures on which we are working are as follows:-

	1957/8	*1958/9*	*1959/60*
Local Authorities and Housing Associations	25,150	20,350	17,500
New Towns	1,450	1,650	2,300
Totals	26,600	22,000	19,800
	(£53.2m)	(£44m.)	(£39.6m)

Cost on basis of £2,000 per house or house equivalent.

As you will see, the figures assume a decline of 26% in 1959/60 as compared with 1957/58, and represents a fall of 45% from the peak year of 1953. It is possible that the rise in interest rates will reduce these figures even further. I have said to the Chancellor that I am most unwilling to attempt to impose any further deliberate cut in the meantime, for the following main reasons:-

(1) Although, as I have said, some authorities in Scotland are within sight of their housing target, others still have a vast programme ahead of them. I am thinking particularly of Glasgow and the authorities in the Clyde valley generally, where the accepted need is for the rehousing of an overspill of 300,000 people—a problem without parallel anywhere.

(2) The contribution which private enterprise makes in Scotland is very small—some 4,000 houses a year—and is unlikely to increase appreciably. Any cut in public housing in Scotland is thus an absolute one, and we do not have the cushion of private building which in England, accounts, I believe, for about half the total programme. Indeed, if we assume that private enterprise output remains at its present level, the decline in the total housing programme (including private enterprise) in Scotland in 1959/60 will be 38% as compared with the present year.

The Chancellor is sympathetic to these difficulties; but he points out that you have indicated your readiness to accept a cut of some 20,000 houses on your estimate for 1959/60, and to slow down approval of tenders in order to achieve this. This means, I gather, that your public housing programme for 1959/60 would be about 20% less than it is at present, against as I have indicated, a corresponding figure of 26% in Scotland.

In these circumstances I very much hope that in view of the very different conditions in Scotland, you will agree as the Chancellor has done that we need not now further reduce our estimate of 19,800 houses in 1959/60 to secure a greater cut than 26%. It is not unlikely, as I have said, that the reduction of the subsidy and the increase in the rate of interest will affect some saving on this figure and I shall, of course, watch the trend closely. [SRO, DD6/1557.]

Letter of Henry Brooke, Minister of Housing and Local Government, to John Maclay, Secretary of State for Scotland, on the Scottish Housing Programme, 20 October 1957.

Thank you for your letter of 10th October about expenditure on public housing in Scotland.

I appreciate that you have some special difficulty, and I recognise that your projected run-down in the total number of houses to be completed in the public sector in Scotland over the next two years would result in a reduction which I have agreed to accept for England and Wales over the same period. If therefore—as I assume—your figures of 22,000 completions for 1958/9 and 19,800 for 1959/60 are to be regarded as definite targets to which you intend to work, I am content and would not wish to press you to make a further reduction. [SRO, DD6/1557.]

THE CONTROL OF SCOTTISH HOUSING, 1958

In July 1958 the Government began a review of its 'social investment' programme for 1959-62. As part of that process the Treasury asked the Scottish Office to reduce local authority housing to 20,000 'starts' per annum. The first extract is from a letter of John Maclay, the Scottish Secretary, to Derick Heathcoat Amory, the Chancellor, outlining the problems he faced in securing a cut. The second is Amory's reply. In the summer, in order to maintain employment, Maclay had specifically instructed his officials not to restrict the local authority building programme. A target range for the programme of between 20,000 and 22,000 houses per annum was subsequently agreed.

Letter of John Maclay, Secretary of State for Scotland, to Derick Heathcoat Amory, Chancellor of the Exchequer, on the Scottish Housing Programme, 20 November 1958.

I have been looking again at the problem of the level of the Scottish Housing Programme in the light of the Financial Secretary's letter of 22nd September and the subsequent Ministerial discussions about capital investment generally.

Following these discussions I obtained a return from local authorities of the number of houses which they propose to put out to tender in the next twelve months. The returns are little help to me, as many of them are clearly inflated. The estimate is for 26,000 houses (for local authorities only), while in fact in each of the last two years only 18,000 have been tendered for. Indeed, I have to go back to 1954 to better the estimate now submitted by local authorities. In these circumstances I have been considering what would be the best line to follow.

The only way of securing an investment cut as suggested by the Treasury would be by the introduction of a system of allocations to local authorities which would impose a severe cut on the proposals of almost all of them.

There are however both administrative and political objections to the introduction of such a system. The administrative difficulties could no doubt be overcome, although they would be more formidable then we have hitherto experienced. Local authorities grumbled at, but nevertheless accepted the allocation system which had to be imposed some years ago during a period of scarcity of labour and materials: they would be less tolerant of such a scheme in a period of plenty like the present. However, at a time when the Government have declared their intention to increase public investment in many fields for reflationary reasons, the political objections to a simultaneous restriction of the housing programme are overwhelming. It might well be that a particular authority would be asked at the same time to spend thousands of pounds on a project covered by the reflationary proposals, but told that they could not begin building what they might regard as a modest housing development, even though they regarded additional houses as the most clamant need in the district. While Government Departments may understand the reasons for such a distinction, the normal local authority are unlikely to do so and to that extent the Government's policy as a whole might be discredited. For these reasons I think you will agree that it is out of the question to contemplate the introduction of an allocations system in Scotland at present.

While I do not think that it is possible now to introduce a system of control of local authority housing, I am in full agreement with you that some measures must be taken to bring Scottish housing to an appropriate level in relation to Government policy. After allowing for the element of inflation in the figures, the returns I have received tend to show that the reduction in the housing subsidies and the increased rates of interest are not sufficient to reduce the amount of housing work which the larger local authorities are prepared to undertake. We thoroughly scrutinise proposals by local authorities and only those needs which appear to be genuine are approved for subsidy purposes. I could not contemplate placing any restrictions on house building for overspill and slum clearance purposes, and in areas of high unemployment so long as that continues. Nevertheless, I recognise that some authorities are prone to formulate their proposals in accordance with the local demand for houses, instead of scrutinising the demand and eliminating the needs which are not really urgent and genuine.

To check this, I feel sure that the right course now is for us to put in hand a review of the present housing subsidies with a view to their revision. Such a revision would exert further pressure on local authorities to increase rents. I am convinced that the key to effective control of the housing programme in present circumstances is not a system of allocations, but further pressure in this way to inject greater realism into the rent structure. We had already agreed to an interim review in the course of 1959 against a possible change in the level of subsidies in 1961. I would propose ... after the turn of the year, to begin an internal study of the problem in order that we might be ready to consult local authorities confidentially, say, in the autumn of 1959, with a view to possible legislation sometime in 1960.

In the light of these considerations, I hope that you will be able to agree that it would be quite inappropriate to introduce a control of Scottish housing investment at the present time. [SRO, DD6/1558.]

Letter of Derick Heathcoat Amory, Chancellor of the Exchequer, to John Maclay, Secretary of State for Scotland, on the Scottish Housing Programme, 15 December 1958.

You wrote on the 20th November about Scottish public sector housing.

If I may take the second half of your letter first, I entirely agree that it would be a good idea to put in hand a review of present housing subsidies in Scotland with a view to their revision. As you say we want to keep up the pressure for an increase in Scottish local authority rents.

But, desirable as this is on its own account, I do not think that it meets my difficulties. The figure you quote of 26,000 houses which Scottish local authorities estimate that they will wish to put out to tender in the next twelve months implies that, in 1960/1, completions will exceed by some 10,000 the total of 21,000 which your officials gave us on the 29th August. If tender approvals continued at this rate in 1959/60, it would mean, in terms of investment expenditure, an increase of some £20m. on the amounts which we have hitherto assumed for Scottish housing. I dare say the local authorities' figures are inflated to some extent, but we cannot be sure that this is so. The assumption of a natural fall in demand has proved badly wrong during the past year or so, even when interest rates have been high. The disturbing feature of the situation is that, on your proposals, we could not stop the local authorities from building this increased number of houses, or indeed even more than this 26,000 a year, if they chose to do so.

I am sure you will appreciate that I cannot accept that Scottish public sector housing should remain uncontrolled, with the risk that it will add some £20m. to the total of investment. The position as you forecast it at the end of August left Scottish public sector housing running at the level of one-fifth of that in England, which we then said we considered a favourable ratio. If house building developed in Scotland as Scottish local authorities forecast it, the ratio would be nearer one-third. I really do not see that anyone could regard it as unreasonable for us to put limits on Scottish local authority housing so that this does not happen. The fact that we now have a rather higher level of unemployment must not blind us to the dangers of overload in 1960/1. I would therefore come back to the suggestion made in the Financial Secretary's letter of 22nd September that you should restrict approvals, on an allocation system, to the rate of 20,000 a year, this figure to include new towns and the Scottish Special Housing Association as well as local authorities.

I do not think that the conclusion of the employment Committee that we should consider whether housing in Scotland can be accelerated in 1959 affects this conclusion. We are trying to operate a policy of short term acceleration and long term caution. We must not allow the first to oust the second. [PRO, T 227/1155; SRO, DD6/1558.]

Chapter Four
HEALTH AND WELFARE

A HOSPITAL COMMISSION FOR SCOTLAND, 1923

In 1923 the Board of Health's Consultative Council prepared a report on hospital services in the south-east of Scotland. It reported a considerable shortage of hospital beds, lengthening waiting lists and a shortage of funds. At the same time the UK Voluntary Hospital Commission was winding up its distribution of a post-war State grant and was generally considering proposals for the future. The extract here is from a submission of the Board of Health to Viscount Novar, the Scottish Secretary, on the issue of hospital shortages and the Commission's proposals. Novar concurred with the submission.

Submission of the Scottish Board of Health to Viscount Novar, Secretary for Scotland, on the Hospital Service in Scotland, 9 March 1923.

So far as the Board are aware, this detailed investigation is the only investigation of its kind that has been undertaken in Scotland. But the main facts are generally known.

There are 90 voluntary hospitals in Scotland with 7,290 available beds; and all the large general hospitals have long waiting lists. The following passage from Sir Napier Burnett's Annual Report for 1921 on the voluntary hospitals in Great Britain illustrates the pressure on the teaching hospitals in Scotland:-

'These 6 teaching hospitals in Scotland with 44% of the total available beds in the 90 voluntary hospitals continue, as in 1920, to be worked at enormous pressure. An average daily occupation all the year round of from 75 to 80 per cent. indicates a full volume of work for any institutions, so that when we get the unusually high percentage of 93.65 all the year round as these 6 hospitals show, one must conclude that some of the hospitals are overcrowded.'

All these hospitals have waiting lists at present (Edinburgh Royal Infirmary, for example, has a waiting list of over 1,200 people, and the three general hospitals alone in Glasgow have at least 1,500 people waiting for admission).

Lord Cave's Committee on Voluntary Hospitals Finance (Report-Cmd. 1335-1921) also stressed the inadequacy of hospital accommodation in Scotland in the following passage:-

Page 7 'It should be added that there is a real need for the extension of hospitals in Scotland, and we were informed that there is little prospect of obtaining the amounts required for that purpose by voluntary contributions.'

Page 35 'Apart from difficulties in maintenance there is a crying need in many parts of the country for further hospital accommodation, and this is especially the case in the poorer parts of the great cities, in South Wales, and in Scotland.'

The Board do not propose to discuss in this memorandum the nature of the inadequacy of general accommodation or the findings of their Consultative Council in regard to the existing accommodation for infectious diseases and mental diseases. It is enough at present to point out that the shortage of general hospital accommodation exists and that if it continues much longer the voluntary system of hospital management may be endangered. There is a formidable body of opinion in Scotland in favour of putting the hospital on the rates; and it will become increasingly difficult to resist that view if adequate accommodation is not provided.

The Board do not care to commit themselves to the view that the voluntary hospitals unaided will not be able to overcome their present difficulty of maintaining existing facilities. The Board have not made an analysis of the financial position of the hospitals; but Sir Napier Burnett's review for 1921 shows that, taking the voluntary hospitals in Scotland as a whole, while there was an excess of *total* receipts over *total* expenditure amounting to £179,589 (compared with £305,071 for 1920), there was a deficit of *ordinary* income over *ordinary* expenditure, amounting to £69,209 (compared with £78,158 for 1920). This represents a deficit of approximately £10 per available bed (compared with £12 for 1920). The difference (£2) in the deficits per available bed was accounted for by a fall in income of £6 and a fall in expenditure of £8 per available bed.

The position for 1922 is not yet known, but it is doubtful if there will be an improvement on 1921; and it appears to the Board that so long as the hospitals are unable to meet their ordinary expenditure out of ordinary income, there is not much prospect that they will commit themselves to large extensions.

The Consultative Council believe the shortage of accommodation could be overcome to a certain extent by co-operation among all the hospitals so as to secure a more effective use of the existing accommodation and facilities, and by concerted effort to develop the resources of the voluntary system. The Board agree with this view.

As this co-operation could only be obtained by means of a central organisation, the Consultative Council recommend that there should be set up for Scotland a separate Hospitals Commission or Trust, and that this central authority should have the assistance of Regional Committees, pivoting on the large central general hospitals, for each of the Regions, N.W., N.E., C., S.E., W., and S.W.

The Consultative Council contemplate apparently that even with the improvements that may be effected through co-operation there may be a need for assistance from Government funds. It is no doubt for this reason as well as for the reason that it is proposed to include the poor law hospitals in the scheme of co-operation that the Consultative Council propose that the Hospitals Commission for Scotland should be appointed by the Board of Health.

These recommendations amount really to a plea that the machinery set up by the Government in 1921 should be made permanent, but that it should be adapted to Scottish conditions and a separate organisation for Scotland established.

At present there is a Voluntary Hospitals Commission for Great Britain with a net-work of local voluntary hospital committees throughout the country. There are thirteen local committees in Scotland. The Voluntary Hospitals Commission is associated with the Ministry of Health; its expenses are borne on the Ministry's Vote, and the members (twelve in all) of the Commission are selected by the Minister and the Secretary for Scotland, the former selecting *eleven* of the members, the latter *one*. The Commission was established by the Government, on the recommendations of the Cave Committee, for the purpose of distributing the temporary Government grant of £500,000 in aid of the voluntary hospitals and for other incidental purposes designed to rehabilitate the finance of the voluntary hospitals, promote co-operation among them and improve the organisation of the voluntary hospital system generally.

The Commission, it was understood, was to be a temporary body whose course would be run with the final distribution of the temporary grant. The final distribution will take place early in the current year. But it is not known whether the Commission will cease when this takes place. The Board were invited recently to assist the Commission in setting up a Consultative Committee for Scotland which is to be merely advisory to the Commission and is to have no executive functions. The Commission propose also to set up a Consultative Committee for England and Wales.

This development may mean that the Voluntary Hospital Commission will continue as the official executive authority for hospitals over England and Wales and Scotland. This runs counter to the established principle of separate executive departments for each part of the United Kingdom, and while the arrangement that there should be one authority for England and Wales and Scotland could be acquiesced in for an emergency purpose and for a limited period the Board consider that it would not be acceptable to Scottish feeling as a permanent arrangement. The Consultative Council Report is in itself a significant expression of Scottish feeling on this matter, for the Board understand that the members, through their association with local voluntary hospitals committees, were aware that the Commission might continue and that this knowledge prompted the submission of their Report at this time.

Apart from national feeling, there are in the hospital systems of Scotland and England clear differences that make separate administration necessary for efficiency. The systems of management, the financial position and methods, the hospital needs, and the methods of securing co-operation of the voluntary hospitals with each other and with the other authorities concerned in the care of the sick, all differ in the two countries. These differences prevent the Voluntary Hospitals Commission from operating with full efficiency in Scotland; and it is improbable that a Consultative Committee for Scotland, with no executive functions, will appreciably affect that position.

Further, the Regional Committees proposed by the Consultative Council would, in the Board's opinion, be much more effective bodies than the existing Local Committees, if for no other reason than that they would operate over wider areas which would be practically self-contained units for hospital purposes.

The Board are in general agreement with the findings and recommendations of their Consultative Council. They consider that the proposed organisation would lead to great improvements in the hospital service in Scotland, and that a small Government grant would be sufficient to give the Central Commission the necessary authority and power to have their recommendations put into effect, and could be administered without detriment to the voluntary management of the hospital. It is not unlikely that the adoption of this policy now will save a much heavier commitment in the future.

The Board recommend that, as soon as the present labours of the Voluntary Hospitals Commission have been concluded, the Commission should be disbanded and its place taken, so far as Scotland is concerned, by a separate national commission or Committee. The Board would be glad to have the President's concurrence in them taking that line at a conference between them and the Voluntary Hospitals Commission which is to be held in Edinburgh on the 23rd March 1923. [SRO, HH65/549.]

APPOINTING A COMMITTEE OF INQUIRY INTO SCOTTISH HOSPITAL SERVICES, 1924

In March 1924 the Secretary of the Voluntary Hospital Commission at the Ministry of Health wrote to the Scottish Office asking that William Adamson, the Scottish Secretary, agree to a commission of inquiry which would cover Scotland as well as England and Wales. The matter was remitted to the Board of Health for consideration and the following extract is from their submission to the Scottish Secretary. Adamson agreed with its proposals and in May the Hospital Services (Scotland) Committee was appointed under the chairmanship of Lord Mackenzie, a High Court judge.

Submission of the Scottish Board of Health to William Adamson, the Secretary for Scotland, on appointing a Committee of Inquiry into Scottish Hospital Provision, 9 April 1924.

1. The letter dated the 26th March from Mr Brock to Mr Lamb asks for the concurrence of the Secretary for Scotland in the following reference to the Voluntary Hospitals Commission:-

'The Voluntary Hospitals Commission are requested to inquire into and report to us upon, the extent of the additional voluntary hospital accommodation required in Great Britain and the best means of providing and maintaining it.'

The letter raises an important question of policy which the Board desire to submit to the President.

2. The main point is that on the 13th March, 1923, the President (Lord Novar) approved a proposal made by the Board that the Voluntary Hospitals Commission should cease to operate in Scotland so soon as its main business of distributing the Government grant of £500,000 was discharged, and that a separate Commission should be appointed for Scotland.

3. Since that memorandum was prepared and approved, there have been no material changes in the position and the case for a separate Scottish Hospitals Commission remains.

4. The only developments have been the following:-

First, a meeting on the 23rd March, 1923, between the Board and Scottish members of the Voluntary Hospitals Commission—Lord Linlithgow, Captain W.E. Elliot and Dr. Buist, accompanied by Mr Brock, the Secretary of the Commission. The following is an extract from the minute of that meeting:-

'Lord Linlithgow stated that at the meeting that morning between the Commission and their Scottish Consultative Committee it has been agreed to advise the Commission to proceed to the final distribution of the balance of funds available for Scotland, thereafter to cease operations in Scotland and to disband the Consultative Committee. The Consultative Committee were also of the opinion, and the Scottish members of the Commission agreed, that if any new body were set up to take the place of the Commission in Scotland, it should be an entirely Scottish authority. Lord Linlithgow also stated that the Voluntary Hospitals Commission would continue as the central co-ordinating body in England. He suggested that, if it were decided to set up a separate organisation for Scotland, joint action between the President of the Board and the Minister of Health should be taken to alter the constitution of the Commission so as to confine its activities to England.

'A general discussion took place in the course of which the position of the existing local committees was considered. It was agreed that they had not been a success and that this was probably due to the fact that they were constituted largely on a county instead of a regional basis.'

Second, a meeting on the 11th May, 1923, between the Board and a deputation from the Scottish Region of the British Hospitals Association to discuss the Consultative Council's Report. At that meeting the Board explained that, as the central authority for health in Scotland, they were seriously concerned about the shortage of hospital accommodation in Scotland, they were in general agreement with the proposals of the Consultative Council to set up a central body to co-ordinate the work of the various hospital authorities so as to make more effective use of the existing accommodation and facilities, but that, because of the popular tendency to suspect any Government offer of assistance to voluntary agencies as part of a design to absorb them, they were diffident about appointing a central hospitals commission without a request to do so from the direct representatives of the hospitals. The deputation agreed that any central commission that might be appointed should be exclusively Scottish, and that it was arranged that before further action was taken the deputation should report to the British Hospitals Association their interview with the Board and that thereafter, if the Association approved, concrete proposals on the subject of the proposed commission would be submitted to the Board. So far the British Hospitals Association have not reported.

5. The case for a central coordinating body rests on, first, the shortage of hospital accommodation, and second, the belief of most of the leading public men associated with the voluntary hospitals that owing to the absence of co-operation among the voluntary hospitals themselves and between them and the public authorities concerned with the provision of treatment for the sick (poor law and public health authorities particularly), the most effective use is not made of the existing accommodation and facilities, and that a central body which had the confidence of the parties concerned would be in a position to effect the necessary co-operation and to act as a clearing house for ideas on construction, accounting methods and management generally. (Finance is

disputed ground: there is a division of opinion whether a central body should interfere in the raising of funds; but if there were Government grants to distribute this division of opinion presumably would disappear.) The idea of a central co-ordinating body was stressed in the Cave Committee Report which led to the appointment of the Voluntary Hospitals Commission. The Commission, although it appears to have had little or no influence in Scotland, has done excellent work in England and has justified its existence there.

6. The case for a separate organisation for Scotland rests on the marked differences in the system of management of voluntary hospitals, in the conditions of effective co-operation among voluntary hospitals and between them and the public authorities, and the hospital needs of the two countries. These immediate practical considerations confirm the general principles of Scottish autonomy in health administration. These are the considerations which appear to have prevented the Voluntary Hospitals Commission and its Scottish local committees from working effectively in Scotland.

7. The above is the necessary background for considering the proposed reference to the Voluntary Hospitals Commission. The inquiry is to extend to the whole of Great Britain. The Board think that concurrence in this would cut across Scottish feeling and expert opinion and would perpetuate a condition which the Board acquiesced in for an emergency purpose and for a limited period only. The reference is for inquiry and advice and does not carry with it executive or administrative functions: but it was contemplated that the first duty of a Scottish Commission would be to survey the whole available accommodation in order to find out exactly what was needed. This has already been done for one area of Scotland (Edinburgh, Fife and the South-eastern counties) by a joint committee of the Board's Consultative Councils, and there is much valuable material, although some of it is out of date, in the report of a survey of hospital services in Scotland which was carried through by the inspectorate of the Scottish National Health Insurance Commission. There is need, however, for a complete survey now on the lines proposed in the reference to the Voluntary Hospital Commission: but, in the Board's opinion, the inquiry in Scotland should not be undertaken by the Voluntary Hospitals Commission but by an independent Scottish body.

8. It appears from the terms of this reference that no further grants are contemplated, at least until the survey is completed and the Commission reports. In these circumstances, it is unlikely that at present the Government would place at the disposal of a Scottish body any funds for assisting the Scottish hospitals. The Board doubt whether a commission which had no funds at its back would succeed in securing the co-operation of all the bodies in the essential elements of a co-ordinated service, inducing, for example, a hospital to act as a clearing hospital for some specified kinds of cases and to handle others to a cure.

There are possibilities of co-operation between the voluntary hospital authorities and the poor law authorities; but even with the development of poor law hospitals into first class hospitals, the restriction to the legal poor sets definite limits, practical and sentimental, to what can be achieved along this line. This is yet another problem which sends roots down to the problem of reforming the poor law, for if the powers of parish councils to provide institutional treatment for general sickness were transferred to the local health authorities, there would be no difficulty in getting the necessary accommodation for general sickness and no difficulty about co-operation between the voluntary hospital authorities and the health authorities who would then be the only other authorities empowered to provide general hospitals free from poor law restrictions. The necessary condition of co-operation would then be solved. The Board's Consultative councils have advised in favour of this reform and it is generally approved by the voluntary hospitals authorities. Even, however, if this were contemplated as an early measure of reform the case for a central co-ordinating body would not be invalidated; in these circumstances, however, the Board themselves might be able to act as the co-ordinating authority.

9. The Board beg to advise the President to arrange with the Minister of Health to limit the proposed reference to England and Wales and to determine the Voluntary Hospitals Commission's jurisdiction in Scotland. They advise also that an authoritative Scottish committee should be appointed to inquire into the whole question of hospital provision in Scotland and that before the terms of reference are finally approved they should be submitted to the Board's Consultative Council on Medical and Allied services and the Consultative Council on Local Health Administration, etc., for their advice. In the Board's view, the limitations of the reference to *voluntary* hospital accommodation is an unnecessary restriction and would prejudice the usefulness of the inquiry. [SRO, HH65/50.]

SCOTTISH CIRCUMSTANCES AND LOCAL GOVERNMENT REFORM, 1925

In November 1924 the new Conservative Government remitted to a Cabinet Committee a review of the rating system and proposals for Poor Law reform. At one of its later meetings, Neville Chamberlain, the Minister of Health, submitted a memorandum outlining his strategy for Poor Law reform. In it he laid special emphasis on abolishing the Board of Guardians and transferring their powers to a reformed County Council and County Borough, which at that time were also the principal local health authority. The extract here is from a note of the Board of Health on the Scottish position. In the event the Cabinet decided not to proceed with Poor Law reform until further discussion.

Note of the Scottish Board of Health regarding the Minister of Health's Memorandum on a Scheme of Poor Law Reform (V.P.C. 12), 27 April 1925.

The Board have not had time to consider fully the various important questions raised in the [Minister's] memorandum but they desire at this stage to point out that the Scottish problem is materially different from that of England. If it should be decided to adopt the principles of transfer of poor law functions to County and County Borough Councils in England it would, in the Board's opinion, be inexpedient to make a corresponding transfer to the existing public health authorities in Scotland. Many of these authorities (especially Burgh authorities) are exceedingly small and a transfer of poor law functions to them is, therefore, out of the question. Instead of such a transfer being to a larger authority as is proposed in England, it would actually be to a smaller authority so far as Burghs are concerned, inasmuch as most of the parishes which contain Burghs have also a landward area. An outstanding example of this is the parish of Culross, with a population of 3,261, including the Burgh of Culross, with a population of 508. In this case, therefore, instead of the poor law being administered by one authority (the Parish Council) transfer of functions to the public health authority would involve splitting up the parish into two areas,—one-sixth of the population being placed under the Town Council and the remaining five-sixths being transferred to the District Committee of the County Council. Take again the parish of Elie, which has a total population of 2,448 and includes the burghs of Elie (population 1,507) and Earlsferry (population 745). In this case the transfer would involve splitting up the present area of administration into three, namely two burgh areas and a landward area, the last of which would form part of the district committee area. A similar splitting up, though perhaps to a lesser extent, would take place in most of the 200 parishes which contain burghs within their boundaries. Transfer of functions to burghs might, of course, be confined to burghs over a certain population—the remaining burghs being grouped with the county districts. The Board are, however, of opinion that any scheme of poor law reform by way of transfer of functions to the public health authorities ought to proceed concurrently with a scheme for the reform of the public health areas. In this respect the problem in Scotland is much more difficult than it is in England. Moreover there is the further complication that in respect of education and lunacy, these services in Scotland are administered by *ad hoc* bodies (the Education Authorities and District Boards of Control) who are quite independent of the Town and County Councils.

The Board would, therefore, suggest that it might be pointed out to the Cabinet Committee that the solution of the problem for Scotland will have to be separately considered in the light of the special Scottish circumstances. [SRO, SOE6/1/34.]

HOSPITAL ACCOMMODATION UNDER MATERNITY AND CHILD WELFARE SCHEMES, 1926

In December 1925 the Hospital Services (Scotland) Committee reported to Sir John Gilmour, the Scottish Secretary. Amongst its recommendations was the need to increase accommodation for maternity and child welfare cases. Gilmour remitted the Report to the Board of Health and the first extract is from its submission to him on what action the Government should take. The second extract is from Gilmour's subsequent letter to Winston Churchill, the Chancellor of the Exchequer, on the issue of maternity and child welfare grants. Churchill agreed that Gilmour could 'approve moderate and well-considered schemes when satisfied that a case has been made out'.

Submission of the Scottish Board of Health to Sir John Gilmour, Secretary of State for Scotland, on Hospital Accommodation under Maternity Service and Child Welfare Schemes, 30 August 1926.

The Board have before them from different areas in Scotland a number of proposals which involve expenditure on hospital accommodation for maternity and ailments of children. Some of the proposals have reached the stage when the Board are being urgently pressed to say definitely whether they will approve them for grant purposes; others have not yet been formally submitted for approval. But in all of them, it is necessary for the Board to decide at once their general line of approach, whether of encouragement or discouragement.

It would not be proper to consider each proposal separately without regard to the needs of the other areas. This memorandum, therefore, gathers up the information before the Board about all the proposed new hospital accommodation in Scotland as it affects the maternity and child welfare service. It is submitted to the President for the favour of a ruling on the policy which the Board are to pursue.

The shortage of hospital accommodation in Scotland for maternal conditions and diseases of children is fully established. The President is aware already of the terms of the relevant portions of the Reports of the Puerperal Committee and the Hospital Services Committee; but the following passages may be quoted here:-

Puerperal Committee Report: 'Our witnesses are unanimous in their evidence that the most important avenue to the prevention of maternal mortality and morbidity is through antenatal care....' (par. 44).

'We are satisfied that the maternity hospital provision is not adequate for the number requiring admission, and that especially in its facilities for antenatal care and teaching it is seriously deficient....' (par. 96)

Hospital Services Committee:

'There is a clear inadequacy for abnormal confinements, again particularly in the industrial areas.... There is evidence that the authorities of the maternity hospitals are forced to discharge patients sometimes dangerously soon after confinement.' (par. 30).

'For maternity we estimate that about 600 beds and for children about 400 beds are needed in Scotland.' (par. 41).

'We think that the local authorities under their schemes of maternity service and child welfare might reasonably be expected to provide a proportion, if not all, of the additional beds that are needed for maternity.' (par. 106).

'The position of hospital accommodation for children under 5 years is much the same as for maternity.... Children suffering from chronic or semi-chronic illnesses are in the worst plight, as the voluntary hospitals can seldom admit them.' (par. 107).

'As with maternity, we think that the local authorities should provide many of the hospital beds that are required for sick children up to 5 years of age.' (par. 109).

As the Board point out in their Annual Report for 1925, there are no signs of any decline in the deaths from puerperal causes in Scotland.

The following is the position of the various proposals which are before the Board:-

Lanarkshire. Proposals for a maternity hospital and a sick children's hospital in Lanarkshire have been before the Board, on the initiative of the local authorities, since 1919. Several difficulties have interrupted progress in the formulation of a definite scheme. Among them have been, first, the changes in Government policy at different times since 1919, and, second, the Board's desire to clear up, before these projects were undertaken, the difficulties, which arose in the progress of the joint schemes for Tuberculosis, of securing cooperation among the local authorities. On several occasions the Board have received deputations from the local authorities at which the latter have explained their proposals and urged the special needs of the Lanarkshire area for hospital accommodation for maternity and sick children. The Board have never been in doubt about the needs of this area and at different times, notably in 1924, they have expressed their approval of the central object of providing additional accommodation.

Originally the proposals were for three institutions—a maternity hospital, a children's hospital, and a convalescent home—to be provided jointly by the local authorities of the middle ward, the upper ward, and the burghs. But, as some of the burghs have since provided maternity homes to serve their own areas, the proposals have been modified into the following form:-

Middle Ward of Lanarkshire:

Maternity Hospital	..	100	beds.

Middle Ward and Upper Ward and Burghs:

Sick Children's Hospital	..	120	"
Convalescent Home	..	80	"

The Board have no hesitation in endorsing on medical grounds the need for these proposed institutions. The pressure on the County Maternity Hospital at Bellshill illustrates the demand for maternity accommodation. In 1918, 132 women were admitted, in 1925, 1030 women were admitted. The pressure is still increasing and the local authority report that, at the end of May last, there were 150 women on the waiting list for surgical treatment. Recently the difficulty of coping with the demand was increased by the collapse of two of the wards; these wards are being reconstructed temporarily in order to restore the accommodation to 40 beds. The Board's Medical Officer, Dr. Dewar, reporting on this institution on the 16th June, 1926, writes:-

'Even when the new wings which are being rebuilt are again in use, it will tax the accommodation of the hospital if 40 patients are present at a time; and, as the demand is steadily increasing, the outlook is not without anxiety ... Here, if the premises are inadequate, the administrative conceptions are sound; and the arrangements from the clinical point of view are well devised for the welfare of the patients.'

The separate arrangements by the Burghs are by no means ideal for cases requiring major operative interference; but in existing circumstances they may serve, especially if the new institution is built, and, as the Middle Ward Committee propose, is made capable of expansion as required.

The sick children's hospital would accommodate children up to 5 years of age. It would be supported by the convalescent home, which would serve as an auxiliary to relieve the main hospital as much as possible for acute illnesses. The Royal Hospital for Sick Children at Glasgow is the only institution in the West of Scotland exclusively for children. As is well-known, it admits only acute cases; it works under extreme pressure, and there is always a long waiting list. The evidence submitted to the Hospital Services Committee on behalf of this institution was emphatic on the need for local authorities to enter this field to relieve the voluntary hospitals and the conclusion of the Hospital Services Committee on the need for additional accommodation for children applied with special force to an industrial area like Lanarkshire.

It is necessary for the Board to make a definite statement now, one way or the other, on these Lanarkshire proposals.

West Fife. The maternity hospital accommodation in Fife, the President is aware, has given the Board cause for serious anxiety. In the Western area of Fife (population about 100,000) there are no hospital beds for maternity or for children. The nearest maternity hospital is in Edinburgh and it is always severely taxed. The Davaar Maternity Home at Dunfermline (12 beds) is approved by the Board under maternity and child welfare schemes of the local authority of Dunfermline District, Lochgelly and Cowdenbeath. The Home, in size, facilities and staffing, is fitted to deal only with normal confinements; but, owing to the lack of other accommodation, the practice has grown for practitioners to send in also their serious obstetric cases. In January, 1924, following on an outbreak of puerperal fever in the Home, with several deaths, the Board instructed that the Home be closed for a period for disinfection and called for changes in the organisation. These changes have been carried out but the Board still find it necessary to keep the Home under periodic observation by their medical officers. The Board fear that, with the continued use of Davaar for serious cases, there is bound to be another disaster. The position grows worse because of the increasing number of all classes of patients and the growing practice of sending in difficult cases. The local authorities have applied for permission to use the Home also as an infants' hospital, but despite the absence of other facilities in the area, the Board have felt unable to sanction the admission of children who are seriously ill. The Board have investigated the possibility of alternative maternity accommodation in the Poorhouse Hospital at Dunfermline; but they find that this does not offer a solution. On the initiative of the Board a conference of the Board and the local authorities to discuss the hospital service in the area was arranged to take place on the 6th May, but owing to the industrial situation [the General Strike] this had to be postponed. The Board feel that they cannot delay further action to secure as speedily as possible an adequate hospital service for maternity in Fife; and they propose, so soon as the present coal trouble is over, to get in touch again with the local authorities. The Board hope that it may be practicable to find a solution which, especially in view of the need for expansion of general hospital facilities in the area, will be undertaken in cooperation with the voluntary hospital authorities. Probably, at least 20 beds for maternity and 20 beds for children will be required for the area.

Stirlingshire. There are two proposals for the provision of hospital accommodation for maternity and children in Stirlingshire. They are assuming urgency with the progress of the schemes for the extension of general hospital facilities in the county. In both Falkirk and Stirling schemes for rebuilding the local voluntary hospitals on new and adequate sites have made good progress and it is anticipated that the respective managements will shortly be in a position to begin work on the new sites. The Board have been approached on the subject of the relation between the extensions of the voluntary hospitals and the public medical provision in the county. In both Falkirk and Stirling, the managers of the infirmaries are willing to cooperate with the local authorities for the provision of the public services; they require to know, however, for the preliminary work of preparing plans and laying out sites, what part the local authorities will play in the initial cost and in the maintenance of the accommodation and facilities for public services which may be provided within the ring fences of the voluntary hospitals. At informal conferences in both Falkirk and Stirling which were attended by representatives of the local authorities and the infirmaries and to which the Board's representatives were invited, the Board's representatives have explained that the general policy of the Board, on the grounds of economy and efficient medical service, is to encourage cooperation between the public and the voluntary agencies. So far, it has been possible to suppress any indication of the Board's probable attitude towards applications by the local authorities for approval of schemes for institutional accommodation. But the local authorities will shortly put up a strong case for maternity hospital beds at the proposed new infirmaries; and it will be difficult, in view of the needs of the area and the ideal circumstances in which the new schemes will be launched, to resist giving some encouragement. The population of the county is over 160,000 and there are no facilities at present for maternity hospital work. Urgent cases go to Edinburgh and Glasgow, where maternity hospitals are harassed by problems of accommodation. In Stirling the initial capital cost will be met to a large extent from voluntary sources. A Ladies Committee in Stirling have been raising funds to equip a Maternity Home which on completion it was intended to hand over to the local authorities. At the informal conference with the Board's representatives it was pointed out that the need for facilities for abnormal cases was greater than for normal confinements, and the Ladies Committee have agreed to direct their fund to the provision at the new infirmary of a maternity block for abnormal as well as normal confinements provided the local authority meet the maintenance charges for their patients. At both Stirling and Falkirk, the units will be large enough to command the services of specialists and consultants and to justify the most modern equipment. Probably 20 beds for maternity at Falkirk and 20 beds at Stirling will be proposed to begin with. At Falkirk the local authorities concerned are the County Joint Committee for Maternity and Child Welfare (which includes the burghs of Denny and Dunipace and Bridge of Allan) and the burghs of Falkirk and Grangemouth; at Stirling, the local authorities concerned are the County Joint Committee for Maternity and Child Welfare, the burgh of Stirling, the Clackmannanshire Joint Committee for Maternity and Child Welfare authorities from Southern Perthshire.

... Even if all [the proposals before the Board] were undertaken the hospital service for maternity and children in Scotland would still be a long way from completeness; but it would be a substantial contribution. Altogether the ... proposals represent about 250 beds for maternity and 150 for children under 5 years of age and 80 beds for convalescent children. The Hospital services (Scotland) Committee estimated that the shortage amounted to 600 beds for maternity and 400 for children. Several areas, notably the South West (Dumfries and Kirkcudbright) will still have no maternity hospital provision at all, and all the industrial areas will still be deficient. Aberdeen and Glasgow are specially conscious of inadequacy, and the Board are aware that proposals for further provision in the towns for maternity are being discussed locally.

The Board's policy on maternity services and child welfare schemes, as approved by the President on 10th December, 1925, is to examine very critically all proposals which involve large capital outlay and to refuse approval unless in exceptional circumstances. The Hospital Services (Scotland) Committee recommend a change of policy into encouragement of a special effort to overcome the shortage of hospital facilities. It would be difficult for the Board to refuse sanction now to those among the above proposals to which approval in general terms has already been given; and with some to others, as for example in Falkirk and Stirling, it would be awkward for the Board to bar proposals without seeming to prejudice the efforts of voluntary hospitals and the development a cooperative policy between the public authorities and voluntary agencies.

The Board submit this memorandum with a request for the President's concurrence in a policy of encouraging efforts by local authorities, on approved lines, to provide additional hospital beds for maternity and sick children if monetary considerations will permit of the recommendations of the Departmental Committee being given effect to. [SRO, HH65/51.]

Letter of Sir John Gilmour, Secretary of State for Scotland, to Winston Churchill, Chancellor of the Exchequer, on Maternity and Child Welfare Schemes, 19 October 1926.

I have recently had under consideration the position in Scotland in regard to the provision of Maternity and Child Welfare centres, including the provision of hospital beds, which, in my view, is one of the most important developments of preventive medicine at the present time. In December last owing to the financial stringency and the recommendations of the Standing Committee on expenditure I instructed the Scottish Board of Health to examine very critically all proposals involving large capital outlay and to refuse approval in almost any circumstances. Since that date the report of the Hospital Services (Scotland) Committee has revealed a grave shortage of hospital accommodation in Scotland.

The Committee were of opinion that the existing shortage of hospital accommodation might and should be partially met by the provision of hospital beds for maternity and infant cases by local authority and child welfare schemes.

After mature consideration I have come to the conclusion that the policy of extreme restriction of this service which has been in operation since December last should not be indefinitely enforced in view of the cumulative evidence which I have received of the urgent need for expansion and the desire of the local authorities to deal with this problem. Instances have been brought before me from all parts of Scotland where adequate treatment of maternity and other cases has to be withheld owing to the absence of suitable institutions. It will be remembered that the infant and maternal mortality in Scotland are consistently high (Infant Mortality 91 Scotland: 75 England: Maternal Mortality 6.2 Scotland: 3.86 England).

I therefore propose to approve moderate and well-considered schemes as submitted by local authorities where I am satisfied that a case has been made out. This is in accordance with the reservation made by the Minister of Health when the economy proposals were under discussion, that he regarded himself as free to continue even with new proposals after due scrutiny. [SRO, HH65/51.]

THE VOLUNTARY HOSPITAL AND SCOTTISH HEALTH POLICY, 1926

The Hospital Services (Scotland) Committee (above) also recommended a State grant to expand voluntary hospital provision. The first extract here is from a letter of Sir John Gilmour, the Scottish Secretary, to Neville Chamberlain, the Minister of Health, enclosing a draft memorandum for the Cabinet indicating what action he proposed to take. The second extract is taken from the memorandum. Chamberlain disliked the idea of supporting voluntary hospitals independent of Poor Law reform and Gilmour wrote another letter suggesting the Committee of Civil Research should undertake a general fact-finding inquiry into the question of state aid to voluntary hospitals. The third extract is from Chamberlain's reply. Gilmour decided not to pursue the matter.

Letter of Sir John Gilmour, Secretary of State for Scotland, to Neville Chamberlain, Minister of Health, on the Hospital Services for Scotland, 9 November 1926.

I have for some time had under consideration the Report of the Hospital Services (Scotland) Committee of which Lord Mackenzie was Chairman and which reported to me in December last. The Report revealed a serious shortage of hospital facilities in Scotland and recommended a substantial Exchequer contribution towards the cost of the 3,000 additional beds estimated to be required. As important questions of policy are involved I intend to submit a memorandum on the subject to the Cabinet, and a draft, of which I enclose a copy, has been prepared. Before circulating it, however, I should be glad to have your observations on the memorandum, particularly in view of your recent speech in which you remarked upon the improved financial position of the voluntary hospitals in England.

I hope you will agree with me that, so far as the different conditions in the two Countries will permit, we should endeavour to avoid pursuing different lines of policy. [SRO, HH65/51.]

Draft Cabinet Memorandum by Sir John Gilmour, Secretary of State for Scotland, on the Hospital Services for Scotland, 2 November 1926.

1. I have had under consideration the report of the Hospital Services (Scotland) Committee which was appointed under the Chairmanship of the Hon. Lord Mackenzie.

2. The main findings of the Committee that I desire to submit to my colleagues are:-

(a) There is an immediate need for 3000 additional beds in general hospitals.

(b) The voluntary hospitals are unable, without assistance, to finance the provision of these additional beds.

(c) save in Glasgow and Aberdeen (about 300 beds) there is no surplus of Poor Law Hospital beds that could be used for general hospital purposes.

(d) save in a few populous parishes the Poor Law Hospitals provide an inferior service.

3. The recommendations of the Committee relevant to these findings are:-

(a) That the State should make a capital grant towards the cost of providing new beds by voluntary hospitals, and that the grant should be based on the cost of building (excluding land, equipment, &c.) and should be conditional on the locality's raising the balance of funds. The Committee consider that the limitations of State assistance to capital works would ensure that the voluntary hospitals suffer no diminution of their revenues by reason of State intervention.

(b) The Grant should be administered 'by a small and independent Commission (unpaid), appointed by the Secretary for Scotland, so constituted as to command the confidence of the hospitals and other interests concerned. The expenses of the Commission might be borne by the Scottish Board of Health'.

(c) That the responsibility of the parish councils (i.e., the Poor Law Authorities) for hospital treatment should be transferred to the local health authorities.

4. Apart from the carefully sifted evidence that was led before the Committee, I am aware that the continuing shortage of hospital beds in Scotland is having serious effects.

5. The position of the voluntary hospitals has also been the subject of a special inquiry in England, notably by Lord Cave's Committee and the Voluntary Hospital Commission, whose reports have been published. The estimated shortage of beds in England is, proportionately, rather less than the estimated shortage (3000 beds) in Scotland. The Minister of Health has so far made no pronouncement on policy but he has indicated that, in present financial circumstances, he could not at present take steps to remedy the admitted shortage.

6. I have considered the recommendations stated in paragraph 3 and, while I am not prepared, in present financial circumstances, to advise my colleagues to accept these recommendations simpliciter, I am satisfied that a measure of Government assistance is necessary if my responsibility for the health of the Scottish people is to be discharged. As my colleagues are aware the matter is one that has aroused considerable public interest in Scotland and has been the subject of questions in the House, and I have promised to make an early statement of the Government's policy.

7. The additional beds may be provided either by rate-aided Authorities or by the voluntary hospitals. The only rate-aided Authorities in Scotland at present with general hospital accommodation or with power to provide general hospital accommodation are the Parish Councils. The Committee have found that the existing surplus accommodation available to these authorities is limited to about 300 beds in the Poor Law hospitals at Glasgow and Aberdeen. The Parish Councils will not be prepared, particularly in view of the imminent reform of the Poor Law, to provide further general hospital accommodation even if such a course were desirable. On the other hand, when the reform of the Poor Law is carried out it may be that the responsibility for providing hospital accommodation for poor persons will be taken away from the Parish Councils as has been recommended not only by Lord Mackenzie's Committee but also two of the Board of Health's Consultative Councils. I have no doubt that at least the larger Authorities (in whose areas the shortage of beds is most acute) will face their new responsibilities for hospital treatment in a generous spirit and that the public demand for more beds may lead them to embark upon the provision of a complete hospital service for their ratepayers. I do not myself think, nor did Lord Mackenzie's Committee think, that course would be in the public interest. It would throw at once on public funds the whole cost of providing and maintaining the additional beds to repair the shortage: and with the growth of a rate-supported system of general hospitals, it would, by checking the flow of charitable subscriptions, jeopardise the continued existence of the voluntary hospital and might well end by throwing on the State and local authorities the whole cost of the hospital service. At all times the shortage of

general hospital beds constitutes a threat to the voluntary system, but the imminence of poor law reform has given the threat a new force and poignancy.

8. I am driven, therefore, to the conclusion that on financial grounds alone and apart from the more general considerations, it will be unwise to permit the hospital problem in Scotland to develop in that way. To avoid such a development it will be necessary *before the reform of the Poor Law is accomplished* to take such steps as are required to put the voluntary hospitals in a position in which they have a fair prospect of overtaking the shortage of beds. I can see no hope that the voluntary authorities will be able to effect this without some assistance from the State.

9. In present financial conditions the provision of considerable lump sum grant presents grave difficulties, although that is the form of assistance that Lord Mackenzie's Committee recommend. In my view, however, the position could be met by assistance in the form of an annual grant over a period of years based on the loan charges which the hospital authorities would bear if the capital cost of the new provision were met out of borrowed money. Further, I see no reason why the whole programme of 3000 beds should be undertaken at once. If it were proceeded with by instalments the immediate burden on the Exchequer would be still further reduced.

10. I propose, therefore, that as the first instalment a programme of 1000 beds be undertaken, with a further instalment of 1000 beds two years later, and thereafter a complete review of the hospital position as it then is. I propose that the Exchequer should meet 50% of the calculated annual loan charges on the cost of these new beds, calculated on a 30 year loan period.

11. The annual cost of such a grant to the Exchequer would be in the neighbourhood of £20,000 for two years and thereafter of £40,000. I base this figure on the Committee's estimate that the average cost of providing a bed will be £625. The Exchequer payment would of course be conditional on the hospital authority's ability to raise 50% of the funds necessary to provide the beds. Naturally, the preliminary arrangements would occupy some time, and I do not suppose that any material charge upon the Exchequer could mature before the financial year 1928-9 at the earliest. [SRO, HH65/51.]

Letter of Neville Chamberlain, Minister of Health, to Sir John Gilmour, Secretary of State for Scotland, on the Hospital Services for Scotland, 14 December 1926.

I have been considering the terms of reference to the Committee of Civil Research on the question of state aid to voluntary hospitals, which I understand you have in mind.

The difficulty arises where you propose ... that the Committee should consider 'what action, if any, should be taken and along what lines hospital services should be encouraged to develop.' Any such form of words takes the inquiry far beyond the region of statistics. It raises at the outset the question what should be the relation of the voluntary hospital to the publicly provided hospital. It is impossible to consider along what lines hospitals should be encouraged to develop, without determining what part they should play in the general scheme of public health services. This is a vitally important question, but it cannot in my view properly be considered apart from the question of Poor Law reform. The great difficulty which confronted the Voluntary Hospitals Commission arose from the diversity of Institutions controlled by different sets of local authorities, with the result that there was no co-ordinating authority able to utilise vacant beds not required for the purpose for which any particular institution was primarily provided. The difficulty was specially acute in the case of the Poor Law institutions because of restrictions, partly legal, partly sentimental, which so long as the Poor Law system remains, render it impossible to make any effective use of vacant poor law beds. Under my proposals for the reform of the poor law I hope that we shall get all publicly provided institutional services brought under the control of one set of authorities. When this is done, and not till then, it will be possible for the County and County Borough Councils, after taking stock of the institutions under their control, to determine to what extent they, together with the voluntary hospitals, meet the needs of the area, which type of institution whether municipal or voluntary, it would be best to develop, and what relation should be established between the various types.

There is and can be no hard and fast line between the province of the voluntary hospital and the province of the publicly provided hospital. In fact in England the line of demarcation rests on no scientific basis; it changes from time to time; and it varies considerably as between different parts of the country. The question of the part which the voluntary hospital should play in a scheme of co-ordinated health services is in my view one of the most difficult and one of the most important with which I shall have to deal. Before it can be finally decided there must be time for public opinion and especially medical opinion to form itself and one object of my correspondence with the 'Times' was to begin that process.

I think accordingly that I could not agree to the last part of your terms of reference. But if that is omitted I should doubt whether a purely statistical inquiry will help us, since such figures as are available in my Department show that the voluntary hospital position in England and Wales is distinctly better than Onslow's Commission anticipated. The rate of hospital expansion is in excess of the rate of growth of the population, and the arrears of the war period are gradually being made good. The case for State aid is steadily weakening, but as I have pointed out in my previous letters any concession to Scotland would create a demand for a similar concession to England. Such information as we could put before the Committee of Civil Research so far from helping you, would be likely to provide the Treasury with a good deal of ammunition with which to resist any demand on the part of the Scottish hospitals for a subsidy from public funds. [SRO, HH65/5.]

REFORMING LOCAL GOVERNMENT, 1928

In 1928 the Conservative Government announced its intention to reform local government in both England and Wales and Scotland. The first extract is from the memorandum submitted to the Cabinet by Sir John Gilmour, the Scottish Secretary, on the changes he proposed. The Cabinet accepted the memorandum.

Memorandum by Sir John Gilmour, Secretary of State for Scotland, on proposals for Reform in Local Government in Scotland, 23 June 1928.

The main purpose of these changes is to enlarge the units of local authority administration, and to reduce the number of different types of local authorities administering local services in each area. Scotland is pre-eminently a country of small administrative units. There are 869 Parish Councils, 201 Town Councils, 98 District Councils, 37 Education Authorities, 33 County Councils, and 27 District Boards of Control. All of these are independent local authorities for the purpose of the particular services they administer. Many of them operate for areas of very small population and rateable value, and the multiplicity of authorities, in type and number, tends to overlapping and waste. Apart from the de-rating proposals of the Government, there was a strong case for reform of local government on the lines now proposed, but the vested interests of existing authorities imposed a formidable bar. The present moment seems opportune for a change. The de-rating under the Government intensifies the urgency of the problem from the point of view of the financially weak authorities, while the new system of Exchequer grants should go a long way towards minimising opposition.

It is proposed to abolish Parish Councils, District Councils, education Authorities, and District Boards of Control. The functions of these bodies will devolve upon reconstituted County Councils, and upon Town Councils of Burghs with a population of 20,000 or over. It is also proposed to transfer to County Councils the powers and duties of the Town Councils or Burghs under 20,000 population relating to the major Public Health Services, Police and Classified Roads.

Under these proposals, the authorities for Poor Law, the major Public Health Services, and Classified Roads will be the County Council (acting for the

County inclusive of the smaller Burghs), and the Town Council of the larger Burghs.

The Education Authority will be the Town Councils of Edinburgh, Glasgow, Aberdeen and Dundee and elsewhere the County Council (acting for the County inclusive of all the Burghs except those above mentioned). The Lunacy Authorities will be a Joint Committee of the County Councils and Town Councils of the larger Burghs in the area comprised in the Lunacy Districts.

As some of the Councils are very small, it is proposed to take power to combine Councils for all administrative purposes. It is also proposed to take power to combine contiguous Burghs.

Strenuous opposition to these proposals is to be expected from the Authorities to be abolished, and from the Councils of the smaller burghs, whose powers as regards Public Health, Police and Roads will be diminished. There may also be some reluctance on the part of Authorities on whom new duties are to be imposed to undertake the additional responsibilities.

There has however been a movement in Scotland in recent years towards a reform of Local Government which is likely to be much strengthened by the attractive results of the financial side of the Government's scheme, and thus will tend to neutralise the opposition of the vested interests.

It is estimated that the new money required to meet the Grants payable under the [aid of rates] formula in Scotland will amount to £750,000.

All burghs will gain under the formula and in the case of the more industrial burghs the gain will be substantial. The results in the selected counties are also satisfactory from a ratepayer's point of view, more especially in the necessitous areas. [PRO, CAB 24/196 CP(28)201.]

VOLUNTARY HOSPITALS, THE POOR LAW AND LOCAL AUTHORITY HEALTH PROVISION, 1929

After the publication of the Local Government Bill, Glasgow Corporation petitioned Sir John Gilmour, the Scottish Secretary, to introduce a clause permitting the local authority to maintain a general hospital service, separate from the Poor Law. The Voluntary Hospital Liaison Committee immediately objected and sought a meeting with Gilmour. The first extract is from a minute of their meeting with the Department of Health. The second extract is from a subsequent letter of the Department to the Committee, after it had written suggesting the formal involvement of voluntary hospitals in local authority health services.

Minutes of the Meeting of the Department of Health and the Voluntary Hospitals Liaison Committee, on the Hospital Clause of the Local Government Bill, 16 January 1929.

Major Elliot recalled the circumstances under which the Committee had been appointed in December 1927 at the request of the Secretary of State for Scotland. The functions of the Committee were to assist in developing a cooperative hospital policy, to assist in keeping the Department in touch with voluntary hospital opinion and to act in liaison between the Department and the Hospital Area Committee. He contemplated that the Committee would play an increasingly important part in hospital affairs.

Major Elliot explained that the Department had considered it necessary to consult the Committee on the proposal which had been made by the Corporation of Glasgow and other bodies to provide in the Local Government (Scotland) Bill for the removal of hospital treatment from the poor law. This proposal raised important issues for the voluntary hospitals and he invited the views of the Liaison Committee.

A general discussion followed in which the conditions in the different regions were reviewed and the implications of the proposed charge on the hospital services generally were examined.

The unanimous view of the Committee was that hospital treatment should be dis-associated from the poor law and that, therefore, in transferring poor law functions to town and county councils, these authorities should be empowered to provide hospital treatment apart from the poor law. No such power, however, should be conferred without provisions that would adequately safeguard the voluntary hospitals against competition from public authority hospitals. The proposed clause submitted by Glasgow Corporation could not be accepted.

It was suggested that proposals for extension of hospital services by public authorities should be subject to the approval of the Department of Health for Scotland, and that approval should only be given if, after local inquiry by the Department and consultation with the voluntary hospitals of the area, there was not already suitable and adequate provision made by the voluntary hospitals, and under conditions that would ensure cooperation between the voluntary hospitals and the public authorities.

It was also suggested that the Liaison Committee and the Hospital Area Committees might be brought definitely into the machinery of cooperation.

Another suggestion submitted was that provision should be made for cooption of voluntary hospital representatives on the appropriate committees of the local authority.

After some discussion it was agreed that the Departmental officials would draft an amendment to the Bill and, after Major Elliot had consulted the

Secretary of State, a draft would be submitted to the Liaison Committee. It was agreed that, to save the time of the members of the Committee, Sir David Wallace and Col. Macintosh should review the draft in the first place and that thereafter it should be circulated to the Committee.

During the discussion of the Bill a question was raised about the status of the Committee and Mr Jeffrey, Secretary of the Department, stated that, if the Committee desired, steps would be taken to raise the status of the Committee, and that in view of the important work that lay ahead, it might be well to take early action with this object. [SRO, HH65/53.]

Letter of H.A.L. Fraser, Assistant Secretary, Department of Health, to the Secretary, the Voluntary Hospitals Liaison Committee, on the Local Government (Scotland) Bill, 4 February 1929.

I am directed by the Scottish Secretary of State that he is very grateful to the Liaison Committee for the help they have given in drafting the proposed hospital clause. He has considered the suggestion which the Committee submitted in their letter of the 30th ultimo, and while he agrees with the Committee in regarding the machinery of co-operation as highly important, he is definitely of the view that provision in the Bill for the Liaison Committee and local advisory councils would be inexpedient and would not strengthen the position of the voluntary hospitals. Satisfactory arrangements for the Liaison Committee can be made by administrative action; and while local advisory councils could also be set up by administrative action, without any change in the terms of the clause, the question of their constitutions and composition would require full consideration and prior negotiation with all the interests concerned. [SRO, HH65/53.]

IMPROVING MATERNITY SERVICES IN SCOTLAND, 1936

In 1935 the Departmental Committee on Maternal Morbidity and Mortality reported and made a number of recommendations on improving the maternal health service. The first extract here is from the subsequent memorandum of Sir Godfrey Collins, the Scottish Secretary, on the issue to the Cabinet. The second extract is from Cabinet discussion on the matter. The following year the Maternity Services (Scotland) Act was passed. The objection during discussion to the use of doctors came from Neville Chamberlain, the Chancellor of the Exchequer, who was 'firmly of the opinion' that many were 'inefficient'.

Memorandum by Sir Godfrey Collins, Secretary of State for Scotland, on the Extension of Maternal Health Services in Scotland, 7 May 1936.

Following the introduction of a Bill to improve the standard of domiciliary midwifery in England and Wales, I desire the authority of my colleagues to prepare and circulate to the Home Affairs Committee a Bill for the extension of maternal health services in Scotland.

The main proposals which it is desired to incorporate in the Bill are in conformity with the conclusions drawn from a special investigation into the causes of maternal morbidity and mortality in Scotland and approved by the clinical sub-committee of the Scientific Advisory Committee to the Department of Health, augmented by a number of distinguished obstetricians. They are accordingly based on authoritative medical opinion, both official and independent, and are as follows:-

(i) Every local authority must secure that there is available for its area sufficient midwives to act as maternity nurses in association with medical practitioners or, where a woman so desires, as midwives. For this purpose the local authority might make arrangements with voluntary associations or itself employ midwives. To maintain adequate standards efficient supervision of the midwives should be instituted, and they should be required to attend refresher courses where these are reasonably available.

(ii) Every local authority must make such other arrangements as the Department think necessary to secure proper attention for expectant and nursing mothers and women in childbirth.

(iii) Certain general provisions (e.g., the prohibition of unqualified persons acting as paid maternity nurses) already agreed to in connection with the English Bill would be included.

These proposals differ in some respects from those incorporated in the English Bill, but the Scottish problem is in many ways different from that in England. The maternal mortality rate is higher in Scotland. Midwives attend to a much smaller proportion of cases of childbirth than in England—25 per cent. as against 60 per cent.—and doctors attend to a correspondingly higher proportion. The practical impossibility of applying arrangements—e.g., ante-natal and postnatal clinics—suited to an industrial or urban area, to districts such as the Highlands and Islands, and the varying conditions in regard to maternity practice even as between different urban areas make it essential to frame proposals sufficiently broad and elastic to ensure the development by local authorities of services suited to the circumstances of their areas. The aim is to make available to every woman who applied for it appropriate medical and nursing care before, during, and after confinement.

Under the proposed Bill local authorities would be involved in material additional expenditure, and towards this it is proposed that in the first instance the Department of Health should make a grant. Details of the grant are under discussion between the Department and the Treasury. It is estimated that when the arrangements are in full operation the total annual charge on the Exchequer will not exceed £60,000. After a sufficient lapse of time the Exchequer contribution would be included in the block grant under the Local Government (Scotland) Act, 1929. [PRO, CAB 24/262 CP(36)128.]

Cabinet Conclusions, on Maternity Health Services in Scotland, 13 May 1936.

The Cabinet had before them a memorandum by the Secretary of State for Scotland seeking authority to prepare and circulate to the Committee on Home Affairs a Bill for the extension of Maternity Health in Scotland, following the introduction of a Bill to improve the standard of domiciliary midwifery in England and Wales. After setting forth the main proposals of the Bill, which differed in some respects from those incorporated in the English Bill, the Minister stated that when the proposed arrangements were in full operation it was estimated that the total annual charge on the Exchequer would not exceed £60,000, and that after a sufficient lapse of time the Exchequer contribution would be included in the block grant under the Local Government (Scotland) Act, 1929.

In reply to the Minister of Health the Secretary of State for Scotland promised to do his utmost to avoid bringing in his Bill until the Minister of Health's Bill has passed the House of Commons, since the scope of the latter was rather less ambitious and the introduction of the Scottish Bill might lead to a demand for extension. The Secretary of State for Scotland's undertaking, however, was subject to the provision that he was very anxious to get his Bill during the present session.

The Secretary of State for Scotland was reminded that the mortality rate for maternity was much higher in Scotland than in England and there was much ground to believe that this is due to the difference in the practice between the two countries; in England reliance being placed mainly on midwives, and in Scotland on doctors. He was asked not to include anything in the Scottish Bill which would tend to stereotype this system. The Secretary of State for Scotland was also asked to bear in mind the special considerations of the Highlands and Islands in this Bill, which he undertook to do.

Subject to the above discussion, the Cabinet agreed: that the Secretary of State should prepare and circulate to the Committee of Home Affairs a Bill for the Extension of Maternal Health Services in Scotland. [PRO, CAB 23/82 36(36)7th; SRO, HH61/787.]

THE WAR AND THE EMERGENCY HOSPITAL SERVICE, 1939

In September 1938 the Cabinet agreed to a programme of emergency hospital accommodation in the event of wartime air attack. The first extract here is from a joint memorandum by Walter Elliot, the Minister of Health, and John Colville, the Scottish Secretary, the following March, outlining the position then reached. The Cabinet agreed to the Block One proposals, but could not agree on the issue of unified control; Neville Chamberlain, the Prime Minister, invited a group of ministers, including Colville, to review the position. The second extract is from a subsequent joint memorandum. After discussion, the committee accepted the policy of unified control and agreed to authorise the second block of hospital building.

Memorandum by Walter Elliot, the Minister of Health, and John Colville, the Secretary of State for Scotland, on Emergency Hospital Accommodation, 31 March 1939.

The fullest use has now been made of existing hospital accommodation by introducing additional beds and by upgrading institutions not at present equipped for surgical work. By these expedients and by sending existing sick to their homes or to inferior accommodation about 200,000 beds will be provided in England and Wales for civilian casualties in the first 24 hours and another 100,000 a week or so later. But these figures include about 80,000 beds in vulnerable situations which could probably only be used for clearing station purposes. Further, the sick displaced—about 140,000—would soon be succeeded by others requiring hospital treatment for the ordinary illnesses. Thus in England and Wales there are only about 80,000 beds on which we can count for the prolonged treatment of casualties.

In Scotland the position is even less satisfactory. About 12,000 beds could be provided for civilian casualties in the first 24 hours, and about 8,000 more a week or so later. But of this total of 20,000 beds some 50 per cent. are situated in vulnerable areas, and something like a further 10,000 would be needed to accommodate cases of ordinary illnesses, succeeding the cases of sickness displaced on the occurrence of the emergency.

In both countries the existing provision of beds is therefore inadequate. No one can forecast with accuracy the number and location of civilian casualties. But we have been advised by the Minister for Co-ordination of Defence that in Great Britain as a whole air raid casualties in the first two or three weeks might be as high as 17,500 killed and 35,000 wounded every day. On this basis 433,000 beds might be required by the fourth week.

It would not be possible to provide hospital accommodation on any modern basis for such a number of casualties. The task of construction could not be completed within any reasonable time, and there would not be enough doctors or nurses to serve so many beds even if they were provided.

By agreement with the Chancellor of the Exchequer and the Lord Privy Seal, we are already proceeding to approach the hospital authorities with a view to the construction, on land adjoining their institutions, of huts which would accommodate 20,000 beds in selected parts of England and Wales (primarily to serve London, Birmingham and Tyneside) and 6,000 in Scotland (primarily to serve Edinburgh and Glasgow) at an estimated cost of £70 per bed for construction and £10 per bed for bedding and ward equipment. A further review is, however, desirable.

The calculations mentioned above do not take account of hospital accommodation required for—(a) Service casualties and sick brought back from overseas, (b) Service sick, not being air raid casualties, in this country. These Service requirements must be treated as additional to those for the civilian population.

The fact that some additional accommodation will be needed for Service requirements raises also a question of principle, viz. whether the Service Departments should themselves undertake the necessary construction or whether, on the other hand, the Service and civilian requirements should both be met from a joint pool of hutted accommodation, units of which might be transferred to the Services if and when the need arises. In our view the latter is the preferable course, in the interests of economy and uniformity of administration, and the organisation of the additional accommodation required would then be under one central authority. In particular, this method would keep medical and nursing personnel employed to the best advantage and would avoid the immobilizing of some skilled personnel in Service institutions, where they might not immediately be required, at a time when the civilian accommodation was being subjected to maximum strain. [PRO, CAB 24/284 CP(39)77.]

Memorandum by Walter Elliot, the Minister of Health, and John Colville, the Secretary of State for Scotland, on Proposals for Hutted Accommodation, April 1939.

It is proposed to commence a programme based so far as possible on the addition of hutments to existing hospitals, but partly on new hutted units, attached where possible to large private houses which would serve as administrative blocks.

The estimated cost of hutted accommodation when attached to existing hospitals is £70 a bed on the basis of 1/- a cube, but when complete units have to be provided *de novo* the cost rises to £150 a bed exclusive of staff quarters. The cost of construction of the 'Block A' instalment therefore, assuming that it can all be carried out at the lower figure, is 26,000 x £70, or £1,820,000. To this should be added not less than £10 per bed for equipment (= £260,000), bringing the total to £2,080,000.

This programme, however, cannot be regarded as in any way sufficient to meet the needs of the situation, and we should propose to provide forthwith another 20,000 hutted beds in England and Wales, and another 6,000 in Scotland (Block B). Most of these further beds would, it is hoped, be provided at the £70 rate, but in some areas beds at the higher rate will have to be provided. Those in England and Wales would again be attached as far as possible to hospitals. The cost, including the allowance for equipment, would be approximately £1,600,000. Those in Scotland could not be so attached, owing to the inadequacy of existing accommodation, and would have to be provided as complete new hospitals at a cost of approximately £960,000. The total cost of Block B would thus be £2,560,000.

Authority is sought to place contracts now for these 26,000 'beds' over and above those included in the first instalment. The situation will be reviewed when the contracts for these 26,000 beds have been placed. [PRO, CAB 27/659 EHO 1(39)2.]

A SCHEME FOR A COMPREHENSIVE HEALTH SERVICE, 1943

In early 1943 the Cabinet's Reconstruction Priorities Committee, in the light of the Beveridge Report, began consideration of a national health service and invited the Health Ministers to discuss the matter with the various parties involved. The first extract here is from the memorandum by Thomas Johnston, the Scottish Secretary, to the Committee on his Scottish proposals. However, Ernest Brown, the Minister of Health, raised objections to his supra-local government health authority and Johnston was asked to discuss the matter further. The second extract is from his subsequent memorandum which also appended a note summarising the conclusions of the Scottish Committee on Post-War Hospital Problems. The Committee accepted Johnston's health authority and local clinic proposals, but delayed a decision on the management of general practitioner services for a further meeting.

Memorandum by Thomas Johnston, Secretary of State for Scotland, on the National Health Service, 25 July 1943.

My colleagues have before them a Paper (P.R.(43)46) by the Minister of Health dealing with proposals for a new national health service. I have had parallel discussions with the various Scottish bodies concerned and I am in general agreement with the proposals in the Paper but there are certain special Scottish aspects (some of them requiring rather a different approach) to which I think it necessary to draw the Committee's attention.

In regard to the local machinery for the administration of the new service I propose that in Scotland (as in England and Wales) the local responsibility for the service, subject to what I say below, should be vested, in the main, in combinations of the present major health authorities, viz. the county councils and the councils of large burghs. But I am faced with the difficulty that in some of the more sparsely populated parts of the country, the combination of authorities which would be needed to secure a population big enough to justify confidence in the ability of the combination to maintain within its own boundaries a complete range of hospital facilities, would be so large in area as to be unwieldy: in other words 'local' government would be supplemented by 'regional' government. Many of the local authorities concerned would, I think, resent being part of a combination based on a 'regional' conception and I propose, therefore, in the areas affected to be content with small groupings, leaving it to the new authorities to make such arrangements on a 'customer' or other basis as will best meet the needs of the area. I should contemplate for the whole of Scotland some 16 to 18 health authorities.

On the other hand, the Scottish problem in relation to local government units is in an important respect materially simpler than the problem in England and Wales. All the health functions under review are in the hands of the authorities already referred to—the county councils and the councils of large burghs—and I see no necessity to make any statutory provision for setting up district health committees. (It will, of course, be open to health authorities to appoint local sub-committees if they so desire.) As regards delegation of functions by the health authorities, I feel that, at the most, I need go no further than to provide for delegation of certain functions to the present major authorities who will be, of course, partners in the combination.

Paragraph 16(1) of the Minister of Health's paper discusses the question of representation of the medical profession and of the voluntary hospitals on the health authorities and suggests that representatives of those bodies should be admitted to membership of the authorities but without any voting power. The proposals that democratically elected authorities should be specifically required to co-opt as members representatives of sectional interests, even without voting power, raises a question of principle to which, in my view, we should be very careful to avoid committing ourselves. If we conceded the principle of membership to the medical profession, we may not be able to stop there: similar claims will no doubt come from the organisations representing nurses, dentists, pharmacists and opticians. In my view, we should go no further than to secure that the views of interested bodies can be made known to the health authorities through some statutory machinery for consultation.

As regards the domiciliary medical services, I have been impressed with the strong objections of the medical profession to being placed 'under the local authorities'. Those objections will be almost as strongly pressed in relation to the projected new health authorities. I see no way of meeting the views of the profession except by the assumption by the State of direct responsibility for the general practitioner service, including responsibility for the provision and administration of health authorities. I realise that, in theory, the assumption by the State of responsibility for this part of the service is not without its difficulties and that especially it will be said that it makes more difficult the unification of the whole service on which so much stress has been laid. I feel sure, however, that in practice it would not be difficult to co-ordinate the services. I have sounded the associations of local authorities tentatively on the proposal and have found them not unsympathetic. I should be glad to have the authority of the committee to undertake further discussion with the local authorities and with the medical profession with a view to preparing a scheme to be submitted to a later meeting of the committee.

The Hetherington Committee's final report has not yet been received, but I understand that they are likely to recommend that no charge for any part of the hospital treatment should be made against a patient at the time of treatment. This may have a bearing on the recommendation in the Minister of Health's Paper (paragraph 42) that a hospital patient should be liable to pay, if he is able to do so, what Beveridge describes as a 'hotel cost', i.e. the cost of maintenance in hospital as distinct from the cost of treatment in hospital. In the circumstances I should like to reserve my position in this matter until I have seen the actual recommendations of the Hetherington Committee. [PRO, CAB 87/13 PR(43)45; SRO, HH101/2.]

Memorandum by Thomas Johnston, Secretary of State for Scotland, on the National Health Service, 1 September 1943.

I have had a further discussion, on an informal and non-committal basis, with representatives of Scottish local authority associations to obtain their views with regard to the proposals for a national health service which I have already described to the Committee. The discussion covered (a) the arrangements to secure a comprehensive hospital service, (b) the future of the clinic services, and (c) the organisation of the domiciliary service through general practitioners.

Hospital Service. At previous meetings the local authority representatives had expressed general acceptance of the proposal that the hospital service should be administered over larger areas through the medium of joint hospital boards consisting of representatives of the existing local hospital authorities in the area. The representatives present at my recent meeting re-affirmed this attitude. They saw no difference in principle between this proposal and arrangements under which two or more local authorities enter into joint combinations for other public health purposes—arrangements with which they are already well accustomed and which have worked with reasonable efficiency. The representatives noted that the financial arrangements to be made would probably involve the preparation of an annual budget by the joint hospital board for submission to the constituent authorities, whose prior approval would also be required to any proposal by the joint board to incur capital expenditure above a certain amount. They raised no objection to the principle of precepting which this arrangement implies. Nor was the point raised that in the deliberations of a joint hospital board one authority with a substantial hospital interest might be outvoted by the combined weight of the remaining—and less progressive—authorities. On the other hand, they considered that it would be reasonable to provide the constituent authorities of a joint hospital board with the right of appeal to the Secretary of State against the adoption of obstructive tactics by any one of the constituent members.

Clinic Services. One or two representatives—mainly medical representatives—argued the merits of placing the clinic services under the same authority as the hospital services, namely the joint board. In support of this view they stressed the importance of securing the closest possible linkage between these services for the unhampered use at the clinics of the services of consultants and specialists based on the hospitals. On the merits, this arrangement would undoubtedly have considerable advantages, but while it was generally agreed at the meeting that very close liaison must be maintained between the hospitals and the clinics, there was a heavy preponderance of opinion in favour of leaving the clinics with the existing health authorities. This attitude was based on what was felt to be the imperative need of preserving as far as possible the present structure of local government and also on a desire to continue to make use of personal interest and local knowledge in the administration of the clinic.

General Practitioner Service. The representatives frankly recognised the medical profession's hostility to being placed under the supervision of local authorities, and indeed they showed no inclination to have the general practitioner service in their respective areas under their control. They agreed on the need for a better service than at present available in the private surgery of the average general practitioner and they felt that this pointed to the encouragement of a system of group practice in health centres. They took no exception to the suggestion that responsibility for the development of health centres and the general practitioner service generally should be undertaken by a central authority in consultation with local authorities and the medical profession in the district.

Comprehensive Medical Service Scheme. After these further consultations with local authority representatives in Scotland I am fortified in the views which I have already expressed to the Committee, and feel justified in asking my colleagues to give sympathetic consideration to the proposals for a comprehensive medical service which I outlined to them at the last meeting.

Briefly, they contemplate the creation of joint hospital boards consisting of representatives of the existing health authorities (County Councils and Town Councils of Large Burghs) for the administration of a comprehensive hospital service; the creation of a regional hospital council in each of the five regions in Scotland to co-ordinate the hospital service on a regional basis; the retention of the clinic services in the hands of the existing health authorities with adequate arrangements to secure the closest possible liaison with the hospital service, including the consultant and specialist services based on hospitals; central administration of the general practitioner service, including the ultimate provision by the State of health centres for the encouragement of group practices; and the strengthening of the central authority organisation in certain respects.

In connection with the proposal to transfer the administration of the hospital service to joint hospital boards, I would point out that in the main the existing health authorities in Scotland are small authorities with resources in population and finance inadequate to support a full hospital service. In proof of this I need only explain that of the 55 existing health authorities -

12	have a population	under	25,000
20	" "	between	25,000 and 50,000
6	" "	"	50,000 and 75,000
7	" "	"	75,000 and 100,000
5	" "	"	100,000 and 200,000
5	" "	over	200,000
55			

I am conscious that these proposals can be criticised on the ground that they do not achieve that complete unification under a single authority of the hospital, clinic and domiciliary medical services which is ideally desirable. On the other hand, I believe that they will secure the degree of liaison between the services which is necessary for the efficient working of as comprehensive scheme and that they form a satisfactory basis for the discussion for inclusion in the proposed White Paper. As I indicated, the proposals are likely to be favourably received by Scottish local authorities and I am hopeful that the medical profession will not show the same unrelenting opposition to central administration of the general practitioner service as they have shown to control by the local authorities. In these circumstances, I believe my proposals are likely to attract as great a measure of agreement from the various interests concerned as is possible at the present moment. [PRO, CAB 87/13 PR(43)52; SRO, HH101/2.]

Note by Thomas Johnston, Secretary of State for Scotland, on the National Health Service (Report of the Committee on Post-War Hospital Problems), 1 September 1943.

I have now received the report of the Committee on Post-War Hospital Problems, presided over by Sir Hector Hetherington, and as arranged at the meeting of the Committee on Reconstruction Priorities on the 18th August I am circulating copies of the Report for the information of my colleagues.

The Summary of the principal conclusions and recommendations of the Hetherington Committee will be found on pages 29-31 of the Report. I would, however, draw the particular attention of my colleagues to the following points:-

(a) The Committee endorse the references already made by the Government spokesman to the possibility that in certain areas health services may be administered over wider areas by joint committees containing representatives of several local authorities, or otherwise. They think that this device would be conspicuously appropriate in relation to hospital services and they have recommended it on the assumption that these services will be based on administrative areas substantially larger than at present. (Paragraphs 20-30 of the Report)

(b) Apart from the adoption of wider administrative areas, a strong preponderance of evidence tendered to the Committee has led them to the conclusion that the future hospital system of Scotland should be developed and co-ordinated on a regional basis. They therefore recommend the division of Scotland for hospital purposes into five regions, in each of which a regional Hospitals Council should be set up.

A Regional council would consist of members nominated in equal numbers by the voluntary hospitals and local authorities in the region. In addition, there would be a small number of representatives of the medical and medical-educational interests of the region, who would possibly act in the capacity of non-voting assessors.

The functions of the Regional Councils would be of an advisory character and the Secretary of State would not approve any scheme for the hospital service of a local authority without obtaining the views of the appropriate Council. As a means of best serving this end, the Committee suggest that one of the first tasks of each Council should be to study the needs and resources of its region and prepare a provisional but comprehensive hospital plan for the assistance of the Secretary of State and of the local authorities in the region in considering hospital schemes for each administrative area.

(c) The Committee are not unanimous with regard to the financial arrangements which should be made between the State, local hospital authorities and voluntary hospitals. They do, however, agree that voluntary contributory schemes would be an inadequate basis for financing the hospital system. They reject any methods of payment for hospital treatment involving assessment and recovery of charges from patients at or near the time of treatment. They therefore recommend the institution of a compulsory contributory scheme which should be co-extensive with the social security scheme. They further recommend that the compulsory hospital contribution should give a title to free treatment, including maintenance. (Paragraphs 67-78 of the Report.) [PRO, CAB 87/13 PR(43)52; SRO, HH101/2.]

A COMPREHENSIVE HEALTH SERVICE AND THE GENERAL PRACTITIONER, 1943

The extract here is from the memorandum by Thomas Johnston, the Scottish Secretary, submitted to the Reconstruction Priorities Committee on the management of general practitioner services (see above). The Committee accepted his proposal.

Memorandum by Thomas Johnston, Secretary of State for Scotland, on the National Health Service and the General Practitioner, 14 September 1943.

The Minister of Health has submitted a paper—P.R.(43)55—to the Committee, in which he states certain difficulties which he feels about my proposals that the general practitioner service should be administered, not though joint boards or local authorities, but direct by the central department. It may assist my colleagues if I indicate the main considerations that have led me to suggest for Scotland, at least, a service centrally controlled.

In the first place, in meetings with the representatives of the medical profession and in informal contacts with individual members of it, I have been impressed by the strong resistance shown by the profession to being made part of the local government machine. They fear that the practice of their profession may be hampered by the play of local politics and prejudices and that the intimate doctor-patient relationship would be in some danger of being weakened. It is no doubt true that their fears might be based on misunderstandings but it is no use shutting our eyes to the fact that their opposition is real and unrelenting. To introduce the new service, of which the public expect so much, in that atmosphere seems to me to be fatal to its success.

In the second place, the circumstances of Scotland are in a number of respects materially different from those in England and Wales. I cannot, for example, make any suitable provision for incorporating Glasgow and Edinburgh in Joint Boards. That means that in those areas the medical profession would, in the Minister of Health's plan, be under the existing local authorities and if there is one thing crystal clear it is that general practitioners in Scotland will not submit to control by the present local authorities. The combined population of Glasgow and Edinburgh is about one-third of the population of the whole of Scotland and we should therefore start our scheme with the bitterest opposition from about one-third of the general practitioners even if we could persuade those in other parts of the country to work with a new health authority in the shape of Joint Boards. Indeed, I have considerable doubt about the readiness of general practitioners in any part of Scotland to serve under Joint Boards.

In the third place, the Scottish local authorities when I consulted them through the representative associations recently, so far from showing resentment at my proposal or regarding it as an intrusion into the sphere of local government, recognised that local authorities had never had responsibility for the general practitioner service and said clearly that they did not want it. Similarly, informal soundings in medical circles have convinced me that the medical profession would co-operate whole-heartedly in a service centrally administered.

I note that the Minister of Health regards it as fundamental that the same administrative structure should be responsible for the adequacy of the general practitioner service as the hospital and consultant services. I admit my proposals have the effect of placing the three main components of the comprehensive health service under three different administrative controls. I am far, however, from regarding this as a fatal defect. Scotland has already had considerable experience of co-ordinating the different services in the operation of the supplementary medical service scheme. Under this scheme general practitioners throughout the industrial belt refer industrial workers with incipient medical conditions to the regional medical officers of the Department of Health for Scotland, who arrange, where necessary, for diagnostic examinations by consultants and for admission to hospital. General practitioners are unanimous in their praise of the efficiency of this scheme in bringing them into close and effective contact with consultants and the hospitals. My proposal envisages an extended development of this successful co-operation, in which the regional medical officers could serve as the co-ordinating link between the general practitioner and the consultant and hospital services. I am satisfied that this machinery, together with the regional hospital councils and the medical services committees to which I referred in ... my previous paper—P.R. (43)52—would be sufficient to secure an effective co-ordination between the three parts of the service. In any event I personally would rather sacrifice some degree of apparent unity to get our reforms introduced in an atmosphere of goodwill. I feel sure that the liaison arrangements which I have in mind would be sufficient to prevent a situation such as the Minister of Health describes in ... his paper.

To sum up, my proposal remains that in Scotland the general practitioner should be placed under direct central administration with suitable local advisory and co-ordinating machinery in which both the medical profession and the local health authorities would have a part to play. From soundings I have taken I am convinced that, whatever may be decided for England and Wales, my proposal is the most appropriate for Scottish conditions and that it would be acceptable to the mass of Scottish opinion both in local authority and medical circles. I would remind my colleagues that many members of the medical profession in Scotland are accustomed to direct central administration based upon individual agreements with the State in the Highlands and Islands Medical Service. [PRO, CAB 87/13 PR(43)56; SRO, HH101/2.]

THE NATIONAL HEALTH SERVICE IN SCOTLAND, 1945

In December 1945 Aneurin Bevan, the Minister of Health, presented a memorandum to the new Labour Cabinet on his proposals to introduce a comprehensive, free National Health Service. The following extract is from the memorandum by Joseph Westwood, the Scottish Secretary, outlining the Scottish position. The Cabinet accepted his proposals.

Memorandum by Joseph Westwood, Secretary of State for Scotland, on the National Health Services in Scotland, 13 December 1945.

My colleagues have before them a paper by the Minister of Health (C.P. (45) 339) describing his proposals for a National Health Service in England and Wales. With the general shape of these proposals I am in full agreement.

The same objectives and general principles must govern the service in Scotland, but differences of geography and local government structure require certain modifications in the detailed administrative arrangements chiefly in the local organisation. In this note I indicate very briefly the application of the Minister's proposals to Scotland, mentioning in paragraphs 5 and 6 the principal modifications.

Central Organisation.

The Secretary of State in Scotland will take the place of the Minister of Health at the centre. He will absorb the administrative functions of the Scottish Board of Control, leaving the Board, as in England, with its quasi-judicial functions relating to the liberty of the subject.

Scottish central advisory machinery will be established on the same lines as set out in paragraphs 3 and 4 of the statement appended to the Minister's Paper. Scotland will also have its own Central Committee on the Distribution of Medical Practices, working as described in paragraphs 41-42 of the statement.

Administrative arrangements will be made for the liaison between Scottish bodies and the corresponding bodies in England and Wales.

Local Organisation.

Health services in Scotland are in the hands of 55 major local authorities. This compares with only 145 major authorities in England and Wales, so that the average Scottish authority is smaller in population and resources. In consequence the following departures from the Minister's proposals are necessary:-

(a) In order to avoid complicated inter-area arrangements and to secure flexibility and economy, the ambulance service in Scotland will be associated with the hospital service and administered by the Regional Hospitals Board (of which there will be 5 in Scotland). Existing voluntary organisations will be utilised under contract, and air ambulance facilities for the remote districts in the north and west of Scotland will also be included.

(b) Instead of establishing a Local Executive Committee for the family practitioner services in each major health authority area in Scotland (as proposed for England and Wales), burghs other than the four cities will, for this purpose, be included with the counties in which they are situated; and some Committees may cover two or more adjacent counties.

Local authorities have not hitherto been concerned with the general practitioner service, and in Scotland they have not pressed for any part of this responsibility in future. I feel, therefore, that progress could best be made with the development of Health Centres by adhering to the White Paper proposal that the provision, equipment and maintenance of Health Centres in Scotland should be the direct responsibility of the Secretary of State, instead of being the responsibility of local authorities as in England and Wales. The Secretary of State will be empowered to delegate any of his functions in this connection to a local authority. This was accepted both by the Scottish local authorities and by the medical profession in Scotland in the discussions following on the White Paper.

Finance.

The Minister gives, in paragraph 52 of his proposals, estimates of past and future expenditure on health services. Corresponding figures for Scotland, on the same assumptions, are as follows:-

1938-9

Expenditure by -	£ million.	Met by -	£ million.
Local authorities	4.3	N.H.I. contribution	1.5
Voluntary Hospitals	1.4	Taxes	0.4
Central Departments (Highland and Islands medical benefit, &c.)	1.9	Rates	4.4
		Voluntary sources	1.3
	7.6		7.6

NEW SERVICE

Expenditure on -	£ million.	Met by -	£ million.
Hospitals and specialists	10.5	Insurance contributions	4.3
Local authority services	1.3	Rates	0.7
Health Centres	0.2	Taxes	12.0
General Practitioner, dental and eye services	4.5		
Compensation and superannuation	0.5		
	17.0		17.0

If my colleagues agree that these proposals are generally on the right lines I shall proceed to meet the representative bodies of the Scottish local authorities and others for some discussion of the principal points, in the same way as the Minister of Health proposes to proceed in England. On major questions affecting the medical profession and the voluntary hospitals, whose representative organisations are on a United Kingdom basis, the Minister and I should jointly meet delegations representative of the whole country. [PRO, CAB 129/5 CP(45)345.]

THE NATIONAL HEALTH SERVICE IN SCOTLAND, 1946

In February 1946, Aneurin Bevan, the Minister of Health, presented a memorandum to the Cabinet on his negotiations with local authorities and the medical profession. He also proposed to separate university teaching hospitals from local health administration. The following is an extract from the memorandum by Joseph Westwood, the Scottish Secretary, outlining his Scottish negotiations. The Cabinet accepted his proposals.

Memorandum by Joseph Westwood, Secretary of State for Scotland, on the National Health Service in Scotland, 1 March 1946.

Scottish Consultations

The Minister of Health has reported in his paper C.P. (46) 86 on those consultations about our National Health Service proposals that have been conducted on a United Kingdom basis. The Scottish Local Authority Associations have not taken part in the United Kingdom discussion, but I have consulted than separately and I do not think that we need expect serious opposition in principle from the Scottish local authorities to the transfer of their hospitals to the State.

My consultations with the local authorities, the medical profession, and other interests in Scotland on the special Scottish aspects of the proposals have shown general support for the points of difference from England and Wales described in my paper C.P. (45) 345 of the 13th December last—the administration of ambulance services by the hospital organisation instead of local health authorities; the establishment of Executive Councils for the family practitioner services on the basis of geographical counties instead of for each local authority; and the provision and maintenance of health centres by the Secretary of State in the first place, instead of by local health authorities.

Teaching Hospitals

One other special Scottish point has been raised. The hospital facilities used for clinical teaching in Scotland include a much larger proportion of the total hospital resources than in England and Wales. Thus the adoption in its present form of the proposal to establish separate Boards of Governors for teaching hospitals would exclude from the direct concern of the Regional Boards the operation of a very substantial and most important part of the hospital service. In some quarters the view has been expressed, particularly by the local authorities, that in Scotland the Regional Boards should be more directly concerned with the teaching hospitals than the powers exercised by the Board of Governors would permit. In considering modifications to meet this point of view, which I am inclined to share, I will, of course, take care to safeguard the necessary independence of medical education. When the English Bill has been published I propose to discuss the matter further with the Scottish Universities and other interests. [PRO, CAB 129/7 CP(46)89.]

THE SCOTTISH HOSPITAL PROGRAMME, 1948

The following extract is from the Department of Health's memorandum to the Treasury's Investment Programme Committee Working Party on its future plans for hospital and specialist services. The Committee accepted the proposal for an increase in capital expenditure during 1949, but deferred a final decision on larger hospital projects until its next investment review.

Memorandum by the Department of Health, on the Capital Investment Programme, 1948 to 1952; Health Services Scotland, 5 May 1948.

Hospital and Specialist Services

Existing Limits of Planning

So far, the hospital building programme has consisted of proposals put forward by individual and independent hospital authorities, municipal and voluntary. Under the National Health Service, new hospital provision will be a matter for the Department and the five Scottish Hospital Boards. It will, therefore, be possible to have complete integration of the hospital building programme so as to secure that new building is undertaken where the need is most urgent.

1948 Programme

2. As a beginning the Regional Boards were asked to comment on the draft 1948 programme. It has been prepared in accordance with the policy laid down in the White Paper on Capital Investment in 1948 and provides for an expenditure of £765,000 as compared with £695,000 for 1947.

3. It consists almost wholly of improvements and alterations to existing hospitals—to provide additional maternity accommodation and better nursing and domestic quarters and to bring the war-time hospitals up to peace-time standard. The only new unit of any size is one 100 bed maternity hospital at Paisley due to begin this summer.

1949 Programme

4. Many of the projects in the 1948 programme are still in the early stages, so that they will run on into 1949 and as they build up demand a bigger effort in 1949 than in 1948.[1] To allow for this £800,000 must be included in the programme for schemes carried forward from 1948.

5. Experience has shown that there are always many small projects (under £2,000) which have to be put in hand at relatively short notice, some essential maintenance, some to tide-over until major development can be undertaken. For these about £75,000 was allowed in 1947 and £100,000 in 1948. The advent of the new hospital authorities is bound to create demands for works of this kind as much of the initial reorganisation will involve alterations—for example, to provide clinics in district and cottage hospitals in which the services of specialists can be provided to reduce the pressure on the main centres and obviate long journeys, and to provide offices for the Board of Management in

1 [Note in memorandum:] The 1947 and 1948 programmes include no allowance for maintenance and other work undertaken by the staffs of hospital authorities. The value is probably not less than £650,000 and a labour force of 500.

the main hospital of the group. Not less than £150,000 can be allowed for these smaller schemes in 1949.

6. Thirdly, some allowance should be made for projects over £2,000 starting in 1949. The projects to be started in 1948 account for £450,000 in the programme for this year. On that reckoning the minimum for 1949 seems to be £300,000

7. The 1949 Programme, therefore, would consist of:-

(i) Projects continuing from 1948	£	800,000
(ii) Minor Projects		150,000
(iii) Projects to be begun in 1949		300,000
(iv) Maintenance		450,000
Total		£1,700,000

8. This programme will include a considerable variety of work. In addition to the kinds referred to in paragraph 4, it will include:- (a) The improvement of poorhouses transferred to the new hospital authorities. Most of these are approaching a century old and will need better ancillary staff accommodation if they are to be used as hospitals for any length of time. (b) Extended out-patients facilities to permit additional consultant work by specialists and to obviate long delays and crowding. This seems to be the point at which the existing services are most vulnerable to criticism in the new conditions. (c) The provision of admissions blocks at mental hospitals to allow of the early treatment of mental illness separately from the chronic cases. This should in time reduce the numbers of the latter class and the burden of providing accommodation and services for them over a long period of years. (d) Improved laboratory and radiological facilities. The integrated laboratory service, based mainly on the hospitals, for which the new Act provides, will entail replacement of some of the existing small units by extensions to the larger units and also new units, which are needed, for example, in Inverness, Fife and the Borders. Many of the radiology and radiotherapy departments are working to capacity. Re-equipment and expansion are already overdue and the new Service is certain to increase the demands. (e) Increased provision for the teaching of medical students and medical auxiliaries. The tendency is to use an increasing number of hospitals for undergraduate medical teaching. At present, these hospitals lack facilities for the purpose. (f) A recent survey has confirmed that most of the general hospitals have no proper facilities for medical rehabilitation. If patients are to be brought back to a state of fitness in which they can resume full activity, a substantial expansion of physiotherapy departments and gymnasia will have to be put in hand.

9. To make a reasonable start with these various lines of development, a provision of £300,000 is very modest and the total 1949 programme outlined in paragraph 8 seems to be the irreducible minimum for that year.

10. If it is practicable to expand this programme, the main object should be to accelerate the start of some of the larger hospital projects which are now beginning to take shape. Some of these may be mentioned briefly:- (i) A maternity hospital in North Lanarkshire at first of 60 and then 120 beds. There is no modern maternity unit in the whole of this county with a population of half a million. (ii) A combined hospital of some 900 beds to serve Dumfries and Galloway. This would be built in successive blocks—maternity, infectious diseases, general—to replace a number of inadequate and obsolete units scattered over the three counties concerned. (iii) A State institution for defectives. There is no specific provision in Scotland for defectives with criminal tendencies. Some are housed with other defectives, some are in prison and for others there is no institutional accommodation of any kind. Temporarily about 150 will be housed in buildings which were erected as a Criminal Lunatic Asylum although these are badly needed for their original purpose. The intention is to erect a new institution for 400 defectives on the lines of Rampton and Moss Side. (iv) A general hospital in Dundee. The municipal general hospital is an unsatisfactory poorhouse conversion. The voluntary general hospital is urgently in need of reconstruction. The two together are inadequate as the centre for a region and as the main teaching hospitals for an expanding medical centre. (v) A chest hospital for Renfrewshire. This is needed to replace a number of small obsolete and isolated units which now present a hopeless problem of staffing and cannot provide modern standards of treatment.

11. The total capital investment involved in these five units would be of the order of £6 millions. None of them is likely to be ready to start until the latter part of 1949 and the average period of construction is unlikely to be less than four years.

12. Additional provision could also be made in 1949 in the categories referred to in paragraphs 4 and 9. The scale of work provided for is hardly above the present level and it is certain that the Regional Boards will be anxious to undertake a good deal more. If possible, another £50,000 should be allowed for small projects and £150,000 for larger projects.

13. With these additions, the 1949 programme would be as follows:-

(i) Projects continuing from 1948	£ 800,000
(ii) Minor Projects	200,000
(iii) Projects to be begun in 1949 excluding major new developments	450,000
(iv) Major new developments (of the kind referred to in paragraph 11)	100,000
(v) Maintenance	450,000
Total	£2,000,000

Programmes for 1950, 1951 and 1952

The programmes for 1950, 1951 and 1952 can only be conjectural at this stage. The carry-over of work from previous years should increase, the rate of increase depending on the rate at which major new developments are brought into the programme. To that extent the later programmes are governed by decisions taken in regard to 1949. What follows assumed that the 1949 programme will be as in paragraph 8 and that the major projects referred to in paragraph 11 will come in from 1949. The allowance for minor projects cannot be reduced below the 1948 level. On this basis the programmes would be of the following order:-

	1950	1951	1952
Major projects	£1,750,000	£2,250,000	£2,250,000
Minor projects (under £2,000)	150,000	150,000	150,000
Maintenance	450,000	450,000	450,000
Total	£2,350,000	£2,850,000	£2,850,000

[PRO, CAB 134/446 IPC(WP)(48)73.]

THE NATIONAL HEALTH SERVICE AND PUBLIC OPINION, 1948

In autumn 1948 the Cabinet asked Aneurin Bevan, the Minister of Health, and Arthur Woodburn, the Scottish Secretary, to prepare a review of the new National Health Service, inaugurated on 5 July. The following extract is from the memorandum submitted by Woodburn. The Cabinet took note of its contents.

Memorandum by Arthur Woodburn, Secretary of State for Scotland, on the National Health Service, 29 December 1948.

In Scotland, as in England, the new administrative organisation has been brought into being with remarkable smoothness. On the latest information I have, 94 per cent. of the population were on the doctors' lists at the end of October. Almost all the general practitioners, some 98 per cent., were taking part in the Service and it is only in some of the cities that there are still a few doctors engaged entirely in private practice. Nearly all the 1,200 dentists in general practice in Scotland have joined the Service; nearly all the 1,800 chemists and 800 opticians are taking part. During the first four months of the new Service 10 per cent. of the population (about 500,000 persons) received glasses. All the hospitals in Scotland of any consequence, with the exception of three Roman Catholic mental deficiency institutions and a Red Cross Sanatorium, have been taken over—425 in all with 62,000 beds.

One would not expect Scots to be slow in taking advantage of the free services provided but in considering the present very large demand I think we have to remember, first, that a good many people postponed the purchase of spectacles, dentures or other appliances until after 5th July and secondly, that we are now meeting, often once and for all, genuine needs which people were unable to afford before. For example, we have had one-legged patients coming for an artificial leg who never had one before. We have sometimes had the tragedy that it is now too late to fit limbs and all we can do is to supply them with wheeled chairs. I am sure that for many appliances we are now facing the peak of the demand but, whether that is so or not, the very magnitude of the demand is significant of the need for the new Service and of the gaps that formerly existed. There are, of course, abuses which it will take time and possibly some tightening up to eliminate, but in relation to the whole they are very small.

The estimated cost to the Exchequer of the Service in Scotland is approximately as follows:-

	5th July, 1948, to 31st March, 1949 (nine months) £ million	Financial year 1949-1950 £ million
Hospitals and Specialists	15.5	25.3
Doctors (General Practitioners)	4.0	5.3
Dentists	2.3	4.0
Chemists	1.5	2.0
Ophthalmic Services	1.5	2.3
Local Authority Services	1.0	1.1
Miscellaneous (Executive Council Administration, Superannuation, &c.)	1.2	1.9
Gross Charge against Exchequer	27.0	41.9
Appropriations in Aid (Contribution from National Insurance Fund Charges, &c.)	6.0	7.4
Net Charge against Exchequer	21.0	34.5

The figure for 1949-50 works out at 2s. 8d. per head of the population per week.

A rough estimate of what was spent in Scotland before 5th July on the kind of things that are now provided in the National Health Service is £25 million. The gap between costs of the old services and the new seems to be slightly greater in Scotland than in England but this is what I would expect. There is no doubt that the levels of remuneration—which account for so much of the total expenditure—tended in Scotland to be lower for all classes of worker in the Health Service than they were in England and Wales. I have thought it right in a National Service for which everyone is paying and to the benefits of which everyone is equally entitled that the same services should carry the same rates of remuneration throughout the United Kingdom and the adoption of this principle is an essential condition of the working of the new Whitley procedure on an United Kingdom basis.

I am impressed by the extent to which the total expenditure on the National Health Service is governed by the levels of remuneration for the health service personnel and it seems to me, therefore, important that the Health Departments should devote particular care and attention to the negotiations which take place under the new Whitley procedure so as to avoid excessive expenditure.

It is too early perhaps to make any general assessment of the positive achievements of the new Service, as distinct from the undoubted success we have had in putting it effectively into operation, but it would be easy to undertaken the benefits to the ordinary man and women of having ready access to all these services and the relief which many of the professional people feel at the removal of financial considerations in deciding on the treatment of their patients. And, in the hospital services, there is already definite evidence that the new regional organisation will bring the most highly skilled resources to the help of the individual patient, especially in the smaller towns and villages, in a way that they have never and could not have been brought before. I quote for what it is worth a passage from a recent report from a Regional Hospital Board:-

'The impression has been gained that there is a quiet but genuine satisfaction on the part of the general public that the hospital and specialist service is now more freely available to all, irrespective of social position. There is already evidence of the wisdom of vesting in one body the general oversight of the hospitals in the Region in the fact that the Regional Office, with its knowledge of the hospital resources of the Region, has been instrumental in arranging the appropriate hospitalisation of many cases whose admission to hospital in other circumstances would have involved considerable delay and difficulty.' [PRO, CAB 129/31 CP(48)308.]

NATIONAL HEALTH SERVICE EXPENDITURE, 1949

In early 1949 the Treasury became alarmed at the prospect of a £50 million supplementary estimate in the UK Health Service budget for 1949-50 and the Cabinet invited the Health Ministers to review 'progress'. The extract below is from the memorandum by Arthur Woodburn, the Scottish Secretary, on the Scottish position. Although both Ministers vehemently opposed the imposition of charges, the Cabinet agreed to delay a decision on the estimate until the Treasury and the Health Departments met to discuss further mechanisms of financial control. Woodburn thought that he would require an additional £5 million.

Memorandum by Arthur Woodburn, Secretary of State for Scotland, on the National Health Service, 10 May 1949.

I find myself in the same position as the Minister of Health, obliged to report that the money provided in the 1949-50 estimates for the National Health Service in Scotland is almost certainly inadequate to enable the service to be carried on without restriction of facilities to the public. These estimates provide for gross expenditure of £39.6 million, which is £2.3 million less than the figures quoted in my earlier paper (CP (49) 308), the difference being accounted for mainly by cuts relating to the hospital and specialist service and to the dental service, which were suggested by the Treasury.

There are two main reasons for the inadequacy of the estimates. The first, which chiefly affects the general practitioner services and especially the dental service, is that demand has not receded as far as I had anticipated from the high level of last autumn. In the dental service, cases involving dentures (and these are the most expensive) are now coming in at the rate of half a million a year: this is only two-thirds of the rate last October, and I feel sure that it must fall further still. On the other hand, cases of conservative treatment are still running nearly at the 750,000 a year level, and I do not think much decrease, if any, is to be looked for. In cutting the original estimate, I relied partly on a more rapid reduction of demand, and partly on the further reduction in the scale of fees, which cannot now be effective for much more than half the cases coming for payment this year. It is thus clear that the final estimate is well short of the mark, although at this early stage I cannot put a figure on the deficit.

As regards the other general practitioner services, I think that, while the present claim by the doctors is seriously overstated, we shall be obliged to concede something to them: the family doctor, who is after all the foundation of the whole service. The cut in fees for oculists and opticians will, I hope, make it possible to keep very close to the estimated figure for the eye service: especially as the current demand (which is running at the rate of almost one million sight tests, 20 per cent. below the October peak) surely cannot be maintained for another twelve months. For the chemists, I am afraid my estimated provision is inadequate, even allowing for minor savings and precautions against abuse. The volume of prescribing now seems to have been abnormally low at the start, and delays in making payments last year mean that arrears have to be met in the current year.

The difficulty in estimating the cost of the hospital and specialist services is not related so much to speculative assessments of demand as in the case of the general practitioner services, but reliable figures of past experience in the hospital field have, as the Minister of Health points out, been very hard to obtain. I would like to emphasise that as the new hospital organisation settles down and the accounts come forward in a standard form for all hospitals, the hospital authorities and my Department will, for the first time, have precise and detailed information on hospital expenditure. It will be possible to frame next year's estimates on the basis of firm figures; and—equally important—from the costings returns to detect and inquire into all exceptional rates of expenditure.

Even so, the main items for which shortages are likely to appear in this year's estimates are the items for salaries and wages of staff whose remuneration has been improved by recent discussions. For nursing staff alone, the improvements about to be effected will cost in Scotland nearly £1 million in the current year. For student nurses, the recent increase granted after the estimates had been framed will cost £¼ million, and domestic increases associated with these improvements will cost another £¼ million. We have had particular difficulty in assessing the cost of the specialist services, for the doctors concerned are only now being graded: but having regard especially to the need for retrospective payments in these cases right back to 5th July, I am afraid that the provision for this item is about £½ million short.

While it is not yet possible to frame really accurate forecasts of the total expenditure for the year, it is clear that increased charges of this order cannot be met out of the original estimate without very substantial savings in other directions. These would involve not only suspension of maintenance and development work, but in all probability the closing of wards and dismissal of staff as well. It is my firm view that we should not be afraid of capital expenditure on such items as redesign of working space and improved equipment in hospitals, which by saving labour can pay their own way as well as provide better services for the patients. Similarly, capital expenditure on improved out-patient departments would be an economy in the long run, for, given proper amenities at these places, the needs of many patients could be met without admitting them to much more costly in-patient care. Apart from these special cases, I think we shall have to increase the volume of capital expenditure: we have taken over very large capital assets, and already there has been practically no replacement for ten years. The present rate of expenditure is short of net replacement, to say nothing of expansion.

I therefore associate myself with the Minister's hope that our colleagues will agree to the provision of additional money, failing which we shall need guidance as to the services to be selected for curtailment. [PRO, CAB 129/34 CP(49)106.]

INVESTMENT IN THE SCOTTISH HEALTH SERVICES, 1949

In October 1949, in response to the devaluation of sterling, the Government agreed to a substantial reduction in public investment. The extract here is from the Department of Health's memorandum to the Investment Programmes Committee Working Party setting out a revised health services plan for 1951-2.

Memorandum by the Department of Health for Scotland, on Scottish Health Services: Investment Review, 1951-2, 30 December 1949.

The following tables show the estimated actual expenditure on health services in Scotland in 1948 and 1949, the programme for 1950, and alternative programmes for the years 1951 and 1952. By far the greatest part of the expenditure is on the hospital and specialist service, other items accounting for £.1m. under new work and £.1m. under repairs and maintenance, with further £.1m. for burial grounds, in 1949, and being retained at that figure in the suggested programmes.

	New Works	*Repairs and Maintenance*	*Plant*	*Burial Grounds*	*Total*
1948	0.9	0.9	-	-	1.8
1949	1.1	1.2	-	0.1	2.4
1950	1.4	1.2	-	0.1	2.7
(a) 1951	1.4	1.2	-	0.1	2.7
1952	1.4	1.2	-	0.1	2.7
(b) 1951	1.9	1.3	-	0.1	3.3
1952	2.1	1.3	-	0.1	3.5

While the estimated actual expenditure in 1949 is slightly below the approved programme for the year (£2.6m.), repairs and maintenance have accounted for a larger proportion of the total. Because of the obsolete conditions of many hospital buildings, the demands for maintenance work will continue to be heavy and no reduction below the 1949 figure is possible in estimating for the next three years.

The programme under alternative (a) is a repetition in each year of the 1950 figures. While it is expected that continuing work on projects begun before the beginning of 1950 to the value of about £1m. will be included in that year's investment, a full reduction to the rate set out in I.P.C.(49)6 should be achieved over the year.

The programme under alternative (b) is an apportionment, without alteration for any change in prices, of the totals proposed in I.P.C.(49)2, which recommend an investment of £3m. in 1950 rising to £3.5m. in 1952.

Hospital work, being by far the largest part of this programme, is likely to suffer most from reduction to the investment level of alternative (a). At that level it is impossible to start a single new hospital of any size and the development of the Service on a regional basis, a major objective of the National Health Service legislation, in so far as it requires new building, will be brought to a standstill. This is a serious situation which should, if possible, be avoided. Outside the hospital service, the highly desirable health centre experimental work will be reduced to a minimum and work to carry out the Government's policy in providing accommodation for old people may, in the latter part of the period under consideration, have to be held in check. [PRO, CAB 134/452 IPC(WP)(49)112.]

CHARGES, PRIORITIES AND THE HEALTH SERVICE, 1950

In March 1950, the Cabinet resumed its consideration of Health Service finance. The following is an extract from the memorandum by Hector McNeil, the Scottish Secretary, on the matter. In the event, with a memorandum from Aneurin Bevan, the Minister of Health, outlining his objection to any charges, the Cabinet remitted the matter to a ministerial committee under the Chairmanship of the Prime Minister.

Memorandum by Hector McNeil, Secretary of State for Scotland, on the National Health Service (Scotland), 31 March 1950.

I understand that the Chancellor of the Exchequer seeks to recover from patients for treatment some £42 millions. This represents on the Great Britain total net estimate a recovery of over 10 per cent; and the same percentage applied to expenditure on Scottish services means that we should seek to recover in Scotland the sum of about £4½ millions. I understand and accept the Chancellor's contention that a recovery of approximately this size is necessitated by the present state of our national economy. There is, as far as I can see, no hope of achieving reduction at all remotely approximating to this total by economies or by tightening of the administration. It means that we must admit publicly, with all its political consequences, that we are deserting the conception of a universal free service.

Another fact must be faced. There is a conflict between the rate of expenditure within which the Chancellor proposes the National Health Service should run and the savings which can be secured in the year 1950/51. It is quite possible, as I seek to show, to secure the saving of 10 per cent in the 1951/2 expenditure by taking several drastic decisions; but whatever we may decide upon there is still a substantial backlog of orders in dental, ophthalmic and other appliances which plainly we must discharge under existing arrangements. By our calculations no proposed economies on these sectors of the service would begin to show until about January of next year.

One other point should be made. I still am not persuaded that we can make reliable estimates of what demands upon our ophthalmic and dental services will be in twelve months from now. There are some signs that demand is dropping. For example, I am told that sight-testing in Scotland for the first quarter of this year is only 55 per cent of what it was in the same quarter of the previous year. On the other hand, I must admit that there is no apparent diminution of the demand in Scotland upon the dental service. Nevertheless it may prove to be true that later in the year our figures will show how we might keep within the level of expenditure which the Chancellor postulates by less drastic cuts than at present seem necessary. So that, even if the Cabinet agree that the Chancellor should be authorised to announce a ceiling to our expenditure, there are arguments, I submit, for deciding that we should not at this stage give any indication what methods we will use to ensure that we will be running at the rate proposed by the Chancellor and what is the earliest practicable date, i.e. January, 1951.

In our search for the economies, three broad principles, I suggest, should guide us. We should economise least at the expense of those services which bring us a potential return in the shape of improved national health, e.g. it probably is better to give children priority of treatment if we cannot provide for all. Secondly, having decided upon that, we should also seek to recover where the hardship will be least felt, e.g. there will always be classes we want to exempt, such as old age pensioners, widows, and the completely unemployed. Thirdly, in attempting to be guided by these two principles, we would still rationally search for methods that can be best justified from the political point of view.

It is most tempting to look for savings in the hospital service since the estimates here amount to about 60 per cent of the gross expenditure. My colleagues, however, I submit, must appreciate that this is the area in which least economy can be achieved unless the service is to be cut. I am quite sure that my colleagues, like myself, would not for a moment justify the shutting down of wards or the reduction of essential staff. If this is accepted, then the possibility of savings inside the hospital service becomes small indeed.

Minor savings are, of course, possible. For example we can restrict the reimbursement of travelling expenses of patients more narrowly than at present. But the total cost of this item in Scotland is not more than £150,000 and other practical economies within the present policy framework are of the same kind of dimension. The best prospect seems to be a return to the tentative suggestion of the Beveridge Report that there might be a 'hotel charge' for hospital in-patients. Even here there are administrative difficulties. We could hardly expect in any circumstances to collect a charge from long-stay patients such as those in mental hospitals and mental deficiency institutions and this type of case occupies about 40 per cent of our hospital beds. Moreover it should be remembered that [national insurance] sick benefit is reduced by approximately 10/- per week after eight weeks in hospital. At most, therefore, we could only recover for this period.

The general practitioner service seems to me more likely to yield a number of economies without hardship, although the size of each economy is relatively small, e.g. there is the proposed shilling charge for prescriptions. I still am not certain that this was the best initial method of seeking to secure a saving. Moreover, we are already committed to it and politically it would seem to me almost as difficult to escape from it as to implement it. A scheme has been worked out which gives exemption to old age pensioners, people in receipt of National Assistance, and disability pensioners. This would give us about £500,000, which the Chancellor has already taken into account.

Then there is action to restrict the prescribing of proprietary drugs, to which the Minister of Health has already drawn our attention and upon which a report is expected from the Committee of which Mr Henry Cohen is the Chairman. There is also another idea which I still think quite reasonable, although I have not so far found my colleagues receptive. I think there is a range of drugs such as aspirin, laxatives, cold creams and proprietary ointments and articles such as cotton wool and adhesive tapes, which could be banned from prescription and which might yield a figure approaching half as much as the 1/- charge. Together these items might give us a saving of between £500,000 and £600,000.

The family doctor service in Scotland costs £5½ millions a year, mostly by way of capitation payments to the doctors. I think I must resist any attempt to save here. But the general dental service costs almost as much—about £5 millions in Scotland in a full year—and on broad grounds I feel most strongly that this is open to criticism as not representing equal value for money. We are seeking to make a cut of about 10 per cent in dentists' fees; which might save £500,000 a year. But the real trouble in Scotland at any rate is that demand for treatment is far in excess of the capacity of the dental profession, and the present arrangements do not concentrate the limited amount of dental care available on those groups in the population who stand to benefit most by it—children and adolescents. There is no prospect that the number of dentists will increase sufficiently to meet the demand for many years to come.

There is, therefore, much to be said for taking our courage in both hands and cutting back the dental service to cover only the most important groups. Mothers could be looked after through local authority maternity services with dental services attached, and children up to school leaving age could be taken care of by school health arrangements, while to cover adolescents we might retain the general dental service for people up to the age of 21.... The saving from this scheme would be about £2½ millions.

However, if this is thought to be too drastic, another remedy would be to impose a flat rate charge of £1 for the supply of dentures. This would bring in approximately £500,000 a year; and exemption for the same classes as before would, it is thought, be offset by the deterrent charges lowering the demand for inessential dental services. A further modification, which I scarcely think worth while advocating, would be to limit the charge only to the replacement of dentures; this would bring in something like £200,000 a year.

There remains the supplementary ophthalmic service. This is estimated to cost in Scotland some £2½ millions in 1950-51. Under the original Acts, this is explicitly a temporary service, to operate until such time as the hospitals can take over. Abolition of the service now would not save the whole sum included in the current estimate, because a proportion of the demand would in fact be met through the hospital service; but the inconvenience of resort to the hospitals as at present organised, together with the actual economy in provision through hospitals, is such that the saving might be put at not less than £1½ millions a year. Mothers and children should continue to have their needs met through the local authorities and school health service.

Short of suspending the service, there is again the possibility of levying a flat rate charge, say 10/- per pair of spectacles. On the assumption that exemption for the same classes as before would be cancelled out by the deterrent effect of the charge, the annual saving would be approximately £400,000. Or we might limit the classes of spectacles frames supplied free of charge to the less expensive varieties at present in use. This would avoid any need for exemptions and would not even need legislation, but the saving would be considerably less.

To sum up:- (1) the savings which the Chancellor contemplates could not be achieved in the current year unless by repudiating the contracts we have already made with a great section of the population; (2) in any year the saving he contemplated could not, as far as I can see, be achieved merely by charges and administrative economies; (3) savings of the kind he desires could be achieved by limiting the dental service and by suspending the ophthalmic service as I have described.

The political effects would, of course, be substantial, but it seems equally true to me that the political effects of continuing at the present rate of expenditure would also be substantial. Smaller savings, it is fair to say, of perhaps about £2 millions a year in Scotland, could be achieved by imposing charges which are more or less nominal, but even these, it seems to me, would have political repercussions which might not be very different. We ought, therefore, to be prepared to re-organise the scheme to give us reasonable savings.

However, since the 10 per cent saving which the Chancellor postulates cannot be effected in the current year, and since in six months time we may be better able to estimate the future level of demand upon the dental and ophthalmic services (and the demand on the ophthalmic service is already diminishing), there certainly are arguments that it would be expedient meanwhile to defer taking or announcing final decisions in favour of any substantial departure from the principle of a comprehensive National Health Service. [PRO, CAB 129/39 CP(50)57.]

TUBERCULOSIS IN SCOTLAND AND SWISS SANATORIA TREATMENT, 1950-1

In Summer 1950 some press publicity was given to the large number of empty beds in Swiss Sanatoria for TB patients. The first extract here is from a letter of Hector McNeil, the Scottish Secretary, to Sir Stafford Cripps, the Chancellor of the Exchequer, on the matter. Hugh Gaitskell replied on Cripps's behalf and indicated that he would consider the proposal if its cost could be 'met within the ceiling'. The second extract is from a personal note McNeil then sent. The third is from a subsequent letter of McNeil and the fourth the reply of Douglas Jay, Gaitskell's Financial Secretary. At that time, with a proportionately lower waiting list, Aneurin Bevan, the Minister of Health, remained unenthusiastic about the scheme. The following February McNeil agreed with Hilary Marquand, the new Minster of Health, a package of economies within the 'ceiling' and a UK scheme to send 400 TB patients to Switzerland, half from the Scottish waiting list.

Letter of Hector McNeil, Secretary of State for Scotland, to Sir Stafford Cripps, the Chancellor of the Exchequer, on Swiss Hospital Treatment for Scottish Tuberculosis Patients, 1 August 1950.

Ever since the War, the incidence of respiratory tuberculosis in Scotland has been a major reproach to our health services. In most countries of Western Europe, including enemy occupied countries, notifications and deaths from this disease quite quickly resumed the general downward trend of pre-war years. But in Scotland the number of cases notified has shown a continuous increase each year since 1939, and even the death rate showed no improvement until 1949. The situation has been worst in Glasgow and the surrounding industrial districts where it has intensified the housing problem—as the Treasury has recognised more than once in agreeing to finance additional allocations of houses to the areas most affected.

The need for hospital beds has far outrun the available accommodation. There are fewer than 5,000 beds available for respiratory tuberculosis in Scottish hospitals, and the waiting list for admission has risen from 1,639 at the end of 1945 to 2,877 at the end of 1949. These figures represent not only hardship and suffering for individual patients, but are evidence of an increasing number of foci of infection in the population liable to give rise to yet more cases. We have done what we can to increase the hospital beds, but the limiting factor is nursing staff. By using beds in fever hospitals and in general hospitals, where nurses are already available, we have done a good deal to increase the facilities and we are still actively pursuing this policy. The most recent figures of notifications and deaths (for the first half of this year) suggest a more favourable trend for the country as a whole, and it may be that the worst is over. But this is speculation, and some medical opinion considers that no significance can be attached to the figures yet; certainly public concern with the position is increasing rather than diminishing in intensity.

It is in this atmosphere that the recent publicity about surplus sanatorium beds in Switzerland has broken. Especially in Scotland we must expect that public opinion will fasten on the contrast between empty beds in Switzerland and waiting lists here. In the past there have been currency difficulties about expenditure in Switzerland, and in addition there is no power under the National Health Service Acts to incur expenditure on treatment abroad. I understand however, from discussion my officers have had with the Treasury, that the currency issue would not now be an insuperable obstacle to spending say £250,000 a year on maintaining patients in 250 beds in Swiss sanatoria; and that the Treasury would be prepared to authorise expenditure in anticipation of amending legislation, which would be drawn tightly so as to restrict expenditure of this kind to respiratory tuberculosis (by reference to the need to remove foci of infection from the population), and which would be temporary in form on the expectation that facilities and needs in this country could be brought into balance in a period of three or four years. But the Treasury felt bound to stipulate that the expenditure involved should be found within the present National Health Service ceiling.

Now I cannot promise to do this. I am making all possible economies within the present policy framework. I am sure there are no major savings possible within the hospital service, but I am impressing on hospital authorities the need for looking twice at every penny before spending it and taking trouble to achieve every economy however small. Even so, as I have told you and repeatedly told the Prime Minister's Committee, I believe a supplementary estimate is inevitable this year for the National Health Service in Scotland as a whole, mainly on account of continuing high demand for dental treatment—uncontrollable without power to make charges, and persistently high volume of prescribing—in which public demand plays a big part, although formal responsibility rests with the doctors.

Yet I think there is a very strong case, in the light of what I have said above, for authorising expenditure on the treatment of suitable selected patients at State expense in Swiss sanatoria, on the assumption that expert investigation confirms the availability of beds and nursing staff and endorses the standards of care provided. For the current year £100,000 would be an outside figure on expenditure for Scottish patients, and for the next year or two we might go up to £250,000.

I should be happy to discuss this question with you as soon as you have been able to consider it. Nye Bevan should no doubt have an opportunity of joining in any such discussion, and I am sending him a copy of this letter. [SRO, HH102/316.]

Personal Note of Hector McNeil, Secretary of State for Scotland to Hugh Gaitskell, Minister of State for Economic Affairs, on Swiss Hospital Treatment for Scottish Tuberculosis Patients, 26 August 1950.

I should stress that I am not replying to you officially. This is a personal letter; but I hope I may be writing you again officially on the subject. I must say, however, that I feel I am being a little unfairly treated. You and I both know that it is quite impossible to get inside the ceiling expenditure for this year. I have repeatedly made this plain both at the Cabinet and at the Prime Minister's Committee, and, indeed, have gone further and tried to show you the only way of getting inside the ceiling.

Now, my advice has not been accepted and yet, because my advice has not been accepted, you officially make this the reasons for turning down what is an eminently desirable objective, i.e., securing additional beds for the treatment of tubercular patients.

I quite see your difficulty, of course, but I hope you will see mine and understand my slight feeling of resentment and my very definite feeling of frustration.

In my view, tuberculosis is so disturbing socially that we have no right to refuse to find the relatively modest sums that would be necessary to use this Swiss capacity in a limited fashion.

However, I should say that because I appreciate your difficulties I am making another attempt to resubmit the scheme to you. I cannot, I repeat, find the money inside the ceiling, and to be blunt, neither can you. But I am asking my people if they will try and find cuts in order to find expenditure equivalent to the amount that would be needed for Switzerland. I promise you that these would be real cuts. I am quite prepared to defend in the House of Commons or elsewhere the cutting out of perhaps a less essential service or the deferment of hearing aids or dentures to find the sum required, on the argument that while these are essential the need for tubercular treatment is imperative. [SRO, HH102/316.]

Letter of Hector McNeil, Secretary of State for Scotland to Hugh Gaitskell, Minister of State for Economic Affairs, on Swiss Hospital Treatment for Scottish Tuberculosis Patients, 25 September 1950.

You will now have seen my latest expenditure report to the Prime Minister's Committee, in which I draw attention to the success we have achieved in controlling the hospital service expenditure to date. It seems clear that our policy of constant pressure through Regional Hospitals Boards to secure all possible economies however small is paying dividends, and that in the absence of any further unexpected charges the hospital service is likely to show a small margin of saving in comparison with its estimated cost. This is in spite of unexpected charges such as increased prices for fuel and other supplies. Moreover the prospective margin is more than we should require for Swiss tuberculosis treatment this year.

My paper also brings out the point that the items on which excess expenditure has arisen are those not susceptible to financial control in the same way as the hospital service. If we are to operate by reference to an overall ceiling, this means that the controllable items are to suffer, irrespective of their importance, just because they can be controlled. In other words, you would have us say that we cannot afford to arrange for tuberculosis treatment in Switzerland because the demand for free replacement dentures is running at such a high level. We cannot expect the people of Scotland to accept that argument, and my colleagues have not so far accepted my proposition that we should secure savings on the dental and eye services by radical measures. That being so I really think that the prospect of a margin on the hospital service by itself justifies me in asking the Swiss project should be authorised, irrespective of the excess which we still anticipate on the Vote as a whole.

I am sure we should all agree that expansion of tuberculosis accommodation in this country, if and when staff can be obtained, is one of our highest health service priorities. The Swiss project has the advantage that it would make no demands on our limited medical, and especially nursing, strengths. I do not, of course, envisage it as a permanent part of our service, but unless we do something at once to get tuberculosis more firmly under control we are merely piling up trouble for ourselves in future years by leaving far too many infectious cases in the community to spread the disease yet further. It is therefore no more than elementary wisdom to spend a little now in order to save more—perhaps much more—later on. [SRO, HH102/316.]

Letter of Douglas Jay, Financial Secretary, to Hector McNeil, Secretary of State for Scotland, on Swiss Hospital Treatment for Scottish Tuberculosis Patients, 12 October 1950.

Before he left for Paris and America Hugh Gaitskell asked me to reply to your letter of 25th September about sending to Switzerland of tuberculosis patients from Scotland.

The Minister has a good deal of sympathy with this particular proposal, and, so, indeed, has the Chancellor. In view, however, of the present position of discussions on the financial position of the National Health Service in England and Wales and in Scotland, he does not see how he can sanction a scheme which cannot be financed within the individual ceilings. Nor does he think it practicable that the scheme could be brought within the Scottish ceiling if the measures necessary to secure the necessary funds elsewhere were such as could hardly be applied in Scotland alone and were unacceptable, as at present advised, in England and Wales.

The Minister suggests that the only course which appears to be open is that you should consider the provision for this sort of service in next year's estimate, for which as yet no ceiling has been fixed. If you regard this sort of provision as of high priority so far as Scotland is concerned, and if your estimates as a whole come out at a figure which is reasonable, it might then be practicable to agree this scheme for Scotland without running into the difficulties of comparison with England and Wales which seems unavoidable in the current year. [SRO, HH102/316.]

TUBERCULOSIS AND THE GLASGOW MASS RADIOGRAPHY CAMPAIGN, 1955

In October 1953 the Department of Health began a number of short 'community surveys' inviting people to attend for TB X-ray examination. However, the numbers attending remained 'disappointing'. The extract here is from the letter of James Stuart, the Scottish

Secretary, to Iain Macleod, the Minister of Health, on the issue of broadening the campaign with the assistance of English X-ray units. Macleod agreed to loan the equipment and staff, but because additional units could not be secured in time from the Army and with the need to ensure full Glasgow co-operation, the campaign was delayed until March 1957. Some 800,000 people were X-rayed, with over 8,000 TB cases discovered.

Letter of James Stuart, Secretary of State for Scotland, to Iain Macleod, Minister of Health, on the Proposed Glasgow Mass Radiography Campaign, 4 May 1955.

We are exploring the possibility of a big new effort against tuberculosis which, as you know, is still one of our biggest health problems in Scotland. In view of current trends and our recent experience with mass radiography surveys we believe that we could now get good results from a sustained three-year campaign against tuberculosis, using to the full all the resources of our chest service and of mass radiography, backed where necessary by the diversion of staff, beds and other medical resources from other fields.

If this campaign is to be successful, we shall need your help with mass radiography for Glasgow. We envisage that our three-year campaign should begin with a five week mass radiography drive in that city in May of next year. Glasgow has been chosen because it has by far Scotland's largest tuberculosis problem in terms of sheer numbers of people affected and is therefore the largest single reservoir of infection. And a big campaign in Glasgow will launch the national programme in a way no campaign elsewhere in Scotland could.

We believe that five weeks is probably about the maximum period for which a sustained public response can be expected; and the best estimate we can make on past experience suggests that up to 400,000 people may present themselves for X-ray in Glasgow in this period if sufficient units are provided. Even allowing the high rate of 2,000 people per unit week, this means that for the Glasgow campaign 40 units will be needed, against 10 available in Scotland.

The purpose of this letter, then, is to ask you to consider whether you could make arrangements for 30 of the mass radiography units at present operating in England to be lent, with staff, to our Western Regional Hospital Board for a period of approximately five weeks beginning about 10th May, 1956. We would of course undertake full responsibility for all the detailed arrangements, including the welfare of the English staff.

I do appreciate that this is a large request, and I am putting it to you only after the most careful consideration. It seems to me that it is only by measures of this radical sort that we can hope to bring tuberculosis in Scotland under better control, and that the time has now arrived when these measures can be practicable and effective. Your co-operation and the co-operation of the English hospital service will put us deeply in your debt.

I shall not be surprised if you find it impossible to reach a definite conclusion on this request before the election, but I should be most grateful if you would arrange for the necessary enquiries to be put in hand now, so that we—or our successors—will be able to reach a quick decision after the election, and thus allow the essential planning work to go ahead in time for the opening of the campaign in Glasgow next May. [SRO, HH102/120.]

PUBLIC EXPENDITURE AND THE HEALTH SERVICE, 1956

In February 1956, Harold Macmillan, the Chancellor of the Exchequer, as part of the Government's policy of public economy, asked the Cabinet to review Health Service expenditure. The Cabinet immediately established a Ministerial Committee, including James Stuart, the Scottish Secretary, to review the position. The first extract is from Stuart's memorandum to the Committee, which received a similar memorandum from R.H. Turton, the Minister of Health. The Committee could not reach agreement, but invited Stuart and Turton to examine further the issue of hospital 'boarding' charges. The second extract is from their memorandum. The third is from a subsequent letter of Stuart to Macmillan, after Macmillan had requested that he look again at other issues. Later the Committee agreed to increase the cost of dentures and the cost of a prescription (to one shilling per item). However, Stuart remained adamant that a 'boarding' charge in Scotland would be 'retrogressive' and others felt it 'wrong on medical and humanitarian grounds'. As a result the Committee referred the matter to the Cabinet, which decided against a hospital charge.

Memorandum by James Stuart, Secretary of State for Scotland, on Economies in the National Health Service, 13 April 1956.

The search for economies in the National Health Service has previously been pursued so thoroughly and so often that I see no prospect of any significant saving being achieved without some drastic change of policy that would be equally unwelcome to my colleagues as to myself. In particular I do not believe that we could possibly reduce the level of expenditure on the hospital service below the figures forecast in S.S.(56)7 if we are to make any pretence of keeping abreast of modern developments in hospital care, and at the same time maintain our existing assets so as to avoid very much heavier costs in future years.

Reduction in Scope of Service. We could I suppose legislate to suspend altogether, for the general population, the dental service or the optical service, leaving local authority maternity and child welfare services, and school health service, to look after those up to school leaving age. In Scotland these steps might save, respectively, £3 million a year (£33 million in Great Britain) and £0.7 million a year (£8.5 million in Great Britain). If the scope of the National Health Service must be cut, I think these are the fields where this would do least harm to the basic essentials. But we could not pretend we were doing anything other than departing from the principle of a comprehensive health service, and we should have to amend the National Assistance Act to allow the National Assistance Board to help people in need to obtain this kind of care privately.

Move towards Insurance Basis. An alternative method of reducing the scale of the Service might seem to be to restrict the provision of certain items (e.g. dental and optical) to persons covered by the National Insurance Scheme and their dependants. The cost would then be transferred from the Exchequer to the National Insurance Fund, and met by an increased contribution. This would, however, not be a major reduction in aggregate expenditure from public funds, for about 94 per cent of the population would still qualify; and those left out include some groups whose need for subsidised provision is particularly great—e.g. old people who were never insured, the student population, and adults maintained by their parents either to care for these parents or because they themselves are invalids. National Assistance Board aid would thus again be necessary.

Whether it is preferable, from the standpoint of the country's economy, to finance a given service from general taxation or from an insurance contribution is not a question to which I myself know the answer. But I do know that any move towards insurance finance would be opposed as transferring the burden to shoulders less able to bear it than those on which it rests at present. Moreover, the insurance basis has the unfortunate result of stimulating the desire of contributors to get value for their contributions. For this reason I think any such move would be unwise; indeed in my opinion the National Health Service has already suffered in this way because a small part of its cost (now less than 10 per cent) comes from the National Insurance Fund, and in consequence there is still a widespread misunderstanding that the weekly insurance stamp represents payment for the Service.

Extension of Charges. If there is no acceptable way of reducing the scope of the Service, its cost to public funds could be curtailed only by extending the charges at present made to users of the Service, or by introducing new ones. There is no scope for material savings by this means in the services run by local health authorities, including (in England) the ambulance service. Nor is there room for more than marginal increases in the charges for dentistry and optical services unless we modify substantially the existing freedom from charge for dental treatment enjoyed by the priority classes (expectant and nursing mothers and persons under 21). This would be diametrically opposed to the Guillebaud recommendations, and although the abolition of this priority class benefit might save +£0.5 million a year in Scotland (£3.5 million a year in Britain) it would be almost as hard to justify as suspension of the whole service.

The shilling prescription charge could be more readily be increased; even to levy a shilling per prescription, instead of per prescription form, would bring in about £0.4 million a year extra in Scotland (£5.5 million in Great Britain). In addition, now that the waiting list has been largely overtaken, we could impose a charge for the initial supply of hearing aids. This seems justified by the analogy with spectacles, but the yearly produce (for new issues not replacements) would be a mere £5,000 in Scotland, and perhaps £50,000 in Great Britain. These alterations could be effected by regulations subject to annulment only. A bottle system for medicine bottles has superficial attractions but would not, I think, enable us to reduce significantly our payments to chemists.

Hospital Charges. As regards new charges, the only important possibility brought to light in earlier studies was that of a 'hotel charge' for hospital in-patients—with the possible exception of patients in infectious diseases and mental hospitals. As some of my colleagues will recall, this was thoroughly examined in 1954 and rejected, mainly because a charge at the rate of 3s. a day (the maximum we thought reasonable) could not be relied upon to produce a new saving of as much as £10 million a year in Great Britain; and this we did not think worth the serious trouble and controversy that would be involved. I think this conclusion is still valid. A substantially higher rate of charge would present a fundamental departure from the basic principles of the Service, and for that reason should not in my opinion be contemplated.

Charges to Non-Residents. There remains one field in which I should favour the introduction of charges, not for the sake of the sum realised or for the direct reduction in demand to be expected, but for the psychological value in protecting the Service against exploitation, and in showing our determination to effect every possible saving that involves no hardship to the community. What I have in view is the institution of certain charges in respect of the use of the Service by foreigners (perhaps excluding Commonwealth citizens) not ordinarily resident in Great Britain, in cases where it would have been reasonable that the foreigner should have returned to his own country for the treatment or should have sought treatment there before he left. This would not require legislation, for sufficiently wide regulation-making powers were taken by the Labour Government in the National Health Service (Amendment) Act of 1949. Reciprocal rights to health service benefits under existing international agreements would of course be safeguarded. [PRO, CAB 134/1327; SRO, HH101/2743/3.]

Memorandum by James Stuart, the Secretary of State for Scotland, and R.H. Turton, Minister of Health, on a Hospital Boarding Charge, 14 June 1956.

At their meeting on 4th May, the Social Services Committee invited us to examine further the case for imposing a 'hotel charge' on hospital in-patients.

The pros and cons of a hospital boarding charge are set out in the Guillebaud Report (paras. 385-8).

The main argument for the charges mentioned in the Report is that, since there is some saving in home expenses while a patient is in hospital (particularly feeding costs), it would be reasonable for the patient to meet some part of the cost of boarding him in hospital. The Committee also point out that it was the custom long before the National Health Service for both voluntary and municipal hospitals in England and Wales to make a charge to hospital in-patients (for treatment as well as board), and the possibility of making a 'hotel' charge was raised in the Beveridge report.

The main arguments set out by the Guillebaud Report against a charge, which led the Committee to recommend against its introduction are:- (a) when a patient is in hospital he and his family have to meet a number of incidental expenses (including the cost of visiting) which may offset any savings. Moreover, if he is already a long-stay patient and is insured, the home saving is already taken into account through the reduction of his insurance benefit after 8 weeks with a further reduction after a year: (b) it is a bad time to subject a patient to possible financial worry when he is in hospital; and his recovery might be retarded; (c) many patients would require assistance from the National Assistance Board or would need to be exempted (there are various other classes with claims for exemption); (d) the cost of collecting the charges.

It has also to be borne in mind that the pre-1948 practice of charging patients did not apply in Scottish hospitals and only to a small extent in Scottish local authority hospitals. Even in England and Wales, charges before 1948 were not normally made upon persons suffering from infectious diseases or from tuberculosis. The institution of a hotel charge would thus be a radical departure from long-established practice in Scotland, and, for the types of patient mentioned, in England and Wales.

As regards the proposed charge, comparisons may be drawn with the charge levied by local authorities upon residents at welfare homes, including homes for the aged. The current prescribed minimum charge which has to be paid by these residents (assisted if need be by the National Assistance Board), for full board and lodging and other services, is 32s. 6d. a week for an adult (from 12s. to 17s. a week, according to age, for a child).

Having considered the various possible alternative courses of action, we regard the following plan as the least objectionable way of imposing a hotel charge: (a) a flat rate of 4s. a day. This is higher than the average weekly cost of provisions for each patient on average. (There are, however, wide differences between the cost at different types of hospital). It is also higher than the average weekly expenditure on food per head in the household; (b) the charge to be limited to the first 8 weeks of a patient's stay in hospital. This would avoid the need for interfering with the existing insurance benefit reduction after 8 weeks, though admittedly those reductions are currently substantially lower from the 9th to the 52nd week and, on the other hand (for a person without dependants), slightly higher thereafter, than the proposed new hotel charge. Limitations of the charge to the first 8 weeks would also limit the volume of National Assistance Board work for long-term indigent patients. It would also avoid the difficulty which arises on a scheme for exempting certain types of patients of finding wholly satisfactory definitions for the exemptions, since, notwithstanding pre-1948 practice, no exemptions would be proposed except those mentioned in (c) below; (c) exemption to be granted only to war pensioners treated for their accepted disability, service patients treated in National Health Service hospital and children under the age of 16 or still in attendance full-time at a secondary school.

The net increase to the Exchequer from such a charge might be about £10ml. a year in Great Britain. [PRO, CAB 134/1327 SS(56)25.]

Letter of James Stuart, Secretary of State for Scotland, to Harold Macmillan, Chancellor of the Exchequer, on Economies in the National Health Service, 31 May 1956.

In your letter of the 28th May to the Minister of Health you made a number of suggestions for health service economies. I do not myself regard a charge of 1/- per item as the furthest we can go in the way of increasing the prescription charge of 2/- per form. I estimate that this would yield in a full year a saving of approximately £700,000 in Scotland and, in the current year, perhaps as much as £350,000. Nor, as I indicated in my previous letter of 10th May, should I oppose an increase of 1/2d. per pint in the charge for welfare milk. But I do not believe that it is possible to achieve significant economies in the hospital services without reducing the scope of the service.

Time and again I have drawn the attention of the Chairmen of Regional Hospital Boards to the need for maximum economy, the latest occasion so recently as last October. I am quite sure that we cannot do more than we are already doing in this direction, and I fear that a further appeal now to the Board might very well do more harm than good. All along I have had the full co-operation of the Boards, but I can maintain this position only if the Boards see that I am dealing fairly with them and trusting them to do their bit. All the evidence I have makes it clear that the Boards are doing their level best by keeping the closest possible grip on running costs.

You suggest particularly that it should be possible to defer considerable expenditure in the field of replacement equipment and the like. I am sorry, but I cannot see any prospect of this at all. When I myself met the Regional Board Chairmen last October, the need for some further expenditure on replacement of completely outworn hospital equipment was one of the strongest pleas that they put to me; and it was against this background that an additional allowance—and a very small one at that—was included in the estimates settled in discussion with you and Turton earlier this year. In the same way I fear that there is no possibility of further cutting back expenditure in the current year on x-ray and similar equipment. Specialised equipment of this kind is obtained in Scotland by central purchase, and all demands for equipment are most closely scrutinised by the Department. Our estimated needs for the current year were heavily out at estimates time, and we shall be able to do little more than replace dangerous and wholly inefficient sets. Moreover practically all the items for supply this year are already on order, and we are therefore wholly committed.

We shall of course, as we would in any event, urge the hospital authorities to reduce stocks generally to the minimum; but the effect of this must be entirely marginal and relatively insignificant, for the process is one we have already pressed very far in recent years. In the same way we shall maintain all our efforts to secure the most efficient use of staff, but all our experience over the years makes it clear that no appreciable contribution is to be found in this way. A most elaborate review in 1952-53 not only took many months to carry out, but produced most disappointing results; and since then financial pressure in support of the maximum economy has remained very strong.

You suggest, if necessary, the withdrawal of the specific allowance included in the Estimates to meet the net additional cost of expansion and improvement of the service in the current year—in Scotland a mere matter of £250,000. I can only say that this would have quite a disastrous effects out of all proportion to the money involved; in any case the Boards are already almost entirely committed to the extent of their respective shares of our Scottish total. As things are, the Boards have been faced with the greatest possible difficulty in trying to contain within the strictly limited allocation the net cost of improvements due to come into effect this year, and many urgently needed schemes have had to be deferred. We cannot expect to run a hospital service without some margin for improvement, much of which is necessarily the consequence of advances in medical science and changes in techniques. And we merely lay ourselves open to ridicule when capital expenditure on badly needed improvements is rendered nugatory because money for the related running costs is not provided; even as it is, I expect to be faced with this situation in some degree in the current financial year, however good our management and whatever the gloss we can put upon it for the purposes of public presentation.

I am sorry to appear so unhelpful, but you will agree that there is no reason to expect different services to be susceptible of economies to the same degree without drastic changes of policy. So far as the national health service is concerned, I have indicated to the Social Services Committee what these would have to be, and I do not gather that there is much disposition on the part of the Committee to recommend that we should incur the odium attaching to them. It is not in the least surprising that administrative economies cannot be found; what would be surprising would be the contrary experience, after all the limelight that has been focused on the service in recent years and the consequent meticulous attention given to it by the responsible Ministers. [SRO, SOE6/7/77.]

PUBLIC EXPENDITURE AND THE SCOTTISH HOSPITAL PROGRAMME, 1958

In summer 1958, Derick Heathcoat Amory, the Chancellor of the Exchequer, informed the Cabinet that to reduce taxation before the next election the Government would have to curtail its planned growth in social investment. The Cabinet immediately remitted the matter to a Ministerial Committee, including John Maclay, the Scottish Secretary, for discussion. The following extract is from the Department of Health's memorandum to Maclay before the Committee's second meeting. In the event the Committee was unable to reach agreement and resubmitted the matter to the Cabinet, which, while agreeing a reduction for the English programme, imposed none on Scotland. Over the period 1959-62 Amory had wanted to reduce capital expenditure by 40 per cent.

Memorandum by the Department of Health for Scotland, on the Scottish Hospital Programme for a Meeting of Ministers on Social Investment, September 1958.

The Report by officials points out that the 1960/61 programme for hospitals is about £30m. (G.B. figures), an increase of more than £7m. over 1958/9. It submits as one of the issues for the consideration of Ministers whether officials should re-examine the Education and Hospital programmes to see how a reduction of £10m.-£15m. in these could be combined with elements of a forward policy for both.

The Scottish Hospital programme for 1958/59 amounts to £3m. and the programme for 1960/61 is £3.4m. This represents an increase in 1960/61 of 13 per cent. over 1958/59. The G.B. figure, in the other hand, shows in the same period an increase of almost 30 per cent. In fact, throughout the years in question the Ministry of Health propose to increase the rate of capital expenditure at a greater rate than is proposed for Scotland.

If, therefore, Ministers decide that some reduction in the Hospital programme is desirable, the Department would argue that it should fall to a very large degree on the English, rather than on the Scottish programme.

The main arguments for the increase in the rate of capital expenditure on the Hospital Service in Scotland are—(1) We have to meet in 1960/61 very substantial commitments on major projects already in hand, the cost of which has been increasing because of rises in wages and prices. (2) We are under increasing pressure to begin the long overdue improvement of the major teaching hospitals. (3) We are anxious to provide modern facilities, e.g., for the treatment of out-patients and for day hospital work in the mental field, which do not involve a new expansion of the hospital Service but would enable us to deal with patients more effectively at no greater cost and perhaps even more economically to the extent that we achieve a net reduction in in-patient treatment which is relatively expensive.

It should perhaps be kept in mind that the Hospital programme, even on the expanding scale proposed by the Health Departments, is relatively small. It is only about one-seventh of the Housing programme and one-third of the Education programme. The Health Departments are in fact proposing to spend very little more than is proposed to be spent in a handful of New Towns. From this point of view it would be most unfortunate if the Hospital Service were cut simply because this particular field of expenditure is more closely under control. It is also the case that over the last 10 or 12 years both Education and Housing have proceeded at a relatively high rate of expenditure, whereas the Hospital expenditure has throughout been very severely restricted. [SRO, DD10/110/1.]

INDEX

Scottish Secretaries for the period 1916-62 were: Robert Munro (Coalition Liberal), 1916-22; Viscount Novar (National Liberal in a Conservative Government), 1922-4; William Adamson (Labour), 1924; Sir John Gilmour (Conservative), 1924-9; William Adamson (Labour), 1929-31; Sir Archibald Sinclair (National Liberal), 1931-2; Sir Godfrey Collins (National Liberal), 1932-6; Walter Elliot (National Conservative), 1936-8; John Colville (National Conservative), 1938-40; A. Ernest Brown (National Conservative), 1940-1; Thomas Johnston (Coalition Labour), 1941-5; 6th Earl of Rosebery (Conservative), 1945; Joseph Westwood (Labour), 1945-7; Arthur Woodburn (Labour), 1947-50; Hector McNeill (Labour), 1950-1; James Stuart (Conservative), 1951-7; John Maclay (National Liberal and Conservative), 1957-62.

The Board of Health (Scotland) Act, 1919, created a Parliamentary Under Secretary for Health for Scotland. The Secretaries of State Act, 1926, created a Secretary of State for Scotland and a Parliamentary Under Secretary of State for Scotland. It abolished the posts of Secretary for Scotland and of Parliamentary Under Secretary of State for Scotland. The Defence (Parliamentary Under Secretaries) Regulations, 1940, created a second Under Secretary of State for Scotland on a temporary basis. The Supply Vote (Scottish Affairs), December 1951, enabled payment for a Minister of State for Scotland, sitting in the Lords. The Ministers of the Crown (Parliamentary Under Secretaries) Act, 1952, made permanent the appointment of the second Under Secretary of State and added a third.

★

SCOTTISH HISTORY SOCIETY

OFFICE-BEARERS AND COUNCIL
1991-1992

MEMBERSHIP

Membership of the Scottish History Society
is open to all who are interested in the history of Scotland.
For an annual subscription of £15.00
members normally receive one volume each year.
Enquiries should be addressed to
the Honorary Secretary, whose address
is given overleaf.

SCOTTISH HISTORY SOCIETY

105th ANNUAL REPORT

Presented to the Annual General Meeting by the Council, 14 December 1991

Members of the Society will have been saddened during the past year by the death of Professor Ian Cowan, just before Christmas 1990. Ian served the Society admirably as Treasurer for a quarter of a century, but he will be remembered also as unofficial membership secretary and distribution secretary. It is a tribute to his sterling work over many years that it has taken three people to replace him. An obituary of Ian Cowan, written by Dr John Durkan, will appear in the 1991 *Calendar of Fearn* (see below).

Due to unforeseen delays in the completion of the third volume of the new Fifth Series, *The Calendar of Fearn: Text and Additions, 1471-1667*, edited by Professor Robin Adam, a volume due to be circulated to members in 1990, Council decided to alter the order of the 1990 and 1991 volumes, and all paid-up members should now have received the *Miscellany XI* volume as the Society's 1990 publication. The obituary notice of Dr T.I. Rae has been transferred from the *Calendar of Fearn* volume to *Miscellany XI*, which also contains: 'A plea roll of Edward I's army in Scotland, 1296', edited by Cynthia Neville; 'Letters of John Graham of Claverhouse', edited by Andrew Murray Scott; 'Some late seventeenth-century building contracts', edited by J.G. Dunbar and Katherine Davies; and 'Correspondence relating to Millburn Tower and its garden, 1804-1829', edited by Clare Taylor. Thereafter the Society's publications will follow the course outlined in the 1990 Annual Report. *The Black Book of Coldingham, 1298-1430*, edited by Dr Joseph Donnelly, will be the 1992 volume: a survey of rentals gathered from the muniments of the Dean and Chapter of Durham, including a survey of the lands of Durham's cell at Coldingham, compiled c.1298; later surveys date from 1412-30. These rentals throw much light on the agrarian society of south-east Scotland in this period. The volume will also include, as an appendix, the Kelso rentals (already printed in the *Kelso Liber* but without modern scholarly apparatus). It will be followed in 1993 by *The Scottish Office: Depression and Reconstruction, 1919-1959*, edited by Dr Ian Levitt.

The new Honorary Treasurer of the Society, replacing Professor Cowan, is Mr W.W. Scott. Dr Norman Macdougall retires from the position of Honorary Secretary, and his place will be taken by Dr E.P.D. Torrie. In addition, Council recommends that a new post be created among its office-bearers, that of Honorary Membership Secretary, responsible *inter alia* for membership lists and close liaison with the Honorary Treasurer. Dr Allan Macinnes has undertaken this task throughout the past year, and has indicated his willingness to continue in the post. Council therefore seeks the approval of members to amend paragraph 7 of the Constitution, which at present reads:

> The Office-bearers of the Society shall be a Chairman, a Secretary, a Publication Secretary and a Treasurer, all of whom shall be elected by the Council for such periods as it may determine.

If the membership approves, this paragraph will be altered to read:

> The Office-bearers of the Society shall be a Chairman, a Secretary, a Publication Secretary, a Membership Secretary and a Treasurer, all of whom shall be elected by the Council for such periods as it may determine.

Three members of Council retire by rotation this year—Mr C.J. Davey, Dr R.A. Mason, and Dr A. Macinnes. To fill their places, Council recommends the election of Mr I.E.F. Flett, Mr W.D.H. Sellar and Dr I.G.C. Hutchison.

During the current year the membership records of the Society have been thoroughly reviewed. Current membership is 633, including 142 libraries or other institutions.

The Society's immediate financial position is healthy, largely due to publication delays and comfortable bank balances at a time of high interest rates. This picture is certain to change during 1992, and Council is considering the need for a new membership campaign.

ABSTRACT ACCOUNT OF CHARGE AND DISCHARGE OF THE INTROMISSIONS OF THE HONORARY TREASURER

1 October 1990 to 30 September 1991

CHARGE

			£
1	Cash in Bank at 1 October 1990		
	a Sum at credit of Savings Account with Bank of Scotland		9500.00
	b Sum at credit of Premier Account with Bank of Scotland		26475.23
	c Sum at credit of current (Treasurer's) account with Bank of Scotland		517.09
			36492.32
2	Subscriptions received		9106.19
3	Past publications sold		864.00
4	Interest on Savings Account		978.45
5	Interest on Premier Account		3525.89
6	Interest on Current (Treasurer's) Account		615.79
7	Income Tax refund (1988-89)		507.65
8	Miscellaneous (refund of AGM expenses)		115.75
9	Sums drawn from Bank Savings Account*	10493.45	
10	Sums drawn from Bank Current Account	816.69	
			52206.04

* Sum transferred to Premier Account

DISCHARGE

			£
1	Subscriptions refunded		42.00
2	Cost of publications during year		nil
3	Costs of printing book lists etc.		66.82
4	Costs of insuring stock of unsold books		74.88
5	Costs of AGM		282.99
6	Costs of postage re AGM		125.00
7	Office bearers' honorariums and secretarial expenses		190.00
8	Subscriptions and Donations		35.00
9	Sums lodged in Bank Savings Account	993.45	
10	Sums lodged in Bank Premier Account	14019.34	
11	Sums lodged in Bank Current Account	11194.38	
			816.69
12	Funds at close of this account		
	a Sum at credit of Premier Account with Bank of Scotland		40494.57
	b Sum at credit of Current (Treasurer's) Account with Bank of Scotland		10894.78
			52206.04

STIRLING, *11 November 1991.*

I have audited the Account of the Honorary Treasurer of the Scottish History Society and certify that I am satisfied that proper records appear to have been kept and that the above Account is a correct statement of the transactions recorded during the year.

H.B. PEEBLES, CA, ACMA
Auditor